IN THE LION'S MOUTH

IN THE LION'S MOUTH

Black Populism in the New South, 1886–1900

Omar H. Ali

Foreword by Robin D. G. Kelley

University Press of Mississippi / Jackson

*Margaret Walker Alexander Series
in African American Studies*

www.upress.state.ms.us

The University Press of Mississippi is a member
of the Association of American University Presses.

Copyright © 2010 by University Press of Mississippi
All rights reserved
Manufactured in the United States of America

First printing 2010

∞

Library of Congress Cataloging-in-Publication Data

Ali, Omar H. (Omar Hamid)
In the lion's mouth : Black populism in the New South,
1886–1900 / Omar H. Ali ; foreword by Robin D. G. Kelley.
p. cm. — (Margaret Walker Alexander series in African
American studies)
Includes bibliographical references and index.
ISBN 978-1-60473-778-3 (cloth : alk. paper) —
ISBN 978-1-60473-780-6 (ebook) 1. African Americans—
Southern States—Politics and government—19th century.
2. Populism—Southern States—History—19th century.
3. Southern States—Politics and government—1865–1950.
I. Title.
E185.6.A28 2010
322.4'4097309034—dc22   2010015113

British Library Cataloging-in-Publication Data available

For
Dr. Jessie Fields
and
Cathy L. Stewart

Organizing the unorganized,
one person at a time

The Lord stood with me, and strengthened me; that by me the preaching might be fully known ... and I was delivered out of the mouth of the lion.

—2 TIMOTHY 4:17 (New Testament, King James Version)

Contents

xi	Foreword by Robin D. G. Kelley
xiii	Preface
xvii	Acknowledgments
3	Introduction
13	Chapter One **ROOTS AND EARLY DEVELOPMENT**
48	Chapter Two **THE COLORED FARMERS' ALLIANCE**
78	Chapter Three **ESTABLISHING THE "NEGRO PARTY"**
113	Chapter Four **INDEPENDENT, COALITION, AND FUSION POLITICS**
150	Chapter Five **COLLAPSE AND AFTERMATH**
168	Epilogue
177	Historiographical Essay
183	Notes
217	Bibliography
237	Index

Foreword

Robin D. G. Kelley

Omar H. Ali has thrown down the gauntlet. He rescues the Black Populist movement, particularly the Colored Farmers' Alliance, from its longstanding place as a footnote to Populism writ large, and restores the men and women who built this powerful movement to their rightful place within the black radical tradition. In an age when black farmers are still struggling with the federal government to receive just reparations for their collective loss of land through discriminatory lending practices and outright theft, this book stands as a potent reminder of just how long and deep this struggle has been.

In the Lion's Mouth: Black Populism in the New South, 1886–1900 breaks new ground by locating a distinctive politics of culture deeply rooted not only in the black radical tradition, but also in agrarian culture, with groundings in African culture and the experience of slavery. Ali correctly resists the common tendency to see Black Populists as either an offshoot of the white Populist movement or as a failed effort at interracial organizing. Rather, he paints a compelling portrait of an independent movement. But understand that by independent, he does not mean separatist. It is an important distinction, for if we follow Ali's arguments and the evidence he marshals seriously, we can only conclude that the white Populist movement, more than any, exhibited separatist tendencies. Ali flips the script, if you will, and compels us to rethink the entire history of late-nineteenth-century southern politics. Moreover, he insists that the real story of these different movements is not a simple matter of two separate strands of Populism operating side-by-side, but conflicting ideals about fairness, equity, and the construction of a democratic, caring political economy.

Rural African Americans felt the financial crunch more severely than their white counterparts, as black men and women endured mass evictions and the loss of civil and political rights. Thus it shouldn't surprise us that sharp philosophical and political differences divided the two Populist movements. Black Populists had advanced beyond printing more money or demanding free silver; they sought a more radical redistribution of wealth. Indeed, they had a vision of a new society and offered a path for the emancipation of the nation as a whole, not just black folk. As such, theirs was not interest-group politics but a black-led movement broad enough for all farmers and working people to follow. Tragically, most whites chose white supremacy over liberation—a story repeated over and over again in the course of our nation's history.

Ali's *In the Lion's Mouth* makes another critical contribution to our understanding of the era. It adds further voice to the burgeoning scholarship that challenges the characterization of the late nineteenth century as a low point—the nadir, as Rayford Logan famously called it—in the black freedom movement. Allegedly, the post-Reconstruction era was marked by African Americans turning inward, embracing self-segregation rather than direct opposition, following Booker T. Washington's injunction to "cast down your buckets where you are." Ali paints a radically different picture. The independent black movement he describes was a collective act of self-determination; it challenged the economic and ideological structures of the day and offered a democratic alternative the nation might have followed.

But Ali goes further. He reveals the contradictions of class within black communities and political formations. It is not enough to examine how Black Populists differed from whites; he points out how some black Republicans and various "representative" race leaders also took issue with the movement's militant tactics and support for a third party—the People's Party. These class conflicts had a profound affect on the ability of black agrarian organizations to build solidarity and strength. Ali shows us how much is revealed once we shift our focus away from questions of whether this was a failed black and white alliance to the *internal dynamics* of a movement. In the end, we need this book and we need it now. As Ali reminds us, social movements do make a difference, even when they might lose the larger battle.

Here we stand in 2010, facing an economic crisis whose depths are not unlike that which America faced in the 1890s. And here we are, with an African American in the White House for the first time in the nation's history, a black president who speaks boldly about a new "green" economy, and yet black farmers continue to be denied their just and legally sanctioned compensation for decades of racial discrimination. As a result of a 1999 settlement, the U.S. Department of Agriculture was required to pay out about $400 million in total damages for violating black farmers' civil rights. The majority of black farmers covered by the suit were eligible to receive $50,000 and the cancellation of any USDA debt. It was a paltry sum, to be sure, but few black farmers had even received that amount. Instead, the USDA directed its energy to denying black farmers' claims, eventually turning down nearly 90 percent of those who sought restitution.

So what are the lessons here? Land still matters. The fight for democracy still matters. We still need movements. We still need a more expansive vision of a caring and just society. We still need dreamers. And we especially need to read Omar H. Ali's *In the Lion's Mouth*.

Preface

The struggle for post-emancipation civil and political rights by men and women of African descent has taken a range of forms throughout the Atlantic and Indian Ocean worlds. Within these African Diasporas, there have always been men and women—whether free, enslaved, or occupying a status somewhere in between—willing to place their lives, livelihoods, and the security of their family and friends on the line in order to ensure or extend emancipation. In the Atlantic world, the abolition of slavery was achieved over the course of the nineteenth century; in the Indian Ocean world, where there existed a much broader range of un-free forms of labor than in the Atlantic, freedom did not come to most people held in bondage until the twentieth century. Regardless, in both areas of the world, freedoms needed to be actively protected post-emancipation, as colonial, neocolonial, or otherwise ruling-class efforts to control black labor required ongoing vigilance and tactical response.

Both prior to and following emancipation black people in the Americas created their own fraternal orders and mutual-benefit societies that formed the basis of independent black action. In the Caribbean and South America, black associations, such as the Afro-Cuban *cabildos de nación* or the Afro-Brazilian *irmandandes*, had their counterparts in North America, in the form of Black Masonry or other African American lodges. Such bodies, which were often closely tied to black churches, not only brought a sense of solidarity to communities of black men and women, but also served as political staging grounds. Such was the case in the U.S. South, where African Americans organized to ensure and advance newfound liberties gained during Reconstruction that were either being curtailed or reversed outright (voting rights, sitting on juries, holding of public office). Among the ways African Americans sought to protect and extend their interests included independent politics: establishing third parties, promoting insurgent candidates, and running fusion campaigns (where two parties run a shared slate of candidates). Such tactics not only fueled the Abolitionist movement of the antebellum era, but were used by African Americans in the decades after the Civil War. The present study details the rise and fall of one of the largest independent black political movements: Black Populism in the New South.

Between 1886 and 1900—within a decade following the end of Reconstruction and before the consolidation of Jim Crow—African Americans mobilized tens of thousands of black farmers, sharecroppers, and agrarian workers to action. They demanded higher wages, debt relief, government ownership and regulation of railroads, a farmer subsidy program, the protection of civil and political rights, and electoral reform. The movement grew out of established networks of black benevolent associations, fraternal orders, and churches that served as centers for the recruitment, education, and leadership-training of African Americans in the post-Reconstruction South; it took organizational form in 1886 with the creation of various mutual-aid societies and labor unions, including the Colored Agricultural Wheels, the Colored Farmers' Alliance, the southern branch of the Knights of Labor, and the Cooperative Workers of America. In 1890, the movement began to shift toward the electoral arena. African Americans would help to establish and then grow the People's Party with white independents to challenge Democratic Party authority in the South. African Americans ran insurgent and independent candidates for office and participated in fusion campaigns with the Republican Party. Some of their candidates won; certain concessions and reforms were even briefly put into place (including election reforms and greater funding for public education). However, by the late 1890s, and mostly under Democratic-led attacks, Black Populism collapsed.

Despite the many thousands of African Americans who actively participated in building Black Populism from the mid-1880s through the late 1890s, the movement remains a little-known chapter in the history of post-emancipation black political struggle. Overshadowed by the much better known history of the white-led Populist movement of the same period, Black Populism was neither an offshoot nor a reflection of the white movement, but was a separate movement, with its own history. While the two movements did overlap when tactics required doing so, African Americans followed their own leaders, had their own organizations, and made demands derived from their own particular experiences.

In the following study, the boundaries of the term "Black Populism" have been expanded to include individuals affiliated with a number of groups and political parties often competing with one another and not usually referred to by scholars as "Black Populist" per se. That is, most scholars limit "Black Populist" to only mean African Americans who joined the ranks of the People's Party; they do not include, for instance, dissident black Republicans and African Americans working with other parties and associations. The limitation does not allow for the multiple ways in which African Americans practically and collectively asserted their independence during the final two decades of the nineteenth century. Analogous to this would be to only consider members of the National Association for the Advancement of Colored People as proper participants in the modern civil rights movement (and exclude, for instance, members of the Congress for Racial Equality, the Women's Political Council, or the Student Nonviolent Coordinating

Committee). Like the modern civil rights movement, there was an array of organizations, parties, and unaffiliated individuals involved in Black Populism; moreover, and more often than not, African Americans were simultaneously members of different groups.

A broader perspective of Black Populism is proposed here: overlapping networks of black men and women and their organizations, beginning with agrarian-based associations and labor unions and continuing with electoral parties, were aspects of a larger whole, a larger movement. Ultimately, *In the Lion's Mouth* offers an additional storyline among the many that comprise late-nineteenth-century U.S. history—in this case, one which places southern African Americans front and center in the historical narrative, with white Populists serving as the background, instead of the other way around.

Acknowledgments

Seeing or hearing the old-time Piedmont trio the Carolina Chocolate Drops performing "Cornbread and Butterbeans" one gets a glimpse of the rhythmic banjo—an instrument of African origin—fused with lyrical traditions of the British Isles, as quintessential America. Theirs are among the many African American musical performances that incorporate multiple traditions. In this way, so were the efforts of Black Populists: African Americans bringing to bear various traditions in creating their own, in their case, political performances in the American South.

Over the last ten years I have benefited from many people in researching and writing the following history of Black Populism. The University Press of Mississippi director emerita Seetha Srinivasan provided essential encouragement and direction. Acquiring editor Walter Biggins picked up where Seetha left off; Deborah Self brought her many years of copy-editing experience into the project as I tied off various outstanding and new research tidbits; and Anne Statscavage brought the final product home as managing editor.

There were many people outside of the University Press of Mississippi involved in the production of *In the Lion's Mouth*, beginning with Winston James and Eric Foner under whose supervision I completed my dissertation. Farah Griffin and Manning Marable added valuable comments and insightful suggestions. It was in Marable's graduate seminar on black leadership in America in which I first turned my attention to the Colored Farmers' Alliance. Phyllis Goldberg a dear friend and editor not only taught me how to write, but also how to think about writing. Edward Ayers provided valuable input early in the project, as did Barbara Fields and Daryl Scott. Gerald Gaither and Tony Adams were ever supportive, even as they maintained their own views of Black Populism. Their annotated bibliography on the subject should be consulted by anyone seeking to pursue the subject. Charles Payne also offered valuable comments in an early draft of a chapter on the movement. Other scholars, including Bruce Baker, James Beeby, Patrick Dickson, Blake Wintory, and Ronald Yanosky, contributed to my understanding of some of the figures and events that constitute the movement.

I am deeply indebted to North Carolina archivist Fann Montague and several descendents of Black Populist leaders, notably Walter H. Pattillo, Barbara Jeanne

Williams, and George M. Shuffer Jr., all of whom were so generous with their time. My closest friends, Christopher Street, Cecilia Salvatierra, and Carrie Sackett, encouraged me over the course of many years as I worked on the project on and off, finishing up another book in between. Leah Worthington read through the manuscript and offered helpful suggestions. Valuable research assistance came from Molly Pryor, Sarah Moeller, and Shana Gass. Funding from several sources, including research grants from the Center for the Study of the American South at the University of North Carolina, Chapel Hill, and the Institute of Southern Studies at the University of South Carolina, Columbia, in addition to a subvention from the College of Liberal Arts at Towson University made this work possible. At Towson, I was given ongoing and collegial support by Robert Rook, Akim Reinhardt, and Emily Daugherty, among others.

Finally, my family—Diana, our two little ones, Pablo and Samina, and my parents, Meer and Lucy—deserve many (many) thanks for their love, support, and good cheer over the years. I thank each and every person who helped me.

IN THE LION'S MOUTH

Introduction

Great hopes paraded down the main street of Raleigh, North Carolina, on the afternoon of September 29, 1892.[1] The recently formed People's Party, also known as the Populist Party, organized a show of strength that day for all in the community to see and to join.[2] Cheered by crowds lined along the main dirt road leading to the city's Brookside Park, the parade featured the new party's presidential candidate, James B. Weaver. Flanking Weaver, a brevet brigadier general in the Union army twice elected to Congress on the Greenback Party ticket, were some 350 men on horseback and mules, 50 of whom were African American.[3]

The white-led Populist movement, of which the People's Party was its most visible expression in the electoral arena, spanned the last two decades of the nineteenth century. The movement mobilized farmers and workers across the nation. Those who joined the movement were largely poverty stricken and indebted; their leaders demanded sweeping reforms, including government regulation of businesses, subsidies for farmers, a minimum wage for workers, and a more open and equitable electoral process. Populists targeted points of exploitation. Agricultural prices had fallen precipitously over a period of fifteen years; capital was increasingly scarce or controlled by fewer people who charged exorbitant interests on loans; meanwhile, railroad costs for transporting goods to market were becoming nearly prohibitive. Movement leaders rallied against planters, merchants, landlords, and creditors (often one and the same people), as well as "Wall Street," bankers, and railroad barons.[4] During the 1880s Populists formed a string of agrarian and labor organizations which included cooperative ventures and credit programs to counter high interest rates, low wages, and low commodity prices. By the early 1890s, many in the movement turned to the electoral arena and helped to establish the People's Party—an "antiparty" party.[5] The party demanded structural political reforms; in the South, it attempted to break the Democratic Party's monopoly; in other parts of the country, the Republican Party was the dominant party to be challenged.

The People's Party saw modest gains during its first four years, its candidates winning public offices in the West, Midwest, and in some parts of the South. Populist presidential candidate Weaver received over one million votes at the polls; meanwhile, electoral reforms were enacted in parts of the South through fusion with Republicans. By 1896, however, Populism, and the party that helped to give mass expression to it, had lost its edge. A combination of factors led to the movement's collapse. The popular issue of "free silver"—the reintroduction of silver in addition to gold as specie—was adopted by the Democratic Party's candidate, William Jennings Bryan. His appeal on this issue, which would have (likely) alleviated some of the debt burden among farmers if such a policy were enacted, led to the People's Party endorsing his candidacy in 1896. In addition to what amounted as fusion between the People's Party and the Democratic Party (in essence leading to the folding of Populism into the ruling party of the South), class divisions among Populists (between the landless rank-and-file and much of the landed leadership) had already been splintering the movement; in the South, Democrats exercised their social, political, and economic authority to destroy independent leadership—especially in those instances of black and white coalitions. Anti-fusion laws in the Midwest (where the People's Party garnered some of its largest votes) coupled with Democratic attacks in the South—changing election laws where it could, using various forms of intimidation, including brute force—effectively destroyed the movement by the turn of the century.

Although the history of Populism has been well established by scholars as a white-based and white-led movement (with dozens of regional and state-based works having been published since the 1930s), the role of African Americans within the movement is considerably less known and understood. When referenced, African Americans, mostly concentrated in the South, are treated as a side story in the narrative. With most scholars conducting their studies through an interpretation of the activities and views of white Populist leaders, certain biases took hold—and early on.[6] In 1931, John Hicks, in his widely influential book *The Populist Revolt: A History of the Farmers' Alliance and the People's Party*, described the Colored Farmers' Alliance—one of the largest black organizations of the era—as having been "little more than an appendage" to the southern white Alliance. Since Hicks's characterization of the black organization, dozens of other scholars have followed suit. Southern historians C. Vann Woodward and Lawrence Goodwyn, among others, while more attentive to African Americans and Populism, wrote about "biracial alliances" in the movement—but maintained that African Americans were minor partners in such alliances (ultimately coming to the same conclusion as Hicks). Despite the efforts of historians such as Jack Abramowitz, William Holmes, Gerald Gaither, and Gregg Cantrell to highlight black political agency within Populism, the image and perspective persists of black people, and the Colored Farmers' Alliance in particular, as "an appendage to the postbellum southern white Farmers' Alliance movement," as one author noted in the 1990s, using language almost verbatim from the 1930s.[7]

From the vantage point of white Populists, the view promoted by Hicks, and subsequently adopted by most scholars of the movement, is correct: African

Americans were marginal to white Populists and their organizations. Most white southerners were not concerned with the plight of black farmers, sharecroppers, and agrarian workers in the way that they were their own. So who were the African Americans in the People's Party parade in Raleigh? What were they doing both in and along the procession? What interests did they have in being there? And, how may have studies on Populism—largely refracted through the words of its white participants—shaped the ways in which scholars have come to understand African American political action in the late nineteenth century?

I first came across a reference to the Colored Farmers' Alliance in an interview published in the journal *Race & Reason*. Herbert Aptheker, a pioneer in the study of African American slave revolts, was responding to a question about areas of research that he believed needed further attention. He briefly noted that while leaders of the Colored Farmers' Alliance claimed an extraordinary membership of over one million men and women, little else was known about the organization.[8] I decided to pursue the subject, broadening the scope of my research to include African Americans in the Populist movement as a whole. Over the coming years, however, the more I focused on the activity of African Americans and their organizations, the more I began seeing a disconnect between the lives of rural African Americans in the New South (the period between the end of Reconstruction and World War I) and how black people were being characterized by scholars of Populism.[9] The evidence seemed to indicate that African Americans had, in fact, been engaged in a series of interconnected organizations that were separate and distinct from those of their white counterparts. But was there a case to be made for a new perspective of African Americans and Populism? Was there such a thing as "Black Populism" as a movement unto itself—that is, independent of the white-led Populist movement?

Three assumptions appeared to be guiding the scholarship on African Americans and Populism: (1) African Americans and their organizations were an offshoot of Populism; (2) "Black Populism" was limited to African Americans affiliated with the People's Party; and (3) African Americans operated principally under white leadership. Scholars, it seems, have too closely followed the words of white Populists in both their descriptions and analysis. As the North Carolina historian Joe Creech observes, "Page after page of Populist correspondence and Populist news print discussed the ebb and flow of Populist success as if [the] massive black voting bloc never existed. Perhaps these Populists, like many of their historians, were simply unaware of the numbers. Perhaps they were aware but chose not to advertise the fact in order to avoid more Democratic condemnation."[10] Thus, for example, the 1890 North Carolina *Progressive Farmer* assertion that African Americans have "always [functioned with] the aid of white leaders," would become the dominant and repeated view.[11] While the term "Black Populism" was used by scholars as early as the 1940s—first appearing in a master's thesis by Douglass Perry in 1945 entitled "Black Populism: The Negro in the People's Party in Texas"—the perspective offered is that of white Populists bringing African Americans into *their* organizations, under *their* leadership.[12] Such a perspective ultimately positions African Americans as pawns (and victims) of southern white men's efforts to gain or retain power.

With few exceptions, it remains the case that when historians, political scientists, and other scholars refer to Black Populism they are either implicitly or explicitly referring to African Americans in a movement understood to be fundamentally white in its composition and white in its leadership. However, given the *de facto* segregated institutional arrangements in the South (before the advent of *de jure* segregation, i.e. Jim Crow), if African Americans were going to challenge the authorities who ruled over them, would they not have had to organize themselves independently—as had those who organized the southern black churches, fraternal orders, and benevolent associations of the same period?

Rather than try to fit southern African Americans and their organizations into preexisting categories of what may be considered "white Populism," I began to develop a concept of Black Populism as a regional movement with its own integrity. In 2003 Steven Hahn published his *A Nation Under Our Feet: Black Political Struggles in the Rural South from Slavery to the Great Migration*.[13] Hahn's elegant study, combined with others since, most notably Charles Postel's *The Populist Vision*, in which he acknowledges "two Populisms, black and white," along with Gerald Gaither's revised *Blacks and the Populist Revolt* (renamed *Blacks and the Populist Movement*), Matthew Hild's *Greenbackers, Knights of Labor, and Populists*, and Joseph Gerteis's *Class and the Color Line*, indicate a new academic consensus: southern African Americans in the post-Reconstruction era were not only actively organizing against (not simply victims of) Democratic rule but developed their own lines of independent black political organizing.[14]

Incorporating the latest scholarship, and building on new strands of evidence, what follows is a history of Black Populism as an *independent movement of black farmers, sharecroppers, and agrarian workers*. As early as 1938, Girard T. Bryant implied that African Americans were independent of the white Populist movement; he titled the fifth chapter of this master's thesis "Colored Populism." That independent notion of African Americans, however, appears to have been buried, not to reappear for nearly half a century. In 1992 Ayers would, in passing, note that "Blacks [of the Colored Farmers' Alliance] ... did not think they could count on white fairness; they saw themselves as a group self-consciously opposed to whites, willing to organize for its members' protection," further suggesting the movement's independence. Patrick Dickson makes the strongest case for the independent origins of the Colored Farmers' Alliance. Dickson challenges a fundamental assumption about the Colored Alliance made by the most cited historian of the white Populist movement, Lawrence Goodwyn: "Goodwyn believed [that the rapid expansion of the white Farmers' Alliance in the mid-1880s] 'generated a self-confidence and enthusiasm among [white] Alliance lecturers... that made organization of black farmers a distinct possibility.'" But, asks Dickson, "How reliable is this assertion?" He continues, "There is little or no evidence that [white] Alliance lecturers were the driving force behind organization of the Colored Alliance," delving into Goodwyn's footnotes to make his point. Dickson's study, however, does not delve into the development of Black Populism beyond the early 1890s.[15]

In addition to the eleven former Confederate states of the South, the following study includes the activities of African Americans in Kansas and Missouri. These two states were in many ways an extension of southern black life; African Americans from the South migrated to Kansas and Missouri in substantial numbers after Reconstruction. Maryland and Kentucky (likely areas for this study, given their proximity to the rest of the South) had different histories; independent black politics never took hold in these latter border states the way that it did further south and west. The origins of this partly lie in policies enacted during Reconstruction.[16] As has been the case with other periods in American history in which black political agency has had to be reconstructed (i.e., the slave revolts and conspiracies of the colonial era or the work of black abolitionists in the first half of the nineteenth century), the quarter century following Reconstruction has required new research and reconsideration regarding African Americans in the South. Despite the growing number of studies showing otherwise, American history textbooks continue to give the overall impression that African Americans were politically passive in the decades following Reconstruction, that is, until the modern civil rights movement.[17] Far from being passive in the years following Reconstruction, black men and women took great measures—and, at times, at great costs—to carry out a range of tactics to advance the political and economic interests of their communities.

Beginning in the late 1870s African Americans built new institutions or strengthened existing ones. For instance, Prince Hall Grand Lodges (the Black Freemasons), originating in the Northeast, were formed across the South, assuming political functions. As the historian Corey Walker describes: "African American appropriation of Freemasonry was a crucial component in a complex political struggle that did not dichotomize the political and cultural ... African American Freemasonry was part of a larger political strategy—what can be termed the 'politics of culture'—that employed various cultural formations in an ever-expanding arsenal of political weapons designed to aid African Americans in articulating their discontent with a political system that marginalized their political choices and opportunities."[18]

Other fraternal orders of the late 1870s and early 1880s included the Colored Granges in Texas and Tennessee, the United Order of True Reformers, founded in Richmond, Virginia, and the Grand United Order of Good Samaritans, also in Virginia, and the National Order of Mosaic Templars of America, established in Little Rock, Arkansas. The historian Michael Gomez has also noted the continuation of uniquely African-derived fraternal orders such as the Sande and Poro in the coastal Carolinas and Georgia. Likewise, a variety of benevolent associations were established in the period with chapters across the South. These included the United Friends Association, the Union Band of Brothers and Sisters, and the all-female United Daughters of Ham and the Sisters of Zion.[19]

Far more extensive than these fraternal orders and benevolent associations, however, were the Black Baptist and African Methodist Episcopalian churches that formed broad networks of support. The black churches—the "womb" of black society, as C. Eric Lincoln described—would serve as the primary bases in the development of black political action.[20] Along with the mutual aid groups, black churches were essential for the stability and sustenance of African American communities in the post-Emancipation period. Writing in 1897 W. E. B. Du Bois observed, "Next to the churches in importance come the secret and beneficial organizations."[21] Fraternal orders and benevolent associations (whose memberships often overlapped) usually met in black churches—as was the case, for instance, with one black Methodist church in Abbeville, South Carolina, which in September 1886 sponsored a literary society, a singing society, and held meetings of the Colored Farmers' Alliance (considered both a mutual benefit association and a union). As the historian Orville Burton describes, "Independent black churches offered an opportunity to meet together away from the constant scrutiny of whites . . . Rural churches housed such Afro-American institutions as the Masonic lodges, benevolent societies, burial organizations . . . and sponsored schools, fairs, and social gatherings."[22] Black churches provided other vital support in the community: care for the sick and for orphans, loans for those without credit, pensions for widows, and funding to help cover funeral expenses. Together with benevolent associations and fraternal orders, the black churches were therefore natural springboards for what became Black Populism.

Beginning in 1886 and continuing through 1900, African Americans built their own movement for economic and political reform. Black Populism neither mirrored nor derived from the parallel white-based movement, although it did share in common certain demands. Black Populists maintained their own organizations, put forward their own leaders, and developed their own set of tactics. They distinguished themselves from the white movement by demanding nondiscriminatory legislation, an end to separate-coach laws, higher wages for black agrarian workers, better credit for black farmers (along with lower interest rates on loans), an end to the convict lease system, the inclusion of black jurors in court cases involving black defendants, and federal support and oversight regarding both public education and the electoral process.

During the two decades following Reconstruction, Black Populism would assume a variety of organizational forms. Black agrarian groups had been established in some parts of the South before the mid-1880s, and notable black electoral participation continued beyond the late 1890s. For instance, a "Negro Alliance" had been formed in Prairie County, Arkansas, as early as 1882, and African Americans in North Carolina's second congressional district remained active in the electoral arena beyond 1900.[23] However, Black Populism—as a regional movement—consisted of a specific period of discernible movement-building. While leaving the South (that is, "voting with one's feet") or working with the Democratic Party were also strategies employed by African Americans during the period, Black Populists distinguished themselves by challenging Democratic rule. In addition to launching independent and insurgent campaigns against the Democratic Party, Black Populists established farming exchanges, raised money for schools, published newspapers, led boycotts and strikes, and lobbied for political reforms. Within half a decade the number of people participating in the movement grew from handfuls to several hundred thousand—exact membership figures are impossible to verify since membership lists were almost never made for fear of reprisal from white authorities should they be discovered.[24]

Black Populism took shape in 1886 with the emergence of a cluster of organizations, including the Colored Farmers' Alliance, the Colored Agricultural Wheels, the southern branch of the Knights of Labor, the Cooperative Workers of America, and the Colored Farmers' Union. As Gerald Gaither notes, the movement of African Americans was not "a sudden political aberration but the culmination of a pattern of agrarian protest that had existed at least since Reconstruction."[25] The establishment of formal organizations in 1886 therefore serves as an approximation of the starting point of the regionwide movement; it does not mean that movement-building efforts were not already underway. By the early 1890s, Black Populism—whose participants had been up to this point largely engaged in the formation of farming cooperatives, instruction to improve agricultural techniques, demanding higher wages for agrarian workers, and lobbying the government for economic reforms—shifted toward the electoral arena. African Americans established third parties alongside white Populists, ran insurgent and independent candidates for office, and created fusion or coalitional campaigns. In addition to working with white independents, most notably, members of the People's Party, Black Populists selectively worked with the Republican Party.

As Black Populism expanded across the region, it met different kinds of resistance—and from a variety of sources. Not only did individual white planters, merchants, landlords, and employers oppose the movement (sometimes through force), but political resistance came from wealthier and more established African Americans who disapproved of the movement's increasingly militant tactics (the use of boycotts and strikes, followed by independent electoral politics). Some black Republican leaders who opposed a third-party strategy tried to undermine politically independent initiatives. Many African Americans would even support Democratic gubernatorial candidates over either Republican or People's Party candidates—as in Alabama in 1893 and Georgia and Texas in 1896—with the hope of either gaining or retaining political patronage.

Under increasing attacks and pressure, Black Populism began to buckle in 1896. White Populist and black Republican leaders who had temporarily allied themselves with black independents turned away or were driven apart. By 1900, in the face of fierce opposition—propaganda campaigns, political intimidation, and physical assaults on black leaders and their followers—the movement fully collapsed. Isolated challenges by Black Populists to the Democratic Party continued for several years (as in parts of east Texas), but Black Populism as a region-wide movement had been destroyed.

The development of Black Populism may be best illustrated through the work of some of its leading organizers. Among the most prominent of these men and women were W. J. Campbell of Alabama, the Reverend George W. Lowe of Arkansas, the Reverend Henry S. Doyle of Georgia, the Reverend John L. Moore of Florida, Lutie A. Lytle of Kansas, Oliver Cromwell of Mississippi, the Reverend Walter A. Pattillo of North Carolina, Sherman McCrary of South Carolina, John B. Rayner of Texas, and William H. Warwick of Virginia. Their collective struggles, achievements, and failures form part of the history of what was the largest movement of African Americans in the United States until the modern civil rights movement.

The first chapter in this study, "Roots and Early Development," details the political and economic origins of Black Populism. Here I examine how various groups contributed to the foundations of the movement as it gained traction in the mid-1880s. Organizations sometimes complemented and at other times competed with one another for members. The chapter traces the development of the Colored Agricultural Wheels, the Knights of Labor, the Cooperative Workers of America, and the Colored Farmers' Union, and how these were largely consolidated regionally through the Colored Farmers' Alliance. The works of grassroots organizers such as the Reverend George W. Lowe of Arkansas, Sherman C. McCrary of South Carolina, W. J. Campbell of Alabama, and Romeo Telfair of North Carolina help to illustrate the early period of the movement.

The second chapter, "The Colored Farmers' Alliance," focuses on the Colored Farmers' Alliance—how it was funded, who made up its membership, and the various tactics its leaders pursued. The activities of Oliver Cromwell of Mississippi, Richard M. Humphrey of Texas, Benjamin Patterson of Tennessee, and the Reverend Walter A. Pattillo of North Carolina are detailed here, displaying the movement's regional differences, its local successes, and its limitations. The Colored Farmers' Alliance emerges here as the most important organizational expression of Black Populism in the late 1880s and the early 1890s, playing a key role in the movement's transition towards independent electoral politics.

In "Establishing the 'Negro Party,'" chapter 3, I describe the leadership role of African Americans in creating state-based People's parties in the early 1890s, which led to the formation of the national party. Black Populism may be viewed in this period through the participation of African Americans in several other electoral parties—these included the Union Labor, Prohibition, Alliance, and Republican parties—all of which attempted to challenge the Democratic Party's authority in the South and in areas of the Midwest. In most states, the People's Party was the movement's primary electoral vehicle. In some areas, however, African Americans exerted their political influence through fusion or coalition campaigns with the Republican Party. Black Populists, such as the Reverend Henry S. Doyle of Georgia, William H. Warwick of Virginia, and the Reverend John L. Moore of Florida, figure prominently in establishing and helping to advance the independent political strategy.

Chapter 4, "Independent, Coalition, and Fusion Politics," describes the development of Black Populism from the mid-1890s to the end of the decade. Emphasis is placed here on Georgia, North Carolina, South Carolina, and Texas, showing a variety of experiences among African Americans across the region. As in previous chapters, descriptions and analyses of the work of key black leaders, including George W. Murray of South Carolina and John B. Rayner of Texas, help to demonstrate the complexities of local circumstances. The chapter concludes with a discussion of the collapse of Black Populism due to a combination of internal divisions and heightened political attacks from Democrats.

In the fifth chapter, "Collapse and Aftermath," I provide a final analysis of Black Populism and explore its legacy. What happened to Black Populists after the movement was destroyed? What was its impact on subsequent generations of African Americans in the South? How did northern black leaders view Black Populism during the late nineteenth and early twentieth century? And how did African Americans continue to challenge the Democratic Party in the region?

Chapter One

ROOTS AND EARLY DEVELOPMENT

The Democratic party [in] the South is something more than a mere political organization striving to enforce an administrative policy. It is a white man's party, organized to maintain white supremacy and prevent a repetition of the destructive rule of ignorant negroes and unscrupulous whites.

—*Greensboro Daily Record,* August 19, 1892

The brutality of southern paramilitary politics that began in the antebellum era, and took its deadliest toll during the Civil War, continued beyond Reconstruction. Violence permeated the ongoing struggle over black labor in the final two decades of the nineteenth century. Quasi-free labor had replaced slave labor through sharecropping and tenant farming and almost anywhere rural African Americans asserted their rights, they were met with armed force. Nowhere were the reactions more explosive than in Mississippi, where African Americans comprised the majority of the population. There, in the early 1880s, the combined votes of African Americans with white independents posed a numerical threat to Democratic rule, leading to deadly violence against what had become a black and independent alliance.

In the summer of 1881, J. J. Spellman, a black veteran of Mississippi Reconstruction politics, declared his candidacy for secretary of state as a Republican. A coalition of black Republicans and white Greenbackers soon formed around his candidacy. The Greenback Party had been established a decade earlier to promote currency expansion to assist debtors but the coalition surrounding Spellman in 1881 sought a series of additional economic and political reforms that, if enacted, would benefit rural African Americans: legislation to regulate labor relations, an end to the convict-lease system, protection of existing civil and political rights, and the creation and enforcement of a more equitable electoral process.[1]

Reporting on separate Republican and Greenback state conventions taking place in Jackson on August 25, 1881, the *Huntsville Gazette*, a black-owned and operated newspaper based in Alabama, wrote: "Jackson is in a blaze of excitement tonight. Bands are playing and speeches are being made." The paper further noted that "the democrats express disappointment that the two conventions could harmonize on a platform and common ticket, and every shade of opposition to bourbonism is enthused."[2] Mississippi's Greenback Party, whose members were almost exclusively white, had drawn only 5 percent of the vote in 1880. While most of their demands did not address the specific concerns of African Americans, their support for a "free ballot and a fair count" was in sharp contrast to Democratic attacks on black political rights. By joining with Greenbackers, black Republicans would be poised to go on the electoral offensive.[3]

John R. Lynch, a former slave and two-term congressman who fought to ensure passage of the 1875 Civil Rights Act banning discrimination in public accommodations, helped to engineer the Republican-Greenback coalition. Lynch and other African Americans had seized the opportunity to work with white independents to push for electoral reform. As the *Gazette* observed: "If the fusion between the Republicans, Greenbackers, and Independents in Mississippi succeeds, we may look for an awakening . . . They fight for a free ballot and a fair count."[4] As election day approached, the Bourbon's *Daily Democrat* launched a series of editorials deriding Lynch as a "clever little didapper darkey"; over the next weeks, the attacks in the Democratic press mounted.[5] Republicans and Greenbackers were soon tarred with the same brush as the "miscegenation alias republican-greenback ticket"—race-mixing language used to instill a sense of white solidarity against those who would dare oppose Democratic rule.[6]

The specter of "Black Republicanism" had loomed large in the consciousness of Mississippi Democrats throughout the summer and fall of 1881. By the day of the election—November 8, 1881—the stage was set: a sheriff's posse in Meridian had gathered as a show of force to intimidate fusion voters. The white posse grew to nearly one hundred men, which was soon matched by the same number of African Americans who came to protect fusion voters. A pitched battle for the ballot began.[7] Shots were first fired near a downtown polling site. The fighting soon moved to nearby Marion, alongside the Sowashee Creek. African Americans were outnumbered and outgunned; some were able to escape on horseback. One group, however, "entrenched themselves in the house of [Ed] Vance, their leader, in which several more lives were lost," reported the *Gazette*. Surrounded by the sheriff's posse, the black men "fought desperately all day."[8] In the end, they and their fusion candidates were defeated; their resistance destroyed. During the battle, the sheriff had been injured; five white men lay dead in the aftermath. The number of African American casualties went unreported.[9]

Battles over the ballot were waged elsewhere in Mississippi, albeit in less violent form, but with equal political impact on statewide returns. The state Democratic Party claimed victory by some 25,000 votes. Nevertheless, the Republican-Greenback coalition received 10,000 *more* votes in 1881 than the total number of votes received in the previous election when Republicans and Greenbackers ran separately against the "party of the fathers." The Republican Spellman, who received 49,021 votes, trailed the rest of the statewide ticket by only 1,000 votes, strongly suggesting that both black and white voters supported him.[10] Fearing the electoral prospects of the Republican-Greenback coalition, Democrats exercised lethal force. As one Democratic editor pithily observed, "The Democratic party [in] the South is something more than a mere political organization ... It is a white man's party, organized to maintain white supremacy and prevent a repetition of the destructive rule of ignorant negroes and unscrupulous whites"—the "repetition" being Reconstruction.[11]

Revolutionary strides in black civil and political rights were made during the early period of Reconstruction, which began in 1863 and ended in 1877. As Union forces advanced and took control of Confederate-held territory during the Civil War, the federal government, under Republican control, took measures to rebuild not only the South's infrastructure but its political institutions. The federal government would establish pro-Union state governments in the South, provide aid to war refugees (through the Freedman's Bureau), and through an infusion of capital and credit help rebuild the roads, buildings, and other transportation and communication services that had been destroyed in the region in the course of the war. During this period, Radical Republicans pushed for the passage of the abolition of slavery (1865), the extension of citizenship to all African Americans (1868), and adult black male suffrage (1870) in the Thirteenth, Fourteenth, and Fifteenth Amendments to the U.S. Constitution; these amendments were strengthened by a series of Civil Rights Acts between 1866 and 1875. The region and period also saw the first public school system established, and the accumulation of small plots of land among African Americans. However, much of the more substantial land that was initially promised to African Americans was either never given or, when secured, stripped away soon after the war.[12]

Black communities collectively created an array of organizations in the wake of the Civil War—including black churches, fraternal orders, and benevolent associations. Spurred by these organizations, and charged politically by Union Leagues (a pro-Republican organization) and calls made by a variety of state and regional black conferences in the late 1860s and 1870s, Reconstruction saw a dramatic expansion of black electoral participation in the South. During this period, African Americans exerted a considerable measure of power—including repealing Black Codes designed to undercut black economic autonomy, shifting the tax base from poll taxes to property taxes, and forming the ranks of armed black militias. Over two thousand African Americans would hold public offices during the period, with hundreds more white Republican allies being elected to offices with black support. By the mid-1870s, however, federal enforcement of Reconstruction policies began to falter as the nation sank into an economic depression.[13]

Within four years of the "Panic of 1873" (a depression caused in part by the collapse in the value of railroad securities), the price of cotton fell by nearly 50 percent and sources of credit in the South evaporated. Northern political commitment to Reconstruction waned as southern Republicans were increasingly forced to defend themselves against Democratic accusations of mismanagement and corruption. African Americans became the targets of roving bands of white terrorists allied to the southern Democratic Party; Republican leaders—black and white—were physically intimidated, assaulted, and even assassinated. Meanwhile, moves were made within southern Republican leadership circles to marginalize and then purge "Negro" elements (which included white sympathizers) from their ranks. Within this context, expectations about what Reconstruction could accomplish were steadily lowered and eventually abandoned altogether.

The end of Reconstruction came with the departure of the last federal troops from South Carolina and Louisiana as a result of the Compromise of 1877. In a political deal negotiated between the Democratic and Republican parties over contested electoral college votes in the 1876 presidential election between Republican Rutherford Hayes and Democrat Samuel Tilden, the Republicans took the presidency in exchange for Democrats resuming control of the South by allowing the withdrawal of the remaining federal troops from the region.[14] The end of Reconstruction meant the end of protection against violations of civil and political rights. It also meant the end of federal and state Republican patronage for African Americans. While patronage assisted only a relatively few people directly, the social impact of patronage was key for black communities as a whole. Daily issues faced by African Americans, from road repair to criminal justice, were more likely to be addressed equitably with African Americans holding local offices and administrative positions than they would be under white Democratic appointees. The loss of federal protection and patronage signaled a new period, one in which African Americans would have little political or legal recourse to counter a range of abuses and crimes: exorbitant interest rates and fees, the deprivation of wages, beatings, harassment, and even murder.[15]

The end of Reconstruction saw Republican legislators and officeholders systematically, sometimes brutally removed from office by Democrats who sought to "redeem" the South from Republican authority. These Redeemers, as they came to be known, equally terrorized local black populations through "rifle clubs" and paramilitary organizations such as the White Leagues and the Red Shirts, which served as adjuncts of the Democratic Party.[16] Led by white planters, Democrats took office and reasserted their antebellum privileges and prerogatives. They would now do so as the "Southern Democracy"— the network of courts, banks, militias, sheriffs, and newspapers supporting redemption. Helping to ensure their control over black labor and much of the southern political economy was the system of sharecropping—a new economic arrangement in the region as a whole. Under the new system, sharecroppers owed a "share" of their crop to landlords after each harvest, although cash rents were sometimes collected; in practice, the system led to debt peonage.

Economic dependency resulting from obstacles and abuses faced by African Americans in trying to secure their own land lay at the crux of black disempowerment both during the latter part of and following Reconstruction.[17] In a predominantly agrarian society, ownership of land guaranteed a degree of autonomy. In spite of major advances made in black political representation during Reconstruction, the growth of sharecropping—leading to black dependence on white landowners—undermined and then derailed that progress. Former slaves were legally free yet (in practice) sharecropping mimicked economic and social aspects of previous slave/master relations. With the best land increasingly monopolized by white farmers, debt induced by the system of sharecropping gripped millions of landless men and women. In an environment where casting one's ballot was neither secret nor discreet, the system ended up politically tying African Americans to those to whom they were in debt.

Sharecropping emerged when confiscated land had been placed back into the hands of wealthier white southerners following the Civil War. In 1865, the Freedman's Bureau controlled over 850,000 acres of "abandoned land." Much of that land, however, was returned to white plantation owners under Lincoln's successor, Andrew Johnson.[18] On the surface, sharecropping appeared to be a kind of economic compromise between white planters, who were determined to control black labor, and African Americans, who needed land to live. Black sharecroppers, like their white counterparts, however, shouldered the bulk of the burden of the inequitable arrangement.[19]

Sharecroppers borrowed money or credit from their landlords against future harvests to purchase tools, seed, fertilizer, and other supplies. But landlords and "furnishing merchants" (often one and the same people) demanded grossly inflated interest rates and costs for supplies. Related to sharecropping was the increased use of crop liens by small landholders. These were claims on future crops as a guarantee for supplies bought on credit. Like sharecroppers, small landholders using crop liens to receive supplies did so at a high cost. In the Cotton Belt, the more farmers concentrated on growing cotton, the more it glutted the market and drove prices down, adding to the financial crisis. Poor harvests, costly supplies, and false accounting, in conjunction with high interest rates and falling crop prices, often combined to form insurmountable debt among small farmers and sharecroppers.

One rural black family after another became ensnared in the system of sharecropping. By 1880 in Georgia already 44 percent of farms were being worked by tenants while the rest were owner-cultivated.[20] A decade later that number increased almost an additional 10 percent. In a state where African Americans comprised well over 40 percent of the population, a direct correlation could be made: the higher the percentage of black people in a county, the higher the percentage of tenant arrangements. While the trend in Georgia was evident throughout most of the South, there were exceptions: in parts of Virginia the level of black tenancy and sharecropping remained approximately the same between 1880 and 1890; in Granville County, North Carolina, black-owned farms increased between 1872 and 1898. But for every black sharecropper, there were at least two African Americans who worked for low wages on farms or carried out other agrarian-related wage labor.[21] Agricultural workers were usually the most vulnerable of all rural groups with their livelihood being dependent upon the vagaries of white planters, creditors, and merchants. Thomas Hall, a former slave from North Carolina interviewed at the age of eighty-one, recalled the plight of African Americans: "[We] still had to depend on the Southern white man for work, food, and clothing, and he held us, through our necessity and want, in a state of servitude but little better than slavery."[22]

Black landowners who were financially independent were only a small percentage of the rural population. During the two decades following the collapse of Reconstruction, the adult population of African Americans in the rural South could be grouped into three categories: small landowners (approximately 144,000 people, or 8 percent of the African American population); sharecroppers (464,000, or 27 percent); and agrarian laborers (1,170,000, or 65 percent). In other words, upwards of 92 percent of adult African Americans were landless.[23] As Postel notes regarding black sharecroppers, "Dependent on landowners for housing, supplies, and mules, [they] usually owed their share of cotton well before harvest and might not even touch money from one season to the next."[24]

Among African Americans who did own a few acres of land, it was usually not enough to be commercially self-sustaining, forcing them into either sharecropping arrangements or seasonal forms of wage labor. In 1890 only 7.1 percent of the rural black adult population owned the land on which they worked (approximately 121,000 people).[25] Economic pressures in the New South were such that even commercial black landowners had to struggle to make ends meet. As a correspondent for the *Progressive Farmer* noted in the fall of 1890, Willie Best of

North Carolina, "probably one of the wealthiest colored men in Wayne county" with some thirty acres of land, netted less than $100 annually from cotton farming.[26] Given these conditions, it is not surprising that many African Americans, if and when they could, left the land they lived and worked on in search of better opportunities.[27]

In the wake of Reconstruction, tens of thousands of African Americans in the rural South set out to find better economic conditions. They migrated to urban centers, to western and northern lands within the South, or out of the region altogether. Seeking more promising opportunities—if not a Promised Land—entire black communities of "exodusters" followed people like Benjamin "Pap" Singleton, a former slave from Tennessee, to new settlements. Between 1879 and 1881 at least 20,000 African Americans migrated to Kansas alone.[28] The U.S. Census Bureau would list 48,929 African Americans migrating from the South to the Midwest and North between 1870 and 1880. Tens of thousands of men and women also migrated *within* the South (for instance, from North Carolina to Texas).[29] Overseas migration, such as efforts to settle in Liberia, were considerably less successful. Between 1877 and 1880, fewer than 400 African Americans made the voyage to West Africa.[30] Economic hardship was among the principal reasons for migration. Recurring crop failures in South Carolina in 1881, for instance, led to mass migration from that state to Arkansas. In response to oppressive labor conditions, African Americans in North Carolina threatened to "depopulate" parts of the state.[31] As one contemporary observer noted, "The migrating negroes complained that their efforts for ten years to obtain a living and improve their condition had failed on account of the exorbitant rents and prices of provisions." He went on, "their political rights were denied them, their ballots not counted, and they were not even permitted to sign petitions against passage of the stock law, which would make existence impossible for them."[32]

Whether moving within the United States or some even going abroad, the impulse among African Americans to relocate was driven as much by economic conditions as it was by political repression.[33] State constitutional conventions held by Redeemer-run governments in the period following Reconstruction were organized to consolidate Democratic power by stripping African Americans' civil and political rights. African Americans, in turn, met in conventions to determine which courses of action to pursue. One convention held in New Orleans on April 17, 1879, brought together two hundred black men and women to discuss migration as a possible solution to the economic and political marginalization of their communities. Pickney B. S. Pinchback, the former black Republican governor of Louisiana, who initially opposed the Kansas Exodus, addressed the convention. Speaking to the assembly, he asked why so many people wanted to leave the area. "The answer," he later said, "was that they were starving; that they were swindled;

[and] that they were afraid of the [outcome of the Democratic Party-controlled] Constitutional Convention." Pinchback would use his newspaper, the *Louisianan*, to encourage migration.[34] For most African Americans, however, leaving home was untenable, as financial debt and personal obligations kept them from moving, at least in the short term. Nevertheless, African Americans did spread the call for migration through local organizations, including churches, plantation councils, militia district clubs, schoolhouses, and benevolent associations.[35]

Some African Americans, however, unwilling or unable to leave their communities or homes behind, pursued electoral coalitions with white independents to challenge Democratic authority. In doing so, they risked not only economic reprisal, but also physical assault, as events surrounding the 1881 election in Mississippi made plain.

African Americans faced a reconstituted and formidable Democratic Party in the New South. Democrats engaged in various forms of electoral fraud (ballot-stuffing, miscounting, and denying votes with no legal cause) were willing to use violence at almost any point to maintain their political authority.[36] Economic dependency—with rising debt, poor wages, and lack of capital—had left the rural poor susceptible to Democratic manipulation and coercion. This *de facto* erosion of political and civil rights would lead some African Americans to seek out white independents as allies in the electoral arena. Black voters in the North had done so in the antebellum period, beginning in 1840 with the Liberty Party; African Americans, this time in the South, would do so with the Greenback Party.

In 1875, African Americans were among those who helped to establish the Greenback Party. That year, black delegates led by C. W. Thompson of the Virginia Tobacco Laborers' Union traveled to Cleveland, Ohio, for what would be the party's founding convention.[37] Although predominantly white in their composition, the Greenback and Greenback Labor parties offered hope to black farmers. In the South, where money was particularly scarce, Greenbackers called for greater printing and circulation of "greenbacks" (paper dollars) to ease debt. The contraction of paper currency favored creditors, who stood to lose if there were to be greater circulation and therefore inflation. The country's severe contraction of the money supply, which was based on a gold standard (and was limited by virtue of the supply of gold), was compounded by it being largely concentrated in the hands of lenders. In the decades following the Civil War, the opening of vast silver veins, such as Nevada's Comstock Lode, greatly increased the supply of silver in the nation and aided the Greenbackers' cause.[38]

Following the first national Greenback convention held in Cleveland, African Americans in Texas began to meet with white independents in order to launch their state's Greenback Party. Black Greenbackers in Texas would play a particularly important role in helping to ensure the party's commitment to improve education and oppose disfranchisement.[39] Among the forty delegates at the first convention of Greenback clubs held in Austin on March 12, 1878, at least ten of the delegates were black. Delegates adopted a platform asserting "The object of our republican government is to protect alike the rights of every individual in the union, irrespective of section, State, riches, poverty, race, color or creed"—in effect, a call for further black recruitment into the party.[40]

The presence of Greenbackers in Texas grew significantly over the course of 1878. By August of that year, a statewide Greenback Labor Party convention brought together representatives from 482 chapters, of which 70 were all-black chapters. African Americans would constitute the majority of Greenback chapters in several east Texas counties. In the November mid-term election, over 56,000 black and white voters cast their ballot for Greenbackers, including those from predominantly black counties. Greenbackers and Republicans—the former being predominantly identified as white, the latter as black—would maximize their support by fusing (running a shared candidate, or slate of candidates for office). Fusion allowed African Americans who were either unwilling or unsure of leaving the Republican Party to gain political leverage. By joining forces with Greenbackers, candidates with African American endorsements won several local and statewide offices.[41] Beyond voting, African Americans continued to participate in conventions with Greenbackers; up to 20 black delegates attended the Greenback Party's state convention in 1881.[42] The following year, black Republicans and white independents in east Texas—where independent politics and black participation were greatest in the state—won a series of local offices through fusion. The black and independent coalition, however, was short-lived as Democrats soon drove coalition members out of office or out of electoral politics altogether.[43]

In neighboring Alabama, the Greenback Party served similarly as the political nexus of disaffected black and white farmers and laborers in the late 1870s. In northern Alabama, black sharecroppers and former white Whigs in Lawrence County established a Greenback Party and ran a fusion slate with Republicans.[44] As in other states to the North, the Greenback Party became closely associated with labor organizations, specifically the Knights of Labor. In the district of Birmingham, African Americans formed their own separate Greenback Labor clubs and became part of a short-lived black and independent coalition—despite widespread violence and intimidation. Violence was directed not only toward African Americans. The Greenback Labor Party's 1880 gubernatorial candidate, Reverend James Madison Pickens—a Confederate veteran and Disciples of Christ preacher—decried massive election fraud on the part of the Democratic Party when election returns revealed that he had been defeated by over three-quarters of the vote (a lopsided defeat, given the strength of the party in the state). By February 1881, the outspoken white candidate was found shot dead. A black Republican observer noted that the defeat of Greenback Labor candidates was the result of "every species of fraud that depraved human ingenuity could devise." Still, twenty-two Greenbackers (including several "Independents"), mostly from northern Alabama, were elected to office in 1882. At least one of the Greenback-Independents who took a seat in the state assembly was African American. Williams (no first name listed) was from Madison County, where the voting population was evenly divided between black and white voters.[45]

African Americans were active in Greenback circles in small pockets elsewhere in the South. For instance, in Arkansas, particularly in Little Rock, African Americans played an important role in the Greenback Labor Party, which fused with the Republican Party.[46] In South Carolina, some fifteen African Americans were elected to the state assembly through an alliance between the Republican and Greenback parties in 1882.[47] Such black and independent partnerships produced a spike in political support for independent candidates across much of the South. Between 31 and 52 percent of voters in Alabama, Florida, Georgia, Mississippi, and Texas cast their ballot for independent and third-party candidates between 1880 and 1884 (including "Independent," Greenback, and Readjuster candidates).[48]

In supporting white independents—be it individual independent candidates or parties (Greenback or Greenback Labor) or in fusion bids (via the Republican Party)—African Americans were leveraging white political discontent to challenge the Democratic Party. While Democrats crushed most of their challengers, at least one black and independent alliance temporarily seized power at the state level. Under the leadership of William Mahone (a veteran of the Confederate army, known as "Little Billy") poor black and white farmers in Virginia came together in the Readjustment Party. They wanted to "readjust" the lingering Civil War and Reconstruction bonded debt downwards. In 1879, riding a wave of political discontent, the independents took over their state's legislature; two years later, they took over the governor's office. Ironically, because Reconstruction was less extensive in Virginia than in other states farther south, the independent upsurge produced less of a reaction among Redeemers. There in the Old Dominion—a former slave-holding bastion where African Americans comprised approximately 42 percent of the population—independents could compete in the electoral arena with less fear of violent reprisal.[49] Virginia's Readjusters demanded that the burden of debt be shifted from individuals onto corporations; they wanted to see the poll tax eliminated, an increase in funding for public education, and protection of voting rights for African Americans (on whom white coalition partners depended for votes). When Readjusters swept into power in 1879, policy changes followed that directly and positively affected African Americans: the poll tax was removed, black schools were established, and the "whipping post," a grisly reminder of slavery, was abolished.[50]

By 1879, the Greenback Labor Party had sent three Greenbackers from the South to Congress. But the independent and fusion efforts of the late 1870s and early 1880s, which included a sprinkling of victories, were not to last. Democrats quickly moved in to contain the challenges to their authority.[51] Just as violence was used in Mississippi in 1881 to suppress the black and independent Republican-Greenback coalition from exerting its numbers at the polls, Democrats came after African Americans and their white allies elsewhere in the South. Those who voted with the Greenback Labor Party in Louisiana and South Carolina were targeted with particular vengeance. The *New York Times* ominously reported that in Louisiana "colored men have been given to understand that they must vote for the Democratic candidates or take the consequences"; two African Americans scheduled to testify before a grand jury regarding the "election troubles" were abducted on the way to court and lynched by a mob. In neighboring South Carolina, other voters and candidates were harassed, beaten, and killed by Red Shirt companies.[52]

Redeemers must have felt vindicated in their use of violence when the federal government made clear its unwillingness to redress the injustices taking place in the South. The October 15, 1883, U.S. Supreme Court ruling which stated that the Civil Rights Act of 1875 was unconstitutional, gave southern Democrats legal fodder. The highest court in the land had effectively decided that the Fourteenth Amendment did not forbid citizens, only states, from discriminating against people based on race.[53] The decision to strike down a fundamental feature of federal protection of black civil and political rights sent a clear message: African Americans could be treated as second-class citizens in both practice and the law.

Independent politics would be temporarily crushed. Between 1878 and 1881 African Americans had worked with Greenbackers in Mississippi, Texas, Alabama, Arkansas, Louisiana, and South Carolina (or in the case of Virginia, forming the Readjustment Party). The Republican-Greenback fusion efforts would foreshadow an explosion of independent electoral activity within several years. African Americans would return to independent politics, but with stronger organization. As the historian Matthew Hild notes, the Alliances and the Knights, among other associations, "would provide the organization and mobilization of farmers and laborers in the region [during the middle to late 1880s] that was largely lacking during the Greenback era."[54]

In the mid-1880s growing numbers of black farmers, sharecroppers, and agrarian workers began forming economic cooperatives where they pooled their resources, educated themselves in better farming techniques, and banned together to demand better wages. A series of droughts, mounting debt, and poor wages had combined to devastate rural black communities across the South. Both small landholding farmers and sharecroppers were increasingly vulnerable to eroding prices for crops that faced foreign competition (notably, Egyptian, Brazilian, and East Indian–grown cotton); wages for agrarian labor continued to decline along with commodity prices; compounding this vulnerability to the market were the extortionist and discriminatory practices of the southern "furnishing merchant"—often the only local source of credit, tools, seed, and other necessities. It was in this context that African Americans gravitated toward cooperation and other forms of collective support in their communities. By the mid-1880s, the contours of Black Populism were beginning to appear through the formation of a series of agrarian-based organizations; fundamental to these new organizations, which included both farmer and sharecropper associations and labor unions, were the bases of support out of which they grew—most notably, the black churches.

The Black Baptist and African Methodist Episcopalian (AME) churches were not only seedbeds of African American political activity from the antebellum era through Reconstruction, but also provided much of the organizational impetus and leadership that would help develop Black Populism. Many of the movement's most important leaders were Christian ministers—including Walter A. Pattillo of North Carolina, Henry S. Doyle of Georgia, John B. Rayner of Texas, and John L. Moore of Florida. With so many African Americans receiving their initial leadership training first in the "invisible institution," and then openly following Emancipation, black churches became staging grounds for Black Populism.[55] Most African Americans in the nation were Christian. However, some scholars, most prominently, Michael Gomez, contend that there was a degree of Islamic presence in the life of southern black communities, whether cultural in form or explicitly religious in practice—and as diminished as that presence might have been by the latter half of the nineteenth century.[56] Larger still was the presence of syncretic spiritual practices that incorporated Christian beliefs. This was the "hoodoo and voodoo, an underground world of peasant cosmology" in southern African American culture, as described by Tiffany Patterson.[57] Christianity, whether of the Black Baptist or AME variations, however, dominated black religious life in the South. These black churches would serve as critical communication hubs, meeting places and sites for the dissemination of information within African American culture and society; they were instrumental in maintaining morale, providing material support, and nurturing the communities out of which post-Emancipation leadership would emerge.[58]

Drawing upon biblical images ranging from Exodus of the Old Testament to concepts of freedom in Paul's epistles in the New Testament, black ministers "eschewed the line between sacred and profane when it came to politics."[59] For African Americans, the church was *the* central social and political institution in the black community—the primary public sphere for black men and women. In the churches, African Americans found and practiced what Bishop Daniel A. Payne of the AME Church described in 1886 as "the freedom of thought, freedom of speech, [and] freedom of action."[60] By 1890, there were over 1.3 million black Baptists in the South. This was three times as many as any other Christian denomination; the AME churches claimed membership of 310,000 in the South, while the AME Zion church counted 366,000 members.[61] Black women, comprising the majority of the African American population, also constituted the majority of members.[62] Among these women, selected "church mothers" and "gospel mothers" led the day-to-day activities of their congregations. As a result, they were intimately involved in the recruitment and training of cadre—collectively constituting a skilled mobilization force to move the black community to action when necessary. As the historian Steven Hahn observes, black churches "unif[ied] rural African Americans across district and county lines [and to] this extent, they were by definition political institutions."[63]

At least one in three African Americans was a member of a black church in the South.[64] Through these black churches, congregants learned about local, state, and national issues. News was discussed and newspapers were read aloud, especially for the benefit of members who were illiterate (in 1880, black illiteracy rates ranged from 70 to 82 percent in the South).[65] And while some ministers attempted to steer clear of electoral politics, many viewed their role, and that of their congregation, as an essential part of black political struggle; for some it was a sacred responsibility. The official policy of the AME was to regard politics as an "imperative duty"; Baptists left political initiatives to their individual congregations to decide. According to Hahn, "The churches did not simply open their doors to the world of politics; they assimilated politics into their very rhythms of worship and community life."[66] In a fundamental sense, therefore, Black Populism was an outgrowth of black evangelical life, extending "Christian American freedom," in which lines of distinction between republican citizenship and religious conviction were blurred.[67]

For at least some African Americans, Black Populism, and its principal organizations in the 1880s and 1890s—the Colored Farmers' Alliance, followed by the People's Party—were discussed in religious terms, forming part of an evangelical drive to reform society. As the historian Joe Creech describes:

> [E]vangelicals worshipped a God who, through "moral governance," was intimately involved in human affairs though guiding people to obey divine laws of morality, economics, and human government; and while the ultimate end

of evangelicals ... was eternal life in the arms of Jesus, for most that hope also included the establishment of Christ's visible rule on earth through human initiative, otherwise known as the millennium. *In the Alliance and People's Party, the political and economic goals of Populism fused with evangelicals goals of salvation and the establishment of the millennium* (and in the case of the millennium, many Populists made Christ's earthly reign actually contingent on those Populist reforms). The result was a movement imbued with a religious fervor to match the ultimate, eschatological certainty and seriousness of the ideals and hopes that propelled it.[68] (emphasis added)

A new generation of post-Reconstruction black leadership had begun to assert itself in the mid-1880s. African Americans born in the decade before the Civil War who were old enough to have experienced the promise of Emancipation and the collapse of Reconstruction began to create local organizations in order to foster solidarity and economic cooperation within their communities. By 1886, a new movement was visible through a confluence of agrarian-based organizations in Alabama, North Carolina, South Carolina, Florida, Louisiana, and Texas. These included the Colored Agricultural Wheels, the Knights of Labor, the Cooperative Workers of America, the Colored Farmers' Union, and the Colored Farmers' Alliance. Thousands of African Americans would soon be participating in what became a regional movement encompassing broad networks of like-minded agrarian-based organizations. Black Populism spread at varying rates, its development shaped by social, political, and economic factors on the ground.

At root, Black Populists promoted the political and economic welfare of rural African Americans. They were "populist" by virtue of their opposition to planter, business, and political authorities and elites; their demands for economic and political reforms reflected their various constituents: farmers, sharecroppers, and agrarian workers. Regarding agrarian workers, Black Populists called for higher wages and the establishment of a national bureau of labor to oversee labor abuses. In the case of farmers and sharecroppers, Black Populists demanded overturning discriminatory stock laws, enacting a single tax on property, and creating government controls on land speculation, regional trading exchanges, and federal agricultural loan programs (the "subtreasury plan"). Black Populists made still other demands that cut across the black community as a whole: an end to lynching, the convict-lease system, and separate coach-boxes; they also wanted the inclusion of black jurors in cases involving black defendants, and, later, an equitable electoral process, including the secret ballot and county elections (as opposed to governor-appointed positions).

By the early 1890s, Black Populism included at least several hundred thousand adherents—men and women who affiliated with one of a number of organizations that gave expression to the movement. Predictably, retribution by white planters and merchants for the actions of these African Americans was severe. This was the case during the Louisiana Sugar Plantation Strike of 1887, the Leflore County, Mississippi, boycott in 1889, the Cotton Pickers' Strike in Arkansas in 1891, and during the mobilization of black voters in North Carolina in 1894. And while Black Populism was principally a black-led movement, several white leaders may be counted among its ranks. In this it was reminiscent of earlier movements that brought together black and white organizers—the Abolitionist movement of the 1830s and 1840s, and Reconstruction in the 1860s and early 1870s.[69] Black Populism would also foreshadow later movements, from the black sharecroppers' movement in the 1930s to the modern civil rights movement of the 1950s and 1960s.[70]

Like the broad masses of rural black southerners, most of whom were landless or held only small amounts of land, Black Populism's base of support largely comprised the poorest black farmers and agrarian laborers in the region. In the words of one of the first scholars to focus on African Americans and Populism, Girard Bryant, "The movement was born in the poorest section of the United States . . . [and] the poorest of the poor in the South were Negroes."[71] Many of the movement's leaders, however, either occupied well-regarded positions of authority in the community, such as ministers or teachers, or were small property-owning farmers with enough land to hire others to work. The president of the national Colored Farmers' Alliance, Jacob John Shuffer, for instance, despite having been born into slavery in Louisiana, would acquire 235 acres of the Lopez League in Texas by 1887; moreover, at least seven of the sixteen founding members of the Colored Farmers' Alliance, all of whom were black or listed as "mulatto," held property themselves or belonged to landowning families.[72]

Divisions within the black movement became apparent as its ranks grew. Disputes, which primarily arose over specific tactics, tended to fall along class lines. In the early 1890s, small black landowners opposed the use of strikes by black agrarian laborers. There were other divisions. In areas where there was already a relatively strong black Republican presence, there was disagreement over whether or not a third party should be formed or supported. African Americans also came into conflict with white Populists during the Lodge Bill controversy, regarding federal oversight of elections, and during the regionwide Cotton Pickers' Strike—both in 1891. But when the interests of black and white Populists coincided, African Americans did support the latter's initiatives—such as cooperative exchanges or the subtreasury loan program.[73]

Direct opposition to the movement came not only from white planters and merchants but also from other African Americans. In Georgia, North Carolina, and Texas, some black Republican leaders opposed measures taken by Black Populists for fear of losing local power. However, it was white planters and merchants, threatened by black-led boycotts, strikes, and elections (whether through fusion, running third-party candidates, or supporting insurgents or individual independents) who mounted the greatest and most vicious opposition.

Redeemers drove a wedge between black and white southerners by invoking the specter of "social equality between the races." In 1886 the *Charleston News and Courier*, echoing the *Daily Democrat* in Mississippi several years earlier, charged: "Social equality means miscegenation . . . [leaving] the Southern country in the possession of a nation of mongrels and hybrids."[74] Similarly, the threat of "Negro rule"—the myth fabricated by Redeemers that during Reconstruction white southerners had been subject to black domination—was promoted throughout the white press to frighten its readers. As the historian Melton McLaurin notes regarding resistance to independent black organizing, "[white] opposition always resorted to two basic issues—economic interests and social mores. [The] organization of blacks threatened whites in both areas. Of the two, economic interests aroused the most violent opposition. And, as has always been the case in the South, social mores were manipulated to serve economic ends."[75]

With few exceptions during Reconstruction, African Americans were in fact only a minority of the electorate and elected (or appointed) public officials in the South. Nevertheless, the alleged "threat" toward white southerners was used in the late 1880s and early 1890s to demonize and further marginalize Black Populists by conjuring up distorted images of Reconstruction. As Reverend John L. Moore, the leader of the Florida Colored Farmers' Alliance observed in 1891, "let the Negro speak once, and what do you hear? Antagonizing the races, Negro uprising, Negro domination, etc. Anything to keep the [white] reading public hostile toward the Negro."[76] The notion of "Negro domination" was the false claim that African Americans ruled over the white population during Reconstruction. However, not all white southerners took the bait. As an editor of the white Alliance's *Southern Mercury*, commenting on the "trick" of the alleged threat, noted, "[The] same old cry of Negro domination that has been made to do service so many times before . . . is too transparent this time."[77] Such warnings against "social equality" or of imminent "Negro rule" were accompanied by other forms of intimidation, including threat of violence and outright assaults—political responses to the growth of Black Populism.

At issue was the Redeemers' dominance over the majority of the population in the South. For all the legal, political, economic, and paramilitary strength wielded by the white planter and merchant class, the formation of black and white alliances threatened their authority and, therefore, control over labor; the Southern Democracy rested on dividing the region's poor and working class. For their part, African Americans sought allies across the color line: As the black Knights of Labor leader Frank J. Ferrell pointed out, the movement against Redeemer rule sought the "abolition of those distinctions which are maintained by creed or color."[78] The movement, which consisted of a post-Reconstruction generation of African Americans, would take visible form in the creation of black agrarian organizations.

The Colored Agricultural Wheels were among the first organizational expressions of Black Populism in the mid-1880s. Dedicated to the economic improvement of black farmers, Colored Wheels helped to facilitate cooperative enterprises, such as food stores, and used their collective bargaining power to try to purchase farming implements from manufacturers at the lowest prices possible.[79] The first Colored Wheels were formed in 1886—a year that also saw the formation of the Cooperative Workers of America in South Carolina, the Colored Farmers' Alliance in Texas, and an expansion of the Knights of Labor across the Upper South. And just as the Greenback and Greenback Labor parties in the late 1870s served as independent political precedents for the People's Party in the early 1890s, so too would the Colored Wheels have their precedents in the late 1870s and early 1880s: Texas had the Colored Farmers' Association and the Dallas-based Colored State Grange; Tennessee, like Texas, also had a Colored Grange; meanwhile several "Negro Alliances" were formed in Arkansas.[80]

In terms of the Colored Granges, as early as 1867 white farmers began to organize themselves into the Order of Patrons of Husbandry (a.k.a. the Grange), a fraternal order which sought to improve the economic conditions of farmers through education and the pooling of resources. Granges thrived across the North and South. Several Colored Granges were formed, but details on them are scant. It appears that African Americans saw an opportunity to work with white farmers for mutual benefit but may have been reluctant to invest in their development; for a generation emerging out of slavery and white social, political, and economic domination, African Americans may not have been too eager to support organizations that were insufficiently independent of white control.

The white Northern Granges had pushed their southern orders to admit African Americans, but it seems with little success. Dudley W. Adams, National Master of the National Grange, noted, "The Constitution [of the Grange] is silent in regard to color, and only prescribes that applicants must be of good moral character, and must be interested in agriculture. If a Grange chooses to admit Negroes it may do so, as there is nothing in the Constitution to prohibit it"—the notion of African Americans having "good moral character" to be determined by white leaders.[81] A "Council of Laborers" was formed to attract black farmers to a "separate" organization from the Grange. With few exceptions, however, African Americans do not appear to have been particularly interested in working with white Grangers. One exception was in Louisiana's northern uplands, where black farmers tried to work with their white counterparts.[82] According to an 1873 newspaper account, "The negroes who were instrumental in forming [this] first Grange asked no special favors; they hoped to maintain their standing in the order by their voting power. In the meetings, both whites and blacks met together on a basis of mutual interest and common defense of the farming classes against the political jobbers and monopolists." The *New Orleans Daily Picayune* optimistically noted, "[The Grange] seemed sure to settle the difficulty between the two races."[83] African Americans were likely a bit less optimistic about the state of race relations in Louisiana.

The Colored Wheels picked up elements of what the Colored Granges began but did not develop. Like the Colored Granges, and later, the Colored Farmers' Alliances, the Colored Wheels were officially nonpartisan and dedicated to "self-improvement." Nevertheless, individual leaders and members of the organization ran for public office. Reverend George W. Lowe, a Black Baptist minister and president of the Arkansas Colored Wheel, won a seat in his state legislature, as would the president of the Texas Colored Farmers' Alliance, Alex Asberry. Others registered their political concerns indirectly. In May 1888, several leaders of the Colored Wheel in Arkansas issued a protest when a county fusion ticket of eight Republicans and Greenbackers added four Democrats to it. Colored Wheeler M. C. Darthord maintained that African Americans were keenly aware of what was going on. As he put it, they had "open eyes" to Democratic machinations.[84]

By the late 1880s, African Americans and their white allies had not only formed Colored Wheels in Arkansas, but also had established chapters in Alabama and Tennessee. Colored Wheels were only loosely associated with the regionwide, and segregated, white Agricultural Wheel. While most of the records on the black order appear through the lens of white leaders, they nevertheless reveal important aspects about how the black organization was conceived. J. W. Allen, editor of the *Alabama State Wheel*, saw the Wheel as a chance to create a "brotherhood" of black and white agrarian laborers and farmers.[85] In 1888, D. A. Gibson, the secretary of the Agricultural Wheel in Oakville, Alabama, reported, "Our colored wheel was organized with eleven charter members [and since] that time, we have increased to thirty-eight members, and are gaining ground." He continued, "[We] are meeting with considerable oppositions, and have some bitter enemies, but we know that our cause is just, and that right will prevail."[86]

African Americans expressed enthusiasm for the Wheels, pointing to the leveraging power that could be gained by entering into alliances with their white counterparts. As George W. Custer, a black leader of the Colored Wheel from

Town Creek in northern Alabama urged: "Now wheelers, we have a good opportunity before us; if we will take advantage. We must unite as a band of brothers, all pull one way and after the same thing."[87] Support for the order appeared to be widespread in the black community, as all-black chapters began to flourish. According to Paul Horton, by mid-April of 1888, "the [Alabama Colored] Wheel's black membership exploded and blacks began to support the *State Wheel* in increasing numbers."[88] Madison County's Colored Wheel No. 20, which claimed 250 members, was one of a number of key Wheels organized and led by black farmers in the state. Other Colored Wheels in Alabama included chapters 1, 10, 29, 30, and 76.[89]

In neighboring Tennessee, members of the Colored Wheel reported news of local, county, and state chapters in their publication *The Weekly Toiler*. In both Nashville and Memphis, African Americans bought and sold goods through the Wheel's State Business Agency. In July 1888, Tennessee's black and white Wheels decided to meet in parallel conferences near Clarksville. There, the two organizations held a joint session and exchanged representatives to discuss how they could better serve their respective memberships. But even as members of the Colored Wheel worked with the white Wheel, African Americans took precautions to maintain their organizational autonomy. James Y. Bernard, president of the Tipton County Colored Wheel, and later president of the statewide organization, insisted on solely deploying African American organizers to set up new chapters.[90] Presumably, not only would black farmers be more receptive to fellow African Americans, but Bernard's decision to use only black organizers ensured the Colored Wheel's integrity as a black organization. The separate identity and status of the Colored Wheels is underscored by the ongoing recruitment of black farmers and agrarian laborers in Tennessee and Alabama several years *after* the white Wheels merged with the segregated Southern Farmers' Alliance in 1888.[91] In the course of the various recruitment drives, one black organizer stood out: the Reverend George W. Lowe.

Born into slavery in Hardeman County, Tennessee, near Memphis in 1847, Lowe escaped from the fields in 1863 and joined the Union army, where he rose to become a chief musician.[92] He served three years before being discharged in 1866. Returning to Hardeman, Lowe worked the land before becoming a teacher. In 1870 he married Winnie A. Williams. Two years later, the couple moved to Marshall County, Mississippi, where Lowe was elected justice of the peace. Following Reconstruction they moved to Arkansas, where Lowe was again elected justice of the peace—but declined to serve, dedicating the better part of his time and energies to ministering. He served as pastor of the St. James Baptist Church in Lamberton from 1883 to 1887, followed by St. Luke's Church in 1888. That same year Lowe was elected president of the newly formed Colored State Agricultural

Wheel and as a Monroe County representative to Arkansas's General Assembly. "[R]egarded by all as an able representative," according to one biographical sketch, Lowe was reelected to both positions two years later—a sign of his popularity and an indication of the interconnections between black churches and agrarian organizations in the formation of Black Populism. He won reelection to the assembly running on the Union Labor ticket, serving in the state legislature—in total—from 1888 to 1892.[93] During this time, Lowe simultaneously pursued another path on behalf of members of his community: emigration. He wrote letters of support for some 500 African Americans who wished to emigrate to Liberia. Between 1890 and 1892 over 3,500 black men and women declared their intention to leave Arkansas for West Africa. He offered a succinct reason for this desire to the secretary of the American Colonization Society, William Coppinger. As Lowe wrote Coppinger in the fall of 1891, "There is a great restlessness among [my people] on accoun [sic] of discriminating laws that are being made."[94] For African Americans in Arkansas, as elsewhere in the South, multiple options would be explored in responding to increased political and economic marginalization.

One of the most important features in the development of Black Populism in the mid- to late 1880s was competition between similar agrarian associations in recruiting black farmers and agricultural workers to their orders. Not only did such competition reflect the vitality of the movement, but it spurred its growth.[95] During the summer months of 1888, organizers of Tennessee's Colored Wheel and the state's newly formed Colored Farmers' Alliance, which had entered into the western part of Tennessee, vied with one another for new members. The *Weekly Toiler*, which was to be designated the official organ of both the Tennessee Colored Wheel and the Colored Farmers' Alliance, reported that the general superintendent of the Tennessee Colored Farmers' Alliance, C. A. Vaughn, had been actively recruiting African Americans throughout that summer. (Vaughn, who was white, was replaced after several years as state general superintendent by J. W. Brown of Prospect, Tennessee.) Writing from Tipton County on July 4, Vaughn placed a bold advertisement in the *Weekly Toiler*: "Wanted—1,000 white or colored men to organize for the Colored Farmers' National Alliance and Cooperative Union."[96] Two weeks later, the same paper reported that "a great many of our [black] brothers belong to both orders [the Colored Farmers' Alliance and the Colored Wheel]."[97] As the historian Gerald Gaither notes, "the combined movement of the two orders ... achieved a notable degree of general success, reporting 387 Colored Wheels and Alliances by October 1888," mostly in the western and middle part of the state, where cotton production was most concentrated.[98]

While the Tennessee Colored Wheel and Colored Farmers' Alliance were willing to work with their white counterparts in the state, they were not willing to give up their separate existence. Tipton County Colored Wheel president James Y. Bernard, who also served as the organization's statewide president, was rightfully accused of not wanting "any white man to know [the] secret work" of the black organization. The accusation came from the white Wheel's leader, John H. McDowell, who served as the editor of the *Weekly Toiler* in Nashville. According to the historian Connie Lester, African Americans may have needed the relatively stronger white organization to financially establish and maintain the local institutions of cooperative buying and selling. However, the white organization needed black support for their reform agenda. African Americans would not be swayed into folding their organization into that of their white "brethren," just as white Wheelers would not possibly think of folding into the black organization. The fact that they both agreed to racial exclusion from each of their respective orders speaks of their distinctive interests (African Americans tended to own less land and were therefore in a subordinate economic position to the white leaders of both the Wheel and the Alliance). This uneasy alliance between black and white rural reformers continued for years to come.[99]

Both black Wheels and Alliances were operational until the summer of 1892. Only then did their membership begin to languish (as it will be later discussed, a trend seen among agrarian organizations throughout the South during the movement's transition toward electoral politics). Beginning in the mid-1880s the growth of the Colored Farmers' Alliances and the Colored Wheels in Texas, Tennessee, Arkansas, and Alabama had given Black Populism momentum in the region. Of equal importance in fueling the agrarian movement was the concurrent growth of the most successful labor union of the era: the Knights of Labor.

Established in the North in the wake of the Civil War, the Knights of Labor would become the nation's largest union by the mid-1880s—even before entering the South.[100] Unlike the Colored Wheels and Colored Farmers' Alliances, the origins of the Knights of Labor were not rooted in rural agrarian society but in urban industrial labor. Officially called the Noble Order of the Knights of Labor, the union was established in 1869 as a secret organization by a group of garment cutters in Philadelphia. That same year, African Americans founded the Colored National Labor Union (CNLU). However, along with its white counterpart, the National Labor Union, the CNLU was soon eclipsed by the Knights of Labor in attracting workers and forming locals.

The Knights of Labor became a key ally of southern black workers as it entered Virginia, North Carolina, and South Carolina in the mid-1880s. Its organizers used a combination of strikes and boycotts to make their labor demands. The majority of Knights of Labor members in the South were agrarian workers or, in the case of domestic laborers, worked for wages in the homes of those who lived in rural areas. Black and white southern Knights (from sugarcane workers in

Louisiana, lumber workers in Florida, to cotton compress workers in Virginia) struck for better wages, hours, and working conditions nearly two dozen times during the mid-1880s.[101] By helping to consolidate the growing networks of black workers in the South, the Knights of Labor became the most important regional expression of Black Populism before the regionwide organization of the Colored Farmers' Alliance in 1888.[102]

By the mid-1880s the Knights of Labor, which had grown throughout the North in the decade prior, had a successful and unique track record of unionizing both skilled and unskilled workers, men and women, black and white. While the union remained in the hands of white leaders at the regional level, several all-black divisions and hundreds of all-black locals were established in the South, including in North Carolina and Virginia. For instance, Richmond's District Assembly 92 consisted of thirteen all-black locals. In order to help ensure that all-black locals were fairly represented, African Americans encouraged segregation at the district level, not unlike their Colored Wheel associates in Tennessee.[103] The impetus for these kinds of actions was in keeping with the conventions of all-black churches and fraternal orders, North and South, which had been formed as a way for African Americans to maintain control over their own resources, membership, and affairs.

As was the case with the Colored Wheels, black autonomy was reinforced in the Knights of Labor by the recruitment of black workers by fellow African Americans. Demands for "colored organizers" poured into the national headquarters of the Knights of Labor in 1885. Over the next two years, black organizers were dispatched across the countryside establishing local chapters—in practice, more fraternal political organizations than collective-bargaining units per se.[104] Some chapter organizers, like W. J. Campbell, a barber from Warrior, Alabama, used his occupation to facilitate his organizing. Being self-employed, Campbell had a greater degree of freedom than black agrarian workers to recruit workers into the Knights, as jobs could easily be stripped by planters at the first sign of organizing efforts by recruiters. Campbell soon became an official "State Organizer" for the Knights, establishing black locals in Huntsville and Montgomery.[105] Other black leaders emerged from the process of recruitment, making the Knights an organized force across the region. Black Knights that were engaged in setting up locals included W. A. Brooks, J. W. Robertson, and Alexander Walker in Alabama; Frank Johnson and W. J. Woodward in North Carolina; Andrew Allen in Georgia; and Lee Nelson in Virginia. Black organizers were also in the field in South Carolina, Florida, and Louisiana.[106] The development of this black agrarian leadership, and the expansion of Knights membership, accelerated the growth of Black Populism—complementing and overlapping with networks formed by the Colored Wheels and the Colored Farmers' Alliance.

By 1886, approximately 60,000 African American men and women had joined the Knights of Labor. They came together in more than 400 all-black locals, averaging 150 members each.[107] It was the same year as the Great Southwest Railroad Strike, the largest clash between organized labor and railroad management during the nineteenth century. Launched by Knights in Texas, at its height, the strike involved over 100,000 workers, including black section hands, who struck against the Missouri-Kansas-Texas Railroad Company initially for the firing of a foreman. Unknown numbers of African Americans joined in the strike, which turned violent and was soon crushed. The white press warned of both the role of black workers in the strike and their participation in independent political conventions underway, as an "army of blacks" had grown under the command of Knights.[108] Over the next five years, the southern branch of the Knights organized thousands of tenant farmers, agricultural day laborers, and domestic workers—with increasingly fewer white workers participating in the region's order. At the general assembly of the Knights of Labor in Richmond in 1886, African Americans represented locals in Georgia, Florida, Virginia, North Carolina, and Alabama. While most of these locals were urban based, by the following year, most black workers recruited into the union were being drawn from rural areas. As the historian Melton McLaurin concludes: "The organization became basically a black union in the South and one composed of the economically weakest blacks," with the "weakest" being the landless in the countryside.[109]

Reflecting the growth of the black Knights was the invitation extended to its best-known leader, Frank J. Ferrell, to introduce Grand Master Workman Terrence V. Powderly at the general assembly of the Knights of Labor in Richmond in 1886. The introduction of the white labor leader by an African American apparently inspired some while outraging others. After the address, and in a show of solidarity against the segregationist policies of the South, Ferrell led a group of black and white Knights to see a local theater performance together. While Ferrell and his coworkers were permitted to enter the theater, the act provoked a strong reaction. The following evening, a mob of armed white men assembled at the theater to prevent any more African Americans from entering. The notion of "social equality between the races" was not going to be tolerated.[110]

As the Knights of Labor spread across the South the organization encompassed growing numbers of black female workers. Throughout the mid-1880s African American women either joined local assemblies with men or formed locals of their own. Between 1885 and 1887, there were at least sixteen all-black female Knights assemblies in the South: eight in Virginia (four in Norfolk, two in Richmond, one in Petersburg, and another in Danville); three in Arkansas (in Little Rock, Galloway, and Argenta); one in Louisiana (in Morgan City); one in North Carolina (in Raleigh); and two in Florida (in Jacksonville and Pensacola).

Additionally there was an all-black female assembly of domestic workers in Washington, D.C. Two of the assemblies in Norfolk, Virginia, included laundresses, housekeepers, and chambermaids; the one in Argenta, Arkansas, female farmers; and the one in Pensacola, Florida, chambermaids and laundresses. As Knights assemblies, their aims would have been to assert collective bargaining power for better wages and better working conditions. As important, the organization of black workers—whether women or men—gave particular meaning to the lives of those who participated in them, serving both economic and social functions. However, the existence of such black labor organizations, as was the case with black political organizations, proved a threat.[111]

Fear among white authorities of a new "Black Reconstruction" grew alongside the spread of the southern Knights.[112] By November 1886 two asemblies of black Knights had been formed in Durham with a reported total membership of two thousand African Americans. Within six months black Knights organized north of Durham in Oxford, Granville County (home of the Black Populist leader Reverend Walter A. Pattillo), came under attack. Black Knights in Oxford had helped to unseat local Democratic officeholders through a Republican-Independent coalition. Political repercussions followed.[113] During the spring of 1887, a black Knight from Oxford reported in a letter to the editor: "[The whites] pointed at us with scorn, and kept crying 'Nigger! Nigger!' until the two words 'Nigger' and 'Knights' became synonymous terms."[114] From its inception, the local assembly faced outside disruption. According to another member, "No stone was left unturned to create ill-feeling against us." Reminiscent of alarms of "slave conspiracies" sounded during the antebellum era, black Knights were accused of setting fire to their own town. Despite no evidence of arson being presented against those accused—and even after the persons guilty of the crime were discovered—attacks continued. The Knights local master workman narrowly escaped being lynched, only to be imprisoned on false charges soon thereafter.[115] Despite such attacks, North Carolina's black Knights continued to build their organization. As correspondence in 1890 between two white Alliance leaders, H. H. Perry and Elias Carr, attests, "the Knights of Labor are organizing [black workers] in every county."[116]

Attacks against organized black workers were not confined to rural areas. In 1887, industrial Birmingham—the "Pittsburgh of the South"—witnessed the failure of a strike by black ironworkers seeking higher wages. The strike failed because white ironworkers refused to join in, despite direct orders to do so from the Alabama state master workman, Nicholas Stack, who was also white.[117] On this occasion, white workers, who earned more than their black counterparts, made plain their hostility toward African Americans. After Stack ordered the white workers to leave their posts, opposition mounted against him and the striking black workers; at one point, Stack was even barred from entering the

Knights of Labor Union Hall. By the end of August 1887, white workers had successfully pressed him to call off the strike.[118]

While Stack lent his support to the striking black ironworkers in Birmingham, he was also embroiled in a dispute with W. J. Campbell, the state's leading black organizer. Just as the strike had been weakening at the end of the summer of 1887, Stack attempted to remove Campbell from office; in a letter to Grand Master Workman Powderly, Stack called Campbell "entirely ignorant of his duties."[119] Campbell, however, had already established himself as a competent, even popular statewide organizer by helping to initiate locals in several cities over the previous year. Such conflicts between black and white labor leaders reveal some of the political tensions and forms of opposition that black leaders encountered—namely, the conditions under which African Americans were operating and the degree to which white leaders were willing to either follow or fight black leadership.

Antiblack policies and practices were also reflected at the national level. The national leadership of the Knights of Labor refused to support black leaders' efforts to racially integrate the southern movement. So while Uriah Stephens and Terrence V. Powderly (each serving consecutive terms as grand master workman of the Knights of Labor) did not openly oppose the formation of integrated orders in the South, neither did they further the growth of an integrated movement. Powderly remained reluctant on the issue—afraid of alienating southern white workers by demanding integration in the South. Stephens, a Quaker and former abolitionist, revealed the limits of white labor leadership. He advocated "the recognition of blacks as economic but not social equals" (in much the same way that Tom Watson of Georgia later advocated "political equality" but not "social equality" between black and white southerners).[120]

Opposition to the black movement also came from black employers, as seen in the events surrounding an all-black Knights of Labor assembly in Wilmington, North Carolina, in the fall of 1886. In September of that year, William Howe, a black "stevedore boss," had promised to pay his workers up to five dollars a day for stowing cotton aboard a steamer docked at the city's port, the largest in the state. Suspecting that Howe would not be able to cover their wages, the stevedores, who were Knights, refused to work unless they were given written assurance of payment. In response, Howe brought in black stevedores from Norfolk, Virginia, to replace the striking workers. But the black Knights from Wilmington countered by convincing their fellow workers from Norfolk to return home. The small, but successful action, forced Howe and the company to guarantee in writing the workers' wages at the five-dollar rate.[121]

By far, the harshest opposition to the demands of black agrarian workers—whether Knights, or members of the Colored Wheels or Colored Farmers'

Alliances—came from white planters. Many of the planters were actually Populists themselves. According to the historian Robert C. McMath Jr., nearly one-quarter of the leaders of the white Southern Farmers' Alliance were planters.[122] Black agrarian organizing threatened planters' access to cheap labor; for their part, African Americans largely regarded the segregated white Farmers' Alliance, the principal white Populist vehicle, as an obstacle to *their* economic interests. White members of the Farmers' Alliance who employed agrarian workers tried to keep wages as low as possible while raising the prices of goods. The class character of the conflict between the mostly poor African American base of Black Populism (drawn from the landless or virtually landless majority of black people living in rural areas) and the relatively affluent white leadership of the Populist movement was apparent.[123] In 1891, a black Knight from North Carolina reported that "the [white Farmers'] Alliance proposes to see to it, and is instructing its members to pay no more money to wage-workers. They are to be paid in orders in stores." The Knight continued, "We fear that [the white] Alliance . . . means nothing more nor less than oppression and death to the [black] laborer."[124] Such tensions reflected differences between the black and white agrarian movements. Antagonisms between African Americans and white workers often led to black workers being isolated, which at times proved deadly when the former were under attack by bosses and landowners.

Violence and threat of violence were the principal methods used to suppress striking workers. In 1886, when a group of black cotton picker Knights attempted to strike for higher wages just outside of Little Rock, Arkansas, they were met with brutal force. No sooner had the black workers called their strike than a white sheriff's posse, similar to the one in Meridian, Mississippi, several years earlier, was formed. Here, unlike the attack in Mississippi, the posse took preemptive measures, storming one leader's home and murdering him. As black workers proceeded to strike, the posse turned their guns on them as well. Some armed black Knights fired back but most were quickly overwhelmed; the strike was soon crushed.[125] Five years later, the violent scene seemed to repeat itself when a similar series of events took place in Arkansas during the regionwide Cotton Pickers' Strike.[126]

Swift and violent reaction by planters to the demands of African Americans for higher wages came despite a precipitous decline in real wages for agricultural work, which in the 1880s had deteriorated to their lowest levels since Emancipation. Victor St. Cloud, a white organizer from Savannah working with the Knights in South Carolina, commented that the average black agrarian laborer had become "more of a slave than they were before the war." Organizers were often threatened at gunpoint for taking up the demands of the rural black poor. In October 1887, A. W. Jackson, an outspoken black member of the Prohibition

Party and Knight from Milton, Florida, was not only threatened but was shot at point-blank range by white vigilantes when he refused to leave town.[127]

In addition to individual murders, public lynching—sometimes randomly targeting African Americans—was used to terrorize the black community into submission. In 1886, there were over 70 recognized cases of African Americans being lynched in the South. As Black Populism grew, so would lynching, peaking in 1892 with over 160 known cases that year. Many of the murders were organized as public spectacles, with advance notice in local papers, bringing thousands of spectators—men, women, and children—to participate and bear witness to these "events." Adding to the gruesome acts of violence, the charred remains of victims who were burned were sometimes even kept as "souvenirs"—even sold. It was in the context of such horrors, and in response to such atrocities, that African Americans built their movement.[128]

In the fall of 1887, Knights District Assembly 194 in Louisiana's Low Country, comprised mostly of black sugarcane workers, also came under attack when it launched a strike to protest low wages. According to McLaurin, the strike grew to "thousands of workers, including many nonmembers who nevertheless supported the strike." Louisiana's Democratic governor, Samuel D. McEnery, responded to panicked calls from planters by summoning the state militia. Joining forces with the local sheriff's posse, the state militia swept in and shot dozens of black workers. With more than thirty African Americans killed, and twice as many injured, the strike was defeated and the Louisiana sugar region's order of the Knights was largely dispersed. Nevertheless, and as was the case with other African Americans confronting armed force from local or state authorities, black workers continued to organize themselves underground, taking precautionary measures such as meeting late at night and in small numbers. Despite such measures, there were breaches of security, and sometimes at the hands of black spies working on behalf of white plantation owners.[129]

Events in eastern North Carolina would illustrate the need for covert action in the face of hostile planters, many of whom were white Populists. In North Carolina, as elsewhere in the South, the interests of black and white Alliance leaders were often in sharp conflict. Most white Alliance members in the state were farm operators whose financial interests were in keeping their labor costs low.[130] As the ranks of black agrarian workers swelled in the state, due in part to the systematic barring of African Americans from the textile, tobacco, and furniture industries in favor of white workers, black workers turned to the Knights. Throughout 1888 and 1889, African Americans in Pitt County formed assemblies to demand higher wages. And like other groups of black workers, the assemblies were organized in absolute secrecy—that is, until the moment of striking. Still, security was occasionally compromised.[131]

During the fall of 1889, black farmworkers in Pitt County were in the process of organizing an assembly when a local white planter—John Bryan Grimes, a member of the Farmers' Alliance (and a Democrat)—discovered their activities. In violation of the white Alliance's own policy against labor espionage, Grimes paid one of his black workers, George Freeman, to infiltrate a black Knights' assembly in Greenville, where more than a dozen African American men and women had been secretly holding meetings in a church. In September 1889, Freeman was paid to spy on the group. He applied for membership to the assembly and a late-night meeting was arranged to debate his application; two doorkeepers, Gale Moon and Elli Hardee, secured the church's entrance. Freeman was deemed suspect. The assembly's principal leader, Reverend Grimes Jr., along with Romeo Telfair, who served as president, believed that Freeman had ulterior motives. Both opposed Freeman's membership, as would another member, Sam Perry. Appeals were then made by the treasurer, Warren Jayson, and fellow member Henry Allen, who supported Freeman's application. The debate apparently carried on until 2 A.M., when Freeman's application was finally rejected by a full vote of the assembly, including by members Lewis King, Hunter Jones, and two of their female colleagues, Phoebe Cobb and Fanny Glass, also known as "the queen."[132]

Unfortunately, no known documents exist to shed light on what became of the black assembly. But here we catch a glimpse of the Knights' structure and the kinds of precautionary measures that African Americans took to ensure their organization's existence. Knights were able to carefully expand their membership through such methods; in doing so they paved the way for Black Populism's continued growth and the development of new agrarian associations and unions. As the Knights came under further scrutiny and attacks, African Americans would join, or create, new black organizations. In North Carolina, the Colored Farmers' Alliance became the principle vehicle through which African Americans carried on what the Knights had established with local black churches. In South Carolina and Georgia still other black organizations emerged—notably the Cooperative Workers of America (CWA).[133]

The development of the CWA between 1886 and 1887 provides another glimpse into the connection between the various organizations that comprised Black Populism. In South Carolina, the continuity of the organizing process linking the Knights of Labor and the Colored Farmers' Alliance through the work of the CWA may be traced through the actions of its local leadership: Sherman McCrary, Lee Minor, and Hiram F. Hover.[134] Hover, a white organizer of the Knights of Labor, had been recruiting members in towns across North Carolina's Piedmont in 1885. However, he broke from the national order, which had been trying to control his organizing efforts. In 1886, Hover moved to South

Carolina to launch the CWA, a union focused on rural black workers. As the historian Bruce E. Baker describes: "Around the 10th of February, Hover appeared in downtown Spartanburg, a growing cotton mill center, and spoke for two and a half hours to a [large] crowd."[135] Some three hundred African Americans came to hear Hover speak. Hover charged that the national Knights had been "selling out" workers by negotiating wages and work conditions to benefit factory owners instead of its members. Moreover, he charged, the Knights were not sufficiently addressing issues of political reform nor were they fighting for "a free cooperative school system."[136]

While Hover helped to launch the Cooperative Workers of America by establishing an executive board and outlining its aims, African Americans quickly led its expansion on the ground. As Baker notes, it was "a handful of local black organizers who did the legwork of establishing CWA locals."[137] The *Charleston News and Courier* described the typical African American organizer as going through the "country talking to the colored people wherever he could find them alone, in the fields or in the houses . . . and read the labor catechism and constitution to his hearers."[138] The account is reminiscent of Union League organizers in the South a generation earlier who, convening in black churches, schools, and when necessary in the fields or in the woods, began their meetings with a prayer and a pledge to uphold the Republican Party with "a Bible, a copy of the Declaration of Independence, and an anvil or some other emblem of labor" near at hand.[139]

The CWA was part of the series of sequential and overlapping organizations in the South that were developed by African Americans following the Civil War: the black Baptist and AME churches, the Union Leagues, black fraternal orders and mutual benefit societies, and "marching companies"—groups of civilians who paraded, military style, during special celebrations. African Americans continued to organize themselves beyond Reconstruction through other independent associations, including the Colored Agricultural Wheels, the Knights of Labor, and the Colored Farmers' Alliance. Each of these associations served a variety of functions, with membership ranging anywhere from less than a dozen to hundreds of men and women.[140] CWA locals comprised as few as five dues-paying members. Small in size, so as not to draw attention from those who might be hostile to their organizing efforts, members elected a secretary, treasurer, and president. They usually met after midnight, often in churches, with sentinels posted at entrances.[141]

Like the Knights of Labor, from which the CWA was in part derived, the organization attempted to raise wages for agricultural workers, improve working conditions, and reduce the hours that black agrarian laborers were compelled to work during certain seasons—or risk losing employment. The CWA even had plans to establish a cooperative store at which products would be collectively sold.[142] Similarities between the constitutions of the Knight and the CWA are evident: the Preamble of the Knights' 1881 constitution calls for "the establishment of co-operative institutions, productive and distributive" and the need to "secure for both sexes equal pay for equal work." The CWA also called for a repeal of the poll tax, the implementation of a free cooperative school system, and land reform. Its call for an inheritance tax and a guarantee of weekly wages placed it on the left-wing of the political spectrum in the era; yet, its demand for the direct election of U.S. senators and a "free ballot" placed it within the broader Populist camp that would soon challenge the Democratic Party at the polls. (Such radical economic and political demands made by the Knights, followed by the CWA, and then the People's Party, would culminate in the Omaha Platform of 1892.)[143]

One of the CWA's leaders, Sherman McCrary, an agrarian worker from Laurel Creek, came from a politically active black household. McCrary's father, Isham McCrary, was as an outspoken leader during Reconstruction.[144] On July 8, 1871, Isham stood up to the Ku Klux Klan by testifying before a congressional investigating committee charged with looking into acts of violence in connection with the white terrorist organization.[145] Not surprisingly, Isham's two sons became active in the CWA. While Sherman McCrary's elder brother, Aaron, was also active in the black agrarian union, it was the younger brother who assumed a leadership role in it. In April 1887, Sherman McCrary formed a club at the Pleasant View Baptist Church in Fairview, where meetings "guarded by four armed pickets" were held late into the night.[146] Over the next two months, he organized two other clubs in areas south and northwest of Fairview, and by July two additional clubs—in Simpsonville, near Hopewell Church, and in Fountain Inn. As McCrary established these clubs, he trained others, many of whom his senior, to help further spread the organization. Among the names of those he trained were Riley Owens, Allen Dorroh, and Lee Harrison.[147]

Planters' reactions to the growth of the CWA came swiftly. However, it was the white leader Hover, not McCrary, or any of the other black leaders of the organization, who was publicly named as the person to be targeted. In part, this was due to Hover being less careful in keeping his activities covert than his black colleagues, whose collective history cautioned greater prudence; but there may have been another dynamic at play. In targeting Hover as the sole leader of the movement, white planters and farm operators were also reinforcing stereotypes of African Americans being incapable of organizing without such white leadership. It is a bias that continues to be reflected in the manner in which Black Populism is characterized. That is, the independent black movement is written about as having been a movement of African Americans under white leadership, as opposed to a movement of African Americans, principally led by African Americans, but which also included important white leaders.

Over the course of 1886 and 1887, Hover, who had been traveling across the northern part of South Carolina, established as many as twelve black locals. The "Hoover [sic] Scare" that broke out among white planters in the area soon rippled across the broader white community.[148] Attempts to infiltrate and uncover CWA plans were thwarted, which only served to fuel the rumor mill. The notion of a return to "Negro domination" was used to create fear in the white community. Word quickly spread that CWA leaders were organizing "against the whites [and encouraging] hostility between the races"; white militias were formed and deployed, scouring the countryside on horseback searching for suspected black leaders.[149]

Amid the mounting hysteria, an individual CWA member was cornered and ordered to divulge information about his secret organization. Under interrogation, the member revealed a "club list" that included the names of seventeen leaders in the area. Few such lists were ever made for fear that they would be discovered by planters or other white employers. As experience taught black organizers, virtually anything that had to do with mobilizing workers needed to be done underground. Planters launched an inquisition with the capture of the CWA member. Those named were quickly tracked down by vigilantes. The captives were initially brought into a large room over the Peden and Company's store for questioning, but they were then transferred to a grove nearby—a decidedly isolated location. Although one newspaper reported that the local leaders "were assured that no bodily harm should befall them," the move was clearly intended to intimidate them into compliance.[150] Under further interrogation, more names surfaced. It was revealed that the CWA had upwards of two thousand members in the area of Spartanburg alone.[151] More people were rounded up and ordered to disband their locals. While most African Americans complied, a few remained obstinate. In early July, a young barber named Lee Minor spoke at a public meeting in Greenville. More than 150 African Americans—both men and women—gathered in the city park and heard Minor all too emphatically deny that the CWA had ever "made any threats of any kind against the whites or encouraged hostility between the races in any shape or form."[152] In hindsight, knowing that at least some of the CWA members went on to join other black agrarian organizations in the area (based on the subsequent growth of the Colored Farmers' Alliance in the area), one may interpret Minor's words as an effort to simultaneously dissipate tensions while keeping an eye toward further recruitment. It was a fine line southern African Americans had to walk, given the circumstances they were in.

White planters did not take any chances. To discourage further organizing among black workers, planters formed three militia companies (in Cedar Grove, Woodruff, and Dacusville) and distributed additional firearms to the local white population. The fear aroused by the existence of the CWA led the Dacusville militia to swell to over 180 men; the Cedar Grove militia even formed a cavalry division.[153] Ironically, if anyone had anything to fear, it was the black population. After all, it was African American leaders who were being rounded up, held captive, and interrogated. Added to this, African Americans now faced roving armed squads. Despite the massive paramilitary presence, black organizers continued to hold meetings throughout July 1887. New leaders emerged. When D. R. Speer, the attorney who defended Hover in court, failed to appear at a gathering of thirty black workers whom he was scheduled to address, a young man named Tom Singleton rose on behalf of the CWA and spoke out against the machinations of the Democratic Party. Learning of the gathering, a group of party operatives apparently swept in to break up the meeting. No further details are known.

Baker, the historian who has done the most work in shedding light on the Cooperative Workers of America, concludes: "The CWA, as a viable movement with the potential to effect change for laborers in South Carolina, was dead."[154] But while the particular organization may have been destroyed, individual leaders had not been silenced. Hover, among others, kept organizing black workers, despite the increasingly dangerous terrain. During the winter of 1886, he appeared in eastern Georgia where he placed advertisements for upcoming meetings. However, while "speaking incendiary doctrine" at the pulpit of a church in Warrenton, Hover was nearly killed; a group of masked white-robed men rode up to the church and shot him through a window.[155] He survived the attempted assassination, but lost an eye—the bullet lodging in the left side of his face near the back of his ear. Apparently, no one else was injured in the incident. Known thereafter as the "one eyed orator," Hover covered his left eye with a green patch. He fled to New York where he waited for tensions to subside before returning to the South—first Atlanta, then Greenville, South Carolina, and finally Hickory, North Carolina—where he continued to organize black workers until leaving the region once and for all.

Unlike Hover, most African Americans in the South lacked the financial resources to leave the region if they needed to do so. Lee Minor and other black leaders of the Cooperative Workers had family and other social connections tying them to South Carolina. For them, and other rank-and-file members of the Cooperative Workers, there were few options other than to simply return to work after the inquisition and purging of their organization—and no doubt under the suspicious watch of their bosses. Others waited for the hysteria regarding the "hostilities" to subside before making their next move. According to one journalist, when he asked Minor whether or not he was planning to attend a July 4 meeting, Minor "didn't believe it would be best for him to go outside of Greenville . . . until the excitement had died out." Given the ongoing efforts to organize black agrarian workers, Minor's statement—like the earlier one he gave in Greenville in front of the 150-person audience—suggests a tactical retrenchment rather than a signal of final defeat.[156]

The modest networks of workers created by the CWA in South Carolina, and to a lesser extent in Georgia, formed the basis for the continued development of Black Populism. As Gaither succinctly notes: "In South Carolina, the Colored Alliance movement was inspired by a forerunner, the Cooperative Workers of America, [viewed as] a subsidiary of the Knights of Labor."[157] A telling incident pointing to the connections between local black organizations was when Tom Briar of the South Carolina CWA urged his fellow members in 1889 to hear the Colored Farmers' Alliance speaker C. J. Holloway. While Holloway invited members to join the black Alliance, neither the details of his appeal nor the response he received were recorded. The incident nevertheless serves as an important affirmation of the fluidity that existed between various black organizations and their membership.[158] An important underlying connection between such black agrarian organizations—as was the case with the North Carolina Knights and the South Carolina CWA—were the black churches, which served as safe havens: places to meet, plan, and deliberate.

A post-Reconstruction generation of leaders was coming into its own. Black and white, these leaders carried on the work of their predecessors, organizing African Americans in rural areas—and with varying degrees of success. In the Lower South, one of the key organizations that came to represent the demands of rural African Americans was the Colored Farmers' Union. Like the Knights of Labor and the CWA, it would help drive Black Populism, and soon bring thousands of members into the largest of the movement's agrarian organizations, the Colored Farmers' Alliance. While a Colored Farmers' Union had formed in Louisiana under the leadership of A. L. Plummer of Bayou Funny Louis, southwest of Shreveport, African Americans in Florida initially organized themselves as black clubs of the white-led Farmers' Union.[159]

The Florida Farmers' Union—unlike the Knights of Labor and the CWA—was established to organize farmers, not wage-earning agricultural workers. Florida's Farmers' Union had distinct black and white clubs. The majority of black members were in the northern parts of the state; the union was strongest in Alachua, Bradford, and Escambia counties, the latter being directly adjacent to Alabama.[160] In the fall of 1887, the Farmers' Union held a statewide meeting in Gainesville, where delegates discussed whether or not to merge with the all-white Farmers' Alliance. Seventy-seven delegates from across Florida met at Oliver Park next to Alachua Lake in mid-October to debate the possibility of merging with the white Farmers' Alliance. Twenty-eight of the delegates were African American, representing fourteen all-black clubs with a total membership of 1,720 men and women. But while the 49 white delegates represented seven more clubs than their African American counterparts, the white clubs had 554 *fewer* members. The black members, with less resources as a group, simply could not afford to send as many representatives to Gainesville as their membership warranted.[161]

A special committee of the Farmers' Union was appointed to confer with the white Alliance delegation in order to consider a merger of the two groups. The committee reported that it favored "the adoption of a constitution and by-laws for the Florida Farmers Union that . . . recognizes the . . . colored farmers as tillers of the soil and whose interests are identical with those of the whites." Despite such official recognition, the white majority voted in favor of consolidation with the segregated white Farmers' Alliance—a merger that excluded over half of the Farmers' Union's own membership: African Americans. The decision underscored the need for black farmers to maintain their independence from white agrarian reformers, since the latter had shown themselves on more than one occasion willing to sacrifice their interests.

While the exclusion of African Americans from white-led Populist organizations varied from one state to the next, white Populists set racially explicit criteria for membership in their national organization. Section 1 of the 1889 constitution of the National Farmers' Alliance and Industrial Union (encompassing the white-led Northern and Southern Alliances, which together claimed well over one million members) read: "No person shall be admitted as a member of this order except a white person over sixteen years of age."[162] Not surprisingly, an exodus of African Americans from the Farmers' Union followed when the organization merged with the segregated white Alliance, prompting an in-flow into the existing Colored Farmers' Alliance. For its part, the black Alliance retaliated on behalf of its members and issued the following (though largely symbolic) statement: "[if] white organizations shall positively prohibit the [admission] of colored men to its membership . . . colored organizations shall prohibit the admission of white men to its membership."[163]

Black leaders in the rural South responded in various ways to the political and economic plight of their communities in the years following the collapse of Reconstruction. With few exceptions, the largest and often the most productive land was placed (or taken) back into the hands of wealthier white farmers. Meanwhile, the southern branch of the Republican Party had been weakened by the Democrats; moreover, third parties, including the Greenback and Greenback Labor parties, had been defeated or marginalized. Although many African Americans managed to leave the South in the hope of finding better working and living conditions elsewhere, even more attempted to reform existing conditions where they worked and lived.

Thousands of African Americans organized themselves into labor unions and agrarian associations and then linked their activities to regional bodies that shared common economic and political interests. By 1888, the ranks of Black Populism reached into the tens of thousands, spurring the rapid growth of the Colored Farmers' Alliance. At an organizational level, between 1889 and 1892, the black Alliance, which claimed over one million members in 1891, deepened and expanded the work of its immediate predecessors: the Colored Wheels in Alabama, Arkansas, and Tennessee; the Knights of Labor in Alabama, Arkansas, Florida, Georgia, North Carolina, South Carolina, and Virginia; the Cooperative Workers of America in South Carolina and Georgia; and the Colored Farmers' Union in Florida and Louisiana.

Like the "Colored speakers" of the Knights of Labor (such as W. J. Campbell in Alabama and Lee Nelson in Virginia) and CWA leaders (such as Sherman McCrary in South Carolina and Hiram Hover in Georgia) who organized black workers, Colored Farmers' Alliance "Lecturers" took to the road to spread the movement's gospel of economic, and later, political reform. While the black Alliance began by promoting self-sufficiency and sought to educate its members with regard to better farming techniques, it later demanded debt relief, regulation of monopolies, better wages for workers, and a more equitable electoral process. Propelling the movement of black farmers, sharecroppers, and agrarian workers across the South were black Alliance leaders who carried out a range of tactics, depending upon local conditions. How African Americans formed the Colored Farmers' Alliance, the ways the organization grew, under what conditions, and what it accomplished, forms the next chapter in the history of Black Populism.

Chapter Two

THE COLORED FARMERS' ALLIANCE

Salvation rests in neither of the old political parties and [we] are no longer slaves to either.

—Virginia Colored Farmers' Alliance, *Richmond Dispatch*, August 11, 1891

On December 11, 1886, a group of sixteen African Americans and one white farmer met near a cotton farm in Houston County, Texas, where they inaugurated what would become the nation's largest black agrarian organization: the Colored Farmers' National Alliance and Co-Operative Union (Colored Alliance, for short).[1] With the fervor of a religious awakening, the order's leaders drove one of the most dramatic expansions of any reform group—black or white—in the late nineteenth century. The creation of the Colored Alliance in the mid-1880s was a collective undertaking. Hundreds of grassroots organizers tapped into pre-existing networks of black farmers, sharecroppers, and agrarian workers affiliated with black churches, the Colored Agricultural Wheels, the Knights of Labor, the Cooperative Workers of America, and the Colored Farmers' Union. Within two years of its founding, the Colored Alliance consolidated various black agrarian organizations scattered across the South into a cohesive movement encompassing hundreds of thousands of African Americans.

Less than three weeks after its initial meeting, leaders of the newly formed Colored Alliance in Houston and adjoining counties met at the Good Hope Baptist Church in Weldon. There they adopted a declaration of principles: "To promote agriculture and horticulture ... To educate the agricultural classes in the science of economic government in a strictly non-partisan spirit ... To aid its members to become more skillful and efficient workers ... [To] protect their individual rights ... [To raise] funds for the benefit of sick or disabled members, or their distressed families; [and to form] a closer union among all colored people."² The principles were endorsed by the sixteen founding delegates, who were identified either as "Negro" or "mulatto": H. J. Spencer, William Armistead, R. M. Saddler, Anthony Turner, T. Jones, Newton C. Crawley, J. W. Peters, Israel McGilbra, George W. Coffey, Green Lee, Jacob J. Shuffer, Willis Nichols, Jacob Fairfax, Abe Fisher, S. M. Montgomery, and John Marshall. Shuffer and Spencer, both of whom were successful farmers in east Texas—the latter also serving as a clergyman—were elected president and secretary, respectively.³ They, along with Saddler, Nichols, and McGilbra, were also elected to one-year terms as trustees of the organization. The delegates elected the only white person in attendance, Richard M. Humphrey, as the organization's spokesperson and general superintendent. Humphrey, a Baptist preacher and farmer who had long worked and lived in the black community, was noted as being selected because of "his ability" and "confidence [among African Americans] in him as a friend of the race."⁴

The Colored Alliance both complemented and competed with other associations of farmers, sharecroppers, and agrarian laborers in the 1880s. Texas was home to a number of black agrarian groups in the mid-1880s, including the Colored Farmers' Benevolent and Charitable Association and the Colored Farmers' Home Improvement Lodge.⁵ Around the same time that the Houston-based Colored Alliance was established, another competing Colored Alliance was also formed in the state.⁶ Headed by Andrew J. Carothers, a white Allianceman from Lee County, the "National Colored Alliance" organization would, within three years of its founding, claim a membership of 250,000 and chapters in every southern state. As with the Colored Alliance, the National Colored Alliance's membership figure was likely inflated.⁷ However, by 1890 the two organizations had merged, with the Houston-based Colored Alliance assuming de facto overall leadership, and propelling the overall black Alliance membership to its highest levels.⁸

In December 1890, Humphrey was claiming the following Colored Alliance state memberships: Alabama, 100,000; Arkansas, 20,000; Georgia, 84,000; Kentucky, 25,000; Louisiana, 50,000; Mississippi, 90,000; North Carolina, 55,000; South Carolina, 90,000; Tennessee, 60,000; Texas, 90,000; and Virginia, 50,000.⁹ The official membership figures were most likely calculated based on the number of black farmers, sharecroppers, and agrarian workers in each of the states listed, rather than actual dues-paying members of the organization. Dues-paying members, even according to Humphrey, were only a percentage of the men and women who were affiliated with the Colored Alliance. Still, there is little doubt that the organization had grown at an astonishing rate. In Texas, the Colored Alliance issued some fifty-six county charters, with two thousand sub-charters, indicating extensive local infrastructure.¹⁰

The Colored Alliance was in keeping with other "self-help" and mutual aid societies that formed across the South in the aftermath of the Civil War. Its call for agrarian reforms resonated deeply among the region's rural black population in the 1880s. By this time, it had become clear to African Americans that they could only rely on their immediate communities for assistance. While calls for federal assistance continued (for everything from credit and educational assistance to regulation of monopolistic businesses and election oversight), they largely went unanswered. White merchants and planters, already suspicious of any independent black formation in the region, strongly opposed the Colored Alliance, especially as the organization assumed what were viewed as militant tactics and demands—boycotting goods where price gouging was taking place, demanding higher wages for cotton picking, and calling for an immediate end to the convict-lease system. The convict-lease system was both a means of control and a particularly cruel profit-making business in the South. It gave planters, railroad bosses, and other employers who faced labor shortages, free reign to purchase labor from the state (at a small fine and court cost). The labor often came from those convicted of petty crimes and disproportionately marked black men, many of whom were physically and mentally abused in a system with little legal recourse; county officials notoriously looked the other way to abuses of authority, even when deaths were the result. The Colored Alliance's opposition to the system therefore targeted a critical point of contention for African Americans.[11]

Through the largely covert organizing efforts of its grassroots leaders, many of whom were ministers, the Colored Alliance stood alone in its ability to reach tens of thousands of rural African Americans. As the historian Charles Postel notes, "The Colored Alliance was a semi-clandestine movement based primarily in the black churches."[12] Congregations were tapped for membership and material support. Churches served as meeting sites for the organization; when greater secrecy was required, members met elsewhere, in individual homes or in the fields. Members attended local chapter meetings, where they shared agricultural techniques and innovations, coordinated cooperative efforts for planting and harvesting, and shared local and distant news. One report of such activities came from Macon, Georgia, where the Reverend E. F. Love offered a resolution for the formation of cooperative associations, cooperative farms, and storehouses. At a meeting of 350 African Americans, he was quoted as saying: "There is no reason why the Negro should not control the Negro trade and handle the money the Negro has to spend."[13] It was this independent sentiment, which posed a threat to the Southern Democracy.

The Colored Alliance occasionally held public gatherings, but they were usually part of national or regional conventions with other reform-oriented organizations and associations. Most of the recruitment work came down to individual outreach. Black recruiters working on the fringes of plantations or on small farms carried out their work at great personal risk, careful in their approach. As the historian Lawrence Goodwyn describes: "Black lecturers who ranged over the South organizing state and local Alliances did not enter Southern towns behind fluttering flags and brass bands. They attempted to organize slowly and patiently, seeking out the natural leaders in rural black communities and building from there."[14] In each state, Colored Alliance members elected a superintendent, president, vice president, treasurer, conductor, secretary, lecturer (usually with the additional title of "organizer"), and sometimes an assistant lecturer. Additionally, there were three positions for meetings, a "Conductor," a "Chaplain," and a "Door-Keeper."[15] All superintendents, their principal task being to expand the organization, reported to the general superintendent who was elected by the national trustees of the Colored Alliance. All members were asked to pay dues, although from the beginning payment for most proved difficult, debt-ridden and lacking in cash as they were.[16]

According to the national constitution of the Colored Alliance, a state having ten "County Alliances" would be entitled to a "State Alliance"; any county having three "Sub-Alliances" would be entitled to one delegate in a state meeting; and any congressional district having thirty "Subordinate Alliances" would be entitled to one delegate in national meetings—regardless of whether or not the state in which the local alliances were in had already formed a statewide organization. This last arrangement allowed for local county leaders to work with the national order and its state affiliates in advance of having created organization access in the entire state.[17]

The use of secret passwords and salutations required upon entry to Colored Alliance meetings were in keeping with the tradition and conventions of other mutual-aid societies and black fraternal organizations of the time. According to the sociologist Joseph Gerteis, the Colored Alliance was "formed as a secret society following the fraternal and ritualistic model of the Knights of Labor."[18] The Colored Alliance had an assigned seating order for its various elected positions, including a doorkeeper and a chaplain, and used special language for initiation rites, application of new members, and opening and closing of sections of the meeting—all delineated in its bylaws. There were other rituals adhered to, including dress code when a member passed away: "black crape rosette, with a sprig of evergreen pinned above it on the left lapel of the coat—the rosette to be worn thirty days."[19] The extent to which such detailed rules and procedures were followed from state to state, or even county to county is not known; they were likely modified to fit local circumstances.

Like other agrarian clubs and mutual-benefit societies of the era, the Colored Alliance also encouraged its members to learn new farming techniques, purchase land, and form greater bonds between themselves and their communities. The organization sponsored a number of cooperative stores where local members could pool their crops for bulk sales. In the eighteen months following the initial meeting in Houston County, organizers set up dozens of chapters; African Americans by the hundreds joined in.[20] Within two and a half years the Colored Alliance spread across Texas, made its way to the Upper South, and then over to the southeastern Atlantic seaboard states. By 1888 the organization had gained a discernible presence across the entire South. In March of that year Colored Alliance chapter delegates were called to gather in Lovelady, Texas, to convene and formally establish themselves as a regional body.[21]

During the summer of 1888, leaders of the Colored Alliance set ambitious goals for their organization. On July 20, Shuffer and Spencer assigned Humphrey the task of leading the effort to "establish . . . trading posts, or exchanges, for the use and benefit of our order [as] your judgment will be most conducive to the interests of the people."[22] Humphrey spent the next two and a half years helping to establish trading posts in Houston, New Orleans, Mobile, Charleston, and Norfolk—key southern ports on the Atlantic and Gulf Coasts—for the large-scale purchase and sale of staple crops. Ideally, members would be able to buy goods at reduced prices at these "exchanges" and to secure loans to pay off their mortgages.[23] Referring to the initiative underway, a lecturer of the Colored Alliance in Tennessee remarked, "The colored people show an eagerness for information for our cause and principles, which is unsurpassed by any audience I have ever addressed."[24] By October 1890 the Colored Alliance claimed 175 chapters across the South.[25] Despite the enthusiasm for such projects, most of the exchanges faltered as the required infusion of capital was difficult to obtain from the organization's largely poor members. In one plea, members were asked to give direct financial support to the organization's initiatives instead of "buying [Colored Alliance] badges and regalia."[26] Members, however, were apparently more inclined to acquire symbols of ownership, group identity, and collective pride, before supporting the organization's large-scale projects. Badges and regalia, were, after all, relatively inexpensive to purchase than paying for projects that were less immediate in their rewards. Colored Alliance officers, limited by logistical considerations and the ever-present threat of retaliation to their order's members (unlike the white Alliances who had the privilege of holding parades and conducting mass public meetings) were unable to keep up with the demands and growth of their own organization.

By 1891, the Colored Alliance had established chapters in every southern state, prompting its national spokesperson, Humphrey, to claim a "total membership [of] nearly 1,200,000, of whom 300,000 are females, and 150,000 males under twenty-one years of age."[27] The membership figures were probably inflated for propagandistic purposes; one reason to bolster its numbers might have been to gain larger proportional representation when meeting with other reform groups in convention, where African Americans were a minority. (Beginning in 1888, and continuing through 1892, the Colored Alliance took part in a series of national conventions to formulate strategies and assert its particular demands among other reform groups.) Scholars offer various estimates of the actual size of the Colored Alliance: Lawrence Goodwyn estimates that the Colored Alliance membership was closer to 250,000; Patrick Dickson maintains that membership was roughly at one million.[28] Others, such as Gerald Gaither, offer the explanation that membership rolls were simply never purged of inactive members, accounting for the high figures; Postel argues that the Colored Alliance membership roughly corresponded to black congregations in the countryside: "[The] relationship to the churches helps to clarify why the order could claim over a million members."[29]

Consensus on the exact number of African Americans in the Colored Alliance will likely never be reached since such detailed records were either destroyed or not kept in order to protect members from hostile planters, merchants, or others threatened by the order. But while the number of Colored Alliance members remains debatable, that the organization commanded a degree of support beyond formal membership is certain. In 1890 approximately 1,100,000 out of 1,725,000 African Americans who worked in agriculture in the United States were farmworkers (roughly 64 percent).[30] These black agrarian laborers, the overwhelming number of whom were in the South, were the Colored Alliance's natural base and would have found it easy to agree with the organization's goals of better education, more land, economic cooperation, and mutual benefit. Declarations by the organization's local leaders in the press, in conjunction with reports from the national spokesman, are ultimately the only figures through which an approximation of its total membership can be made. Writing to the *Southern Mercury* in December 1888, for instance, Alex John, a leader of Ebenezer Colored Alliance No. 195 in Texas, reported that his local chapter comprised "10 male and 6 female members."[31] Few reports with such specific information like this exist, however. Taking political, economic, and demographic factors into consideration, it may be conservatively estimated that at least 250,000 African Americans participated in Colored Alliance activities during its six-year history.

The Colored Alliance published several newspapers. Most of what remains of these publications, however, are reprinted excerpts found in white Alliance-affiliated newspapers—most notably, the *National Economist*. The Colored Alliance had up to three publications in Texas: the *National Alliance*, the *Colored Alliance*, and the *Alliance Vindicator*. The *National Alliance*, the organization's national newspaper, was published in Houston between 1889 and 1891; Humphrey served as its editor. According to Joseph J. Rogers, the Colored Alliance superintendent from North Carolina, the *Colored Alliance* was first published in Dallas in July 1888. Finally, the *Alliance Vindicator*, which began in February 1892, was edited by Robertson County's leading black Republican and Colored Alliance state president, Alex Asberry. The *Midland Express*, which was published in Boydton, Virginia, from 1891 through 1893, was the official organ of Virginia's Colored Alliance (although the *Richmond Planet* became a semiofficial outlet for announcements for the organization). North Carolina had the *Alliance Advocate*, which was published in Oxford, North Carolina, around 1890; meanwhile, South Carolina had the *Alliance Light* and the *Alliance Aid of South Carolina*, the latter established in Sumter.[32]

The Colored Alliance newspapers variously informed and directed its readers—or listeners, since newspapers were often read aloud to reach larger numbers of people, many of whom were illiterate. As Steven Hahn notes about the distribution of newspapers in the rural black South, "papers circulated more widely still [than their subscription base], as they were passed from hand-to-hand, and household-to-household, and read aloud in groups."[33] Newspaper topics included the workings of transportation, storage, and other monopolies, issues of taxation, pending legislation, discussion about currency flows, and how all these matters affected them through price fixing, inflated interest rates, and driving up costs for farmers while keeping wages low for workers.[34] Members also learned about their organization's latest initiatives: cooperative exchange projects, lobbying efforts, credit programs, and cost-saving measures and techniques that were practiced and suggested. The Colored Alliance even tried to establish "Colored Homestead Companies" to assist African Americans to purchase their own homes, and in some areas, raised money to extend public school terms, in addition to providing financial assistance to individual members and their families in distress.[35]

While the Colored Alliance began as a strictly "non-partisan" mutual-benefit association focused inwardly on economic cooperation and education, it would develop into one of the most radical organizations of the era—it launched boycotts and strikes and then helped to found the People's Party to directly challenge Democratic authority. Some scholars have described the Colored Alliance as a "protest organization," although this characterization does not convey its more complex history and identity. As Ronald Yanosky notes, "[The Colored] Alliance framed public statements of its members' ambitions in terms of a carefully chosen language of domesticity, claiming that black farmers needed the civilizing influence of 'homes.'" Or, as Charles Postel notes, "Black Populism . . . contained a covert element of subversion. The public pronouncements of the Colored Alliance . . . reassured the white South that its members acquiesced in the separate but equal doctrines of white supremacy. But black members such as Reverend J. L. Moore of Florida clearly understood this as a strategem, as a means toward black progress." The organization publicly insisted (at least initially) that it was neither "political" nor "partisan"; it did so tactically as part of a broader strategy until 1890 when leaders began to move the organization into the electoral arena.[36]

As the Colored Alliance's membership grew and began to politically assert itself—abandoning its accommodationist public position—it came under attack from white planters and merchants. Attacks sometimes came from white Populists and African Americans tied to the Republican Party who opposed the organization's labor and electoral demands. As the attacks intensified, the national organization began to fragment: in 1891, one faction attempted a regionwide strike of cotton pickers; another vehemently opposed the strike, while yet another faction moved toward independent and third-party politics. Within a year, virtually all traces of the Colored Alliance disappeared from newspaper accounts. Still, its political impact continued to be felt. Having organized a base and network of support, Colored Alliance leaders redirected African Americans to focus their efforts on either building the People's Party or participating in independent coalitions, including supporting insurgent Republican candidates. By 1891, not only were leaders of the Colored Alliance openly declaring their support for federal supervision of elections and lobbying Republicans to have their leaders nominated for office, but many were also actively engaged in the meetings and conventions to create an electoral party of their own—a far cry from the Colored Alliance's initial nonpartisan stance.[37]

The careers of several notable Colored Alliance leaders illustrate the development and complexities of the organization from the mid-1880s to the early 1890s. They include Humphrey of Texas, Walter A. Pattillo of North Carolina, Oliver Cromwell of Mississippi, William H. Warwick of Virginia, and Ben Patterson of Tennessee. The amount of biographical information on these leaders varies widely. Notably missing from the record are female leaders of the Colored Alliance. With the exceptions of Phoebe Cobb and Fanny "the queen" Glass of the Knights of Labor in the mid-1880s (and later Lutie Lytle of the People's Party in the late 1890s) the vast majority of what is known about Black Populism is limited to the activities of its male leadership. Taken as a whole, however, their stories help to capture some of the local dynamics of the Colored Alliance— its successes, failures, and limitations—while reflecting some of the geographic diversity and range of the movement's leadership. Among the Colored Alliance's initial leadership, all were black (or "mulatto") except for Humphrey.

Known for his years of work as a Baptist missionary among African Americans and described by one contemporary as "an elderly man of large frame and portly person, with plain speech and a free blunt manner," Humphrey proved to be an effective leader.[38] In assigning substantial responsibilities to him, his black peers were acknowledging his skills as an organizer and propagandist. In March 1888, leaders of the Colored Alliance had charged Humphrey with the task of growing their organization on a national basis. His commitment to the interests of the region's most marginalized—landless black tenant farmers and agrarian laborers—was repeatedly affirmed through his actions, even as his sometimes patronizing attitude toward African Americans reflected the prevailing racist views of his white contemporaries.

Born in Clarendon County, South Carolina, on February 14, 1835, Humphrey was the son of Protestant immigrants from Northern Ireland. He attended Furman University in Greenville, South Carolina, between 1854 and 1858 and moved soon thereafter to Alabama.[39] During the Civil War he served as the captain of an Alabama infantry regiment. At the war's end he moved to Texas, where he worked as a cotton farmer, served as a Baptist minister, taught school, and participated in "dissident" (i.e., independent) politics.[40] The plainspoken Humphrey became active in the 1880s with the Union Labor Party, a key independent party in the period between the decline of the Greenback Labor Party and the rise of the People's Party. Along with the Non-partisan Convention, the Union Labor Party was one of the most important independent electoral vehicles to challenge the Democratic Party in the South during the late 1880s—particularly in Texas. In the words of historian Matthew Hild, the Union Labor Party served as "a bridge between the loosely organized farmers-labor political activity of the mid-1880s and the Populist Party of the 1890s."[41] In 1887 a national convention was held in Cincinnati that brought together over four hundred delegates from a range of organizations, including the Agricultural Wheel, the Farmers' Alliances, the Knights of Labor, the Greenback Labor Party, and the Grange. The overwhelming majority of participants at the convention were farmers. Together they established the National Union Labor Party. The Greenback Labor Party, which was an intermediate step in the dissolution of the Greenback Party, dissolved itself soon after the convention.[42]

In the fall of 1886, the Union Labor Party held its first convention in Fort Worth, Texas. Among its planks, the party opposed the monopolization of land, and favored both the direct election of U.S. senators and a single tax. Nationally, and significantly, the party sought to prohibit the convict lease system and demanded women's suffrage (the latter position removed from the Populist Party Omaha platform of 1892).[43] Humphrey was elected a presidential elector from the second congressional district and was later nominated as the party's congressional candidate from the same district.[44] Three days after the convention, the *Southern Mercury* published an article listing sixteen of Humphrey's speaking engagements scheduled to be given between October 20 and November 3. Humphrey's brief statement at the conclusion of the article helps to encapsulate his method of recruitment and reflects his direct manner: "Friends of the labor movement please take notice and meet me."[45] William H. Martin, the incumbent Democratic congressman from Texas's second congressional district, attacked Humphrey during the election for working with African Americans. Like Humphrey, Martin was born and raised in the South and served in the Confederate army (under Robert E. Lee's command, participating in all the battles of the general's army until his surrender in April 1865).[46] But unlike Humphrey, who subsequently sided with the freedmen and women and took up the plight of the black poor, Martin became a staunch supporter of the Democratic Party and its white-supremacist politic and practices. Charging Humphrey with "slipping around at night with lantern in his hand to organize the negroes into alliances, [and] doing so for mercenary and political ends," Martin, with the backing of the Democratic Party, easily won the election. However, he did lose a county—not surprisingly, one with a predominantly rural black population. As it became clear over the coming months, Humphrey's campaigning among African Americans, while unsuccessful in winning the second congressional district seat, would win him an abiding trust among those who soon joined the ranks of the Colored Alliance.[47]

Much of what survives about the character and composition of the Colored Alliance (what it strived to do, who comprised the organization, and how many members it included at any given time or place) comes from Humphrey's written and oral accounts between 1889 and 1891. In the few sketches of the Colored Alliance, the fact that Humphrey is the primary source of information on the organization has had the unintended effect of privileging his role in the Colored Alliance over that of other leaders—notably black leaders. Humphrey's leadership role in the organization was no doubt critical to the Colored Alliance's development, but only in conjunction with others—including Pattillo, Cromwell, Warwick, Patterson, and Shuffer—who carried out the mass organizing of African Americans locally that gave the national organization its relative strength.

Humphrey's accounts include his brief history of the Colored Alliance in *The Farmer's Alliance History and Agricultural Digest*, published in 1891; excerpts of articles from the weekly *National Alliance* newspaper, which he edited for two years beginning in 1889; occasional press statements; and testimony he offered to the U.S. Senate Committee on Agriculture and Forestry in 1890—all of which provide important details about the organization's goals, membership, and activities, as well as how they changed.[48] Other sources on the Colored Alliance appear in letters in the *Southern Mercury* and the *National Economist* from newly appointed business agents, reports from the organization's cooperative efforts in

Virginia and South Carolina, and its public political activities—for instance, a convention of black and white Alliances in Ocala, Florida, in December 1890 and a national People's Party meeting in St. Louis, Missouri, in February 1892, both of which included the participation of Colored Alliance delegates.[49]

As it turns out, class divisions proved to be as great a source of conflict among leaders in the movement as race.[50] Colored Alliance president Shuffer was reportedly "stern and domineering, especially with blacks in his hire." Shuffer's grandson noted that he "readily inflicted whip lashes to [black] slackers [who worked for him] with threats to cut their pay." He continued, while "Blacks throughout the community looked up to him [they did so] more out of fear than genuine respect." However, Shuffer's success as a farmer—he owned some five hundred acres of land—apparently brought him into conflict with local white farmers. The family history helps to explain some of the class tensions that existed among African Americans in the Colored Alliance—that is, between its black leadership and rank and file—and points to the pressures faced by some of the wealthier black leadership in relation to local white farmers.[51]

While the vast majority of the Colored Alliance's presidents, secretaries, and state lecturers were black, there were several white state superintendents, in addition to the organization's general superintendent Humphrey. White Colored Alliance state superintendents included Alabama's Harry G. McCall (who also served as the editor of the *Montgomery Alliance Advocate*), North Carolina and Virginia's Joseph J. Rogers, and Kentucky's F. T. Rogers.[52] Given the racial discrimination that infused the dominant culture and institutions of U.S. society, the role of white organizers in the Colored Alliance—characterized as "an African union" by one of its opponents—was designed to bolster the growth of Black Populism. White leaders such as Humphrey were more easily able to establish ties with segregated white agrarian and labor organizations that shared common interests with black organizations than were their black counterparts.[53] Similarly, white leaders did not face the kinds of barriers that African American leaders confronted when attempting to reach or speak with the white press (although it is also true that white leaders were not fully shielded from discrimination or physical attacks). As national spokesperson, Humphrey was therefore an important asset to the Colored Alliance, as were other white leaders locally.

From the outset, Black Populism proved to be an integrated movement. This was unlike the white Populist movement with its fully segregated organizations, including the white Southern Farmers' Alliance and Florida Farmers' Union—both of which had provisions in their bylaws explicitly excluding African Americans; the former from its inception, the latter beginning in 1889. While the southern white Populist organizations excluded African Americans from their membership, the white Northern Farmers' Alliance did not. And while the national Colored Alliance made a retaliatory declaration in 1888 that it would, as a matter of principal, exclude white members in response to black members being excluded from the southern white Alliance, state-based Colored Alliance chapters did not exclude white participants willing to help grow the organization.

A word on "race" as a political concept and activity: Just as there had been "Black Republicans" during Reconstruction who were white (the term "Black Republican" having been principally used by Democrats to deride their opponents), so had white leaders emerged as Black Populists—their defining characteristic not being their race, but their participation in building the movement to empower black farmers, sharecroppers, and agrarian workers through a variety of tactics. In other words, "Black Populist" designates an activity rather than a fixed racial identity. Under this definition, white men such as Humphrey, Harry McCall, and Joseph Rogers of the Colored Alliance, Hiram Hover of the Cooperative Workers of America, and Nicholas Stack of the Knights of Labor were Black Populists. Other white leaders followed them: J. W. Allen of the Alabama Colored Wheel, Victor St. Cloud of the Georgia Knights of Labor, T. J. Mott of the Florida Knights of Labor, and Garrett Scott of the Texas People's Party. Like Humphrey, who had been accused of "slipping around at night . . . to organize the negroes," in 1889 Mott, who was serving as the Florida Knights' state master workman, was fired from his job for his "insurrectionary movements among the Negroes."[54]

These white men constituted a minority, albeit an effective one, for the movement. But it was African Americans who predominated among Black Populism's leadership and the rank and file. African Americans did the lion's share of expanding the movement on the ground by recruiting new adherents and directing the various initiatives of their respective organizations. Among these black leaders, few stand out more than a former slave turned minister who not only became the principal organizer of North Carolina's Colored Alliance but also helped to lead Black Populism's transition into third-party politics.

Among the most effective Black Populists to emerge from the ranks of post-Reconstruction black leadership was the Reverend Walter A. Pattillo, a "mulatto" Black Baptist minister and educator from North Carolina.[55] Even before the rise of the black agrarian movement, Pattillo was known as an exceptional organizer in Black Baptist circles. Born into slavery in North Carolina on November 9, 1850, Pattillo taught himself how to read and write. It appears that he may have been afforded certain privileges as a young man with relatively light-colored skin—the result of being the son of a white man and his black female slave.[56] An apparent advantage to Pattillo's lighter complexion was not having to work in the field. In the late 1860s he drove wagons and worked in a sawmill. In 1870, however, he was listed as working on a farm (possibly to augment his income); that same year he married Mary Ida Hart, with whom he would have twelve children. In

1874, two years before entering the Raleigh Theological Institute (later renamed, and better known as Shaw University), he received a license to preach. Unlike Humphrey, Pattillo was ordained. The combination of being African American and an ordained minister gave him much greater access to Black Baptist circles, through which he recruited Colored Alliance members, including the Reverend Robert Ikard, who became Catawba County's Colored Alliance leader.[57]

Issues of race and the related concept of "color" among African Americans informed decisions taken by African Americans to elevate or block the rise of certain members of the community. Being lighter skinned likely worked to Pattillo's benefit in a number of ways. As the historian Tiffany Ruby Patterson notes, "Color permeated the consciousness of African Americans ... It was a source of pride and shame, status and beauty ... It defined who was in and who was out in particular social circles. Color, therefore, was about power ... It was a determining factor in who achieved success, position, and recognition."[58] Part of this cultural dynamic may have been at play when Pattillo sought funds to attend Shaw University in 1876. Both black and white members of the community came to his assistance.

Pattillo's home county, Granville, located in the Piedmont, was the only predominantly African American county outside of the mostly black eastern part of the state. In the decade prior to the Civil War the Granville census listed 10,975 "Slaves" and "Free Blacks & Mulattoes" and 10,383 "Whites."[59] There, as in other counties with high concentrations of African Americans, Black Baptist and Methodist churches dotted the landscape and served as centers for the cultivation of black leadership.[60] Local black churches brought together young and older members of the community into a shared environment. Here, junior members took their lead from senior, more experienced members, assuming greater responsibilities. In this way, at the age of seventeen, Pattillo joined the General Association of the Colored Baptists of North Carolina to promote the newly established statewide association. Within a few years he gained a reputation as a "convention stalwart" for strengthening ties between congregations across the state.[61] His studies in theology at Shaw in the mid-1870s would bring him into even greater contact with other black leaders in the region, raising further still his profile. Pattillo, a pioneer of the Black Baptist church, later served as a member of the Home Mission Board of the Baptist State Convention in Granville and was elected president of the Middle Baptist Association; he also edited the *Baptist Pilot* newspaper. As one of his sons later recalled, Pattillo's ministry grew significantly. It is estimated that he delivered "nearly three thousand sermons, including funerals, and baptized about 3,100" people over the course of his lifetime.[62]

Pattillo would use his connections to the black church to organize the African American community and to advance his own standing. In 1883 he ran for register of deeds as a Republican in Oxford, the seat of Granville County, where he commanded a strong following.[63] However, attacks on his candidacy quickly mounted. As light skinned as he appeared, he was still black. His white opponent launched a campaign warning voters that, if elected, the "sleek, oily, negro" would have the authority to issue marriage licenses to white couples—presumably violating the sanctity of their unions.[64] Pattillo lost the election and continued to serve his community; he became superintendent of schools in Granville (overseeing twenty-seven schoolhouses) and helped to establish the state's first black orphanage, the Colored Orphanage Asylum.[65]

In the late 1880s, with growing economic instability in rural black communities—the result of falling crop prices, steep debt, and acutely low wages—Pattillo turned his attention to the agrarian movement sweeping the countryside to his south and west. Pattillo joined the Colored Alliance, which had been established in North Carolina on the heels of the Knights of Labor.[66] Soon, the minister was spreading the Colored Alliance's gospel of reform, bringing a wealth of experience to the task of rallying rural African Americans to the agrarian cause. In 1890, he was formally elected as the Colored Alliance's "State Lecturer and Organizer" and began editing the *Alliance Advocate* in Oxford. Pattillo also took care in fostering cooperation between black and white communities, understanding the need for allies to promote black interests. As his son recalled: "Aside from his ministerial work, [his strength lay] in the middle ground he occupied ... in bringing about peace and goodwill between the colored and white races."[67] Pattillo's success was in part reflected in the phenomenal growth of North Carolina's Colored Alliance, which by 1891 was claiming a membership of 55,000 men and women—a figure which roughly coincides with the number of African Americans in rural Black Baptist congregations.[68]

The Colored Alliance's entry into North Carolina was part of a general surge in the organization's regional membership following the black and white Alliances' conventions in Meridian, Mississippi, in 1888. In the same city where African Americans and white Democrats had engaged in armed conflict seven years earlier, the Colored Alliance and the white Alliances (Northern and Southern Alliances), most of whose southern members continued to be affiliated with the Democratic Party, began to formally cooperate with each other. The spirit of cooperation was short-lived, however.

Meeting separately from the white organizations, the Colored Alliance sent representatives to speak with white delegates in Meridian to determine possible areas of cooperation. Black and white delegates decided that their respective Alliances should join forces against the railroad and banking monopolies from which their members both suffered. With virtually no oversight or regulation, railroad companies charged excessive prices for transporting goods to market while banks and local merchants charged exorbitant fees and interest rates—anywhere from 20 to 200 percent. In forming a united front, the black and white Alliances were careful to avoid the adoption of positions likely to exacerbate differences between them—namely, the mostly landless and laboring membership of the Colored Alliance versus the high percentage of white Alliancemen (particularly at the leadership level within the Southern Alliance) who were either employers or landlords. Despite this fundamental (and ultimately, as it would become clear, irreconcilable) difference between the two orders, cooperation between black and white Populists based on shared interests took place from time to time. As the Southern Alliance noted in a resolution at Meridian, "Whereas, A large per cent of the products of this country are produced by the colored farmers and laborers, and a large proportion of supplies are purchased by them; therefore, Be it resolved, That it is detrimental to *both* white and colored to allow conditions to exist that forces our colored farmers to sell their products for less and pay more for supplies than the markets justify" (emphasis added).[69]

Pragmatic considerations drove the spirit of cooperation between black and white Alliance leaders. Like their white counterparts, black leaders chose to enter into such alliances based on their own particular interests. Within only a couple of years, the Colored Alliance had established itself as a small but growing force in the South; leaders of the white Alliance saw in the black Alliance movement an opportunity to enhance their own by attempting to bring organized African Americans into their fold. Meanwhile, black leaders saw that their demands could be more powerfully expressed in coalition with white allies. But the Colored Alliance was neither subservient to the white Alliances nor was its leadership controllable. The president of the Southern Alliance, Leonidas L. Polk, who later tried to undermine the Colored Alliance's call for a regionwide cotton pickers' strike, admitted that the black order was "an entirely distinct organization"—a statement which echoed one made by North Carolina's white Alliance president S. B. Alexander in which he described the Colored Alliance as "a separate and distinct group."[70] Indeed, according to H. H. Perry, North Carolina business agent of the Craven County Alliance and president of the Riverdale sub-alliance in James City (an all-black town), by May 1890 over three hundred Colored Alliance chapters had been established across the state. Such a widespread base of support, if effectively co-opted, could serve white Populist interests by adding to their numbers.[71]

White Alliance leaders at the state level, like Polk at the national level, praised and even offered money to Colored Alliance leaders in a bid to co-opt them. Joseph J. Rogers, the white manager of the Norfolk exchange in neighboring Virginia, assured North Carolina Alliance leader Elias Carr, for instance, that Pattillo was "perfectly reliable" (i.e., that he could be controlled) as a spokesman.[72]

However, Patillo was cautious in navigating his relationship with Carr, who was offering him an underwhelming sum of ten dollars to help fund his recruitment efforts. Scholars on North Carolina Populism, such as Craig Thurtell, acknowledging that co-optation lay behind Carr's financial support, however, have also concluded that Pattillo was "Carr's obedient agent, which meant, among other things, no disruption of labor." But given Pattillo's career as an independent black leader, which later included his leading the call for a third party, it is more likely that Pattillo was effectively using the opportunity presented by Carr to expand the Colored Alliance for its own sake. Pattillo's diplomacy and tact should not be confused with "obedience," which is a bias that speaks to one of the underlying assumptions guiding existing studies on Black Populism.[73]

Fully aware that his black constituents would protest any arrangement that compromised their order's independence (or appeared to do so), Pattillo carefully treaded the situation with Carr. As Pattillo put it, if African Americans knew "that one cent had [been given] to me in this work, they would not follow me, though they knew I was working for their good." Deciding to take the ten dollars, Pattillo insisted to Carr that their arrangement not be made public. African American leaders in the period were not above the fray of corruption. The interaction between Pattillo and Carr may simply be interpreted as a black leader being bought out for a sum of money by a white leader; it could also be understood as Pattillo seeing a small opportunity to use what money was offered to him (by whomever) to continue his organizing efforts—money to cover transportation costs, for instance. Taking the whole of Pattillo's career, it appears that the minister did what he deemed necessary to build the Colored Alliance.[74]

Pattillo, as with most other black leaders of the era and region, communicated his thoughts and interests to potential southern white allies in supplicating ways. Doing so was in keeping with the practices of the more effective black leaders in the South given both white political and economic domination and accompanying notions of white racial supremacy. Pattillo was equally sensitive to conditions facing black farmers and agrarian workers. In correspondence with Carr two months prior to the exchange over the ten dollars, he wrote: "Please drop me a few lines respecting canvass of the East, if you mean for me to postpone it entirely until September . . . I am ready to work at all times but know now is a very busy time for the farmers and hands."[75] Pattillo traveled across the state, recruiting members into local chapters of the Colored Alliance, working with whomever he could to help grow the organization. His actions express his commitment to building independent black organizations: religious, educational, or, as with the Colored Alliance, with a focus on agrarian cooperation. For African Americans tied to the Colored Alliance, cooperation included working on initiatives with white Alliancemen when such initiatives had the chance of advancing black interests. As the historian Joe Creech notes, Pattillo did not hesitate to work "within the Colored Alliance to procure black political support for [shared white] Alliance demands through the Democratic Party, and as early as 1890 the Colored Alliance had vowed to take independent political action in order to secure reform if the two old parties rejected [its] demands"—a process in which Pattillo would play a key role.[76]

Like Pattillo, other black leaders in the South did not hesitate to reach out to white Alliancemen when necessary. The Reverend John L. Moore, the black superintendent of Florida's Putnam County Colored Alliance, made overtures to his state's white Alliance on the basis of shared economic concerns: "We are aware of the fact that the laboring colored man's interest and the laboring white man's interest are one and the same." Similarly, P. Lawrence, the black superintendent of Alabama's Lee County Colored Alliance, echoed Moore when he asserted that many of the goals of the white Alliances were in line with those of the Colored Alliance.[77] Black and white farmers therefore shared concerns over high interest rates and transportation costs while black and white agrarian workers shared concerns over low wages. The theme of shared economic interests between certain black and white southerners expressed by Colored Alliance leaders prefigured the famous statement by the Georgia white Populist Tom Watson regarding the shared plight of black and white farmers. In October 1892 Watson would write: "You are kept apart that you may be separately fleeced of your earnings. You are made to hate each other because upon that hatred is rested the keystone of the arch of financial despotism which enslaves you both."[78]

Black and white Populists worked on specific initiatives together. In the summer of 1888, black and white Populists in Alabama passed similar resolutions to boycott jute (the coarse material used to wrap cotton bales) after a "Jute Trust" sharply drove up prices. In July of that year, the price of jute jumped from approximately 6.5 cents to 12.5 cents per yard, forcing cotton farmers to pay an additional 42 cents per bale to prepare their crops for market. In response, farmers began using cotton sheets to wrap their bales.[79] In September, demonstrations against the trust were organized in neighboring Georgia. In one such demonstration, a group of young African Americans in Fort Gaines were seen pulling small samples of cotton from a wagon carrying a bale of cotton wrapped in jute, shouting, "Here's your pickery! Here's your pickery!"—"pickery" being a word used in the era to denote petty theft.[80] The jute boycott carried on for two years. In April 1891, the trust finally capitulated to farmers' and workers' demands and brought down prices. By then, however, many farmers faced even greater economic difficulties, having been hit by an especially poor harvest that year. The conclusion of the boycott nevertheless marked a political victory for the thousands of people who participated in it.[81]

Another instance of black and white cooperation took place in Louisiana. Leaders of the black and white Alliances joined forces to try to abolish the state's lottery system. With the promise of quick riches, the state lottery appealed to poor black and white Louisianans. Alliance leaders said that their members were buying into the lottery, and thus diverting funds from their respective organizations. In the process, members were creating even more debt for themselves by borrowing money to play. The Louisiana State Lottery Company, which was founded with a twenty-five-year charter in 1868, brought legal gambling to the state. Although it contributed $40,000 annually to the state treasury for public education and health care, it is estimated that it extracted far greater sums from the state's population, the majority of whom were poor. The campaign to abolish the lottery failed, but the cooperative relationship between the black and white Alliances continued when their mutual goals and interests aligned.[82]

In addition to state-based joint ventures, the Colored Alliance engaged in other work with white Alliances that could more broadly impact rural southerners. In 1890, the black Alliance sent their general superintendent, Richard Humphrey, to Washington, D.C., to lobby members of the Senate Committee on Agriculture and Forestry to enact a "subtreasury" loan program—a program initiated by the white Alliance. The legislation, which passed the House, but was blocked in the Senate, would have provided low-interest federal loans to farmers: warehouses were to be established where farmers could store crops when prices were low. In exchange, they would receive low-interest loans with negotiable notes that would increase the money supply; if market prices rose, the farmers could sell their produce at a profit.[83]

The Senate proceeding at which Humphrey testified sheds light on the dynamics of white leadership in the Colored Alliance. In the case of Humphrey's testimony, he assumes a defensive, even contradictory posture, as he addresses powerful white government officials on behalf of African Americans. At one point, Humphrey declared: "I am a white man, a Southern man, and have not been very friendly always toward the colored people. [However] I am proud to see them succeed. I want them to have justice."[84] He identified himself closely with rural African Americans, telling the committee, "I have worked in the field day after day [with black farmers]; I have ploughed by their side; I have known them ever since I was born." Yet he also distanced himself from African Americans when he came under scrutiny. Questioned by the committee about his assertions that the intelligence of black people was equal to that of whites, as evidenced by their skills in discerning differences between various grades of cotton, he responded: "I do not consider it superior intelligence in the dog that he smells better than a human being."[85] Despite such a racist statement designed to curry favor with the U.S. Senators, Humphrey carried out his assignment on behalf of the Colored Alliances' black leaders who sent him to lobby for the legislative interests of southern African Americans (specifically the subtreasury loan program).

To Black Populists, Humphrey, like other white leaders in the movement, served a practical political function. Whether or not African Americans objected privately to aspects of Humphrey's public manner, they saw him as an instrument for furthering the movement's growth. A general division of labor between black and white organizers of the Colored Alliance formed early on: white organizers, such as Humphrey related to the press, government bodies, and white-led organizations that refused to meet with or obstructed black leaders, while black organizers—such as Pattillo in North Carolina, Moore in Florida, or Lawrence in Alabama—carried out mass organizing among African Americans. However, such divisions of expectations and responsibilities among Colored Alliance leadership were not always clear, nor did they guarantee against internal conflicts erupting within the organization.

Several sharp disputes arose in the early 1890s between black and white leaders of the Colored Alliance. In June 1891, Joseph J. Rogers, the white superintendent of the Virginia Colored Alliance who had been lauded three years earlier for setting up the Norfolk Exchange, was now accused by members of mismanaging the very same cooperative exchange. Norfolk had become a center for regional black protest. Located in the southeastern peninsula, Norfolk was a coastal entrepôt linking northern and southern, as well as domestic and foreign markets. The Colored Alliance exchange opened with stock worth $2 a share and collected over $700 for operations. By 1890, the Virginia Colored Alliance had established organizational breadth; it counted over eight thousand black members in thirteen counties, with two dozen branches across the state.[86] In the midst of this rapid growth a committee of the Colored Alliance's national board was sent to Virginia to investigate the matter concerning Rogers.[87]

Rogers had apparently helped himself to a substantial portion of funds from the exchange. He not only refused to meet with the national investigating committee but subsequently failed to appear at the Colored Alliance's statewide meeting in August 1891. The office of Virginia's state superintendent was duly declared vacant and an election was called pitting Rogers against William H. Warwick, the state's principal lecturer and an African American.[88] Delegates at the meeting largely appeared to represent black farmers, as opposed to agrarian workers. In addition to Warwick, Colored Alliance leaders included Frank B. Ivy of Mecklenburg County (a Hampton Institute graduate who served on the Colored Alliance's board of directors), Reverend Edwin Austin Jr. of Appomattox County, D. C. Beasley of Dinwiddie County (who owned 110 acres of land), and Harry C. Green of Brunswick County (a tax official who owned 107 acres of land).

Delegates unanimously elected Warwick state superintendent and proceeded to pass a resolution calling for the protection of its members against "the deadly fangs of monopoly"—a resolution directed against railroad companies and the American Tobacco Company (which brought together a number of tobacco manufacturers). The historian Jeffrey Kerr-Ritchie described Warwick's election and the resolutions passed as "a hallmark of freedpeople's politics stretching back to Republicanism and Readjusterism."[89] The Colored Alliance noted in its records that day that its membership had grown to a robust 20,000, across forty-two counties.

While internal disputes occasionally flared, external opposition to the Colored Alliance eclipsed any divisions that lay within the organization between its black and white leaders. This was especially true as Colored Alliance tactics became more militant, and more widely known in the South, ultimately provoking the wrath of the Southern Democracy. It had been one thing for African Americans to form organizations of their own that were devoted to education and self-help; lobbying for reforms under the guise of paternalistic white leadership was even acceptable. But it was quite another for black people to carry out boycotts and make demands of their own that directly cut into the profits of white merchants and planters—as the Colored Alliance did under the leadership of Oliver Cromwell, a popular black farmer from Mississippi who, like his seventeenth-century namesake, would also lead a rebellion.[90]

During the summer of 1889, Leflore County, Mississippi, was the scene of one of Black Populism's bloodiest engagements with the Southern Democracy. Leflore, where 85 percent of the population was black, was located in the Yazoo-Mississippi Delta, an alluvial plain running some fifty miles wide and two hundred miles long between the Yazoo and Mississippi rivers. The Delta contained some of the darkest and richest soil in the nation—ideal for growing cotton.[91] As was typical of the Black Belt, local white landlords held the majority black population in an economic stranglehold. During the early summer, Cromwell, described by the *New Mississippian* as a "notoriously bad negro," began encouraging black farmers in the county to trade with a white Alliance cooperative store some thirty miles away in Durant, Holmes County, instead of with local white shop owners who were price gouging.[92] The white Alliance store, while far away, was near the Illinois Central Railroad line. Leflore farmers could pool their orders and send them to Durant to reach the larger market. Cromwell's boycott was ostensibly designed to break, or at least loosen, the grip of local white merchants on the black community; the outcome, however, was a brutal silencing of those who stood up to white authorities.[93]

Targeted for retribution, Cromwell received multiple death threats. In response, a group of seventy-five Colored Alliance members held a demonstration, marching in "regular military style" delivering a message to local white authorities: "Three Thousand Armed Men" were prepared to "stand by" Cromwell if need be.[94] The situation immediately grew tense and a white posse gathered on site. The Colored Alliance's show of righteousness was reminiscent of a parade fourteen years earlier in Clinton. Cromwell was said to have been the "main instigator of [that] affair" and described as "an ex-convict."[95] In a display of black power, Cromwell led a cavalry column at the parade in Clinton—mounted upon his horse, with cavalry saber at his side, he donned a stove-pipe hat topped off with a plume. The parade, which took place over the course of a day, was peaceful and culminated in a community-wide picnic. However, white vigilantes roamed the countryside and attacked African Americans following the picnic.[96] Cromwell was targeted for retribution.

Fourteen years later, African Americans would again be forced to defend themselves. Black Alliancemen were overwhelmed by the onslaught that hit them. Mississippi's Democratic governor Robert Lowry even summoned three white state militias to break up the "resistance." White authorities were now looking to punish and destroy, not simply disperse those who had gathered in a show of force against white business interests. Dozens of African Americans lay dead or seriously wounded as they retreated from fire. The incident was described as a "race riot," as such instances of black resistance to white authority were usually called by the white press. After the initial dispersal of Colored Alliance members, white vigilantes again went into the surrounding countryside where they beat up African Americans, killing several in their homes. The incident was more akin to a massacre, as it would later be called by African Americans. Black men, women, and children fled into the swamps, where they hid for two days. Among those killed were Colored Alliance leaders Adolph Horton, Scott Morris, Jack Dial, and J. M. Dial. Cromwell narrowly escaped only to be tracked down a week thereafter while still on the run. According to family oral history, Cromwell was killed in a standoff, but not before "taking down" five of his assailants—members of the Ku Klux Klan.[97]

Following the massacre, the Alliance store in Durant was ordered to break all ties with Colored Alliance members. The combination of murders of key Colored Alliance leaders and the trauma caused to the black community crushed the local organization; the decentralized structure of the Colored Alliance, however, allowed the Colored Alliance to continue functioning in other areas of the state. (As late as April 1891 there were sporadic reports of a Mississippi Colored Alliance assistant lecturer named McAllister organizing chapters in the state.)[98] While the white press and government officials were quick to bury reports of the massacre, its news traveled swiftly and widely along black networks. For African Americans, Leflore would serve as yet another vivid reminder of the lengths to which the Southern Democracy would go in order to maintain control over black labor and other African American resources. Black Populism, however, contained at least in this section of Mississippi, continued elsewhere—and in other forms.

African Americans lobbied for policies that would benefit their communities and challenged existing and pending legislation on several occasions. In 1889, the Colored Alliance confronted the white Northern Alliance, which—unlike the Southern Alliance—had not excluded African Americans from its order but was lobbying for legislation that would hurt both black and white cotton farmers in the South. The point of contention was the Conger Lard Bill, a measure to impose high taxes and strict regulations on vegetable oil—specifically, oil derived from cottonseed, the "colored man's crop." The Northern Alliance, with its large number of dairy farmers, strongly opposed the admixture of cottonseed to pure lard (animal fat).[99]

In response to the proposed Conger Lard Bill, the newly elected Colored Alliance president, John S. Jackson of Alabama (replacing Jacob J. Shuffer of Texas), sent a telegram to the U.S. Senate Committee on Agriculture. Jackson had emerged as one of the most prominent black leaders of the movement. He served as a negotiator with white Alliancemen, with whom, like Pattillo, he worked carefully. In addition to serving as national president, he would also represent Alabama's Colored Alliance at several national conventions, even addressing the full body of white Alliance delegates at the Ocala Opera House during the separately held black and white Alliance meetings in Florida in 1890. The telegram Jackson sent in response to the proposed bill read: "No legislation ever introduced into Congress, with the exception of the laws fastening slavery upon us, has been so injurious to the colored race as the so-called Conger Bill."[100] The pressing tone of the telegram suggests just how much harm the proposed bill would have caused African Americans, should it have been passed. The dispute over the bill, however, also pointed to regional conflicts between northern and southern farmers, temporarily (and unusually) positioning the Colored Alliance and the Southern Alliance on the same side against the Northern Alliance. A far more intense fight, however, erupted over the Lodge Bill—a highly controversial bill introduced into Congress in 1890 centering on federal supervision of elections. The proposed bill was for southerners reminiscent of federal measures taken during Reconstruction to protect black voting rights.

The Lodge Bill strongly united African Americans and, in particular, black leaders of the Colored Alliance in opposition to the Southern Democracy and its manipulation of elections. On June 26, 1890, U.S. representative Henry Cabot Lodge of Massachusetts introduced into Congress what detractors quickly dubbed the "Force Bill." Lodge's proposed legislation would have allowed federal authorities to oversee national elections if, in a district with at least 500 people, 50 people signed a petition attesting to electoral fraud.[101] Although the legislation technically only applied to federal elections, the bill would have also impinged upon state and local election practices—igniting fierce opposition from Southern Democrats. The implications of such legislation was even too much for some white leaders who had aligned themselves with African Americans, most notably, the Colored Alliance general superintendent Richard Humphrey—a former Confederate. Humphrey's opposition to the Lodge Bill was in sharp contrast to black Colored Alliance delegates who at the Ocala convention in December of 1890 unanimously supported the bill. While Humphrey may have gained the trust of many black southerners, he was not willing to support so powerful a federal mandate. Not surprisingly, white Alliance delegates went on record strongly opposing the bill. While the House of Representatives passed the bill on July 2, 1890, by a margin of 155 to 149 votes, Democrats in the U.S. Senate, along with eight Republicans, went on to defeat it in January 1891. As the historian Donald Grant wrote, "Georgia politicians feared the North was reneging on the 1877 Compromise . . . a northern effort to 'Africanize' Georgia by placing the state under black control."[102]

The erosion of black civil rights was of equal cause of concern to African Americans in the Colored Alliance. Black leaders in the organization variously took up the fight against attempts to roll back legislative gains made during Reconstruction. In the fall of 1890, for instance, Georgia's Colored Alliance appealed to its state jury commissioners that black jurors be included in cases involving black defendants. Georgia's Colored Alliance lecturer and legislative spokesman, J. W. Carter, would also lobby the state government to vote down a bill under consideration for a separate-coach law.[103] As Carter declared, "We don't want social equality. All the Negro wants is [legal] protection. You white people attend to your business and let us alone."[104] Unity, however, as witnessed with the controversy surrounding the Lodge Bill, was not always operative among Colored Alliance spokesmen and leaders. Class conflicts within the organization ran deep. Here, interestingly, Humphrey sided not with the landed elements of the organization, but with its poorest members—field hands and other agricultural workers. The divide between landholders and non-landholders within the Colored Alliance only intensified as time passed; such differences became increasingly manifest as the organization's non-landholding members bore ever greater and more acute economic pressures. Tensions culminated in the fall of 1891 with the launching of the regionwide Cotton Pickers' Strike.

As material conditions grew worse across the South—with falling crop prices and plummeting wages—one faction of agricultural workers within the Colored Alliance resorted to drastic measures. In an effort to secure higher wages for cotton pickers, a group of black Alliance leaders prompted by rank-and-file members pushed for a regionwide strike—highly ambitious in its call, given the logistical considerations in attempting to strike across multiple states. While strikes had been launched previously by black agrarian workers (such as the Cotton Pickers' Strike of 1886 in Arkansas led by black Knights), the scale of the proposed strike in the fall of 1891 was unprecedented.[105] Some black farmers who stood to lose if their harvests were not picked opposed the strike; other black farmers, such as E. A. Richardson, superintendent of the Colored Farmers' Alliance in Georgia, objected to the strike on different grounds. As he put it, "it was not the purpose of our organization . . . we were banded together for the purpose of educating ourselves and co-operating with the white people for the betterment of the colored people . . . such a step as this would be fatal."[106] Moreover, planning for the strike was, at best, minimal. Black agrarian laborers were nevertheless compelled to strike.

Cotton prices had fallen precipitously in the late nineteenth century—from approximately 31 cents in 1866, to nine cents in 1886, and then down to six cents by 1893. The fall in prices had a ripple effect: farmers demanded fair prices for their crops; workers demanded fair wages for their labor—the specific amounts of which depended upon where they were, as both prices and wages varied across the cotton-growing region. In 1886, cotton prices were as follows: Alabama (8.6 cents per pound); Arkansas, Louisiana, and Mississippi (8.1); Florida and Tennessee (8.0); Georgia and South Carolina (8.2); North Carolina and Virginia (8.3); and Texas (9.0). Meanwhile, wages for cotton pickers varied from 30 cents per 100 pounds in North Carolina to 50 cents in Texas.[107] With over two-thirds of white Alliance officers listing their occupation in 1890 as either farmers or planters (as opposed to only 2 percent who were listed as laborers), it is no wonder that they were hostile toward agrarian labor strikes; white Alliance leaders tended to favor antitrust measures, federal subsidies, and monetary reform instead.[108]

As it turns out, white Alliance leaders, many of whom were large landowners, had little in common with either their own membership or the majority of poor, largely landless African Americans. As a result, the economic interests of most African Americans in the Colored Alliance were usually at odds with the white farmers and planters who dominated the white Alliance leadership. Farmers and planters not only sought higher prices and lower transportation costs for their crops, but the lowest wages possible for their workers—as lower wages translated into less overhead and therefore higher margins of profit for employers.

Leonidas L. Polk, the president of the Southern Alliance and a former Confederate colonel, best expressed the white Alliance leadership's perspective regarding labor strikes in general and the proposed cotton pickers' strike in particular. Not for one moment, he declared through his paper the *Progressive Farmer*, did he "hesitate to advise our farmers to leave their cotton in the field rather than pay more than 50 cents per hundred to have it picked." Polk went on to accuse the organizers of the strike of trying "to better their condition at the expense of their white brethren." "Reforms," he stated, "should not be in the interest of one portion of our farmers at the expense of another."[109] The double standard on which Polk's statement rests reveals just how divorced white landowners were from—indeed in direct opposition to—the mostly landless African Americans who comprised the base of Black Populism.[110] Moreover, that white Alliance leadership in North Carolina, beginning with Polk, never objected to legislation that discriminated against sharecroppers and tenants, such as North Carolina's Landlord-Tenant Act, underscores their class bias against agrarian laborers. Thus the *Progressive Farmer* was joined by the *Caucasian*, another white Alliance newspaper, in sternly opposing the proposed Colored Alliance's strike.[111]

Prompted by black cotton pickers to take action, Humphrey called for a strike.[112] Initially directed against white planters in the areas of Charleston and Memphis who refused to pay their workers anything over 50 cents per 100 pounds of cotton picked, the call became regionwide. On September 26, 1891, fueling reports of a widespread strike amassing in the Cotton Belt, the *Cleveland Gazette* warned that a circular had been mailed out from Houston to "every colored sub-alliance throughout the country, fixing the date when the strike of the pickers [would] be simultaneously inaugurated, and how it [should] be conducted."[113] Specific direction and discretion, however, would prove difficult on such a wide scale.

Class dynamics within the Colored Alliance added further disorganization to the strike. Structural divisions between the organization's leaders and rank and file—that is, between its landed and landless elements—became accentuated. While landed leaders of the Colored Alliance opposed the strike, Humphrey and a small group of African Americans formed a separate group, the Cotton Pickers' League, to represent the movement's landless black tenants and agrarian workers. These, the most marginalized African Americans in the South, would soon form the core of the strikers. From his headquarters in Galveston, Humphrey "admitted the existence of the [Cotton Pickers' League], saying it had been induced ... by planters and merchants ... to reduce the price for picking to a very low standard, and that the colored pickers had combined to protect themselves from this dictation."[114] For most, then and since, the Cotton Pickers' League was synonymous with the Colored Alliance, although class differences between the two organizations could not be more evident.

The task of organizing the regionwide strike had begun in the summer of 1891 and ultimately fell on the shoulders of local leaders. The strike itself was to take place in mid-September; the launching date, however, varied by as much as ten days across the South. Pickers in South Carolina and east Texas, for instance, walked out on September 12, while pickers elsewhere held off for another week. The staggering of the strike—as much a function of the variation in peak harvesting times as a lack of coordination on the part of its leaders—led to disastrous results. Local strike leaders were summarily fired while pickers were threatened with force if they did not return to work. Despite the planters' swift retaliation, other outbreaks followed. The most notable took place in Lee County, Arkansas, where Ben Patterson, a thirty-year-old black farmworker, led local cotton pickers to strike.

Patterson, originally from Memphis, traveled in late August to Lee County, Arkansas, to mobilize cotton pickers in the Delta. For three weeks he plied the cotton fields in soaring temperatures, secretly recruiting local leaders willing to join him and help organize others to strike. Reportedly gaining the support of a core group of twenty-five black cotton pickers, he called for the Delta strike to begin on September 20. Assuming that many more pickers would join the strike once it was underway, he both underestimated the strength of planters' control over the local black workforce and overestimated the desire and willingness of black workers to follow his and other organizers' lead. The strike, which began on the plantation of former Confederate colonel H. P. Rodgers, fell short of expectations.[115] In calculating the prospects of their success, most pickers, despite their low wages, saw the possibility of better wages as hardly worth the risks of striking—imprisonment, physical harm, and the loss of current and future work. As was the case in east Texas and South Carolina, dozens of strikers were summarily fired in Arkansas. The adamant few who persisted in their efforts were soon crushed. Planters came after one particular group of black strikers under Patterson's lead who had been scouring neighboring areas in search of recruits.

Fighting quickly broke out between the heavily armed and mounted planter forces and the striking workers—most of whom were only armed with hoes, sticks, and knives. Planters were also aided by fighting that broke out among strikers and pickers. Many workers had decided to ignore the call to strike, viewing the prospects of a successful outcome as dim. Chaos seemed to characterize much of what occurred over the five days of the strike. At one point, so frenzied did fighting become between different groups that a white posse inadvertently burned a cotton gin. In the end, at least fifteen people—including two black workers who had refused to strike and a white plantation manager—were killed. At least six strikers were imprisoned. Of those killed, nine were lynched by white vigilantes at the instigation of planters.[116] Patterson, who had been wounded during a gunfight, was arrested and taken aboard the riverboat *James Lee*—ostensibly to be transported to a jail up the Mississippi before being placed on trial. Before arriving, however, he was taken to shore at Hackney's Landing and executed by a group of white-hooded men.[117]

In the aftermath of the strike, the white Alliance's main newspaper, the *National Economist*, stopped printing excerpts from the *National Alliance*, the Colored Alliance's main newspaper. Torn by competing factions among African Americans—farmers and workers opposed to the strike, and those who had joined the strike—the Colored Alliance was severely weakened. The failure of the strike was in addition to several factors that led to the demise of the Colored Alliance as a regional body: the inability to sustain cooperative stores and local programs, limited results in lobbying elected officials for agrarian reforms, and the inability to create a more public "movement culture."

According to Lawrence Goodwyn, "White supremacy prevented black farmers from performing the kinds of collective public acts essential to the creation of an authentic movement culture." As he notes, "Within the Southern caste system, there could be no vast Colored Alliance cooperatives and no public demonstrations of support for such cooperatives, no wagon trains stretching for miles, no spectacular summer encampments—nor any other public acts of solidarity . . . [in comparison to those of the white Alliances]."[118] Public displays and demonstrations by the Colored Alliance—which did include marches, boycotts, and strikes—were on a much smaller scale and scope than those of the white Alliances, which regularly brought hundreds of white farmers together for publicly held meetings (announced in newspapers ahead of time). Mass rallies of the white Alliances sometimes involved thousands of people; their parades even included politicians' support. The hostile conditions under which African Americans operated in the South simply did not allow for these kinds of public acts by the Colored Alliance; instead, Black Populists met in relatively small groups, in secret, and held relatively few public demonstrations.

The combination of obstacles and failures faced by the Colored Alliance steered increasing numbers of African Americans in the direction of those leaders who had been urging independent electoral political action. Several Colored Alliance leaders had begun running for public office as Republicans in the late 1880s. Lectured Crawford of Georgia's Colored Alliance was elected to his state assembly as a Republican; W. A. Grant, president of South Carolina's Colored Alliance, sought the Republican Party's congressional nomination in the state's first district; and the Reverend George W. Lowe of the Arkansas Colored Agricultural Wheel was elected to his assembly as a Republican and then reelected on the Union Labor ticket.[119] Absent a larger political strategy, however, these isolated forays into electoral politics that depended mostly on the Republican Party could do little to affect the kinds of broad structural reforms that rural African Americans needed.

Black Populists recognized that if they were going to defeat the Democrats at the polls and gain majorities in local or state government, they would have to work with white independents to combine their votes. Drawing on previous Republican-Greenback fusion experience, African Americans, most of whom were affiliated with the Republican Party, began working with white independents (and disaffected Democrats) along a new trajectory, establishing a string of local and statewide third parties in the early 1890s. By building independent electoral alternatives, African Americans would no longer rely on the Republican Party as its only electoral vehicle. The inside-outside tactic of establishing third parties while making use of existing Republican candidacies and organizations—that is, where feasible—not only set Black Populism on a new course but targeted Democrats' control of the electoral process.

The formation of the national People's Party signaled a significant shift in the movement. Between 1889 and 1891, operating through a series of parallel national conventions that brought together delegates of the black and white Alliances and several other reform-oriented organizations (including members of the Knights of Labor and the Women's Christian Temperance Union), African Americans and white third-party advocates established a new national political party: the People's Party. North Carolina's Walter Pattillo, Virginia's William Warwick, Florida's John L. Moore, and Louisiana's L. D. Laurent, were among the Colored Alliance leaders who emerged as key organizers in the conventions leading up to the formation of the national party in 1892.[120] Despite the regional dissolution of the Colored Alliance in the fall of 1891, local chapters continued to shape the course of Black Populism. Local Colored Alliance chapters in Georgia and Texas, for instance, would help feed the growth of the People's Party in the early 1890s.[121] By that time the People's Party—and the electoral tactic of running fusion campaigns with the Republican Party—would become the new means through which African Americans challenged the Southern Democracy.

"Biracial" cooperation existed at times between the two Populisms but had proven difficult to sustain for any substantial length of time. The wealthier white southerners in charge of the white Alliances generally attempted to dictate the terms and conditions of their relationship to their black counterparts—witnessed, for example, in the treatment of African Americans in Arkansas, Mississippi, and North Carolina. The pattern continued into the 1890s, when white Populists saw the political advantage of capturing black electoral support. Black Populists, however, approached alliance making with their white counterparts from their own vantage point. At times, they extended themselves to white Alliancemen even in the face of formidable social, economic, and political pressures from white *and* black southerners. That is, African Americans in the Colored Alliance supported the development of the Southern Alliance when it served their own interests. They did so by patronizing white Alliance cooperative stores, lobbying for the subtreasury loan program, joining the boycott on jute bags, and fighting the Conger Lard Bill. At other times, African Americans stood in opposition to the white Alliance: they endorsed the Lodge Bill, organized the Cotton Pickers' Strike, and made plain their demands for political and civil rights. Many white Populists had supported, or did not oppose, Jim Crow legislation—as had white Alliancemen in the Georgia state legislature in 1891, or the white members of the Louisiana Farmers' Union who supported segregation on trains. These contrasting positions came from the different experiences of black and white southerners.[122]

A lesser-known distinction between black and white Alliancemen and their respective movements had to do with their differing views regarding private property. According to the scholar Ronald Yanosky, African Americans tended to view land in less individuated and more collectivized terms than did white Alliancemen. Reverend I. N. Fitzpatrick, a prominent figure in the AME Church in Alabama, for instance, commented to the *New York World* on June 19, 1892: "Many of the people of my section belong to the Colored Farmers' Alliance, and they have adopted a single-tax platform as the only means of political salvation for our race . . . The success of the single tax may injure me as a landlord, but it will be the consummation of freedom."[123] Yanosky points out that African Americans in the Colored Alliance—despite their emphasis on acquiring property—displayed a commitment to a more collective kind of ownership of land "in which the producer was defined by his guaranteed access to natural resources, rather than his independent ownership of them." He continues, "Unlike the white Populists, the Colored Alliance embraced a platform explicitly addressed to the propertyless."[124] Such differences in perspectives underscore some of the opposing interests between rural black and white southerners—the former largely being landless, while the latter, largely being landowners.

Black Populists distinguished themselves from most white Alliancemen in another critical way. A number of black leaders in the Colored Alliance were among the first to call for a national third party when most African Americans were firmly tied to the Republican Party and most white Alliancemen were unsure whether to break their political ties with the Democratic Party—the party of most white southerners. Walter Pattillo, a delegate to the Ocala convention of 1890, was notably among the first leaders in his state to call for the formation of a third party.[125] More broadly, as the historian Edward Ayers notes, "The black declaration of independence came a year earlier than the white [southern] Alliance dared make the break." Other scholars have noted how the Colored Alliance itself was "an early champion of the third party cause within the [wider] reform movement."[126] Chief among the early third-party proponents was the Reverend John L. Moore, Florida's Colored Alliance superintendent and president from Crescent

City, who within a year would help form the Florida People's Party and serve on its state executive committee.[127] Moore had earlier attempted to build bridges with white farmers based on shared economic interests, but now chided white southern Alliance members for their unwillingness to support an independent course of action:

> The action of the [white] Alliance in this reminds me of the man who first put his hand in the lion's mouth and the lion finally bit it off; and then he changed to make the matter better and put his head in the lion's mouth, and therefore lost his head. Now the farmers and laboring men know in the manner they were standing before they organized; they lost their hands, so to speak; now organized in one body or head, if they give themselves over to the same power that took their hand, it will likewise take their head.[128]

The Colored Alliance's growing attention to the electoral process, and its move toward independent and third-party politics, presented a new challenge to the Southern Democracy. For Black Populists, new possibilities were being created to exert collectively organized electoral strength. After consolidating Black Populism as a regional force by linking and further activating networks of black agrarian organizations across the South, Colored Alliance leaders positioned themselves to shape what would become the People's Party. The formation of the new party, and its selected fusion and coalitions with the Republican Party, not only continued the development of Black Populism, but would pose the most powerful threat yet to the Democratic Party in the South.

Chapter Three

ESTABLISHING THE "NEGRO PARTY"

The fact that a man is colored should not be self-evident that he belongs to any particular party. As a rule the colored people are Republican, the results of which were perfectly natural. But more than a quarter of a century has thrown around him the light of intelligence ... the two old parties have not kept pace with the great demands of the common people ... Now in my view of the above facts ... the one and only advantageous political course of the Negro, under present existing affairs, is to support the People's Party.

—P. K. Chase, "The Colored Man and Politics," *Southern Mercury*, August 11, 1892

The spectacle of two thousand armed white Populists converging to prevent one of Georgia's Black Populists, the Reverend Henry S. Doyle, from being lynched in the fall of 1892 was unlike anything southerners had seen in a generation. Former Democrat Tom Watson, now a white Populist leader from Georgia who issued the call to arms, was dubbed insane by the press for aiding Doyle, a former Republican who worked with the Prohibition Party but who was now building the People's Party. One Democratic newspaper editor shuddered that the South was being "threatened with anarchy and communism."[1] Even high-ranking Democratic officials were compelled to recognize the political revolt underway. North Carolina's Democratic governor, Zebulon Vance, wrote in 1890, "There is an uprising of the agricultural class ... which amounts to little short of a revolution."[2]

The general uprising was not solely that of white Populists applying pressure on particular Democratic officials, such as Vance; more threatening still was the coming together of black and white Populists in tactical alliances via the People's Party—stigmatized as the "Negro party."[3] But while Democrats employed the word "Negro" as a term of opprobrium, intended to remind white southerners of former "horrors" brought on by "Negro rule" during Reconstruction, the enemies of the People's Party were also acknowledging the contribution of African Americans in the formation and development of what became the most significant third party in the nation since the rise of that other "Negro party," the Republican Party.

The outpouring of support in late October for the black minister Doyle from Macon, Georgia, came from white farmers loyal to Watson, who was then running for Congress on the People's Party ticket. Rushing through the night from outlying areas to the village of Thomson, Watson's supporters heeded his call with the urgency characteristic of the agrarian crusade. The next morning, as Doyle described, the village streets were "lined with buggies and horses foaming and tired with travel"; Doyle stood next to Watson on the court steps of Thomson, thanking his supporters for coming out and declared: "We are determined in this free country that the humblest white or black man that wants to talk our doctrine shall do it, and the man doesn't live who shall touch a hair of his head, without fighting every man in the people's party."[4]

Watson, whose bold public pronouncements for political equality were unusual for a southern white man at the time, was apparently hailed as "almost a savior" by African Americans, according to Doyle.[5] There were apparently instances of black women at People's Party campaign rallies holding aloft their children so that they could catch a glimpse of the fiery speaker; some black women went so far as to breach southern etiquette (i.e., the rules of racial conduct) by shaking his hand. Watson spoke passionately about the right of African Americans to exercise their vote. He noted how black and white southerners shared mutually oppressive economic conditions; on that basis they could work together in the political arena. It was a theme he preached often, and which he also penned in an essay entitled "The Negro Question in the South." As he wrote in the essay, "You [black and white southerners] are kept apart that you may be separately fleeced of your earnings. You are made to hate each other because upon that hatred is rested the keystone of the arch of financial despotism which enslaves you both."[6]

From the vantage point of African Americans, Watson was helping their cause; but there was the white Populist side to Watson's words and deeds. When Doyle came to Watson's home for protection, the minister was directed to sleep in a shed near the rear of the house; those white Populists who rushed on Watson's call had not come in support of Doyle but had come to rescue Watson, who they believed was the person in danger. The southern Democratic Press would use the Doyle rescue incident to show how white Populists were betraying their own people. Watson may have believed in political equality but neither did he nor his fellow white Populists advocate social equality. White supremacy was to remain intact. Watson, who had been serving in Congress as an "Alliance Democrat" before breaking from the Democrats, had repeatedly voted against black educational funding; and the practice at People's Party meetings of white Populists sitting on one side of the aisle, and Black Populists sitting on the other, or at the back, underscored social inequality.[7] Black Populism was separate, and for white Populists, fundamentally unequal—a perspective which, within a few years, became abundantly clear as Watson effectively led the charge for black disenfranchisement.

By the turn of the century, Watson became one of the South's most vocal opponents of black political rights, using his eloquence to strip the vote from African Americans.[8] His call for black disfranchisement was made on the grounds that votes cast by African Americans were being stolen by Democratic-appointed registrars and placed in favor of Democratic candidates; using this rationale, it was therefore in the best interest of white Populists to simply eliminate African Americans from the voting rolls.[9] But back in the fall of 1892 Doyle had risked his life to promote Watson's candidacy on the People's Party ticket. Watson's words and deeds as an impassioned proponent of black and independent white voters uniting at the ballot box had served to advance Black Populism, even if Watson was doing so primarily (if not exclusively) to advance white Populist's interests. Doyle delivered over sixty speeches to black and white Georgians that year; it was a campaign wracked with violence—at least fifteen African Americans were killed while scores of others were physically threatened and intimidated. Doyle was among other Black Populists who had helped Watson transform his image in the process of the campaign. As one scholar has noted, "Watson's earlier anti-black voting record in the Georgia Legislature brought him under fire from black audiences when he ran for re-election to Congress in 1892 as a Populist. His attempts to explain his record were apparently met with skepticism, and his supporters were compelled to argue that Watson was . . . a new man."[10]

Widespread violence used during the campaign of 1892 was, in part, a reflection of the political threat posed to the Democratic Party by the coalition of black and independent white voters. Tenuous as it was, a working political relationship had been formed between poor black and white farmers, whose mutual economic interests, it was argued, could indeed be advanced by joining their movement's forces in the electoral arena. Tapping into the Alliance networks created in the 1880s, grassroots organizers across the South would use the People's Party and, in some areas, fusion with the Republican Party to challenge Democratic rule. The opportunity to bring together a variety of fledgling independent parties and independent-minded voters came with the U.S. presidential election of 1892. The national election would serve as the fulcrum around which a variety of groups formed the national People's Party—a moment seized by African Americans to build new alliances in order to advance their interests.

Black Populism had effectively transitioned from agrarian organizing—with an emphasis on lobbying for reforms while promoting economic cooperation—to electoral politics in the early 1890s—with an emphasis on gaining offices through coalition building with white independents. The transition started locally and grew regionwide. By 1890 in Arkansas, for instance, black and white Alliances were meeting (albeit separately) in the state capitol building: the white Alliance met in the house chamber while the black Alliance met in the senate. There was some symbolism to the alliances meeting in the state government building—a move from the countryside to the halls of political power.[11] Although African Americans had been involved in third-party politics with the Greenback Labor parties in the 1870s and continued with the Union Labor and Prohibition parties in the 1880s, not until 1891 did independent and third-party politics become the principal organizing tactic of Black Populism.

Democratic control over the region did not entirely extinguish black participation in electoral politics in the wake of Reconstruction; enclaves of black political power persisted, exercised through the Republican Party. Black Republican strongholds included those in Texas' Black Belt, South Carolina's Low Country, and North Carolina's "Black Second" congressional district in the eastern part of the state, where Republicans regularly received over one-third of the statewide vote during the 1880s.[12] Although few in number, African Americans continued to sit in southern legislatures; the Colored Wheel's Reverend George W. Lowe of Arkansas and the Colored Alliance's Lectured Crawford of Georgia were both elected to their respective state legislatures. Several notable African American congressmen were also elected in the South—George Washington Murray of South Carolina's Colored Alliance was elected to the state's seventh congressional district (in 1893 and 1895), and George H. White of North Carolina was elected to the state's second congressional district (in 1897 and 1899).[13]

While most African Americans were loyal to the Republican Party, some African Americans were looking to diversify their political options by working with white independents. Beginning in the mid-1880s African Americans voted for selected white independents on the basis of candidates' support for agrarian and labor reform, antilynching laws, and the protection of black civil and political rights. A convention of African American leaders in Georgia in 1888 put forth their concerns by condemning the chain gang and convict lease systems, lynching, and the growing practice of segregation in public services and facilities; they deplored the exclusion of African Americans from jury duty and insufficient appropriations for the education of black children, and demanded accurate ballot counting.[14] Two years earlier, John Nichols, a white master workman of the Knights of Labor, ran for Congress in North Carolina's fourth district as an independent in a Labor-Farm-Republican coalition. African Americans saw his candidacy as one that could advance their interests. That fall Nichols campaigned on a platform that included shorter working hours and support for the Blair Bill. The bill, sponsored by New Hampshire Republican senator Henry Blair, called for federal support for public education and was strongly endorsed by the Colored Alliance. In response to Nichols's support for such reforms in labor and education, African Americans came out in force and joined white independents at the ballot box, providing his margin of victory.[15]

A similar coalition of African Americans and white independents formed in Alabama two years later. Under the leadership of *Alabama State Wheel* editor J. W. Allen, members of the black and white Wheels in Lawrence County organized themselves into the Union Labor Party. African Americans in Lawrence County had been active in independent politics since the late 1870s when black sharecroppers, former Whigs, and small white farmers formed the Greenback Party and fused locally with the Republican Party. Once again African Americans drew on independent coalition building to leverage their numbers at the ballot. They fielded a number of candidates, some of whom ran competitive campaigns for local offices.[16]

The example of Nichols in North Carolina, in particular, helps to demonstrate the conditions under which African Americans were willing to support white independents over white Republican candidates. Nichols, a former Republican, was among a growing number of southerners who believed that neither of the "old parties" represented small farmers or laborers, white *or* black. The southern Democratic press vilified white independents like Nichols, calling them, in one instance, "the posthumous bastards of the Republican Party."[17] Despite such political attacks, Nichols went on to win the fourth congressional district seat with the support of fifteen hundred black and white Knights (mostly in the area of Raleigh). North Carolina Democratic newspaper editor Josephus Daniels disparagingly attributed Nichols's victory to a combination of "black support" and "hard times."[18] Winning, however, was no guarantee that Nichols would be effective once in office. As the *Raleigh News and Observer* noted in an editorial, "There is nothing more lonesome or powerless in this world than an independent in an American legislative assembly"—the editors could have added, especially one where African Americans were part of the margin of victory.[19]

The potential for future victories for independent white candidates through black electoral support was not lost on Democratic leadership. In 1888, North Carolina Democrats reacted to the black and independent threat by passing election laws that gave greater discretion to handpicked Democratic election registrars to disqualify potential voters. The new law disfranchised over 25,000 African Americans.[20] When 2,000 African Americans gathered in Goldsboro, North Carolina, to discuss migrating out of the state, white opponents, fearing a hemorrhaging of black labor, called out their militia to prevent an outflow of cheap labor.[21] The pattern of black disfranchisement continued in other parts of the South. In Georgia, independent political efforts challenging or seeking to reform the Democratic Party led to the establishment of "white primaries" in the 1880s, further blocking black electoral participation.[22] African Americans who supported independent candidates and parties would do so, therefore, as much in response to isolated abuses of power as a way of trying to halt the overall erosion of black civil and political rights. Not only were individual politicians perceived as corrupt, but the entire political process was structurally, systematically, corrupt.

The existing political framework made it virtually impossible for African Americans to redress their economic concerns—high interest rates, low wages, lack of credit and capital—through the established political channels and institutional arrangements. Beginning in the late 1880s, the response of Black Populists was to build independent electoral organizations and coalitions with white independents in order to gain political leverage. But African Americans faced several electoral obstacles in doing so, beginning with the Republican Party. Starting in the late 1870s and continuing through the 1880s, black Republicans, along with their white sympathizers, were removed from internal leadership positions within the party's apparatus. Once the beacon of black empowerment, the Republican Party was effectively being purged of its "black and tan" elements by the party's "lily-whites." In the process of this purging, African Americans lost patronage and political influence that directly affected their communities. Nevertheless, the party could still mobilize a core constituency of black voters as "the party of Lincoln."

In the early 1890s, Black Populists, looking to maximize their political options, would use the Republican Party in the few remaining areas of the South where the purging of its African American leaders had not been fully achieved. African Americans asserted themselves through fusion campaigns with the People's Party, whose national platform may have differed substantially with that of the Republicans', but whose common interest was to break up the electoral monopoly of the southern Democratic Party.[23]

In the wake of Reconstruction, ongoing physical threats (directed or carried out by Democratic Party officials and their operatives), combined with ballot-box stuffing, the enactment of poll taxes, and the tossing out of votes, drove increasing numbers of African Americans out of the electoral process.[24] Black voter turnout plummeted as a consequence: in South Carolina, between 1876 and

1888, turnout fell from a high of 96 down to 26 percent; in Georgia, during the same period, turnout dropped from 53 to 18 percent.[25] By the late 1880s, Democrats began enacting "white primaries" across the South to suppress black voter participation—a direct result of electoral challenges posed by black and white independents in the 1880s. Literacy tests, grandfather clauses, and the expansion of poll taxes followed in the 1890s.[26] African Americans who did try to vote faced multiple legal and even life-threatening obstacles as the southern electoral system was now designed not only to favor, but in most cases guarantee Democratic outcomes.[27] Relatively low voter participation among African Americans was therefore a consequence of direct attacks on their voting rights, not simply black voter "apathy"—a term sometimes used to explain low voter turnout among African Americans in this period. "Apathy," however, is not an explanation for political behavior as much as it is something to be explained. The historian C. Vann Woodward, who while detailing the abuses faced by black voters in his classic study *The Strange Career of Jim Crow*, nevertheless states: "Caught between the 'Lily-White' policy of the Republican party and the blandishments of the Southern Democrats, the Negro became confused and politically apathetic." African Americans, however, were neither "confused" nor "politically apathetic," as much as they were living under hostile political conditions that often made it impossible to vote for candidates of their choosing.[28]

Given the political options that existed for African Americans in the 1880s, some took up a defensive position and resigned themselves to working with the ruling Democrats, believing it their best possible choice: a practical opportunity to participate in political decisions of importance to their communities, or simply to get something of value for themselves and their families (which could be anything from cash to some kind of favor, in exchange for their vote). Black leaders in Georgia, including the AME's Bishop Henry McNeil Turner and newspaper editor William Pledger, who later became the chairman of the state Republican Party, lent their support to the Democratic Party, believing it best for the black community at that particular time.[29] In 1890, black leaders in North Carolina were also reported to be considering defection to the Democratic Party as they grew resentful of their marginalized status within the Republican Party.[30] That same year in South Carolina, the Colored Alliance, with the urging of the conservative Black Baptist minister Richard Carroll (later called the "Booker T. Washington of South Carolina") lined up behind Democratic gubernatorial candidate Benjamin Tillman. Though Tillman was an open opponent of black political rights, he nevertheless publicly spoke out against the lynching of African Americans. Tillman won the election, and for a time used his authority as governor to curb lynching—that is, before pulling back.

By that time, however, the South Carolina Colored Alliance had already begun exploring other political options.[31]

It appears that many African Americans, having been pushed aside by Democrats and Republicans, became increasingly disillusioned with *all* elected officials and parties. James H. Powell, an officer of the Mississippi Colored Alliance, added his voice to the growing chorus of criticism against politicians for failing to fulfill their legislative promises regarding civil and political rights once elected. In 1890, in a letter to the *National Economist*, Powell wrote scathingly: "Down with [the] old politicians ... send new men. It is the aim of every colored farmer of Mississippi to send men to our national legislature who will represent the farmer." He challenged African Americans to look elsewhere: "We know that the men who have been sent there before will not do [right] .... if we depend upon our present members [of Congress] to do anything, we are deluded."[32] As Patrick Dickson correctly notes, "Powell's letter demonstrates the growing militancy of the Colored Alliance's political platform and could be read as an early expression in support of the third party movement."[33] Six months later a dispute ignited between black and white independents in Mississippi over two local candidates; the one favored by the state's Colored Alliance prevailed and Powell soon shifted his efforts to help build a third party in the state.[34]

Over the next year, Colored Alliance leaders such as Powell shepherded Black Populism from agrarian organizing to independent electoral politics. The Colored Alliance had already been engaged in local and state issues with legislative assemblies; for instance, a delegation of the Georgia Colored Alliance addressed its state assembly in 1891 urging that it not pass what amounted to be the first proposed statewide Jim Crow law.[35] However, Colored Alliance members were now beginning to join the People's Party to compete directly against existing legislators. As Gerteis notes, following the failed Cotton Pickers' Strike, which saw Colored Alliance membership dissipate, "People's Party clubs sprang up from the ashes of the Colored Farmers' Alliance."[36] Among the most prominent of the black Alliance leaders to move African Americans into third-party politics were Walter Pattillo of North Carolina and William Warwick of Virginia—the latter accused of "introducing politics," and "getting his nefarious [political] work in the secret conclave [viz., Colored Alliance]."[37] As local circumstances did not always permit or favor forming or entering a third party, African Americans in the South sought local branches of the Republican Party that could still be used as vehicles to advance their interests. The most notable example of this was George Washington Murray, South Carolina's Colored Alliance lecturer who was elected to Congress as a Republican in 1893. Whether through an independent party, fusion or cooperation with the Republican Party, or the GOP on its own, African Americans sought a variety of electoral paths to strengthen their leverage against Democrats.[38]

The notion of uniting black and white voters in a new party to compete against the Democrats apparently held mass appeal to the rural black population—at least theoretically. In August 1890, Joseph J. Rogers, a white Colored Alliance superintendent of South Carolina, reported that his state's Colored Alliance, comprising an estimated 40,000 African Americans, was prepared to vote *en masse* for candidates mutually agreed upon with white independents.[39] In December, Colored Alliance general superintendent Humphrey observed, "[From] the inception of the Alliance movement among Negroes[,] they have been in favor of a new political party."[40] And in Virginia, when the state's Colored Alliance was falsely accused of encouraging its members to vote for Democrats in early August of 1891, the organization issued a public statement in the *Richmond Dispatch*: "The colored [people's] . . . salvation rests in neither of the old political parties and [we] are no longer slaves to either."[41]

Political appeal and action, however, were two different things. Despite the limits of the two major parties, most African Americans were not willing to vote for independent candidates as Colored Alliance leaders had made it seem. As a resolution adopted by the Colored State Farmers' Alliance convention in August 1890 that noted "there should be no politics whatever in the order" demonstrates, entering the electoral arena had its opponents.[42] The task of creating a competitive national third party, building on the growth of state-based People's parties (beginning with the Kansas People's Party, followed by those in Texas, Louisiana, Georgia, and North Carolina), would require sustained lobbying efforts by its leading proponents.

The concept of a national "people's party" was forged at a meeting of black and white Alliances in St. Louis during December 1889. A series of national meetings followed over the next two and a half years, which included a number of reform-oriented and labor organizations. Meetings were held in Ocala, Florida, in December 1890; Washington, D.C., in January 1891; Cincinnati, Ohio, in May 1891; again in St. Louis, in February 1892, and culminated in a national nominating convention held in Omaha, Nebraska on July 4, 1892.

Delegates to the 1889 meeting in St. Louis included representatives of the Colored Alliance from Alabama, Florida, Indiana Territory, Kentucky, Mississippi, North Carolina, South Carolina, and Texas.[43] While supporting "race co-operation," the Colored Alliance resisted an attempted merger with the white Alliances in St. Louis. The decision is indicative of Black Populism's independence from the white movement. The next year, Colored Alliance delegates from across the South met in a parallel convention to the white Alliances meeting in Ocala, where the names of nearly one dozen black leaders were recorded.[44] Among the

Colored Alliance delegates were John S. Jackson, representing Alabama; Walter Pattillo, North Carolina; William Warwick, M. F. Jones, and B. Langhorne, Virginia; L. D. Laurent, Louisiana; J. H. Nichols, Mississippi; John D. Norris, South Carolina; James C. Sanders, Tennessee; and H. J. Spencer, Texas.[45]

The *Atlanta Constitution* headlined its story on the Ocala meetings as such: "Black and white will unite in stamping out sectionalism. The Colored Alliance in Ocala ready to join a third party which will lead to the welfare of the farmer." The newspaper went on to note, "The important news today is the discovery of . . . nearly 1,000,000 voters, organized, ready and waiting to follow the lead of the [white] Alliance . . . to strike out in the independent line of the people's party. This body is the Colored Farmers' Alliance."[46] The *Constitution*'s bold pronouncement, however, failed to see or acknowledge that the People's Party was not the sole creation of white Populists; rather, it was a *joint* creation of African Americans and white Populists. The historian Jack Abramowitz similarly pointed out that the *New York Times* missed, or ignored, the implications of African Americans building an independent political coalition with white Populists at the Ocala convention. Instead, the *Times* narrowly focused on the white Alliance's opposition to the Lodge Bill—which would have given a mandate to the federal government to protect voting rights where they were being demonstrably violated. Unfortunately, the uniquely white perspective on the role (or lack thereof) of African Americans and the People's Party would not only persist in the press, but, in decades to come, reflect a fundamental bias in the scholarship on Populism.[47]

Black Populists were not simply "waiting to follow the lead" of white Populists. Rather, African Americans had developed an independent political strategy in conjunction with white political allies; in the South, where white Alliancemen were more reluctant to enter third-party politics (as opposed to the West and Midwest, where farmers were much more willing to pursue independent politics), Black Populists in fact led their southern white counterparts into third-party politics. As Gaither notes, "the 1890 Ocala meeting suggested that black delegates were more receptive to a new party than the whites in attendance."[48] Colored Alliance leaders such as Walter Pattillo were among the first in the South to call for the formation of a national third party. African Americans had moreover helped to establish local People's parties in the South and parts of the Midwest. Beyond this, they participated in conventions leading up to the founding of the national People's Party, and once parties were established, wrote op-eds in favor of the party, attended nominating conventions, campaigned on behalf of the new party, and voted for local, state, and national People's Party candidates.

While St. Louis prefigured Ocala, it was the Ocala meeting that marked the birth of the national People's Party; it also served as a turning point in the development of Black Populism. The formation of a third party with calls for political reform not only alarmed Democrats but raised new concerns for southern white Populists. To the dismay of southern white delegates at Ocala, African Americans (through the Colored Alliance) asserted the importance of fair elections by taking a strong stance in favor of the proposed Lodge Bill to have the federal government oversee elections. Black delegates unanimously supported the bill while southern white delegates vehemently opposed the legislation.[49] However, a considerable number of other white delegates at the Ocala meeting (from the West and Midwest) supported the Colored Alliance's position on the Lodge Bill: over one-third of the white Alliancemen ended up endorsing the bill.[50]

Black delegates at the convention made special efforts to reach out to white Alliancemen, understanding the importance of allying themselves with those who might be sympathetic to their political goals. A Colored Alliance resolution greeted the Southern Alliance delegates and pledged the organization's "fullest co-operation and confederation in all essential things."[51] The resolution was signed by John S. Jackson of Alabama, J. H. Nichols of Mississippi, Walter Pattillo of North Carolina, John D. Norris of South Carolina, L. D. Laurent of Louisiana, H. J. Spencer of Texas, and James C. Sanders of Tennessee.[52] A committee of three white Alliancemen responded to their overture by requesting that the Colored Alliance indeed work in confederation with delegates of the Southern Alliance and the Farmers' Mutual Benefit Association, the latter organization claiming over 200,000 members.[53] The white Alliance noted in its minutes at Ocala, "we visited the Colored Farmers' National Alliance and Co-Operative Union committee, and were received with the utmost cordiality."[54] The spirit of cooperation—politically/practically motivated—had been further fostered by Colored Alliance delegates such as Warwick, who signed an agreement calling for the union of the black and white Alliances on a joint reform-oriented platform.[55] After careful consultation, the two groups adopted a series of measures and agreed to "such action as shall tend to unite our strength."[56] Each organization within the federation was allotted five representatives on an executive council with proportional (weighted) voting strength based on the estimated number of people comprising their respective memberships.[57] Meanwhile, debate carried on among delegates at the respective Ocala conferences over the formation of a third party; by the end of the two conferences there was a call for a conference to be held in Cincinnati on February 20, 1891 that would focus on the question of electoral independence. As one newspaper described, "[a] call was addressed to all who have stood up for independent political action."[58]

Many southern white Alliance delegates had resisted a third-party break, insisting instead on reforming the Democratic Party. Third-party advocates responded by forming a separate body, the Confederation of Industrial Organizations (CIO), to forge an independent political course of action. Humphrey, representing the Colored Alliance, would serve as the body's vice president. At their meeting in Washington, D.C., in January 1891, the CIO—described as "an important precursor to the Populist Party" by Patrick Dickson—brought together a variety of reform organizations under one umbrella, including delegates from the black and white Alliances, representatives of the Knights of Labor, the Citizens' Alliance, and members of the Women's Christian Temperance Union.[59] The meeting of the CIO would help build momentum for a third-party break going into the Cincinnati meeting, which was pushed to May in order to give organizers time to bring out as many delegates as possible.

On May 19, 1891, some fourteen hundred black and white delegates and observers from across the country gathered in Cincinnati for a "National Union Conference." Delegates met at the city's grand Music Hall, where African Americans and their white counterparts deliberated and sang songs. The words to one song went as follows:

> Let us work and vote together, with a due respect to law;
> Let us choose our ablest workmen, to represent our cause;
> Let us say to all monopolies, just loosen up your claws!
> So we go marching on. Glory[, Glory, hallelujah].[60]

When the official call for conference was read aloud by former Union captain C. A. Power of Indiana, he noted that the Colored Alliance was "a million strong and ever ready to do battle." The announcement was immediately followed by "hearty applause" according to a *New York Times* reporter in attendance. Like the D.C. meeting in December, the Cincinnati conference represented a wide range of groups—including the Colored Alliance, the Northern and Southern Alliances, the Knights of Labor, the Farmers' Mutual Benefit Association, the Citizens' Alliance, and the Union Labor Party (it is likely that WCTU delegates were also in attendance given their participation in the D.C. meeting). It was a dramatic scene. At one point, in a show of northern and southern postwar reconciliation, two older white Alliance members, Confederate and Union veterans, went on stage and clasped hands; a couple of steps behind the two white men stood a single black member of the Colored Alliance. The hall roared with applause. African Americans, it was clear, would have to continuously find ways of inserting and asserting themselves into the affairs of white men; they did so independently and to their best advantage. As long as white men were willing to challenge the Democrats in the South, Black Populists engaged in such acts (for some historians, such acts were of humiliation; for those who carried them out, it was a matter of practical politics). Despite the visible drive toward the formation of a national party, internal resistance continued to stymie progress.[61]

Southern Alliance delegates played the most divisive role in Cincinnati. They sponsored a measure that would segregate African Americans on the floor of the convention. Most delegates rejected this move and defeated the segregationist proposal. In similar fashion, the Southern Alliance's insistence on continuing to lobby the Democrats for agrarian reforms before considering a third-party break was voted down. With momentum on their side, Colored Alliance delegates and other third-party advocates pressed their advantage. By the end of the Cincinnati convention, delegates had established a national People's Party committee in preparation for the upcoming 1892 elections. With a single exception—the state superintendent of Georgia's Colored Alliance, E. A. Richardson, who was solely committed to the Republican Party—the regionwide Colored Alliance delegation supported the formation of a national third party. The Mississippi Colored Alliance had initially expressed reservations about pursing an independent political course of action that unconditionally supported *any* party. For them, reform could be "brought about by our own choice of candidates," not necessarily through a particular party—a less partisan, but less powerful stance in the face of bipartisan electoral domination and the visible desire among significantly organized groups of people in favor of a third party.[62] Ironically, the pro-Republican Richardson would, like other black Republicans, side with Georgia's white Alliance leader, Leonidas F. Livingston, a Democrat, in opposing the formation of a national third party. Reverend Henry S. Doyle, among other Black Populists from Georgia, however, stood in sharp contrast to the state's Richardson/Livingston faction. The larger body, meanwhile, had taken its next step toward forming the national People's Party.[63]

African Americans, whose position in the emerging third party was strengthened by, if not a function of the grassroots networks they had built through the Colored Alliances, were well positioned in the early development and strategic thinking behind the formation of the national People's Party.[64] With each national conference or convention, the split between the black and white delegates who favored and those who opposed the formation of a national third party became increasingly apparent. The independents—mostly disaffected black Republicans and disaffected white Democrats, the latter primarily from outside of the South—argued that it was not possible to reform the Democratic Party, given the entrenched political interests of the Southern Democracy as a whole. In fact, they argued, the Democratic Party stood in the way of reform. The anti-third-party white Alliancemen from the South countered by saying that any chance of reform would have to go through the Democratic Party. Their argument was that since it was Democrats who controlled the government in the

South—and held a majority in the House of Representatives, despite there being a Republican president (Benjamin Harrison) and a Republican-majority in the Senate—reform could only go through them. Of course, the very point that black and white independents were making was that without challenging the structure of authority erected by the southern Democratic Party, no reform was possible; Democrats were not going to voluntarily give up control.

Black and white delegates at the 1891 conference in Cincinnati would issue a call for yet another national convention. The meeting was scheduled for February 22, 1892.[65] Reconvening in St. Louis, black and white representatives of the Alliances, as well as temperance and single-tax groups, sat together for the first time—participating in the deliberations as "political equals." Many white Populists, especially those in the Northern Alliance, were apparently interested in creating a movement that would include agrarian workers and farmers. In the 1880s, the Northern Alliance, unlike the Southern Alliance, did not exclude African Americans from its organization. Some significant white leaders of the northern organization even declared their support for "racial solidarity." At the St. Louis convention in 1892 Ignatius Donnelly, the leading white Populist from Minnesota, exclaimed, "We propose to wipe the Mason and Dixon line out of geography; to wipe the color-line out of politics."[66] Ninety-seven, or approximately 14 percent of the roughly 700 credentialed delegates at the St. Louis meeting came from the Colored Alliance. African American delegates in St. Louis included John L. Moore of Florida; E. A. Richardson of Georgia (despite his ongoing opposition to a third-party break); E. C. Cabel of Kansas (and then Virginia); L. D. Laurent of Louisiana; H. D. Cassdall of Missouri; Walter Pattillo of North Carolina; and William Warwick of Virginia.[67] Pattillo served as one of three national representatives of the organization for the conference's credentials committee, a position of considerable authority that reflected not only his individual prominence in the movement but, in particular, the leadership role of African Americans in the development of the national People's Party.

Through measured participation, African Americans shaped the initial character of the new party. At times, black delegates held back in their words and actions; at others, they pressed aggressively to make their voices heard (or presence felt). Black leaders at St. Louis would initiate conversations while inserting themselves into existing debate. At one point, a black representative even addressed the entire body of the convention. Newspapers noted a "colored Populist delegate" named William Morey, who spoke to the national assembly—the contents of his speech, unfortunately, were not recorded.[68] In less direct fashion, but no less significant for its visual impact, during the all-white "ceremony of reunion and solidarity between the Blue and Gray," E. C. Cabel, a Colored Alliance delegate from Virginia, broke tradition and joined the celebrating group of white delegates on stage—shocking some, while delighting others.[69] The scene was reminiscent of the Colored Alliance delegate at the Cincinnati meeting in May 1891 who had similarly physically inserted himself on stage. Some white delegates, however, refused to acknowledge the presence of any black delegates on the floor, placing yet another obstacle in the third-party path. But this time, instead of planning for another meeting to be held elsewhere, the majority in attendance proceeded by simply waiting for the convention to adjourn and immediately held an *ad hoc* "mass meeting" to continue the work of forming a national party.

While the stage was set for the emergence of the national People's Party, African Americans made sure to continue asserting their role within it. At the *ad hoc* meeting, the Colored Alliance vehemently protested their "shoddy treatment" by certain white delegates. Rising from his seat "in a dignified but extremely earnest manner" amid a sea of mostly white delegates, William Warwick of the Virginia Colored Alliance "firmly demanded" that no racially discriminatory practices such as the ones previously proposed by the southern white Alliance be tolerated by the body; Warwick emphasized that such divisive tactics should not be permitted to disrupt the process of forming a national party underway. No sooner did he take his seat than did a white delegate from Georgia at the back of the convention nominate Warwick for the position of assistant secretary of the meeting. Another white delegate, this one from Alabama, moved that the "colored gentleman" be unanimously elected. A motion was put to the floor. Only a single objection was heard in defiance of the "several hundred" voices filling the hall with a resounding "aye" and Warwick was elected assistant secretary.[70] At the end of the meeting a call was put forth for a convention to be held in Omaha, Nebraska; the day chosen for the convention, the 116th Anniversary of the Declaration of Independence, July 4, 1892. There in Omaha the party would hammer out its party platform and nominate its presidential candidate.[71]

Among those whose names appeared on the call to the Omaha convention were Warwick, along with Colored Alliance colleagues L. D. Laurent of Louisiana and H. D. Cassdall of Missouri. Warwick went on to urge the party's national committee that a newspaper be created and edited by African Americans to help reach black voters. Laurent and Cassdall, who had joined Warwick at the Confederation of Industrial Organizations in Washington, D.C., in 1891, were among the handful of Black Populists who had been driving the movement toward independent politics.[72] For several days in Omaha during the summer of 1892, over 1,400 black and white delegates debated what the contents should be for the new party's platform. They built upon the "St. Louis Platform," and after much dialogue ratified their "Omaha Platform" and selected its presidential candidate, James B. Weaver, a Union veteran.[73] The presence of black delegates at the convention was unmistakable. Enthusiasm abounded as one white national committee member declared that the People's Party had the support of upwards of 400,000 African Americans.[74] Among the more notable African Americans at Omaha was a "coal black negro," referred to only as "Brown" of Massachusetts, who marched in the procession during the convention's Fourth of July celebration. As part of the celebration Brown took to the main stage; and with two of his white counterparts, he held up an American flag on a cane. Together, it was reported, the three men formed "[an] apex at the center of the stage," demonstrating (in even more dramatic fashion than Colored Alliance leaders who took to the stage in Cincinnati and St. Louis) the presence of African Americans in the new party.[75]

The platform ratified by the delegates at Omaha called for a comprehensive set of demands: government ownership of railroads, telegraphs, and steamships; a progressive income tax; the direct election of U.S. senators; an eight-hour workday; and a subtreasury loan program. (The Omaha platform foreshadowed two amendments to the U.S. Constitution, various pieces of local legislation, and other key policies enacted in the early twentieth century.) Central to the platform was a call for greater paper currency harking back to the Greenbackers' demand, but this time through the unlimited coinage of silver and gold.[76]

While black and white delegates at Omaha had settled on the nomination of Weaver, they appeased southern white delegates by selecting James G. Field, a former Confederate major and attorney general from Virginia, as the party's vice presidential nominee. Weaver, a former brevet brigadier general of the Union army, had been elected to Congress in 1885 with the backing of the Greenback Labor Party and helped to establish the Farmers' Alliance in the Midwest. Emerging as a natural Populist candidate, he would campaign with black and white Populists alike. White Populists saw in Weaver's candidacy a continuation of their movement; Black Populists, such as those who accompanied him in the Raleigh parade in the fall of 1892, saw a continuation of their own, hoping to create political leverage against the Democratic Party through his candidacy. African Americans were now tactically allied with white Populists. Both would have to rally support in their communities to make the new party competitive. For African Americans, however, the task involved much greater risks.

In building the People's Party, black organizers would need to generate support for white Populist candidates, many of whom had been openly hostile to African Americans. When speaking to potential black voters, they would argue that only by allying themselves with white independents could they have a chance at defeating Democrats. That is, African Americans could most powerfully exercise their vote by supporting the People's Party or by voting for the Republican Party in fusion with the People's Party. Most African Americans continued to support only the Republican Party, skeptical of white independents, who were, after all, mostly disaffected Democrats who continued to deride African Americans. A segment of the southern black electorate, nevertheless, did embrace the People's Party. In the end, numeric support for the third party was far less than either predicted or proclaimed by black or white Alliancemen. Black Populists, from Doyle in Georgia to Rayner in Texas, took the lead in the face of such cynicism (beyond the immediate dangers involved): campaigning for the People's Party locally, training and dispatching speakers, forming party chapters, and mobilizing black voters on election days. Doing so would, of course, also mean incurring the wrath of the Southern Democracy.

As with other political parties, the national People's Party derived its power from its state-based affiliates. African Americans would play a key role in the formation of People's parties in Kansas, Texas, Louisiana, Georgia, and North Carolina. By the time of the national convention in Omaha, a number of other state-based third parties—including the Alliance Party and the Union Labor Party—had either been established or had grown with the participation of African Americans.[77] P. K. Chase of the *Dallas Southern Mercury* argued in an August 11, 1892, editorial the case for black support for the People's Party:[78]

> I have said before and say now, that there is not enough political independence among colored voters. The fact that a man is colored should not be self-evident that he belongs to any particular party. As a rule the colored people are Republican, the results of which were perfectly natural. But more than a quarter of a century has thrown around him the light of intelligence ... the two old parties have not kept pace with the great demands of the common people ... Now in my view of the above facts ... *the one and only advantageous political course of the Negro, under present existing affairs, is to support the People's Party.*[79] (emphasis added)

Independents in Kansas led the way by establishing the first People's Party. Launched under the banner of the Alliance Party in June 1890, it was soon renamed the People's Party. The Reverend Benjamin F. Foster, a black minister and educator, ran for state auditor on its ticket. A string of other People's parties were subsequently formed that included black leadership. In August 1891 Texans formed a People's Party with two African Americans—the Reverend Henry J. Jennings of Collins County and R. H. Hayes of Tarrant—serving on its state executive committee. At the People's Party state convention in Fort Worth on February 9, 1892 black delegates discussed why they were joining the party in Texas. During the first day's session an African American man named "Watson" from Grayson County addressed the body. He declared, "I am an emancipated slave of this state ... It is recognized that the Negro holds the balance of power, and the democrats and republicans are trying to hold him down." Like his fellow Texan, P. K. Chase, Watson implored African Americans to exercise their political independence.[80]

Other examples of black independence were recorded in the South: in October 1891 two black leaders in Louisiana were considered as candidates for state treasurer of the newly formed People's Party; in December 1891 Georgians established their own People's Party and at least two black delegates attended the party's state convention in 1892.[81] In North Carolina, the People's Party, which was founded in August 1892, would go on to win control of the state legislature through a Republican-Populist fusion coalition.[82]

African Americans in Arkansas initially used the Union Labor Party to mobilize independent black support—that is, before the party merged with the People's Party in 1892. The Union Labor Party had been formed in the wake of the 1886 midterm elections by leaders of the Agricultural Wheel to challenge the state's Democratic Party. In 1888 Union Labor presidential candidate Alson J. Streeter, whose "interest centere[d] on agricultural pursuits and the success of the farmer," received a modest 146,935 votes nationally. His vote, however, would help to establish the independent party's presence in the South.[83] Union Labor worked with black Republicans in Arkansas, effectively using fusion—so effectively that Democratic legislators soon passed a state bill disfranchising large numbers of black voters.

In 1888 Confederate veteran C. M. Norwood ran as the Union Labor gubernatorial candidate with Republican support in a coalition of African Americans, members of the Knights of Labor, and Wheelers against the Democratic Party's candidate, James P. Eagle, a wealthy planter. The Republican State Central Committee resolved to decline fielding a statewide ticket that year, recommending Republicans to support the Union Labor candidate instead. Norwood received 46 percent of the statewide vote (84,213 votes to Eagle's 99,214) but it was widely believed that the election was stolen by Democratic registrars who deliberately miscounted votes. Norwood doggedly contested the election results, claiming he had been counted out in a number of counties. When the Democratic legislature required Norwood to supply a $40,000 bond to cover the cost of the investigation, he was finally forced to withdraw his protest. Between 1890 and 1892 Democratic-sponsored legislation in Arkansas in turn proceeded to cut voter turnout by 18 percent. The legislation targeted illiterate voters in the state, which meant mostly black voters, but thousands of white independent voters were also disenfranchised.[84]

With the backing of African American voters, the Union Labor Party ran several key leaders, including Texas Colored Alliance general superintendent Richard M. Humphrey, North Carolina Knights of Labor master workman John

Nichols, and Arkansas Colored Agricultural Wheel president Reverend George W. Lowe. Lowe won reelection to his state legislature through the party's backing. In 1890 the Union Labor Party in Arkansas also nominated the Reverend Isom P. Langley for Congress in the state's second congressional district.[85] The forty-year-old black minister was described by the *New York Times* as both "a labor candidate and a tariff reformer."[86] That same year, another black delegate to the state's Union Labor Party convention asserted that African Americans "heartily supported [Union Labor] because they wanted a party to succeed which would treat the colored man like it treated the white man."[87] As the historian William Gnatz notes, the Arkansas Union Labor Party served as a "training ground for [black]-white cooperation in politics."[88] African Americans had played a significant role in the Greenback Labor Party in Arkansas and would continue to do so in the state's Union Labor Party. Not surprisingly, fusion efforts between the Greenback Labor and Republican parties would also lead to fusion efforts between the Union Labor and Republican parties, bringing black and white independents together into electoral alliances.[89] Over the next two years, Union Labor leaders assisted the newly established People's Party in further organizing black voters. By 1892, Union Labor merged into the People's Party with eleven African Americans serving as delegates to its state convention. One of the black delegates, I. Glopsy, wrote a resolution that was included in the new third party's platform. Explicitly designed to appeal to black voters, the resolution read, "[I]t is the object of the People's party to elevate the downtrodden irrespective of race or color."[90]

African Americans implemented their independent political strategy in Kansas in 1890 by fielding the Reverend Benjamin F. Foster, pastor of the AME church in Topeka, as state auditor on the People's Party ticket.[91] The party brought together members of the black and white Alliances, former members of the Union Labor and Prohibition parties, moderates from the Democratic Party, and disaffected Republicans, black and white. African Americans had felt snubbed by the Republican Party, which appeared increasingly less interested in—if not opposed to—either nominating black candidates or offering patronage to African Americans. During the 1890 campaign, the thirty-nine-year-old Foster gained the support of the nation's leading black newspaper, the *Indianapolis Freeman*, which ran a front-page picture of him accompanied by a biographical sketch. It noted that he had studied at both Fisk University in Nashville and the Chicago Theological Seminary and then served the Lincoln Street Congregational Church in Topeka.[92] When Foster was asked by a reporter from the *Topeka Call* why he decided to work with the People's Party, he responded succinctly: "[I]ts doctrines are in favor of the masses and against monopolies. It is the party of the poor man."[93] Foster's stature among African Americans, combined with his growing presence in the third party, would assure him the chairmanship of an outdoor rally in the fall of 1891. The rally featured the then presumptive presidential candidate of the People's Party, Leonidas L. Polk. Polk, who also served as the president of the Southern Alliance, was briefly joined on stage by Foster, displaying a black and independent coalition in the making.[94]

Foster proved a strong crossover candidate, linking white independents and disaffected black Republicans. While losing the election, Foster ran some 6,000 votes *ahead* of his own "fusion ticket" (no formal fusion existed in Kansas in 1890). In two predominantly black districts, Foster outpolled white Populists on the ticket by a margin of two to one. This combined with the fact that the Republicans tallied 15,000 votes fewer than in the previous statewide election, suggests that a segment of black voters defected from the Republican Party to support Foster on the People's Party ticket; it also shows that Foster commanded independent white support.[95] In 1890 the People's Party won three-fourths of the ninety-one seats in the Kansas state legislature, including the only state senate seat that had been up for election, as well as five congressional seats. The party received votes from a cross-section of voters: Republicans (35.94 percent), Democrats (30.94 percent), Union Laborites (29.35 percent), and Prohibitionists (3.77 percent).[96] The highest percentage of votes came from small towns, with populations of fewer than 5,000 people—pointing to the party's more rural base of support.[97]

Following the 1890 election, Foster and other Black Populists continued to build support for the People's Party. Newspapers reported a slow but growing presence of African Americans in the party over the next two years. The *Topeka Weekly Call* commented in November of 1892: "in some sections of the state there were breaks in the solid colored voters towards the People's Party." Another paper noted how "leaders of the colored people of this city [were] distributing People's party tickets."[98] In July of that year at least one African American was part of the Kansas delegation representing the state at the founding convention of the national People's Party in Omaha.[99] Another Black Populist from Kansas, Lutie A. Lytle, who would later hold the distinction of becoming the first woman to teach law at the university level in the South, served as the party's assistant enrolling clerk in 1895.[100]

Lytle was born in Murfreesboro, Tennessee in 1875. In 1882, her parents, John and Mary Ann "Mollie," her three siblings, and grandmother moved to Kansas as part of the Exoduster movement. Her father operated a barbershop in downtown Topeka and was a leader of the anti-Republican progressive Populist Flambeau Club, which he helped to organize in 1893; the club was an arm of the Kansas People's Party. John Lytle was subsequently nominated by the People's Party for Register of Deeds in Shawnee County as part of a fusion ticket. While he never won public office, the elder Lytle's political activism clearly influenced his daughter. In 1895, at the age of twenty, Lytle was appointed as the People's Party's assistant enrolling clerk in the Kansas state legislature, where she worked with legislators to facilitate political reforms. She is among the few identifiable Black Populist women.[101] Kansas, where the People's Party had carried the state in the presidential election of 1892, winning ten electoral college votes, would remain a hotbed of third-party politics.

Black and white independents in Texas, where the Colored Alliance was founded in 1886, held their first statewide People's Party convention in Dallas on August 17, 1891. The Texas People's Party was, in many ways, a continuation of the state's Union Labor Party, which fought for both urban and agrarian workers' rights and election reform. As a result of having an active third-party predecessor, People's Party membership and influence grew relatively quickly.[102] East Texas, with a large black population, would become the stronghold of the new party. By 1890, the black population in Texas had almost reached 22 percent (488,171 of 2.2 million people); seventy counties in east Texas had populations that were at least 20 percent or more African American; and in sixteen of these counties African Americans virtually determined election outcomes.[103]

One of the two African Americans nominated to the People's Party state executive committee in 1892, the Reverend Henry J. Jennings, reported that he had organized a number of "people's party colored clubs in Texas."[104] Between July 15 and August 14, 1892 the seventy-one-year-old Jennings spoke at political rallies in fourteen counties across the eastern part of the state.[105] Reports from the party's statewide convention the following year conveyed similar levels of black support in other parts of the state. For instance, delegates from southern Texas boasted that "the colored people are coming into the new party in squads and companies. They have colored third party speakers and are organizing colored clubs." Such enthusiasm, however, did not necessarily or immediately translate into votes for the People's Party.[106]

The networks of farmers and sharecroppers organized by the Texas Colored Alliance in the late 1880s would help drive the growth of Black Populism in the 1890s. The Colored Alliance fueled the movement in Texas in the early 1890s by urging its members to join the third party and then mobilizing voters on election day. Notices of meetings held by the Colored Alliance in 1892 in support of the People's Party in Texas would demonstrate the continuity of the Black Populist movement from the Colored Alilances to the People's Party. One such notice appeared in the *Southern Mercury* on June 30, 1892. It was signed by D. H. Stilven and E. S. Eldridge on behalf of the Colored Alliance and called for a meeting in Conroe, just north of Houston.[107] The *Mercury* and other newspapers would also report on the appearance of Colored Alliance speakers at People's Party rallies in several eastern counties during this period.¹⁰⁸ References to the Colored Alliance in the press, however, disappear soon thereafter. The lack of mention of the Colored Alliance after the summer of 1892 may suggest that black chapters of the People's Party—the "colored clubs"—may have been taken over by groups initially organized by the Colored Alliance but were now focused on electoral politics. Local groups with similar aims as the Colored Alliance may have also absorbed elements of the black agrarian organization, such as the Village Improvement Society or the Farmers' Improvement Society, the latter founded by the African American leader Robert Lloyd Smith, who won a seat in the Texas legislature in 1895 as a Republican.¹⁰⁹

African Americans from counties in east and central Texas appeared to be the most energized by the third-party during the 1890s. In some of these counties black voter turnout reached upwards of 90 percent, as in Grimes, San Jacinto, and Waller. While not faring as well in 1892 as many had hoped, the People's Party received an estimated 35 percent of the black vote in 1894 and 50 percent of the black vote in 1896, largely in combination with the Republican Party through fusion arrangements.¹¹⁰ Fusion, as was the case in North Carolina, was effectively employed in Texas. Ultimately, however, the rise of the new "Negro Party," like all other Black Populist organizations, rested on the organizing capacity of its leaders at the grassroots. John B. Rayner, billed as the "Silver-Tongued Orator of the Colored Race," stood out as Texas' foremost black organizer in this period.¹¹¹

Born in North Carolina on November 13, 1850, Rayner was the son of a black slave woman, Mary Ricks, and her owner, Kenneth Rayner, a white planter. The elder Rayner had been active in third-party politics before the war. He was elected to Congress as a member of the Whig Party and served as a leader of the American Party (a.k.a. the Know-Nothing Party). Placed in the care of his maternal great-grandparents, the younger Rayner worked on his father's plantation but was later given certain privileges, including financial assistance to attend the Raleigh Theological Institute (later renamed Shaw University) and nearby St. Augustine's Normal and Collegiate Institute. According to Rayner descendents, the elder Rayner "made no effort to conceal the paternity of his child [John] and his two other mulatto children." As historian and biographer Gregg Cantrell further notes, "To criticize a wealthy southern planter-politician [for having an illicit affair with a slave] nearly always would have backfired, so common was the vice among Rayner's [white] contemporaries." As one former North Carolina slave put it, having such relationships was "a general thing 'mong the slave owners."¹¹²

In 1867, Kenneth Rayner, having lost a good deal of money in the course of the Civil War (he was initially opposed to secession but then reversed himself), decided to move his white family to Memphis, Tennessee, where he held other land. The younger Rayner and his two fellow "mulatto" sisters, however, were left in North Carolina, but not without financial provisions. Having fulfilled what he perceived as his paternal responsibilities, the elder Rayner left North Carolina without any further communication with his black children. As Cantrell poignantly observes, "Such was the legacy of slavery and racism in the South; blacks and whites found their lives undeniably interconnected, yet worlds apart."[113]

As it turns out, John B. Rayner and North Carolina Black Populist leader Walter Pattillo (also the son of a white planter and a black slave mother) were born within the same week in neighboring counties. Like Pattillo, Rayner was light skinned—so light that he was sometimes called a "white nigger" by southern white men; he was also viewed with suspicion by some African Americans, as he could almost "pass" for white. Cantrell describes him as having been "relatively short in stature, but built like a bull." He seemed to be of two worlds: While his accent resembled an upper-class white southerner, he knew and effectively employed the common black vernacular, especially when mass organizing. However, "[his] broad nose and wavy hair," according to Cantrell, "suggested his African ancestry more than did his parchment-colored complexion."[114]

Growing up near each other and having both graduated from Shaw, Pattillo and Rayner are likely to have known each other or, at the very least, known of each other. Growing up, however, Rayner had advantages that Pattillo did not: as Cantrell describes, "Even for a slave boy, reaching adolescence in the Kenneth Rayner household a few blocks away from the state capitol must have provided unusual opportunities to observe politics." The Rayner mansion was apparently a social scene that brought together many of the state's leading political figures. The young Rayner would have been privy to the ways in which white politicians operated at close quarters—lessons that he took with him to Texas, a thousand miles away and nearly a quarter of a century later, where and when he matured as a Black Populist organizer.[115]

Between 1870 and 1872, after completing most of his studies and briefly teaching, Rayner made his first foray into the world of politics. Leaving his home in Raleigh and heading eastward, he decided to settle in Tarboro, Edgecombe County. Edgecombe was a Republican Party stronghold at the time with a particularly large black population—in 1870, two-thirds of the county's 23,000 inhabitants were African American; it was also part of North Carolina's "Black Second" congressional district. There, in 1873, Rayner secured a Republican appointment, serving as a constable of the grand jury of the superior court. In 1875 he was elected justice of the peace in Tarboro, a position he served in for the remainder of Reconstruction, at which point he returned to teaching, while setting his sights on Texas.[116]

In 1881, among the waves of "exodusters" leaving North Carolina, Rayner led a migration of over nine hundred African Americans to Texas. Settling in Calvert, in the central-eastern part of the state, Rayner's new home was like Tarboro, located in a predominantly black county. He stayed out of politics for a number of years, resurfacing in 1887 during a heated campaign to put the prohibition of alcohol on the state ballot. A supporter of the Colored Alliance's basic tenets, although never a member of the organization himself, Rayner attempted to seize what he saw as an opportunity to divide the Democratic Party through the prohibition campaign; he urged white leaders to seek support among African Americans, politicizing a campaign that was initially designed to be "non-partisan." He ran into resistance however from black Republican leaders, especially Melvin Wade, who later worked with Rayner in the People's Party.

A carpenter by trade, Wade began his political career following the Civil War registering voters as a member of the elections board. He grew to prominence in Republican circles during Reconstruction, serving on the party's statewide platform committee while championing black trade unionism. During the mid-1880s he promoted the eight-hour workday and became one of the earliest advocates in the formation of a statewide black labor union. But he also strongly opposed the tactic of Republicans working in coalition with Greenbackers or other independent candidates. By 1892 the political climate had changed and, like other black Republicans thwarted by lily-white Republicans, Wade joined Rayner and the Texas People's Party. However, in 1887 Rayner and Wade were on opposites sides of the table surrounding the issue of prohibition.[117]

Rayner saw an opportunity to exploit existing divisions between "Bourbon" (conservative) and "agrarian" (progressive) factions within the Democratic Party over the issue of prohibition. In January 1887 the Texas Prohibition Party successfully petitioned the state legislature to place on the ballot a measure for an amendment to the state's constitution banning the sale of liquor. Having developed his own networks through the black farmers he had led to the state and in his work as a teacher, Rayner displayed his political acumen advising prohibitionist leaders in the state on how to best capture black voters. Meanwhile, the Republican Wade stumped on behalf of the "wets" (antiprohibition forces), which placed him in step with the Bourbon Democrats. Rayner countered Wade where he could in east Texas, but to no avail. With enormous sums of liquor-money spent on campaigning by the Bourbon forces, the prohibition measure was soundly defeated. Rayner, however, became known as a skilled mass organizer in the eastern counties of the state. Several more years would pass before Rayner's networks, which in time spread across the entire state, became useful to once again challenge the Democratic Party.[118]

The Texas People's Party had been officially formed in Dallas in August of 1891. Two months after the party's formation, Rayner suggested to the white Alliance leader Dr. Charles W. Macune, a physician and the editor of the *National Economist*, that the Knights of Labor in the South could help mobilize black voters. Unbeknown to Rayner at the time, Macune was (and remained) a supporter of the Democratic Party. Both black and white Alliancemen would need convincing if the third party was going to succeed. Rayner was not present at the People's Party founding meeting, which included fifty black and white delegates from different parts of the state; Wade, on the other hand, was among the delegates present. He, along with other African Americans at that meeting, pressed white delegates whether or not they intended "to work a black and white horse in the same field"—that is, have African Americans as equal partners in the party. But when white delegates responded "in platitudes," Wade protested by leaving the meeting. Another black delegate, R. H. Hayes, continued pressing. Hayes, who had been active in independent politics since the 1880s, argued that African Americans would join the third party, but would only do so if black leaders were placed in positions of party leadership. As he put it, if white delegates did not take such affirmative action "the streams would be poised." After one final push by Hayes, in which he took to the floor and declared, "You will lose ... if you do not treat the nigger squarely," a vote was taken and he and another black delegate joined the party's state executive committee.[119]

Despite the visible position of two African Americans on the People's Party's executive committee, the third party received only modest support for its statewide ticket in the 1892 election. About one-third of the black electorate voted Republican while another third voted Democrat; most of the remainder boycotted the election. The People's Party fared much better in the eastern part of the state, where in counties like Robertson, the Greenback Party had previously sunk roots. In its inaugural election, the People's Party had not made its case to black voters, including Rayner, who maintained a low profile in the first couple years of the third party's formation. Some saw the 1892 results as a sign of weakness; others, including Rayner, thought otherwise. He soon joined the party, and over the next four years, Rayner grew the Texas organization like no other leader in the state, black or white. He established dozens of party chapters and ultimately helped the People's Party defeat Democrats (or significantly weaken its political grip) in eastern Texas.

Louisiana, like Kansas and Texas, witnessed a surge of independent black electoral activity just prior to the establishment of the national People's Party in the fall of 1891. A call for a conference to establish a third party was issued on October 3, 1891 to be held in the city of Alexandria, located in central Louisiana, just south of Grant Parish. The call, which was published in the *National*

Economist, was designed to attract a cross-section of the state's voters, especially black voters. It began, "To the voters of the State of Louisiana irrespective of class, color, or past political affiliation."[120] A number of disaffected Republicans heeded the call. Charles A. Roxborough, a prominent "mulatto," had resigned from the Republican Party two years earlier under protest for what he saw as the party's commitment to white supremacy. He had served as an officer of the all-black Odd Fellows' Louisiana District Lodge No. 21 fraternal order and was a member of the Colored Farmers' Alliance. He joined the People's Party and in 1891 was nominated for the office of state treasurer alongside Louisiana Colored Alliance leader L. D. Laurent. Laurent had been actively involved in organizing African Americans into independent politics over the previous two years through the national conventions.[121]

After consulting fellow black delegates, and under pressure from white delegates at the People's Party meeting in Alexandria, both Roxborough and Laurent withdrew their names from nomination for the office of state treasurer. The concern was that "it was not the proper time" for black candidates to appear on the state's ballot. African Americans, it was argued, should support white candidates initially to build the independent party's white ranks. Presumably, having black candidates on the party's ticket would drive away would-be independent white supporters. Black Populists were willing to make such moves for the larger goal of defeating the Democrats at the ballot. Befitting of their leadership role, however, Roxborough and Laurent were subsequently elected to the Louisiana People's Party state executive committee. On February 1, 1892, four months after the meeting in Alexandria, two dozen black delegates participated in a People's Party's state meeting, where they sought to represent the political and economic interests of Louisiana's rural black communities.[122]

During the fall of 1892, the Louisiana People's Party received significant support among African Americans. In the state's fourth congressional district, where nearly 50 percent of the population was black, nearly a quarter of the vote (23.92 percent) went to the third party. In the fifth congressional district, 63 percent of which was black, the party received just under one-fifth of the vote (19.29 percent). Such percentages of support for the People's Party in its first election in Louisiana were indicators of future independent political growth among the state's rural black population—in contrast with Louisiana's highly urban first congressional district comprising New Orleans (with a strong Republican presence), which was 36.2 percent black, but where less than a single percentage of its voters cast their ballot for the People's Party.[123]

The historian Joel M. Sipress describes a black and independent coalition in Grant Parish comprised of African Americans from the River Valley and white independents from the Hill Country. Here, as was the case in other parts of the

South, Black Populism took expression in the early 1890s with African Americans voting for People's Party candidates endorsed by the Republican Party. Despite a growing migrant white population into Grant Parish, as late as 1890 41 percent of the parish population was black. Sipress notes, "Black men continued to vote in significant numbers, and the Grant Parish Republican Party, with its mostly black leadership and the near unanimous support of the black electorate, provided the African American community with an organized political voice. Though lacking the numbers to elect black candidates to parish office, African American voters were able to exert significant political influence through the strategy of bloc voting. The Grant Parish Republican Party used its endorsement process to deliver black votes to those local white candidates, regardless of party, deemed most sympathetic to black interests." Fueling black support for the People's Party in Grant Parish was the Colored Farmers' Union, which had been formed in the parish in 1888 and had developed an extensive membership on plantations along the river valley by 1890. In 1891 the Colored Farmers' Union unanimously endorsed the People's Party ticket. African Americans in Grant Parish would determine virtually the entire slate of the third party's candidates in the primaries, to both positive and negative reception. Positive, in that it signaled independent black electoral strength; negative, in the backlash to such exerted strength by white voters. Black farmers, sharecroppers, and agrarian workers in this part of Louisiana had effectively leveraged their numbers at the ballot box via independent black organization, but their alliance with white independents proved fragile.[124]

African Americans in Louisiana forged a political path within the state's People's Party despite hostility from certain vocal white Populists. In 1892 the editor of the *Louisiana Populist* would criticize "white Populists" of Grant Parish for inviting "colored Populists into their primary for nominating a parish ticket."[125] For these white Populists, Black Populists were not equal partners in the formation of the party; and, certainly there was never going to be a time to field black candidates on the People's Party ticket. These white Populists viewed the party as theirs, despite the inclusivity of the call to conference which stated political, racial, and class-blind acceptance for those who wanted to join the new party. For Black Populists, the question remained how to leverage independent white discontent in the face of lily-white Republicanism, white supremacist Democratic rule, *and* opposition from certain white Populist leaders. Black Populists attempted to maintain as independent a perspective as possible. Roxborough, for instance, made it clear that black voters would, if need be, exercise any number of political options. At one point, he even threatened white Populists that black voters could just as well support Democratic candidates. But Louisiana, like every other state, had its own particular dynamics; here, Roxborough could contemplate such a move, given the relative weakness of the Democrats. Elsewhere, however, African Americans dealt with more rigid political options.

African Americans in Georgia confronted one of the most powerful Democratic organizations in the South. The launching of the Georgia People's Party in the fall of 1891 created a political firestorm. With an estimated 84,000 members (nearly half of the rural adult black male population in the state), the Georgia Colored Alliance was a potentially powerful base of support for the third party.[126] For Black Populists, the possibility of shifting even a portion of the ranks of the Colored Alliance toward the People's Party offered a tremendous opportunity. However, not all of Georgia's Colored Alliance's leaders favored the third party. E. A. Richardson, who represented the organization at multiple meetings culminating in the formation of the national People's Party, remained consistently opposed to a political break among African Americans. A Republican, Richardson argued that a third party would undermine the strength, small as it was, of Georgia's Republican Party.

In July 1892, two Black Populists—maligned in the southern press as "Peek nigger" John Mack and "nigger co-laborer" R. J. Mathews—served as delegates to the first People's Party statewide convention in Atlanta. Observers noted that the two men "participate[d] in deliberations on party nominations, as well as on tactics and demands."[127] Mack seconded the nomination of the white Populist gubernatorial candidate William L. Peek (accounting for John Mack's derogatory name in the southern press).[128] Other African Americans were active in building the party locally. People's Party district committees in Greene County apparently had equal numbers of black and white members; most district committees had at least one black representative. All-black committees were also created to recruit members. From the beginning then, Black Populists, while still a minority, were active in the life of the Georgia People's Party.[129]

Despite the sometimes open hostility faced by Black Populists from Republicans, outright attacks by Democrats, and the indignation of many white Populists, several African American leaders put their own lives on the line to promote white Populist candidates. The Reverend Henry S. Doyle was the most prominent of Black Populists in Georgia willing to support white Populist candidates—in particular, Tom Watson, whom he had come to admire for standing up for poor and working people against the parties and their financial interests. Described as the "young preacher" at the time of the 1892 People's Party campaign, Doyle was born on January 8, 1867, in Eastman, about fifty miles south of Macon, Georgia. He attended Clarke University in Atlanta and Ohio Wesleyan University. He had experienced both social and political equality in Ohio and resolved to challenge southern racial conventions and practices. His contemporaries knew Doyle to be learned and exceptionally bold. Doyle read widely, including theology, history, and political economy, in addition to current events. Included in his readings were Adam Smith's *The Wealth of Nations*, Karl Marx's *Communist Manifesto*, and Henry George's *Progress and Poverty*—all of which he incorporated into his preaching and political organizing.[130]

W. E. B. Du Bois, who did not know Doyle but had studied his life through contemporary sources, described the minister as "an earnest thinker."[131] Apparently Doyle was also a person of great courage, as Du Bois further noted. According to one of Doyle's younger followers, Channing Tobias, he was "the one minister in Augusta who had the courage to challenge racial discrimination, even though he knew that his statements might be used against him by the so-called 'Uncle-Tom' Negro type of leadership." Tobias, an Augusta native, continued: "Not only [did Rayner have] the courage to challenge jim-crowism, he also had the courage to challenge the effectiveness of the dominant political parties." Doyle's work with the People's Party made him famous across the state. As Tobias notes, Doyle's name was "almost as much of a household word as Watson's among the poor whites as well as the Negroes in Georgia."[132] Doyle had come out of the black church; he served as pastor of the Trinity Colored Methodist Episcopal Church, and was among a number of Black Populist leaders who were ministers—including the Reverends Grimes Jr., Walter Pattillo, Benjamin F. Foster, Henry Jennings, and George W. Lowe.[133]

Two other African Americans, Anthony Wilson and Anton Graves, joined Doyle's direction and took to the stump on behalf of the People's Party ticket in the fall of 1892. Wilson, from Camden County in southeastern Georgia, had previously served as a Republican state legislator (and was later reelected to Georgia's assembly with the backing of the People's Party).[134] Like Doyle, he and Graves would work closely with Watson, who traveled with armed guards during the campaign. The campaign proved especially violent: all four organizers—Wilson, Graves, Doyle, and Watson—survived assassination attempts that fall. Their black (Populist) and independent (white) alliance posed a much larger threat than even they had anticipated. In late October, in the face of being lynched and having narrowly escaped death in Jefferson County, where a bullet meant for him killed a white supporter standing nearby, Doyle asked for Watson's help. Watson famously responded by calling his supporters to the village of Thomson, where Doyle had taken shelter—albeit in the back shed of Watson's home.[135] For good measure, armed white Populists called into town by Watson remained on guard for two nights thereafter.[136]

The logic of black and white voters joining forces against the Democratic Party based upon their common economic plight was compelling as it was controversial in Georgia, and elsewhere in the South. As indicated by the throngs of African Americans who cheered Watson when he spoke at campaign rallies, his appeal to economic self-interest helped to galvanize black support for the third party in Georgia. However, African Americans also challenged Watson's picture of a shared plight. Addressing a third-party convention in the summer of 1892, another Watson—a Black Populist from Texas—declared that "it is now useless to tell you my interest is yours and yours mine," pointing to the very real socioeconomic differences that existed between black and white Populists, the former being predominantly landless sharecroppers and agrarian workers, while the latter, farmers, and often with black tenants and workers dependent upon them and their land.[137] Nevertheless, Georgia's Watson inspired many African Americans to support the People's Party in his state, earning him the enmity of the Democratic Party and at least one attempt on his life. Watson additionally faced electoral obstruction and legal manipulation—for instance, in the form of gerrymandering (the redrawing of district lines by the Democratic legislature) when he sought reelection of his congressional seat in the tenth district in 1893. Watson would harbor deep resentment for the political injustices he experienced; in coming years, he expressed his frustration by lashing out against African Americans. He called for the disfranchisement of black voters in order to eliminate (for white Populists) the obstacle of stolen votes by African Americans placed into the Democratic camp by party-appointed registrars.[138]

The details of Tom Watson's life have been extensively explored by others, most notably beginning with Woodward's classic biography *Tom Watson: Agrarian Rebel*. In brief, Watson was born in Georgia into a family of slave owners. He became a lawyer and one of the state's largest landowners. He was elected to the Georgia State Legislature as a Democrat in 1882 and joined the Southern Farmers' Alliance. He was subsequently elected as an "Alliance Democrat" to Congress in 1890 before helping to establish the People's Party in 1892. His later life, marked by his decision to drive African Americans out of the electoral system, has come to overshadow his earlier work as an impassioned proponent of black and white alliance making.

As in Georgia, the message of North Carolina's People's Party was received by African Americans with a mix of enthusiasm and apprehension. Founded in Raleigh, the People's Party held a statewide convention on August 16, 1892, which was said to be "about equally composed of Republican whites . . . negroes and disappointed Democrats."[139] Like the Texas organization, cooperation between black and white Populists in North Carolina was built on a foundation that had been laid by the Colored Alliance. With a strong state Republican Party and without the burden of fighting disfranchisement (unlike Mississippi, where the Republicans were weak and disfranchisement had been enacted through the state constitution in 1890), the emergence of the People's Party in North Carolina would present a unique opportunity for African Americans to leverage their numbers against the Democratic Party through fusion. In 1892, and of particular significance to black voters, the People's Party called for a secret ballot by adding a provision that illiterate voters receive a "fair and honest count." The call was a response to Democratic Party election fraud designed to hobble Republican, insurgent, and independent candidacies.[140]

Black Republicans had grudgingly grown accustomed to discrimination at polling sites. Despite the black Republican stronghold of North Carolina's second congressional district—the "Black Second"—African Americans' efforts to address issues beyond the district were limited by Democrats. African Americans nevertheless set out to make larger changes in the state.[141] Meeting in convention in August 1891, black Republicans made a series of key demands: federal appropriations for education; support for the Lodge Bill; test cases to force the Supreme Court to place African Americans on juries; and county government and election reform. Following the convention, seven African Americans were elected to the fifteen-member Republican state executive committee. They included J. T. Cheshire of Pasquotank County, Abraham R. Middleton of Duplin, Edward A. Johnson and John H. Williamson of Wake, John C. Dancy of Rowan, J. H. Hannon of Halifax, and J. W. Pope of Northhampton.[142] Despite the prominence of African Americans on the Republican's executive committee and the party's avowed support for issues of direct concern to African Americans, black disaffection with the Republican Party had been mounting. As early as 1890, African Americans met in a series of conventions in the South declaring their intentions to leave the Republican Party. One group gathered in Raleigh in a "Negroes' 'Declaration of Independence'" convention, proclaiming: "The white Republicans have been traitors to us."[143] Black voter turnout for the Republican Party between 1888 and 1892 fell from 49 percent to 27 percent—a clear indication of black disapproval and unrest, accounting for much more than Democratic fraud.[144]

Not only were there signs of disaffection among African Americans from the Republican Party, but interest in exploring independent political options began to appear in the press. As early as 1890 the Colored Alliance vowed to take independent political action if their demands were not met by either of the major parties: in Bettie County it was reported that "good, honest men" were going to vote for People's Party candidates "from township constable to President of the United States" in the fall of 1891.[145] In 1892 more than one hundred African Americans attended a speech given by the white Populist leader Marion Butler, who had joined the People's Party after leaving the Democratic Party. That same year in Edgecombe County, located in the eastern and predominantly black populated part of the state, the People's Party slate for office included two African Americans. In Vance County, northwest of Edgecombe, the Reverend Allen P.

Eaton led a black delegation to a People's Party countywide convention, at which African Americans were nominated for general assembly and local office seats. Black organizers recruited African Americans who leaned independent in other parts of the state's eastern counties of Halifax and Warren. And while their efforts brought about little success in terms of convincing black voters to cast their ballot for the People's Party, their presence helped to fuel the Republican-Populist fusion (which was strongly supported by black voters on the Republican side), which led to the Populist takeover of North Carolina's legislature two years later.

Propagandistically or not, opponents of the movement acknowledged the growth of Black Populism in North Carolina. With regard to the 1892 election, one critic noted that "4/5 of the Colored vote will go for the [People's] Party, Legislative, County and Congress[ional] tickets."[146] While overstating black support for the People's Party, the perception of renewed black political participation connected to the rise of North Carolina's People's Party was not without basis. Black political participation in North Carolina grew 19 percentage points between 1888 and 1896.[147] Although most African Americans (possibly even those who were voting for local People's Party candidates) would end up voting for the Republican presidential candidate, the independent party's presidential nominee that year, James B. Weaver, received a warm reception from the black community when he visited North Carolina. The fifty African Americans on horseback who paraded with Weaver in Raleigh in September 1892 embodied a newfound political optimism in the black community.[148] Hundreds of black men, women, and children had joined the parade to Brookside Park, and applauded Weaver elsewhere in the state.[149] The *Raleigh News and Observer* reported that the "procession yesterday was a motley crowd." "[B]y actual count [there were] 175 men and boys and negroes on horse and mule-back," noted the newspaper. It continued, "There were probably 500 negroes present. Taking it all together, we conclude that 1,500 would cover the number of Third party people present."[150] In the days following the parade in Raleigh, newspapers captured the feeling among some black supporters for the independent ticket. "[N]egro marshals filed by," wrote a reporter covering the parade. "'Hurrah for Weaver,' shouted a big buck Negro as he cast a significant smile at T. R. Purnell, the Radical candidate for Attorney General."[151]

African Americans also welcomed the white female Populist Mary Elizabeth Lease when she came to North Carolina. Lease, an attorney from Kansas, known for her powerful speeches (she was famously reported to have said that farmers needed to "raise less corn and more hell!"), was a tireless campaigner for the People's Party. The "People's Joan of Arc" had initially become active in the temperance movement, making her first political speech at a convention of the Women's Christian Temperance Union—one of the reform groups active in the series of conventions leading up to the founding of the national People's Party. Lease ran for office on the Union Labor ticket before joining the white Alliance; she then left Union Labor to join the People's Party, along with a number of other white women in Kansas who had become politically active, including Eva Blackman and Annie L. Diggs.[152] Lease, however, stood out among these women—as well as most white male Populists leaders, for her audacity and oratory. Repeatedly shattering the rules of gender decorum, Lease once called a "gentleman" who interrupted her "a long-eared animal."[153] In one instance, speaking to a racially mixed crowd (a double transgression of southern etiquette), she "eulogized the grand new [People's] party and said a stampede was going on from both the old parties toward it."[154] The reporter from the *News and Observer* went on to report that "[a] crowd of negroes who stood immediately at her elbow on the stand were loudest of all in their applause." Lease, like the majority of her white Populist colleagues, was also a white supremacist; but it was her call for political independence that resonated among African Americans, and could be used to advance their movement.[155]

Rampant fraud during the election of 1892 makes it difficult to determine the actual size of African American defection toward the People's Party; it was likely modest. Between 1888 and 1892, J. Morgan Kousser estimates the percentage of African Americans who voted for the Democratic Party went up fifteen points (from 19 to 34 percent), and only a single point increase among African Americans who voted for independent candidates—that is, from 1 to 2 percent.[156] But as legal testimonies in contested election cases would illustrate, Democrats openly stole votes, stuffed ballot boxes, and intimidated voters, further corrupting an already undemocratic political environment in which laws were designed to keep African Americans from voting.[157] Despite the array of political and legal obstacles set up by the Democratic Party, the People's Party received over 17 percent of the vote (approximately 47,000 votes) and elected eleven members to the North Carolina state legislature. While perhaps no more than a thousand votes were cast for the People's Party by black voters, the 1892 election nevertheless established that the new party had potential; it was as an independent electoral vehicle with white Populists with whom African Americans could partner to challenge the Democratic Party—which they did most effectively through fusion with the Republican Party in 1894.[158]

The development of various state-based People's parties in the South and the Midwest between 1890 and 1892 would feed into the formation of the national party in St. Louis in 1892. Establishing People's parties was one thing; it was quite another to gain black support for them, as Black Populists quickly found out. The task was both laborious and even dangerous, particularly for African Americans.

If the increasingly marginalized black electorate (by dint of fraud at the polls, physical threats, and actual attacks) was going to be persuaded to vote for Republican candidates when fusion could advance the movement, or for People's Party candidates when doing so was more advantageous, black voters would need to be continuously and carefully politicized. The growing dissatisfaction of black voters with the Republican Party that led to lower voter turnout for Republican candidates did not automatically translate into votes for the People's Party in 1892. After one of the most fraudulent elections recorded in the South since Reconstruction, the results that year showed a combination of lower overall voter turnout (a result of intimidation and restrictions at the polls) and an increase in votes for the Democratic Party (through miscounting and ballot box stuffing).[159]

From the vantage point of strictly winning elections, it would hardly seem that the life-threatening risks taken by black organizers—such as Doyle campaigning for the People's Party in Georgia—were worth the extraordinary efforts and risks involved. However, from the perspective of *building the movement*—creating alliances with white Populists and inspiring greater independence in the black community—the campaigns of 1892 were a success. Black and white Populists had divisions among themselves. Both movements had their traditional (or "straight") party proponents (for African Americans, the Republican Party; for white southerners, the Democratic Party). There were African Americans within Black Populism and white southerners among their own movement who did not want to see the development of a third party. But both movements also had their strong third-party (or fusion) advocates. The local and national work of those Black Populists who wanted to diversify their political options (that is, lessen their dependency on the Republican Party) beginning in 1890, and continuing through 1892, would lead to a series of important electoral victories starting in 1894.

As was to be expected, Democrats reacted quickly to Black Populism's turn toward electoral politics and, in particular, the development of the new "Negro Party." The Democratic Party had several reasons for alarm: Populist presidential candidate James B. Weaver polled over one million votes nationwide in 1892 (1,041,028 votes, or 9 percent of the vote), winning twenty-two electoral college votes (and while none in the South, he secured Kansas with ten electoral votes); Populists (some of whom were elected with the help of black voters) sat in Congress, governor's offices, and dozens of local offices in the South and Midwest; all the while, black and white party chapters were being established. In addition to Weaver's votes, other independent presidential candidates received 285,297 votes (an additional 2 percent of the total vote). The People's Party also gained notable support in areas of Louisiana and Virginia; moreover, the party's gubernatorial candidates only narrowly lost in Alabama and Texas (with Republican acquiescence), as well as congressional seats in Georgia, including Tom Watson's; and North Carolina elected 11 (out of 170) independent representatives to the legislature.[160]

Not since the advent of the Republican Party in the mid- and late 1850s had a third party grown so rapidly and achieved such success. The threat posed by the People's Party toward the Democrats' reign over the South was not to be tolerated; the Southern Democracy would move in to quell the rebellion underway. Democrats, provoked by black and white Populists—having now demonstrated their capacity to capture, if not command a following—embarked on a campaign to suppress any form of opposition to their rule. With the election machinery firmly in the hands of the Southern Democracy—backed by the courts, state legislatures, and militias they operated and controlled—the Democratic Party may have appeared invincible, yet black and white Populists resisted, and for a time, even remained hopeful.

Various agreements were adopted between the People's Party and the Republican Party to harness the combined electoral strength of black and independent white voters. Fusion or coalition agreements were carried out in Alabama, Arkansas, Georgia, Louisiana, North Carolina, Texas, and Virginia.[161] A range of outcomes followed: in Mississippi and South Carolina the Democratic Party would prove virtually impregnable; in Texas and Georgia independents would make significant inroads; and in North Carolina, a Republican-Populist fusion would take control of the state legislature, followed by the governor's office. Together, the experiences would reflect the multifaceted electoral strategy of Black Populism in the 1890s.

Chapter Four

INDEPENDENT, COALITION, AND FUSION POLITICS

To the colored man the People's Party in Georgia is largely what the Republican Party was to him in this nation thirty years ago.

—The *Georgia Baptist*, quoted in the *Progressive Farmer*, October 30, 1894

By midmorning of July 25, 1896, several hundred black and white delegates, reporters, and observers from across the nation had arrived in St. Louis for the People's Party nominating convention.[1] Just four years earlier, Colored Alliance delegates had gathered in the city with their white counterparts to establish the national People's Party. After helping to create the third party as an instrument for breaking the Democratic Party's political monopoly in the South, African Americans now found themselves in the position of trying to persuade white delegates not to support the Democrats' nominee. William Jennings Bryan had offered a powerful speech at the Democratic nominating convention at the Chicago Coliseum two weeks earlier in favor of the unlimited coinage of silver, a core Populist demand. As a result, many white Populist leaders saw in Bryan's candidacy an opportunity to advance their own movement. The appeal to silver resonated among white farmers, most of whom were in debt and sought relief through inflationary measures. For African Americans, however, support for Bryan was no less as a political capitulation to the Southern Democracy.[2]

Over the next several days, delegates to the People's Party nominating convention debated whether they should nominate their own presidential candidate or endorse Bryan—that is, fuse with the Democrats. Henry Demarest Lloyd, a reporter from New York at the time covering the third-party convention, said, "The most eloquent speeches were those of whites and blacks explaining to the convention what the rule of Democrats meant in the South." He continued, "A delegate from Georgia, a coal black Negro, told how the People's Party alone gave full fellowship to his race when it had been abandoned by the Republicans and cheated and betrayed by the Democrats."[3] Another delegate, A. W. Ricker from Iowa, recalled "the presence of Negro delegates from the South, one of whom spoke vigorously against the proposed unity with the Democrats." The black delegate to whom they were both referring, S. D. Walton, had seconded Tom Watson's nomination for vice president. According to Walton, voting for Watson "made it possible for the black man to vote according to his conscience." He and other black delegates backed the "middle-of-the-road" Populists, mostly from Texas and Georgia, who were trying to keep the People's Party fully independent by endorsing its own candidates.[4]

African Americans, such as Walton, made plain their objections to fusion with the Democratic Party. Fusion—the tactic employed by African Americans and white independents from 1879 to 1884, primarily through the Greenback Labor and Republican parties, and then again beginning in 1894 with the Republican and People's parties—had challenged the Democrats in various parts of the South; in 1894 a Republican-Populist fusion in North Carolina brought independents to power in that state.[5] But while African Americans—including Black Populists—had at times either tactically threatened to or actually carried out endorsing Democratic candidates in the South (as Charles A. Roxborough of Louisiana's Colored Alliance threatened Republicans in attacking the party's lily-white practices, or the South Carolina Colored Alliance endorsement of Democrat Ben Tillman), Black Populists supported the People's Party by itself or through fusion with the Republicans. For African Americans, it was one thing for the People's Party to fuse with the Republican Party in the South—their common opponents were Democrats—it was quite another to fuse with the Democratic Party, the very instrument of Redeemer rule. As the historian Jack Abramowitz notes, "To [Black] Populists the prospect of fusion with the Democrats was a disaster since it would lead inevitably to the destruction of the new relationship that had begun to develop during the period of insurgency."[6]

The Texas Black Populist John Rayner was among those who forcefully denounced fusion with the Democratic Party. As Charles Postel writes, "Rayner grasped immediately that the endorsement [of a Democratic candidate] threatened to end his role and that of other black Populists in reform politics. The black vote would no longer be a contested vote if Populist-Democratic fusion cemented white solidarity at the polls. At the 1896 Texas Populist convention, Rayner convened a conference of black delegates to decide between 'Republican oppressive conservatism and Democratic rashness.' Faced with such a choice, the People's Party of Texas chose to support the Republican nominee William McKinley."[7]

The fate of the national People's Party and its state affiliates would largely be decided at the St. Louis convention. Would the national party endorse the Democrats, or would it stay the independent course and select its own presidential candidate? Despite protests, petitions, and objections made by Walton and other black delegates, as well as several white delegates, the majority-white convention voted to nominate Bryan. The People's Party nominated Georgia's Tom Watson for U.S. vice president over the Democratic vice presidential nominee Arthur Sewall. However, Bryan never publicly accepted Watson as a running mate, even though Watson supported him. Consequently, Watson's name did not appear on the ballot in a number of places. In fusing with the Democrats, the People's Party convention abandoned the "middle" road, hoping to ride the coattails of the Democratic Party into the White House should Bryan win the election. The gamble of the white Populists failed. Bryan lost the election to Republican McKinley. Having thrown its support to the Democrats, the national People's Party had forfeited a key aspect of its independence. (Tom Watson continued to play a role in the People's Party, but the party became increasingly obscure. In 1908 Watson ran as the party's presidential candidate and received fewer than 30,000 votes.)

The fight over whether or not to employ fusion in the 1896 presidential election would underscore the divergence between the strategic interests of black and white Populists and make plain the political vulnerabilities of African Americans who now wrestled to sustain their movement.[8] Black Populists had forged an offensive approach to the stripping away of black political rights and the worsening economic plight of black farmers, sharecroppers, and agrarian workers. White Populists, whose concern for disfranchisement was less acute than their black counterparts, were more focused on monetary issues—and were thereby more willing to support a Democrat for president who spoke on economic issues that resonated with them, more easily laying aside the fact that the candidate was of the same party with which the Southern Democracy affiliated nationally. As the nineteenth century drew to a close, legalized segregation and disfranchisement of African Americans—Jim Crow—would come to dominate much of the South.

The demise of Black Populism bore a striking resemblance to the end of Reconstruction. In 1877 black Republicans had been marginalized by their party, which entered into an arrangement with the Democrats that effectively gave the presidency to the Republicans in exchange for the withdrawal of federal troops from the South. Similarly, twenty years later, Black Populists were marginalized by their national party. The second time, however, the blow was self-inflicted. Some historians have implied that black political efforts to ally with white southerners were doomed from the beginning, but the fact is that neither Black Populists, nor anyone else, knew what would become of their efforts when, in the spring of 1893, African Americans, in alliance with white Populists, helped to launch their multistate offensive against the Southern Democracy.

Black Populists were politically linked across the South by their desire to defeat the Democratic Party, even as the ways in which they proceeded from one county or state to the next varied—supporting insurgent candidates, running independents for office, or fusing with the Republican Party, depending on what was politically feasible and tactically advantageous to carry out. Underlying their efforts was the recognition that only by reforming the electoral process could they do anything to redress the material hardships most African Americans faced; that is, a fair ballot was a prerequisite for changing economic policy. In addition to systematic intimidation and orchestrated violence, African Americans confronted a barrage of "dirty tricks"—ballot-box stuffing, doctoring of returns, repeat voting, tampering with registration books, using boxes with false bottoms, and altering vote tallies.[9] Black Populists, like their white Populist counterparts, readied themselves for a fight over the electoral process. As the *Louisiana Populist* declared:

> The war of the ballots will be between Populists and Plutocrats. The Populists will have for allies all honest silverites, prohibitionists and socialists; while the plutocrats will be divided into Democrats ... It will be a mighty contest ... between freedom and slavery. There can be no neutrality upon this grave and important question. Those who are not in favor of honest elections are in favor of corrupt elections.[10]

The intensification of fraud, coercion, and intimidation by Democrats was a political reaction to the growing strength of the independent electoral challenge they now faced; Democrats reserved their harshest words and deeds for African Americans, as well as their closest white allies within the electoral rebellion. By the end of 1893 the People's Party, while having lost most of its races, had nevertheless succeeded in establishing itself as a significant political force in the nation. There were visible signs of the independent political impact and presence of the People's Party across the nation, including the South; the over one million votes received by Populist presidential candidate James B. Weaver in 1892, the dozens of congressional seats won by Populists the year thereafter, along with three governors' offices and hundreds of local positions across the nation (with western states gaining the highest percentages of Populist votes in local and statewide contests), and Populist-backed gubernatorial and congressional candidates in Alabama, Georgia, and North Carolina only narrowly losing their races. While

African Americans cast only a small fraction of the votes for the third party in 1892 and 1893, Black Populists were a visible component of the campaigns that urged political independence.

Depending on local political circumstances, Black Populists employed any one of three organizational tactics to maximize their political leverage against the Democrats: (1) supporting the People's Party and its candidates; (2) supporting the People's Party's candidates in fusion with those of the Republican Party; or (3) supporting insurgent Republican candidates. In the context of a largely single-party-dominated South—especially in states such as Mississippi and South Carolina—many Black Populists opted to use the Republican Party as their own vehicle. This notion goes against the dominant scholarly accounts of Black Populism (which place black Republican participation on its own as outside of the movement). The clearest examples of each of the three organizational tactics used by Black Populists may be seen in Georgia, North Carolina, and Virginia, respectively. Throughout the South Black Populists at the state and county levels sometimes carried out a combination of these tactics based upon the relative strength of the Republican and People's parties, and the strength of black leadership within these organizations. Over the next two years, formal and informal agreements were worked out between various state and county-based Republican and People's parties. Most of the arrangements were informal: in separate conventions each party endorsed the other party's candidates, who would then appear together on a joint ticket. When successfully carried out, the tactic combined the total non-Democratic vote instead of splitting it between Republican and Populist tickets (or another independent party, such as the Union Labor Party). While electoral success remained elusive in most southern states, a number of key Populist victories—for instance, in Alabama and North Carolina—resulted from fusion. The North Carolina Republican-Populist fusion of 1894 produced a majority of the seats in the state legislature, along with seven congressional seats. And while the Alabama Populist Reuben Kolb lost his second gubernatorial race, fusion arrangements in the state sent two Populists and two Republicans to Congress and several to the state legislature; three of the legislative seats in Alabama were won only after a special appeal and an investigation were launched.[11]

Fusion in some counties or states was complemented by the use in others of the People's Party or the Republican Party on their own. Black Populists in Texas, Louisiana, and Georgia initially made the People's Party their principal vehicle. Georgia saw a flurry of victories, including Tom Watson's election to Congress in 1890 as an Alliance Democrat (caucusing with Populists), and a few narrow defeats. Meanwhile, in South Carolina and Virginia, where African Americans only had a marginal role in the People's Party (especially after 1893 in the case of

Virginia), Black Populists used the Republican Party to their advantage. Overall, the percentage of black votes recorded as having been cast for the People's Party remained small. For instance, in Choctaw County, Alabama, where black voters were active in the People's Party primaries in 1892, only 14 percent were said to have cast their vote that year for the third party. However, African Americans in Alabama continued to be active in the People's Party. Two years later, ten "colored friends" were recorded as having joined about seventy white Populists at the county nominating convention to select a candidate for the state legislature.[12] Even some white Alliancemen in Alabama were compelled to stand up for the "Force Bill" to provide federal oversight for voting in the South. Though a minority voice, the reasoning of these independent white Alabamans was as forward looking as Radical Republicans a generation earlier: "so [that] the negro could get a fair vote" and that African Americans in the state not be "deprived of the privileges of voting for whom [they] please."[13] Meanwhile, in Georgia in 1894, only 15 percent of African Americans were said to have cast their vote for the People's Party (with so much election fraud, it is difficult to know how many African Americans actually cast their vote for the third party). However, in Virginia in 1893, where the People's Party is reported to have had at least one black representative on each precinct committee, 46 percent of African Americans were reported to have cast their vote for the third party.[14] Again, the high level of fraud and voter manipulation make these figures—either low or high—suspect.

Even the most conservative estimates regard Kansas a leading center of People's Party activism in the nation. The Kansas People's Party won both the popular and electoral college vote in 1892. That year, African Americans were able to help ensure that no fusion would take place with the Democratic Party. As the *New York Times* reported in May of 1892 ("The Kansas People's Party Propose to Go at it Alone") at least one dozen People's Party conventions were held throughout the state to discuss the matter.[15] As in all other states, most African Americans in Kansas were affiliated with the Republican Party. However, dissent from that party among black voters had grown over the course of the 1880s, partly in response to lily-white control.

The Kansas People's Party would receive just as high—even higher—percentages of support in western states in the 1894 elections: 39 percent in Washington State and 41 percent in Colorado. As with several western states, the independent movement in Kansas took the form of cooperation with Democrats, not Republicans. Kansas had taken the lead in forming a "People's ticket" in Cowley County as early as November 1889, precipitating the statewide break from the two major parties among black and white Kansans.[16] African Americans in the West were often completely left out of the People's Party decision making—not surprisingly, as the percentage of the black population in western states (Texas being here considered part of the South) was relatively small. In most western states, African Americans formed less than 3 percent of the total population. Kansas, however, with 49,710 African Americans in 1890, did have a sizable black population (much of which was relatively new to the state, having come up from the South), and exerted their numbers where they could.[17]

In the South, where most African Americans lived, the People's Party received a range of support; Texans and Alabamans saw one quarter to over one-third of their respective state's votes go to the third party. Most black voters did not end up casting their ballot for People's Party candidates, especially in plantation areas where black votes were particularly subject to fraud and electoral manipulation (in addition to intimidation of different sorts). The following table shows the estimated total percentage of votes cast for Populist or fusion tickets in the South in 1892 and 1894—or where noted, 1893, 1895, or 1896.[18]

Election Year	1892 / 1894
Alabama	36.60 / 47.64
Arkansas	8.07 / 19.31
Florida	21.3 / 20.68
Georgia	19.17 / 44.46
Louisiana	5.30 / 43.68 (1896)
Mississippi	19.42 / 27.2 (1895)
Missouri	7.59 / 8.45
North Carolina	15.94 / 53.78
South Carolina	3.42 / 30.43[19]
Tennessee	8.92 / 9.93
Texas	23.64 / 36.13
Virginia	40.8 (1893) / 28.60

Such percentages of votes recorded for Populists or fusion campaigns that included the People's Party in the 1890s must be viewed with caution. There were multiple distortive factors involved in these elections: election fraud, the selling of votes, and laws and practices that disenfranchised voters (especially black voters), discriminatory registration procedures, literacy tests, the "eight-box law," and poll taxes. These factors likely diminished what levels of support may have *actually* existed for the People's Party among both black and white voters. Fraud, it turns out, was not only carried out by Democrats; supporters of the People's Party were, at times, also guilty. However, considering that most elections were under the authority of Democratic registrars, official results disproportionately favored Democratic candidates.

Multivariate regression analyses, specifically those attempting to correlate black population density in congressional districts in the South and voter turnout for the People's Party, ultimately yield inconclusive results since critical data of election distortion (i.e., fraud) cannot be adequately measured and therefore included in calculations. As Edward Ayers notes, "Class or race interests, already complex, become even more so when refracted through the political system. Southern politics in the age of Populism ... were extraordinarily intricate."[20] In other words, percentages recorded cannot be taken as a direct measurement for independent or fusion support.[21] Ultimately, we can only contextualize election results and rely on what anecdotal evidence exist to gain a better picture of what kind of black support the People's Party and its organizers were actually able to generate. Nevertheless, and for a variety of reasons, the fact remains that throughout the South African Americans also voluntarily cast their vote for Democratic candidates. In response, black and white Populists derided these African American voters as "Negro Democrats."

Of the "negro democrat," the Atlanta *People's Party Paper* published the following editorial:

> The negro democrat is a source of inspiration and joy to all who know him. He holds an office. Of course he does—that's what he came for. The purpose of [his] life is to get a higher and better one ... The negro democrat ... cares nothing about the poor and the oppressed of his race. Having sold out his own color in order to get a democratic office, nothing better could be expected of him. He treats the black laborer precisely as the white office-holder treats the white producer—with gushing fondness during the campaign and with contemptuous indifference after the election.[22]

Black Republicans who voted for Democratic candidates provided their own justifications for doing so. In Georgia, black Republicans endorsed Democrat William J. Northern in the 1892 gubernatorial race, citing his favorable record on educational appropriations and his public stance against lynching, which African Americans (the primary victims of this particular form of terrorism) sought to criminalize. That year a number of black "Northern clubs" were formed under the leadership of the Atlanta-based attorney William A. Pledger, one of the most influential black Republicans in the state. As the historian Charles Crowe has argued, the size of the black vote for any given candidate often depended not only on "the personal popularity of that man," but the candidate's "record in matters relating to colored people, *regardless of his political label*" (emphasis added).[23] That is, African Americans broke from their party based on tactical considerations. As the political scientist Michael Dawson underscores, "The movement of African Americans into and out of the Republican party was never blind or random but was based on a realistic assessment of which party would best further black political and economic interests."²⁴

As in Georgia regarding the Democratic gubernatorial candidate William Northern, in Alabama, between 1893 and 1895, black Republicans endorsed Democrat William Oates for governor over the Populist candidate Reuben Kolb. The effort was led by William Stevens and a group of black lawyers, ministers, and editors—the most affluent segment of the black community. White Populist Kolb, they argued, had a record of being hostile to issues of concern to African Americans, specifically, on matters of civil rights and educational funding. Support for Democrats among black Republican leaders was also evident in Mississippi in the 1880s. John R. Lynch, the chair of the Republican Party who in 1881 directed a powerful fusion campaign with white independents, lent Mississippi Democrats his support. For these African Americans, endorsing a Democrat was tactical, in the same way that Black Populists argued that their voting for white Populists was tactical—both seeking benefits, whether through patronage in the form of an appointed office or support for issues of particular concern to the African American community, usually revolving around civil rights and education. The difference lay in Black Populists' desire to work with white independents around issues of electoral reform centering on a fair ballot.²⁵

The "Negro Democrat" could also be extended as a term to describe poorer and working-class African Americans who sold their vote. As the historian Gerald Gaither notes, "Living in an age when wages generally ranged between seventy cents to one dollar a day for 'first class' black laborers, [African Americans] who accepted Democratic bribes probably did so more from efforts to redress economic grievances than as acts of demonstrated faith in the Bourbons." Reports of black voters "holding themselves too cheap" also appear in the press. In 1892, a Black Populist from Zeigler, Georgia, noted ironically how as a slave in the 1840s he had been sold for $1,500, yet black voters were currently being bought for "a glass of cider, a second for a 'two-for-a-nickel' cigar, and a third for a pint of peanuts." In North Carolina, black voters were brought by Democrats on four-horse wagons across the South Carolina border to vote illegally—selling their votes for three to ten dollars, depending on how late in the day it was to the closing of the polls. White Populists were not beyond making bribes to gain votes from African Americans, although there were likely significantly fewer cases of this by virtue of the fact that Democrats won most contests.²⁶

With the combination of African Americans being presented with egregious white Populist candidates (even when such candidates received the backing of the Republican Party), fraud on the part of Democratic registrars, legal disenfranchisement, physical intimidation, and economic incentives offered to support Democratic tickets, it is understandable why so few votes were actually cast (or recorded as having been cast) for the People's Party by black voters. Black Populists faced other obstacles as they tried to build alliances with white Populists in the electoral arena. With slavery having been a direct part of the early life experiences of many black adults in the early 1890s, and with negative recollections of Reconstruction still fresh in the minds of most white southerners, distrust between black and white Populists was not only to be expected, but clearly persisted.

While African Americans did not ever constitute more than one-quarter of the Mississippi state legislature during the course of Reconstruction (in 1870, 30 out of 110 house seats were held by black representatives, and 5 out of 33 state senators were African American), the state remained a symbol of "Negro rule" for white southerners. Reconstruction-era Mississippi U.S. senators Hiram Revels and Blanche K. Bruce, along with Representative John R. Lynch, were the first African Americans to enter Congress; for many white southerners these men, among others serving in government, were an abomination to white society and civilization. As Mississippi's own "Honorable S. S. Calhoon," an esteemed circuit court judge and leading Mississippi Democrat who served as president of the Mississippi Constitutional Convention in August of 1890, made plain about African Americans, "Withdrawn from the envelopment of white civilization, the negro race seems unable to maintain even its own imitative acquirements. It seems unfit to rule. Its rule seems to mean, as it has always meant, stagnation, the enslavement of woman, the brutalization of man, animal savagery, universal ruin."[27]

Disaffected white Democrats in Mississippi who had joined the People's Party were like loyal white Democrats, similarly organized around the "fear" of a return to "Negro rule," and maintained a distance from Black Populists. African Americans following Reconstruction, however, faced warranted fear as a result of some of the most brutal attacks in the South by white vigilantes and law enforcement—from the lethal assaults on election day in Meridian in the fall of 1881 to the massacre of black men, women, and children in Leflore County during the summer of 1889. This history in Mississippi (which had its versions in other states) made it extremely difficult for Black Populists to work with white Populists, and vice-versa. Animosity among African Americans toward white politicians (Populist-allied or not) were only compounded by an amendment to the Mississippi state constitution in 1890, which led to a nearly 25 percent decrease in overall voter participation between 1888 and 1892.[28] Delegates called for the repeal of the Fifteenth Amendment in order to assure that white citizens fully controlled the state government. The legal measures contained therein disenfranchised thousands of white Populists in the process of targeting African Americans; over the next several years, an estimated 100,000 black Mississippians lost their vote as a result of the new constitution, as would some 50,000 white and mostly poor Mississippians.[29]

In November 1890, Mississippi's Democratic-led legislature took the decisive and extraordinary step of legally disenfranchising African Americans through a constitutional amendment; it did so even after being repeatedly charged on federal indictments for election fraud. The "Mississippi Plan," as it came to be called and followed elsewhere in the South, would serve as the regional model over the course of the next decade to minimize, if not completely eliminate, black participation in the electoral process. African Americans were hard pressed to find independent white coalitional partners in the state to challenge the Democratic Party. A People's Party of Mississippi was formed in 1892 under the leadership of white Allianceman Frank Burkitt, but it remained almost exclusively a white organization. While purportedly seeking to represent the interests of all small farmers, the Mississippi People's Party did not intervene on behalf of African Americans as Democrats trampled their Constitutional rights. Unlike white Populist leaders in other states, Burkitt did not actively seek the support of black voters in his state. Despite being a majority black state, white Populists in Mississippi were simply willing to forego black electoral support, seeking to create a "whites only democracy" instead. In 1890 only six black legislators remained in the Mississippi assembly; after their removal, no other African American would serve in the state legislature for almost eighty years. In South Carolina, as was the case in Mississippi, African Americans were virtually locked out of a third-party option, prompting Black Populists to use the Republican Party to advance their interests.[30]

Black voter turnout had begun to be legally suppressed in South Carolina as early as 1882 with the "eight-box law," requiring separately marked ballot boxes at the polls for each office. The law was designed to induce illiterate black voters to cast their ballots incorrectly, thereby providing a legal pretext for invalidating their votes. In 1892 Ben Tillman boasted that despite the "enormous negro majority ... under our registration and eight-box laws[,] two-thirds of the negroes can't vote."[31] The impact of the eight-box and other registration laws were significant: whereas 70 percent of black South Carolinians (adult men) were voting in 1880, by 1892 that percentage had been driven down to 22 percent.[32]

Black Populists in South Carolina were, at best, met with indifference by white Populists in the early 1890s. As J. W. Bowden, a white Populist leader, remarked: "We are not considering the negro [in South Carolina]. This is a question the negroes will have to settle for themselves. [Nevertheless] I have reason to believe that thousands of them will not go with the Republicans any longer. Especially do I believe this will be the case among the Colored Alliance."[33] Most African

Americans in South Carolina, including members of the Colored Alliance, did end up supporting the Republican ticket in 1892; no People's Party ticket made an appearance in 1894 (in fact, a functional People's Party never existed in the state), instead a dissident white faction emerged, largely known as "Independents," garnering a sizable 30.4 percent of the vote.[34] Democrats maintained tight control of the electoral process in South Carolina.[35] Still, pockets of black Republican dissent persisted. Without a functioning, let alone effective, third party in South Carolina, Black Populists turned to the Republican Party as their electoral vehicle. It was through the Republican Party that South Carolina Colored Alliance state lecturer George Washington Murray not only grew to statewide prominence, but by 1893 found himself elected to the U.S. House of Representatives—the last African American from South Carolina to hold such a high-level office until well into the next century.

Born to slave parents in Sumter County, South Carolina, on September 22, 1853, Murray was orphaned at an early age. He attended public schools during Reconstruction, where his teachers were black, and he studied at the State Normal Institute at Columbia and the University of South Carolina. With the collapse of Reconstruction in 1876 Murray and several other black students were expelled from the University of South Carolina on account of being African American. Led by former Confederate general Wade Hampton, Redeemers seized control of the government. Red Shirt paramilitary companies under the general's command patrolled the streets on election day to ensure that African Americans did not vote. Murray's hopes of completing his higher education were dashed. In order to make a living he turned to farming and supplemented his income by teaching. He dedicated much of his energies to growing cotton and corn, acquiring as much property as he could over the next four years. By 1880 he owned some forty-nine acres of tilled land and an additional fifteen acres of forest land. By that time he had also distinguished himself in his community. He decided to enter the electoral arena and was nominated to serve as a Sumter County delegate to the Republican state convention.[36]

Over the course of the 1880s, Murray continued to make a name for himself. Soon after the Colored Alliance entered the state in May of 1888 he was elected "State Lecturer" of the organization. Murray is the best-known Colored Alliance leader of South Carolina, but he was joined by several other notable leaders, including T. E. Pratt, John D. Norris, W. J. Grant, and Isaiah D. Williams. Williams, like Murray, would personify much of what the Colored Alliance hoped to achieve among its men and women. Born in Marion, South Carolina, in 1860, Williams attended Hampton Normal and Agricultural Institute in Virginia and subsequently taught in Savage, Ariel, Oakton, Campbell's Bridge, and Bostic—all in Marion County, where he counted a total of 360 students, one of whom, he boasted, had become a teacher, like himself. Williams, however, lamented the fact that his students had neither enough books nor teachers to really "make a success" of themselves. He resolved to better the educational opportunities for those in the community; he would do so by building the Colored Alliance, by accumulating land, and by spreading his wealth. In line with the Colored Alliance philosophy of "self-help" he, like Murray, saw acquiring land and wealth as the way to improve conditions for rural black men and women. Williams would go on to accumulate a sizable share of property: 160 acres of land worth $480, with "buildings" worth $250. When asked to send in an alumni update to Hampton Institute, Williams proudly noted his membership in the Colored Alliance. Writing circa 1890, he gave "farming and merchandise" as his immediate aim. He remained surprisingly optimistic about the state of African Americans in South Carolina: "The condition of [my] people is favorable, considering their circumstances." But unlike Murray, who was not so optimistic, Williams did not enter the political arena.[37]

Murray saw electoral politics as a vital course of action to pursue for the betterment of black farmers; he saw this early on. After all, it was the Democratic takeover of government that had—among other things—stripped him of his chance to complete his studies at the University of South Carolina. Murray, having sensed a desire for a populist revolt against Democratic authority, took the lead in shaping Black Populism in South Carolina. Drawing on his personal networks via the Republican Party, students he had taught, and contacts he had made over the 1880s through farming, Murray began recruiting African Americans into the black Alliance in earnest; for him, it was a political base, as much as it was an organization for mutual benefit.[38]

Murray joined other black leaders in building the Colored Alliance. T. E. Pratt of Cheraw was one of the earliest leaders of the Colored Alliance in the state. Pratt had built a number of black sub-alliances, several having been formed by September of 1888: at Cedar Creek in Lancaster County; Gadsden, Mill Creek, and Congaree in Richland County; and possibly another in Chester County. Even at that early stage of the organizing the sub-alliances in Lancaster and Chester counties were considering a protest to raise wages for cotton pickers to a minimum of fifty cents per pound.[39] Over the next year, the Colored Alliance flourished in South Carolina; during the winter of 1888–1889, the organization spread through the Piedmont and into the rest of the state. Union County alone had twelve sub-alliances by April 1889. John D. Norris, the leader of Union County's Colored Alliance, was like Murray and Williams also a schoolteacher. Norris organized a meeting on April 25 at the county courthouse, describing the black Alliance at that meeting in strictly nonpartisan terms. As he put it, the object of the Colored Alliance was (among a number of things) designed "to elevate the colored people . . . to be more obedient to the civil and criminal law and *withdraw their attention from political partisanship*" (emphasis added).[40] However, there appears to have been more to the seemingly nonpolitical statement. As Edward Ayers notes, "black farmers saw different meaning in such phrases; they saw the organization of the Colored Alliance as a chance to show their love for their country, homes, and family by taking a stand against those who kept them down." Perhaps in the same way that black Alliancemen in Arkansas met in their legislative assembly a year later, South Carolina's black Alliancemen were actually pointing to the power that lay in organizing their ranks by holding their meeting in a seat of political authority even as they purported to be uninterested in politics.[41]

In June 1889, less than two months after Norris's meeting at the country courthouse, Colored Alliance delegates from twenty counties met in Sumter to officially form a statewide organization. The June meeting was held near Murray's home, and took the form of a large barbecue, which grew rapidly over the course of the day. The meeting reportedly swelled to an estimated nine hundred people—including families. Murray and other leaders insisted on making the gathering public in order to build a sense of agrarian solidarity within their own communities and with white Alliancemen and their friends and family.

Taking their cue from the Texas organization, the South Carolina Colored Alliance continued to present itself as a nonpartisan organization for the betterment of African Americans. Speakers at the June meeting addressed the large crowd; food was served, while black and white farmers and their families mingled. Murray's own speech was given particular attention. He urged African Americans to work with white farmers toward mutual benefit, highlighting running themes in the agrarian movement, including self-help, education, and economic improvement. From the veranda of an old house from which speakers addressed the crowd, Murray declared that "a new era [has] dawned in which white and colored farmers [can] pull together for the good of South Carolina." A band of black musicians performed "Dixie" in a gesture to make white guests feel welcome; in turn, those white Alliancemen in attendance passed a resolution of gratitude to their black hosts. But the spirit of unity was not to last long; the Southern Democracy would simply not permit such fraternizing between the races to go on—it was simply too political. African Americans, nevertheless, continued to organize their communities: by November 1889 the Colored Allaince reported 112 clubs in South Carolina; by February the organization boasted 237 clubs in the state. One Colored Alliance lecturer, Thomas Powers, reported a total membership of thirty-thousand in 1890, by which time both a state exchange with capital stock of $2,500 and a newspaper, the *Alliance Aid of South Carolina*, were established.[42]

Meanwhile, Murray's prominence in state Republican circles landed him an appointment as inspector of customs at the port of Charleston, where the Colored Alliance had been building a state exchange. Continuing his work in the Colored Alliance, which boasted forty thousand members by the fall of 1890, allowed him to simultaneously build his base of political support. During 1890 there were efforts to make the Colored Alliance a political organization to support sympathetic Republican candidates. That year Norris represented the Colored Alliance at the Ocala meeting in Florida where independent politics was being discussed. A resolution was passed by the Marlboro County Colored Alliance in support of Tillman for his antilynching stance. The organization seemed to be inching its way into electoral politics. But there were also divisions regarding this; W. J. Grant, a black Alliance leader in Charleston, appears to have opposed Murray and others' intentions to explicitly make the organization a political entity, and led a schism of the organization at the port city.[43]

Over the next two years, as Murray's public profile continued to grow he decided to launch a bid for Congress. He was the outside candidate in a field that included three veteran Republican politicians seeking the same office. Murray was considered temperamental and independent by his Republican colleagues, despite his years operating in their midst. He supported "free silver" and reached out to white independents; he had organized his own independent base of support through the Colored Alliance; he was not a typical black Republican. Murray campaigned vigorously in the seventh district, the "Black District," as it was called, and ended up defeating the three veteran Republicans, including the notable Robert Smalls—African American Civil War hero and Reconstruction congressman.[44] With Murray's candidacy secure on the Republican line, he continued his campaigning and went on to defeat the insurgent Democrat Edwin M. Moise in the general election. To his demise, Moise (of the Conservative faction of the South Carolina Democratic Party, a "Grover Cleveland Democrat") had resisted control by state Democratic boss Ben Tillman. Tillmanites were apparently instructed not to vote in the election in order to let Murray win.[45] Unlike other elections in which Republicans had their votes changed or invalidated, in this case, state board of election canvassers in the Tillman camp refrained from tampering with the returns—political payback against Moise—and Murray was declared the winner. The small yet significant Colored Alliance's endorsement of Tillman in 1890, Murray's strong grassroots support, and the particular intra-Democratic Party politics of 1892–1893, combined to give the Colored Alliance leader his victory.[46]

As Murray's star rose, the state's Colored Alliance seemed to be quickly losing members. Most scholars account for the organization's overall precipitous decline after 1891 as a result of the failed Cotton Pickers' Strike that year.

However, the development of an independent electoral strategy may equally account for the Colored Alliance's dissolution. By the time Murray entered the congressional race, the South Carolina organization claimed fewer than 25,000 members (down from 40,000 two years earlier). Black Alliancemen appear to have increasingly turned their attention to electoral politics, as one of its chief organizers, Murray, had done.[47] Now Congressman Murray would soon assume much of the responsibility in combating the Democrats and their efforts to legally disfranchise African Americans in the state; he had gone from organizing black agrarian cooperation in the community to becoming the leading voice of Black Populism in the state against the Southern Democracy in Congress. To the surprise of most, given the state of politics in South Carolina, Murray went on to win and eventually be seated in a second term, as well—a testament to both his popularity and political acumen.[48]

Serving in Congress from 1893 to 1895, Murray was an active member of the House Committee on Education. He dedicated himself to the task of legislating on behalf of the interests of both black and white poor, but there was little he could do in the face of southern Democrats who were intent on undermining him. He persisted, symbolizing the pride of African Americans, and campaigned for a second time. He was battling South Carolina's Democrats to disenfranchise African Americans. He eventually won the next congressional election on appeal, after requesting state board of election canvassers to overturn the election in the fall of 1894 amid a slew of reports of fraud, corruption, and other flagrant violations of the law. In Charleston, where election managers (appointed by the Democratic Party) prohibited ballot-box inspections prior to the election and then privately counted ballots after the polls closed, Murray received only 397 votes (5 percent of the total), even though the city had over 8,000 eligible black voters. Citing a mountain of evidence in the form of testimonies and other firsthand accounts, Murray's attorneys appealed his case all the way up to the Congressional House Committee on Elections. Incredibly, the election was overturned, his rival, William Elliott, unseated, and "amid loud applause from the Republican side of the aisle," Murray entered Congress on June 4, 1896—just seven days before the end of the first session.[49]

Throughout his tenure, Murray aligned himself with Populist-oriented colleagues and condemned corporate interests opposed to the "producing and laboring masses," on whose behalf he proudly claimed to speak.[50] "The Black Eagle of Sumpter," as he came to be known, was, however, best known as the leader of the resistance to the Democrats' campaign to legally disfranchise African Americans. Murray's staunch opposition to disfranchisement pitted him directly against the Tillman forces in the mid-1890s and propelled him into the position of principal leader of South Carolina's struggle to protect black voting rights. He introduced and tried to pass legislation guaranteeing federal protection of voting rights and presented several petitions on the floor of Congress calling for a return to a "republican form of government."[51] In February 1895, as the situation grew worse in his state, he took a leave of absence from Congress and returned to South Carolina to help organize the campaign against the rewriting of the state constitution.

Murray spoke out against the injustices of the existing political system: laws designed to have election managers represented by only one party, intimidation of voters at the polls, ballot boxes stuffed or miscounted, and discriminatory registration procedures upheld in the courts. Tillman's political forces passed a temporary registration law to prevent African Americans from voting in a referendum on calling a disfranchisement convention. He then ensured the convention would proceed by having ballot boxes stuffed as well as striking a deal with "upper class" South Carolinians otherwise opposed to him to disfranchise many poor white voters along with African Americans. A new state constitution was quickly proclaimed.[52] Despite Murray's efforts to counter the Tillman forces, state legislators followed the "Mississippi plan" and rewrote the state constitution in 1895, disfranchising virtually the entire black voting population within a few years through the use of poll taxes and the understanding clause (where registrars were permitted to ask voters to "correctly" interpret segments of the Constitution as a requisite for voting).[53]

Tillman would later state: "We have done our level best [to prevent blacks from voting] . . . we have scratched our heads to find out how we could eliminate the last one of them. We stuffed ballot boxes. We shot them. We are not ashamed of it."[54] Murray gave a lengthy rebuke in Congress, declaring: "I know that the Sumners, Logans, Lincolns, Jeffersons, Grants, and Conklings are dead and sleeping beside the liberty of a class of their countrymen in whose behalf they have spoken and labored, but I do not despair. I have no apology to make for the truth, upon whose adamantine walls I am always willing to live or die."[55] Populist-oriented colleagues from the Midwest, including Indiana representative Henry Underwood Johnson, were supportive, arguing to give Murray additional time to address Congress. But time, it seems, had already run out in South Carolina as disfranchisement was set into law.

In other areas of the South where disfranchisement was less advanced, relatively successful black and white coalitions were formed behind the People's Party. In Georgia, the third party threatened Democratic authority in 1892 and 1894. In both of those years, African Americans held official positions in mass county meetings, participated in statewide conventions, and supported white Populist candidates as a way of advancing their own movement.[56] The percentage of votes cast for the People's Party between those two years more than doubled—from

19.17 percent in 1892 to 44.46 percent in 1894. Alongside this, Georgia's black voter turnout nearly doubled in 1892, reaching over 41 percent, from four years prior.[57] Of the nineteen counties that the People's Party captured in 1892, ten had more black residents than white; in the tenth congressional district—the center of Georgia Populism, black and white—nine out of ten counties carried by the third party had a black majority.[58] African Americans would provide the margin of victory for the People's Party in 1892 in several areas of the state, supporting local party candidates in higher numbers than those on the national ticket. In other words, African Americans split their vote in favor of Republicans at the top of the ticket (for president), and People's Party candidates below.[59] Two years later, despite strict enforcement of the poll tax and heightened political violence, 15 percent of African Americans voted for the People's Party, some of whom had been organized through Colored Alliance chapters.[60]

It has been estimated that more African Americans went to the polls in Georgia in the early 1890s than at any other time since Reconstruction, pointing to mobilization of black voters with the rise of the People's Party.[61] African Americans supported the People's Party, despite the fact that it did little to support them: reflecting the interests of yeoman and small planters, and not those of tenants and sharecroppers, the party never objected to the poll tax nor did it ever try to reform the crop lien system.[62] In the midst of this, as Democrats repeatedly demonstrated, they did not hesitate to employ military-style force against African Americans when threatened in Populist strongholds. One measurement of the relative strength of both the People's Party and of the fusion tactic in the South was the ferocity of the Democratic counter-movement to suppress what had become an electoral rebellion. The extent to which Democrats resorted to force and fraud would, in part, reflect the degree to which they felt politically threatened. In 1892, Georgia's Democratic Party organized a series of attacks against the People's Party, their candidates, and supporters. As one white Populist wrote with great alarm in the *People's Party Paper*,

> The leaders of the Democratic party have touched a depth of infamy in this campaign which is almost incredible. They have intimidated the voter, assaulted the voter, murdered the voter. They have bought votes, forced votes, and stolen votes. They have incited lawless men to a frenzy which threatens anarchy. They have organized bands of hoodlums of both high and low degrees to insult our speakers, silence our speakers, rotten-egg our speakers, and put lives in danger.[63]

Such violence was almost always backed by the threat of economic reprisal. African Americans, most of whom either worked for white employers or were tenants on white-owned farms, were threatened with losing certain "privileges" or being fired outright if they did not vote for Democratic candidates.[64] Despite the politically oppressive atmosphere, white People's Party candidates in Georgia in 1892 won 15 seats in the State House (out of 220 total seats) and one in the Senate—small but not insignificant outcomes that were used to further grow the presence of the party in the state over the next two years.[65] Witnessing the growth of the People's Party, black Republicans who had been unwilling to lend their support to the third party in 1892 would change their minds as the 1894 elections approached. They, like increasing numbers of white leaders of the People's Party, had grown to accept fusion as a possibility after adamantly refusing to do so in 1892. However, vocal opposition to fusing with Republicans remained among white Populist leaders; even after the Republican convention refused to nominate its own candidates that year, giving tacit support to Populism, Tom Watson rejected fusion. Watson's refusal suggests the unique role of black independents, who, at least in Georgia, tended to be more open and willing to bridge racial and partisan lines towards advancing the movement.[66] The *People's Party Paper* reported, "Several colored ministers and teachers, who misunderstood the principles and purposes of the people's party ... openly avow they are [now] with the populists."[67] And while most African Americans—62 percent—did not vote in the election, at least some African Americans believed that the People's Party could serve as an effective vehicle against the Democratic Party.[68]

A correspondent for one of the South's leading black newspapers, the *Georgia Baptist*, boldly remarked in late October 1894: "To the colored man the People's Party in Georgia is largely what the Republican Party was to him in this nation thirty years ago." The paper went so far as to add that the independent party had "delivered the colored voter in Georgia from political bondage."[69] African Americans were reported to have participated in People's Party county and state nominating conventions in Georgia, selecting congressional nominees, and then organizing support in the party's open primaries as well as voting for the party's candidates.[70] That the People's Party—despite its unwillingness to counter the poll tax and institute crop lien reforms—held open primaries sent a message of inclusiveness to Georgia's black voters, who were institutionally excluded by the Democrats' closed "white primaries." As E. I. Taylor, a black worker from Wadley, enthusiastically wrote in September 1894, the People's Party had "done more for [African Americans] than anybody else has done ... they have opened their primaries."[71] In May of that year, two dozen Black Populist delegates representing eleven counties attended the Georgia People's Party convention. Although the meeting was itself conducted in a segregated manner, E. V. White, one of the African Americans elected to the party's state executive committee, would introduce a successful resolution asserting that it was "the right of every man, without regard to his race or color, who has qualified under the law to vote, to cast his vote according to the dictates of his judgment, and that it shall be honestly counted when voted."[72]

Black Republican leaders finally lent their support to the People's Party in 1894, helping to bolster (if only slightly) the third-party movement. The Republican state convention that August gave its implicit support to the People's Party by refusing to nominate any of its own candidates for office. Republican delegates declared that the "democratic party of Georgia is unworthy of the support and countenance of the people of this state and should be retired in the interest of good government."[73] Weeks after the convention, black Republican leaders in Pierce County were more forthcoming in their support. "[I]t would be wise to endorse the People's party platform, as this was the first to recognize the Negro and attempt to let him sit on the juror's bench." Moreover, they noted, the People's Party was "the first to condemn lynching, and we feel that for these things alone we should endorse their platform."[74]

Black Populists—unlike most black Republicans—were willing to support the nomination of white candidates by the People's Party in order to leverage electoral strength against the Democratic Party through the votes of white Populists. Democrats were very clear about the threat posed by a black and independent alliance at the ballot box. As a way of creating divisions between black and white Populists, Democrats prodded African Americans to be given a place on the People's Party ticket, knowing that white Populists were unwilling to do so. Eight black delegates attended the People's Party nominating convention in Bullock County. Despite such prodding by Democrats, the black delegation stood by their endorsements of an all-white People's Party ticket.[75] This strategy, as William Gnatz points out, was in marked contrast to lily-white Republicans who may have offered token offices to African Americans in return for their support, but held little promise of mustering white votes—that is, beyond the diminishing number of black votes the party was receiving—to combat the Democrats.

While white Populists may not have regarded African Americans worthy of party nomination or appointment, from the vantage point of Black Populists, the issue (as the Bullock County black representatives demonstrated) was how to best undermine the electoral strength of the Democratic Party—*even if it meant supporting white candidates who were unwilling to support them.* Thus, Black Populists appear to have taken a real politick perspective of why the People's Party merited their support. Some white observers, however, were more optimistic in their assessment of the People's Party. The Reverend W. J. White, editor of the *Georgia Baptist*, wrote in 1894:

> Already the People's Party in Georgia has been a great benefit to the masses of the colored people. This party opened the way to the ballot box for the colored men of Georgia two years ago as it had never been opened before. In many counties colored men went to the ballot box and voted as they pleased

... the first time they had done so in twenty-five years ... It is to the political interest of the colored voter to cast his lot with any party that will recognize his political manhood. The democratic party of the South has never recognized the colored vote except as a purchasable commodity in the market.[76]

African Americans were credited by the Democratic press—which had a vested interest in exaggerating black support for the People's Party to mobilize support against the black and independent alliance—with providing the margin of victory for the People's Party in a number of counties: in Butts County, "Negroes voted solidly for the populist candidate"; in Pike County "Three-fifths of the third party vote [came from] negroes"; in Laurens County "the negroes ... secured a populist victory"; and in Gwinnett County "Negroes ... held the balance of power and voted with the Populists."[77] On October 5, 1894, the *Atlanta Constitution* even announced in a headline, "The Negroes Voted Solidly with the Third Party." Clearly, African Americans did not vote "solidly" for the People's Party—61 percent were recorded as having not voted at all, 23 percent voted for the Democratic Party, and 15 percent voted for the People's Party (while no Republicans ran for office that year).[78] Due to electoral fraud, exact black voter turnout for the People's Party is impossible to verify. Nevertheless, newspaper reports suggest that at least a portion of the black community supported the independent party; whether their votes were legally counted is another issue.

The strong showing among African Americans at the polls led Democrats to intensify their manipulation of the electoral process. Fraud was so rampant in Tom Watson's congressional race in 1894 that his Democratic opponent, James C. C. Black, was eventually compelled to resign his seat and agree to a second election (albeit seven months later). In Richmond County, the Democrat received 14,000 votes—nearly 2,000 more votes than the total number of registered voters.[79] In the tenth congressional district, another Democratic candidate received more than 3,000 votes from a pool of 500 African Americans.[80] The 1894 election also saw new types of fraud, including Democrats paying under-age African Americans to vote their ticket. In Augusta, nearly one-third of all the black voters registered for the election were said to be twenty-one years old—an exceptionally high (and probably false) concentration of young voters.[81] Nonetheless, the People's Party in Georgia fared better in 1894 than it did in 1892, winning forty-one legislative seats in the House and six in the Senate.[82]

African Americans were mobilized to vote for the People's Party through a combination of county organizations divided into "militia districts," local chapters of the Colored Alliance, and Republican Party organizations.[83] For instance, there were reports in both the *Savannah Tribune* and the *People's Party Paper* of "colored committees" organized by the Colored Alliance mobilizing support for the People's Party.[84] Similarly, local black Republican county organizations drew African American support into the People's Party by tapping into their existing political networks. The combination of Colored Alliance and Republican mobilization efforts for the People's Party, while not enough to defeat the Democrats in 1894, indicates Black Populism's strategic development. As the historian Jack Abramowitz put it, the 1894 campaigns "demonstrated the outstanding success of Populist tactics."[85]

Black Populists helped to elect a number of white Populists to the Georgia House and Senate in 1892, 1894, and 1896 (the total membership number in each chamber is contained in the parentheses):[86]

	House	Senate
1892	15 (175)	1 (45)
1894	41 (176)	6 (45)
1896	30 (176)	6 (44)

Georgia Democrats responded to the outpouring of black support for the People's Party in 1894 by enacting a new law. Under the new law, Democrats would control twice the number of seats than any other party sitting on district committees that regulated voter registration. Along with the enforcement of the existing poll tax, which was cumulative, the new registration law ensured virtually full control of the voting process, minimizing the threat of any future challenges by the People's Party or any other potential independent political force. Twenty-five black delegates attended the party's statewide convention in December 1895, and two of these delegates were elected to the state executive committee.[87] But with the election machinery firmly in the hands of Democrats, the People's Party had less chance of winning offices in 1896.

Fraud, undemocratic election laws, intimidation, and violence would make it extremely difficult for Black Populists to sustain voter support in Georgia. Compounding these difficulties, black Republican leaders reversed their support for the People's Party in the 1896 election. They complained that they had gone "un-rewarded" and endorsed the reelection bid of Governor William Y. Atkinson, a Democrat, instead. Not surprisingly, support for the People's Party among African Americans decreased significantly in 1896. There was less than 20 percent overall black voter turnout—a nearly 60 percent reduction from four years earlier; additionally, white Populists lost 11 seats in the state legislature (from 41 to 30, out of 176 total seats in the House).[88]

Political conditions in the South, in terms of political rights and basic civil rights for African Americans, had taken a turn for the worse by the mid-1890s:

the U.S. Supreme Court sanctioned the doctrine of "separate but equal" in *Plessy v. Ferguson*, validating Jim Crow segregation. In 1896, the Supreme Court ruled that Homer Plessy, a resident of New Orleans who was "one-eighth Negro," could be legally forced to ride a segregated black train coach. The ruling provided the legal underpinning for segregation by race across the entire South, a process that was already underway with segregation on railroad cars being legalized in Louisiana in 1890; Alabama, Arkansas, Georgia, North Carolina, Tennessee, and Texas in 1891; and South Carolina in 1892.[89] In 1898, the U.S. Supreme Court accelerated Democratic Party control in the South in its *Williams v. Mississippi* ruling, which stated that poll taxes and literacy tests did not violate the Fifteenth Amendment. Two years later, the North Carolina state legislature passed a law requiring literacy tests for all voters except those whose grandfathers had voted prior to the Civil War. The "grandfather clause" excluded most African Americans.[90] In coming decades, white-ruled South Africa would send delegates to the American South to observe the implementation of Jim Crow as part of setting up their own system of racial segregation, Apartheid ("separateness" in Afrikaans). Meanwhile, political terrorism in the form of lynching continued to escalate in the United States, especially in the South.

At least 2,522 African Americans were known to have been lynched in the United States between 1889 and 1900 (African Americans comprised 78 percent of the 3,224 total number of people lynched in this time period). However, the numbers of actual persons lynched—that is, beyond official reports—was most likely much higher.[91] Lynching, mostly carried out against black men, was most acute in the cotton uplands of the South, where, for instance, 129 African Americans were killed between 1889 and 1894 in 103 separate incidents. Although most lynchings were carried out on individuals, small groups of African Americans were sometimes lynched simultaneously in order to instill even greater terror in the black community (or among those white southerners who may have sympathized with the plight of African Americans). Between 1889 and 1894, the number of black southerners lynched in the cotton uplands was followed by those in the Gulf Plain (95 in 60 incidents), which was followed by the river counties (85 in 63 incidents) and central plateau (83 in 74 incidents).[92]

In addition to the looming possibility among African Americans in the South to become victimized (and almost always without any form of punishment to the perpetrators—some lynchings being advertised *beforehand*), the nation's economic depression, which began in 1893, hit black farmers and agrarian laborers particularly hard. Mounting debt, low wages, and poor crop prices kept most African Americans in a state of chronic poverty. Within this distressing social, political, and economic climate, Black Populists continued to organize opposition to the Democrats. In some states, African Americans fared better in trying to oppose the ruling party, as was the case in North Carolina.

In North Carolina, where a coalition between a relatively strong People's Party and a relatively strong Republican Party made possible a united front against the Democrats, black and white Populists succeeded in taking over the state legislature in 1894—the result of two years of political negotiations between African Americans and white independents. African Americans began working with white Populists during meetings in the spring of 1892. In August of that year the *Progressive Farmer*, a white Alliance newspaper edited by Leonidas L. Polk, indicated that there were black representatives participating in the state convention.[93] As Joe Creech notes, "To the surprise of Republicans and to the consternation of Democrats, blacks gave massive support, especially in the east, to the Populist ticket." He continues, "Because most historians have relied on county rather than precinct returns in assessing Populist voting patterns, they have often overlooked this high level of black support, since resistance to Populism among blacks and other Republicans in urban precincts observed these high levels of rural black support." Black Populism was therefore strong in rural areas. Creech characterizes this Black Populist support as "black Republican support for Populism," which he concludes was "in many cases unanimous [in rural precincts]." But he goes further: "In addition to voting the ticket, blacks sometimes ... took roles in county organizations and in mobilizing black voters. Some counties [even] placed blacks on ballots, and blacks were present at Populist rallies and in local Populist nominating conventions." These were the African Americans who paraded on horseback and mules with Weaver in Raleigh during the fall of 1892.[94] African Americans voted "en masse" for the People's Party in 1892 in the first and second districts of the eastern part of the state, where the majority of black counties were. Black voters in both Hyde and Wilson counties, for instance, gave near unanimous support to the third party ticket. Black Populist support was also strong in townships in Edgecombe, Nash, and Johnston; meanwhile, the western county of Chatham saw equally strong electoral support for the People's Party.[95]

North Carolina's black and independent alliance was further strengthened over the next two years. Marion Butler, the chairman of the North Carolina People's Party would hold a series of meetings with black and white Republican leaders, including the former black congressman Henry P. Cheatham. By July 1894 the terms of fusion—who would run for a particular office on the joint ticket—were largely hammered out. At the heart of the coalition of black and white independents was a shared focus on overturning discriminatory election laws enacted to keep state and county government control in the hands of Democrats. The County Government Act, passed in 1877, for instance, still allowed the state legislature to appoint local judges, who, in turn, appointed county commissioners. As a result, control over local budgets was tightly held by the Democratic machinery.

In the fall of 1894, voters—led by the black and independent alliance—elected a new government.[96]

The alliance of African Americans and white independents in North Carolina had a more realistic chance of succeeding electorally in the state since, unlike most areas of the South, the statewide Democratic vote in North Carolina exceeded the Republican vote by only a small margin. Only in one gubernatorial election since 1876 was the difference between the Republican and Democratic vote more than 20,000 ballots, or 8 percent of the total vote.[97] African Americans could therefore enter into the balance of power with even a small split of voters from the Democratic Party or existing white independents. A combined Republican and People's Party vote, with a joint slate of candidates, could numerically defeat the Democrats. Political divisions among the Democrats in 1893 would make a Republican-Populist fusion even more viable.[98] African Americans had been a critical part of the fusion strategy by virtue of their large numbers in the Republican Party: fully two-thirds of Republicans in North Carolina were African American.[99] In fifteen out of the state's ninety-six counties, African Americans comprised 50 percent or more of the population; fourteen out of fifteen of these black belt counties would support fusion tickets in North Carolina during the mid-1890s.[100] Black Populists, however, had been forced to contend with certain black leaders in the Republican Party—almost exclusively wealthier and more politically established urban leaders—who had opposed fusion in 1894.

The black urban elite, a combination of professionals and businessmen, distinguished themselves as a separate class from black farmers and agrarian laborers. Joseph C. Price, the president of Livingston College, as well as the president of the Afro-American League and the National Equal Rights Convention in 1890, expressed the black elite perspective when he remarked, "There is no social equality among Negroes . . . Culture, moral refinement, and material possession make a difference among colored people as they do among whites." Other voices from the black community—i.e., "Negro Democrats"—included North Carolina educator Dr. Ezekiel Ezra Smith and fellow North Carolinian minister Reverend Garland H. White. Smith, an agent for the American Colonization Society, served as principal of the Fayetteville State Normal School. According to one biographical sketch, Smith "remained a Democrat, even in the face of disfavor." But there were pragmatic reasons for doing so: "The fact that he was a Democrat helped him in at least one respect," notes the sketch. "The [Democratic dominated legislature] favored him and voted for increased appropriations for [his] school."[101] Along this line, Reverend White argued that "the best thing for the colored people to do is to unite with the governing class of white people in this section who are Democrats who we have to depend upon in emergency." What White failed to recognize, or chose to ignore, was that for poor and landless African Americans living in rural areas, "emergency" conditions already prevailed.[102]

Driven by a combination of political defeatism and practical considerations—namely, interest in local patronage, of which the Democratic Party was positioned to deliver—hostility by some black Republican leaders toward Black Populists (who either supported fusion via the Republican Party or supported the People's Party directly) was framed in ideological terms.[103] Occupied with programmatic differences between Populist and Republican platforms, some black Republican leaders were vehement in their opposition to fusion. Nationally, the Republican Party favored the gold standard, a protective tariff, pro-banking legislation, and other legislation partial to the wealthier elements of the business community. In contrast to the Republican Party platform, Populists demands included election reform, the government ownership of railroads, telephone, and telegraph companies, the Alliance subtreasury program, and free and unlimited coinage of silver—policies almost diametrically opposed to the principles of the Republican Party.[104] As one black Republican declared, "Expediency is the only bond of union [between the Populists and Republicans]. I have tried to reconcile it with conscience and principle. I can't do it. Being, as I am, Republican to the core, I can't be a Populist even skin deep." Such sentiments were in marked contrast to the position of Black Populists, who may not have been in ideological agreement with white Populists but focused instead on the need for structural political reforms. Gerald Gaither makes careful note that despite the lure of money or special favors offered to African Americans to vote for Democratic candidates, "[black] voters still supported the Fusionists and their program in their eagerness to overturn somehow the seemingly irresistible Democratic hegemony."[105]

The call for reform would unite "pro-tariff piedmont industrialists, merchants, businessmen, small farmers, and African American laborers," a disparate group.[106] The coalition is reminiscent of black Abolitionists working in the unusual coalitions that culminated in the establishment of the Republican Party—remnants of the Liberty Party, northern Whigs, Know-Nothings, Barnburner Democrats, Free Soilers, and white Abolitionists.[107] From the vantage point of Black Populists, here was an opportunity to leverage power beyond what African Americans could wield on their own against the Democratic machine. As Creech notes, "Blacks, including those in the Colored Alliance, believed an economic level playing field and fair elections were the means to racial uplift ... the Colored Alliance [in North Carolina] appears to have lent its support to the People's Party because of its reform priciples."[108] But African Americans needed to move quickly to seize the moment that brought seemingly antagonistic forces together in opposition to the Democrats. As the historian Craig Thurtell notes, "The challenge to the mechanisms of power [through a Republican-Populist fusion] contained the potential to disrupt the advantages enjoyed by landlords." Taking away such "advantages" from white landlords, which involved both political and economic power, naturally appealed to black tenant farmers and agricultural workers upon whom they depended.[109]

In reaction to the formation of the black and independent alliance, Democrats resorted to their usual array of tactics. Attacks by Democrats, especially against African Americans who made their support for the People's Party known, rose sharply as election day approached. During the election in Anson County, in the southern Piedmont bordering South Carolina, African Americans who tried to register, let alone vote, for the People's Party risked being beaten, or even killed. Congressional testimony by Lewis N. Jones, a forty-two-year-old member of the Anson County Colored Alliance who worked in a mill grinding corn, suggests the kinds of dangers he and others faced. In the case of Jones, a local white merchant struck and then shot him in the leg in broad daylight. Described by his Democratic assailant as "an infernal scoundrel," Jones, not to be intimidated, would later testify in court about the abuses and outright crimes committed against African Americans when they tried to exercise their right to vote.[110]

Black support for fusion in North Carolina, by either voting for the People's Party or the Republican Party, is made clear through further testimony offered in the case of *Martin v. Lockhart* (a case in which white Populist candidate, attorney, and Baptist preacher Charles H. Martin successfully contested the congressional election of Democrat James A. Lockhart in the Sixth District). Forty-six-year-old Elias M. Thompson, a farmer and preacher from Black Swamp, Robeson County, voted for Martin, noting widespread support in his community for fusion; thirty-nine-year-old H. W. Pope from Maxton, also in Robeson County, agreed with Thompson; similarly, twenty-nine-year-old D. L. Maultshy, a black schoolteacher from Lumberton, spoke of support among African Americans for the People's Party candidate. Some African Americans, however, were careful to distinguish themselves from the white Populists, even as they supported Martin; forty-four-year-old Lemuel Simmons of Rockingham emphasized that he was neither "a Populist or Democrat" but did in fact support fusion. Still other African Americans were less concerned about perceived fealty to the Republican Party. Enoch McCallum, of Robeson County, was among these voters, declaring his support for Martin and fusion as a member of the People's Party.[111]

Fusion in 1894 resulted in a stunning statewide victory—especially in light of the systematic attacks on African Americans and their white coalition partners. The victory was soon followed by a spate of electoral reforms passed by the fusionists in office. Such structural political changes had not been seen in the state since Reconstruction. People's Party candidates had won control of the state senate and, together with the Republicans, a majority of the assembly. Three

Populists, three Republicans, and one independent won congressional seats, the latter with the coalition's support.[112] Populists and Republicans consequently held congressional seats in the first, fourth, fifth, sixth, seventh, eighth, and ninth districts.[113] North Carolina's fusion constituency, comprising the poorest elements of the population, black and white, with a hodgepodge of business and industrial allies who viewed Democrats as holding back progress through monopolistic political and economic control, had effectively overthrown the state's Democratic government.

By focusing on their shared interest in political reform, Black Populists in North Carolina had leveraged the votes of African Americans to strengthen the presence of the independent movement, overturn Democratic rule, and help change legislation statewide. Concrete measures were taken in North Carolina's legislature to carry out the Populist call for "Equal rights to all and special privileges to none."[114] Among other changes, the elected Republican-Populist majority revised and simplified election laws, making it easier for African Americans to vote; they restored the popular election of state and county officials, dismantling the appointive system used by Democrats to keep black candidates out of office; and the fusion coalition also reversed discriminatory "stock laws" (that required fencing off land) that made it harder for small farmers to compete against large landowners.[115] The reform of election and county government laws, in particular, undermined planter authority and limited their control of the predominantly black eastern counties.[116] Legislative changes also led to a significant expansion of the African American electorate, which grew statewide over the period of two years from 278,000 to 330,000 (an increase of 18.7 percent).[117]

While legal changes to the electoral process did make available a large number of minor state and county positions to African Americans, they did not immediately lead to a surge in black officeholders.[118] No African Americans were elected to the state senate in 1894; only five were elected to the state assembly. As some scholars have noted, in comparison to North Carolina's legislatures during Reconstruction, which had an average of nineteen African Americans in both houses between 1868 and 1874, the number of African Americans elected to office in 1894 appears minimal. The significance of what Black Populists accomplished with both white Republicans and white Populists through fusion lay instead in the political reforms their government enacted to help further erode Democratic power.

The tactical emphasis by Black Populists on a "free ballot"—in addition to critical issues such as public funding for education, legislation banning the convict-lease system, the criminalization of lynching, the repeal of separate-coach laws, or the requirement that African Americans be represented on juries in cases involving black defendants—reflects the growing political sophistication of the movement. The recognition among black and white Populists that the political process was paramount to necessary changes (the prerequisite for social and economic reforms) had grown out of the experiences of black and white independents engaged in ongoing battle with Democrats. In pointing to the overall trend among independents toward placing greater emphasis on matters regarding the political process, Edward Ayers observes: "The fine points of policy could be worked out later, for the immediate goal was to break the hold of the two major parties on the country's development."[119] Following the election of 1894, the North Carolina People's Party reported that Democrats had stolen over 40,000 votes—underscoring the need for a "free ballot."[120] As M. C. Birmingham conveyed to fellow white Populist Marion Butler in a letter in 1896, "a free ballot and a fair count was yet more to be desired than free silver." Marion Butler, who served as the president of the white National Farmers' Alliance and Industrial Union and was elected to the U.S. Senate through the People's Party in 1895, had helped to effect the successful fusion agreement in North Carolina on the white side of the negotiations (he would soon help to effect the disastrous fusion agreement with the Democratic Party on a national level).[121]

Black Populists in other areas of the South had been among the first to call for an equitable electoral playing field; some expressed their desire to work with whomever and whichever party that could advance this agenda. In March 1891, Reverend John L. Moore, the Florida Colored Alliance leader, declared in a Jacksonville editorial which was reprinted in the *National Economist* newspaper:

> As members of the Colored Farmers' Alliance we avowed that we were going to vote with and for the man or party that will secure for the farmer or the laboring man his just rights and privileges, and in order that he may enjoy them without experiencing a burden. We want protection at the ballot box, so that the laboring man may have an equal showing, and the various labor organizations to secure their just rights, we will join hands with them *irrespective of party* ... I for one have fully decided to work for that party, or those who favor the workingmen, let them belong to the Democratic or Republican, or the People's Party. (emphasis added)[122]

True to form, the Democratic Party resorted to electoral fraud where it could. In Charlotte, North Carolina, the Democrats erased eligible voters from the registration books and removed People's Party ballots from the boxes in which voters had deposited them. Several hundred eligible black voters were arrested by Democratic functionaries prior to the election or were forced to flee for not paying their taxes. Failure to pay the poll tax was made a misdemeanor by Democratic legislators in order to keep as many black and white independent voters from appearing at the polls. In another letter to Butler, and despite the fusion victory of 1894, W. A. Guthrie, a former Republican who ran and then dropped out of the contest on the People's Party ticket for governor in 1896, lamented that North Carolina had still not seen "a fair election in over twenty years."[123]

Black Populists in coalition with white Populists and Republicans saw yet another major electoral victory in 1896. The task was accomplished through a full-scale mobilization of African Americans to vote the Republican-Populist ticket. With 87 percent black voter turnout, 59 percent of African Americans cast their vote on the Republican side of the ticket, while 8 percent cast their vote on the People's Party side (with 20 percent going to the Democrats). White voters, with 85 percent voter turnout, cast only 31 percent on the Republican side and 9 percent on the People's Party side (with 45 percent going to the Democrats).[124] The result shook the Democratic Party establishment, with the fusion ticket capturing a majority of the state legislature that year. Black support for the People's Party was exceptionally high in some districts: according to one report, prior to an agreement to fuse in the sixth congressional district, approximately 80 percent of African Americans had committed themselves to supporting the People's Party (over the Republican Party). Statewide, 59,000 more Republicans—mostly African Americans in the eastern part of the state—voted than had four years earlier.[125]

The growing political participation of African Americans in the state made some white Populists nervous, although the latter benefited at the polls from the presence of the former. One white Populist bemoaned the fact that African Americans were becoming increasingly active in the electoral process, deliberating and "pass[ing] [resolutions] in Negro school houses in the dead hours of night."[126] The statement was reminiscent of the response to black Knights a decade earlier when African Americans began organizing locals in the state. Over the next two years, white voters were whipped into a frenzy by Democratic politicians and newspaper editors desperate to overturn the fusion government. One of the most violent reactions to the rise of African Americans holding local political office centered in Wilmington, the main port city in the eastern part of the state, located at the mouth of Cape Fear River.[127]

In 1897, the Republican-Populist fusion legislature revised Wilmington's charter, giving the new governor, Daniel L. Russell, a white Republican, the authority to appoint five of the city's ten aldermen. Russell, who advocated electoral reform and an end to lynching, used his authority to place dozens of African Americans in minor offices. White Democrats reacted with a vengeance. "Red Shirt companies," like the paramilitary organizations used in South Carolina during Reconstruction to keep black and white Republicans from voting, were revived—this time to destroy the new city government.[128] The campaign was systematic and thorough. South Carolina's Democratic U.S. senator (and former governor) Ben Tillman, who had been present at the Hamburg Massacre in 1876 when Red Shirt companies murdered black Republicans, was even brought in to "consult" on how to remove the independents from office.[129]

The effort to overthrow the duly elected Wilmington government began in early 1897. Democratic politicians and editors launched a campaign against African Americans to incite fear and panic in Wilmington's white population. By the fall of 1898, the stage was set for the Democratic takeover of the government. Jane Conly, a white resident of Wilmington who watched events unfold in the city, noted that black men were "threatened with dire things if they dared vote. A secret committee of twenty-five now began pointing shot guns at helpless Republican heads and requiring them to write letters announcing their intention to vote the Democratic ticket."[130] So bent were the Democrats on winning the election that they forbade the Populists and Republicans to so much as publicly announce their candidates. Not surprisingly, when the election came, the Democrats won by an overwhelming majority. However, winning was apparently not enough; they wanted to assume their "elected" offices right away and not wait for any transition to power—which would have been a matter of weeks. Determined to root out all political opposition, Democrats called for the immediate resignation of every fusionist in office.[131]

Following the election, on November 10, 1898, resentment against fusionists erupted into violence. A small but vocal section of the white population of Wilmington comprised of Democratic Party leaders stirred what quickly grew into a citywide antiblack hysteria. African Americans were physically attacked, beaten, and shot in street fights that left dozens killed. The pretext for the attacks: a recently published editorial written by Alex Manly, a young mulatto editor with a razor-sharp talent for cutting through the myths propagated about African Americans. Mississippi-born Ida B. Wells and other antilynching crusaders had been vigorously protesting the increasingly more common practice of lynching in the South by documenting and publicizing them. In 1895 Wells compiled statistics to counter the claim that lynching of black men was done to protect white womanhood—demonstrating that in 1893 alone fewer than one-third of those lynched were accused of rape or attempted rape.[132]

Wilmington, with a strong black middle class of lawyers, teachers, and public officials, had two black-owned and operated newspapers. On August 18 one of the two papers, the *Daily Record*, had published Manley's editorial, which subsequently became the focal point of the hysteria.[133] Manley, the son of a former white governor of North Carolina and an African American woman, asserted that it was not always clear that poor white women "are any more particular in the matter of clandestine meetings with colored men, than are the white men with colored women." He continued, "Meetings of this kind go on for some time until the woman's infatuation of the man's boldness brings attention to them, and the man is lynched for rape."[134] For white Democrats, Manley's editorial constituted a direct assault on the sanctity of white women and the honor of white men.

At first, little mention was made of the editorial itself. However, as the fall elections drew near, it was reprinted and then widely distributed, not only in Wilmington, but throughout the state—over 300,000 copies were made. As Edward Ayers notes, "Everything about Manley's statement infuriated white men, from its claims that white men were at fault, to the charge that white women secretly longed for black men, to the implication that Manley himself had firsthand knowledge of white women's secret desire."[135] The presumed threat posed by black men to white womanhood, growing out of the changed political dynamics of the city where black and white independents governed, was an effective propaganda piece for white Democrats who argued that it was the direct result of "Negro rule." In an eleventh-hour effort to quell the most reactionary elements in the Democratic Party who threatened violence, a committee of white Democrats resolved to demand that Manley leave Wilmington. The young journalist agreed, fully aware that his life was in danger, but word did not reach the four hundred armed white men (including white working-class men demanding control of certain jobs in the city) who had marched behind some of the city's leading white professionals and businessmen to the *Daily Record* office.[136] Shots were fired in an adjacent street. Most African Americans were blindsided by the attack. The few African Americans who happened to be armed, shot back, but were soon overwhelmed by the white mob. As the fighting poured into residential areas, African Americans found themselves entrapped. Black elected officials, fearing even more bloodshed, agreed to resign from their offices on the spot. The Democrats had regained control.[137]

The return of Redeemer rule to Wilmington and the intense white reaction against African Americans signaled the demise of Black Populism in the state. Regionally, however, there remained a few strongholds of independent black power. East Texas, where the Colored Alliance had been launched in 1886, was one such stronghold—and, as it turns out, the last in the South.

In the summer of 1891 organizers of the Texas People's Party began what became an eight-year crusade against the Democratic Party. The crusade, fought out in a series of battles across the eastern counties of the state, gained a significant following among African Americans. Organizers drew on the membership of the Colored Alliance and tapped African Americans disaffected with the Republican Party as well as those who had been previously affiliated with either the Union Labor or Prohibition parties.[138] From the founding of the People's Party,

African Americans participated in its local meetings and statewide conventions. Colored Alliance speakers addressed People's Party rallies in several counties.[139] And while the party did not fare well at the polls in its opening year, over a dozen counties were reported to have had Black Populist participation by 1894. In some places, African American participation was substantial earlier on. Going into the 1892 election, fully one-third of the delegation from Gonzales County (west of Houston) were African Americans.[140] Organizing black support for the People's Party in 1892 had been complicated by the endorsement of Democratic gubernatorial candidate James Hogg by prominent black Republican leaders who used their influence to sway African Americans not to vote for the third-party's slate of candidates. The situation was similar to the one in Alabama in 1893, when black Republican leaders lent their support to Democrat Reuben Kolb, and in Georgia, three years later, when black Republicans endorsed the Democratic candidate William Atkinson.[141]

The run-up to the 1894 election was marked by the mass mobilizing efforts of John B. Rayner in both black *and* white communities. The *Texas Advance* began publishing his speaking schedule in March of that year; "Rev. J. B. Rayner, colored, our Populist orator," was on the move and word soon spread of the "traveling negro." According to Rayner's biographer, Gregg Cantrell, the Black Populist spoke at a range of venues: barbecues, picnics, political meetings, conventions, county courthouses, local opera houses, as well as in isolated black settlements. From April through June 1894, the "Silver-Tongued Orator" traveled across eastern Texas, setting up Black Populist clubs and helping to consolidate fusion agreements with the Republican Party. One report from a town near Austin read: "The colored people of Elgin turned out [en] masse on last Saturday to hear J. B. Rayner . . . The opera house was filled with white and black and Rayner made many colored Populists by his address. We are growing in numbers and influence." Not only did Rayner organize African Americans and disaffected white Democrats into the party, he also directed white colleagues on how best to reach would-be adherents.[142]

While there are no records to indicate just how many People's Party chapters Rayner established, he was personally credited with bringing an estimated 25,000 African Americans into the ranks of the party.[143] Rayner's skill as an organizer lay in his ability to articulate a political perspective that allayed the fears of white Populists (who were susceptible to being organized around the generation-old rallying cry of "Negro rule") while simultaneously addressing the most immediate concerns of African Americans. His message was clear: "Vote the People's Party ticket; we will get better wages for our work and we will have better times in the South."[144] African Americans were especially drawn to his message about reforming the convict-lease system. The notoriously exploitative system thrived on all-white Democratic-appointed juries and judges sending African Americans into slave-like conditions.[145]

Rayner's organizing pace "preaching the [People's Party] doctrine" was frenetic and apparently relentless. He reportedly made three speeches for every one delivered by his leading white Populist counterparts. Moreover, Rayner often spoke in the face of danger, displaying, as one commentator put it "physical bravery," threatened as he was on a number of occasions.[146] His efforts did not go unnoticed—or unrewarded. On June 19, 1894, Rayner and other Black Populists joined twelve hundred other People's Party delegates in Waco for the party's state convention. At the convention, the popular white Allianceman Harrison "Stump" Ashby introduced Rayner, who in turn addressed the body. By this point Rayner was the most widely recognized African American independent in Texas—the undisputed leader of Black Populism in the state. Rayner's extraordinary recruitment efforts were formally acknowledged by the Texas People's Party, which elected him as a member-at-large of the party's executive committee. Equally important to his joining the fifteen-man board was being named to the party's platform committee. He used the position to sharpen the party's platform regarding issues of concern to African Americans—including the convict-lease system, the lack of "fair elections and an honest count," the need for "an efficient lien law" to protect agrarian workers, and public education.[147]

Educating voters about the electoral process and particular tactics to be used was critical to building black support for the People's Party. Rayner's Black Populist chapters, which he purportedly formed with the help of a "corps of colored assistants," served as venues for political education. William Teague, a Black Populist from Tilmon (in Caldwell County, south of Austin), for instance, noted in the *People's Party Paper* in April 1894 that a large chapter had been organized in his county. According to Teague, African Americans in the chapter were studying and "investigating subjects related to politics."[148] Through this process, Rayner was joined by increasing numbers of African Americans at conventions in 1894 and 1896.[149]

Black Republicans were slow, if even willing, to support the People's Party. After years of opposition, Norris Wright Cuney, one of the most prominent black Republicans in the state and grand master of the black Free Masons of Galveston, finally supported fusion with the People's Party—but only after lily-white Republicans had driven him out of his own party.[150] His argument in favor of fusion in Texas in 1896 echoed the call made by African Americans in other parts of the South over the years: "[T]he combined vote of the two parties was far greater than that of the Democrats." Most black Republican leaders in Texas nevertheless continued to oppose fusion, including William "Gooseneck" McDonald, who reasoned, as did some of his black Republican colleagues from Georgia, that programmatic differences between Republicans and Populists simply rendered a meaningful alliance between the two parties impossible.[151] For his part, Rayner rallied African American support for the People's Party despite such black Republican opposition.

The investment in local political recruitment and training translated into a modest set of victories for the People's Party. While in 1892 the People's Party won only 8 out of 128 seats in the state legislature; two years later, the party nearly tripled its representation by winning 22 seats.[152] By 1896, voter turnout in the governor's race approached 86 percent, with the People's Party and Republican Party fusion ticket receiving 46.5 percent of the total vote. Notably, African Americans voted nearly fifteen percentage points higher than their white counterparts in 1896, with approximately 50 percent of African Americans voting Republican as part of fusion agreements statewide and 3 percent of black voters casting their vote directly for the People's Party.[153] Despite the fusion movement's growth in Texas, members of the People's Party, in conjunction with Republicans, were unable to gain enough seats in the state legislature to effect changes in the law—that is, in the way that their counterparts in North Carolina had been able to do.[154] Changes, however, did take place locally and nowhere more visibly than in Grimes County, east Texas. There, beginning in 1898, a coalition of black and white Populists succeeded in overturning local Redeemer rule. But as in Wilmington, they would be removed from office through force of arms. The historian Lawrence Goodwyn recounts the events surrounding the rise and then violent demise of Black Populism in what was the last stronghold, not only in the state, but the South at large.[155]

In Grimes County, sixty miles north of Houston, where the Colored Alliance had been launched, African Americans in alliance with white Populists, took control of local government. Once in office the black and independent alliance carried out a series of reforms that led to the election of a black district clerk, Jim Kennard, and several black deputy sheriffs appointed by a white Populist sheriff, Garrett Scott. The independent government—headed by Scott and Kennard—became the target of Democratic political reaction. Scott had previously been active in the Greenback Party and was elected sheriff in 1882 through a coalition of Republicans and Greenbackers. The coalition remained intact and in office through the mid-1880s, until, under the banner of white solidarity, the Democratic Party took over.[156] In 1892, with the rise of the People's Party in Texas, the independent coalition in east Texas was organized once again, this time under the leadership of Scott and Kennard. They were joined by Morris Carrington, a school principal, and Jack Haynes—two African Americans described as "staunch advocates of Populism in the black community," along with several other white allies.[157] Together, they would lead the People's Party to victory in Grimes County in 1896 and then again in 1898.

As in other counties where the People's Party had a strong presence, the Democratic press denounced Grimes County as being under "Negro rule."[158] In response, Democrats created a paramilitary organization—in much the same way that Democrats responded to the success of Black Populism in North Carolina by forming Red Shirt companies—to destroy the newly reelected black and independent government of Grimes County.[159] In the spring of 1899, a defeated Democratic candidate for county judge, James G. McDonald Jr., along with several other defeated white Democrats and prominent local white citizens, organized the White Man's Union Association—apparently inspired by a similar organization formed in Wharton County called the Jaybird Association. McDonald had been voted out of office as county judge (a position he had held for four years) by black and independent white voters in 1896. His second defeat two years later was apparently intolerable. He and his fellow Democrats had become determined to restore themselves to government by destroying the coalition; they would do so through sheer terror. The White Man's Union began organizing itself clandestinely but soon began to openly boast its aims, which was not only to unseat the newly elected government through its own slate of candidates but to forcefully remove black voters from the electoral arena.[160]

In the fall of 1899 newspapers began recording increasing numbers of violent incidents in the county and printed warnings of imminent danger to African Americans. Two African Americans had already been lynched in the county earlier in the year; more deadly violence erupted in the coming months. By the spring of 1900, night riders were regularly roaming the county and threatening black voters and their families—telling them to leave the county or face untold consequences. Then in July, only blocks away from the Grimes County courthouse in Anderson, the Black Populist leader Jim Kennard was approached and in broad daylight shot off his horse. His murderer was widely rumored to have been the leader of the White Man's Union, Judge McDonald. Soon another prominent Black Populist, Jack Haynes, was murdered—this time in his cotton field where he was working. Two leading African Americans of the People's Party were now killed, and openly.[161]

Sheriff Scott tried in vain to persuade white farmers to take up arms to protect other possible black targets. African Americans, fearful of what might follow, began fleeing Grimes County. It was reported that scores of people left "by train, by horse and cart, by day and by night." In fact, thousands of African Americans, as well as white Populist allies would forever leave the county. They began doing so before and immediately following the election, which easily saw the White Man's Union's slate of candidates (including Judge McDonald) sweep into office.

The terrorist campaign had succeeded in restoring Democratic rule and eliminating black voters from the electoral process: reportedly, while 4,500 people voted in the county in 1898, the 1900 election saw fewer than half—only about 1,900—go to the polls. In some places, such as Plantersville, north of Anderson, votes for the People's Party dropped from 256 in 1898 down to 5 in 1900 (a 98 percent decrease). Although the Democrats were back in office, it appeared that the terrorist campaign would not stop until Scott was himself either driven out of the county or killed.[162]

Ambushed by a group of heavily armed members of the White Man's Union, the now ousted Scott and his deputies took cover in Anderson's jailhouse, where they came under siege. Outnumbered and after nearly two days of fighting, an exhausted Scott and his men surrendered. With rifles trained on Scott (who was still bleeding, having sustained a bullet wound) the attackers looked on as members of his family carried the former sheriff out of town on a wagon. The black and independent alliance had been crushed. Four days after the battle, a company of light infantry from Houston's Volunteer State Guard marched into the once Black Populist stronghold, greeted by the newly restored Democratic regime.[163]

What began in the early 1890s with the launching of an independent electoral strategy by African Americans to challenge the Southern Democracy ended with the defeat of the movement itself. The opening decade of the new century saw the near complete elimination of African Americans from the electoral arena in the South and the beginning of an extended period of black political retrenchment in the region, but not without attempts at picking up where Black Populists had left off. With few exceptions, the Democrats had proven themselves impervious to the challenges posed by Black Populists and their white allies. In the end, Black Populists were defeated virtually everywhere they had asserted themselves.

Chapter Five

COLLAPSE AND AFTERMATH

Be watchful, stand firm in your faith, be courageous, be strong . . . I urge you to be subject to such men *and to every fellow worker and laborer.*

—I Corinthians 16:13–16, final sermon, Reverend Walter A. Pattillo, Granville County, North Carolina, c. 1908

With the exceptions of North Carolina and east Texas, Black Populists were unable to produce democratic political reforms, greater funding for public education, or a revival of black officeholding. By the summer of 1891, tens of thousands of African Americans across the South were actively participating in local chapters of the Colored Alliance, the People's Party, or other organizations of the movement. Moving beyond its initial focus on agrarian cooperation and economic reform in the 1880s, Black Populists in the 1890s called for reforming the electoral process itself. As Gerald Gaither succinctly notes, "political reform [would need to] precede economic reform."[1] Black Populists and their white allies argued that economic reforms would simply not be affected at the ballot box without engaging the process through which reforms were enacted; Democratic control over the electoral process would have to be dislodged. But how?

The People's Party offered hope. Proclamations of massive black support for the party were largely speculative. Those who offered specific numbers did so propagandistically—but not without reason or basis. At the People's Party national convention in Omaha during the summer of 1892, newspapers reported that some "400,000 blackmen have been enlisted in the organization."[2] That number, like other membership estimates—from the Colored Alliance's claim of 500,000, noted in the spring of 1891, to the 1.2 million figure stated later that year—remain impossible to verify.[3] In place of membership records, we have declarations by spokespersons restated in the press of the day. In the end, because of the necessarily covert and decentralized organizing process of Black Populism, it is likely that scholars will never know the precise number of people who were involved in the movement. What survive in the historical record are the names and some of the details of the most prominent Black Populist leaders: the Walter Pattillos, George Washington Murrays, and John B. Rayners of the movement. The specifics of the lives and political work of the rank and file of the movement, however, can only be indirectly surmised: from the Colored Alliance men on horseback vowing to protect their leader Oliver Cromwell, to those riding alongside Weaver, their candidate; from the men who stood guard at meetings of the Knights of Labor, to the black women holding up their children at People's Party rallies.

Trying to quantify Black Populism is an elusive affair. Attempts at correlating census and voting data yield inconclusive results in determining estimated black participation in the People's Party, for instance, given that unquantifiable factors—namely, varying types of voting fraud—render regression analysis unreliable. From what can be gathered from the historical record, the number of active participants in the movement (those who attended meetings regularly, or later on, voted for particular Black Populist–supported candidates) conservatively reached into the tens of thousands. Hundreds of thousands more black men and women in the South probably agreed with the need and demands made by Black Populists for economic and political reforms but hesitated to demonstrate their support either out of fear of reprisals for their involvement or simply because they did not see the movement as tenable. Ultimately, the actions of Black Populists were circumscribed by the realities of grinding poverty, potential and actual violence, and legal tactics used by Democrats to counter any threat to the Southern Democracy.

The extent to which Black Populism threatened the authority of the Democratic Party may in part be measured by the reaction to the movement.[4] One reaction took the form of southern state legislatures pressing (successfully) for legal disfranchisement. The loss of the ballot was more than just a vote on election day; it meant the loss of the right to hold public office, to sit on juries, and to allocate tax dollars for schools and other services in rural black communities. Democrats pushed for disfranchisement in multiple ways: through local and state election laws, constitutional amendment, or the complete rewriting of constitutions. Mississippi Democrats organized a state constitutional convention in 1890 in which a new constitution was written and passed targeting African Americans, but with the effect of disfranchising both black and white voters. As a result, overall voter turnout in the state was more than halved: from 43.3 percent in 1888 to 18.7 percent in 1892.[5] Accompanying this drop, were the number of African Americans registered to vote in Mississippi, which plummeted from approximately 190,000 in 1890 to 8,615 in 1892—a decrease of 95 percent.[6] Elsewhere in the South, poll taxes were used to disfranchise black voters: in Florida (1889), Tennessee (1890), and Arkansas (1891). However, the "Mississippi Plan" was carried out by Democratic legislatures in South Carolina (1895), Louisiana (1898), Alabama (1901), and Virginia (1902). Finally, state legislatures of North Carolina, Texas, and Georgia disenfranchised African Americans through constitutional amendments—in 1900, 1902, and 1905, respectively.[7]

By the beginning of the twentieth century, virtually every southern state legislature had amended its constitution or enacted municipal or state election laws to disfranchise black voters and legally segregate African Americans in public establishments and services (including street trolleys, restaurants, theaters, and schools). The effect of literacy tests, poll taxes, white primaries, "understanding" and grandfather clauses, and other measures to disqualify black voters from participating in elections was particularly acute in the Lower South. As in Mississippi, Louisiana black voter registration fell dramatically between 1890 and 1900—from 127,923 to 5,320. By contrast, voter registration among the state's white population during these years fell only slightly—from 126,884 in 1890 to 125,437 by 1900. Within the last four years of this period, black voter registration fell 96 percent—from 130,344 to 5,320.[8] While disfranchisement in Mississippi and Louisiana took accelerated form, disfranchisement in South Carolina (in terms of voter turnout) took slightly longer, but was just as thorough: from 96 percent black voter turnout in 1876 to 11 percent in 1896. In all three states, the near complete elimination of black voters from the electoral process was achieved by the turn of the century.[9]

Driving the attack on African American voting rights were the fears of the southern white elite that Black Populism would bring about the kinds of democratic changes enacted during the heyday of Reconstruction. Democratic leaders invoked the specter of "Negro rule" and "social equality" to rally poor whites into joining their fight to suppress African American electoral participation and the coming of a "second Reconstruction." The Republican-Populist victory in North Carolina fueled these fears, as did other challenges to Redeemer rule—as did those made by Black Populists in Georgia and Texas. Using the Democratic Party as their principal vehicle, and relying on paramilitary force (state militias, posses, and vigilante groups) to back their political actions, African Americans were systematically removed from the political process.

Democrats were not the only ones calling for black disfranchisement; by the late 1890s many white Populists, including former Black Populist allies, had joined them. Their logic was simple: as the Democratic Party—by means of fraud, coercion, and manipulation—consistently nullified African Americans' votes, including those that went to the People's Party, it became in the interest of white

Populists to remove black voters from the registration rolls. African Americans were to be deprived of their right to vote (in direct violation of Section 1 of the Fifteenth Amendment to the U.S. Constitution). As one white Republican from Virginia noted ironically: "The remedy [of disfranchisement] suggested here is to punish the man who has been injured [in order] to prevent the Democratic election officials from stealing their votes[!]"[10] Before the close of the century, the twisted logic for black disfranchisement was adopted by, among others, Tom Watson, who had earlier preached that the combination of black and white votes in the People's Party could defeat the Democrats at the polls. With excessive fraud and legal disfranchisement, Watson no longer believed this to be possible, or even desirable, and joined the drive toward the elimination of black voter participation in the South.[11]

Along with Democrats and growing numbers of white Populists calling for black disfranchisement in the late 1890s, there were also white Republicans who sought to remove African Americans from elected office. Integral to the lily-white Republican strategy was the elimination of black Republicans from internal party positions. African Americans, according to this plan, were to be reduced to voters, and nothing more. The long-term aim was apparently to build up a strong enough base of white Republican voters to win national elections, which would eventually translate into political power and patronage at the state level for white Republicans. Republican tickets would necessarily need to be purged of African Americans if lily-whites in the party were to attract support from disaffected white Democrats and new white voters. That the basic civil and political rights of African Americans were of no consideration in the calculations of so many white Populists, underscores why Black Populists had, from the very beginning, organized themselves separately from their white "brethren."[12]

George Washington Murray led the counterattack on black voting rights in South Carolina while African Americans elsewhere tried to petition their state legislatures to counter disfranchisement. Booker T. Washington, who had emerged as the most visible black leader in the nation with the passing of Frederick Douglass in 1895, petitioned the Alabama state legislature for political relief and redress (a lesser known fact about his career, which has been painted as rejecting all political activities). Some African Americans took a more confrontational stance: for instance, a black convention in Birmingham threatened mass migration to states where "the rights of manhood will be respected."[13] But such demands, appeals, and even threats fell on deaf ears. Some African Americans in the North attempted to intervene, but their energies were directed toward condemning black disfranchisement, instead of supporting those in the South—namely, Black Populists—who were attempting to engage the Southern Democracy. As it turns out, few prominent African Americans in the North acknowledged the importance of Black Populism as either a countervailing political force to the Southern Democracy or a movement to stem the rising tide of Jim Crow.[14]

An elderly Frederick Douglass was unwilling to lend his support to the third-party effort. He wrote shortly before his death: "We have a chance of getting a better man from the Republicans than from the Democrats or Populists."[15] A partisan loyalist until the end, Douglass's position remained fixed: the Republican Party was the ship, all else the sea. His biographer Waldo Martin notes that Douglass's "stalwart Republicanism contributed to his failure to explore more carefully and fully alternative political possibilities for his people's struggle, such as the third party insurgency of Populism."[16] Like Douglass, the antilynching crusader and journalist Ida B. Wells-Barnett, who had been forced to flee to the North after her life was threatened in Tennessee, did not lend her support to Black Populism. Black independents in the Midwest, such as George Edwin Taylor, a labor leader and newspaper editor from Wisconsin who would go on to run for president on the National Negro Liberty Party in 1904, would look to his east for black labor allies, not south. A more prominent African American labor leader in the North, however, indicated his support for the People's Party. T. Thomas Fortune, the outspoken leader of the National Afro-American Council, remarked that "none of them [the two major parties] cares a fig for the Afro-American," noting that "another party may rise to finish the uncompleted work [of Reconstruction]."[17] While Fortune initially expressed support for the People's Party, he later changed his mind; generally, he said, he had "no faith in parties"—moving toward a nonpartisan stance.[18] Notably, the People's Party received support from prominent white labor leaders. In 1894, Eugene V. Debs (who would run multiple times as the presidential candidate of the Socialist Party) declared during a Pullman strike meeting: "I am a Populist, and I favor wiping out both old parties so they will never come into power again . . . I want every one of you to go to the polls and vote the people's ticket."[19]

In the early twentieth century the black scholar, journalist, and political activist W. E. B. Du Bois reflected on the independent political movement. He wrote, "The Populist Movement which swept over the West and South . . . was a third party movement of deep significance." The movement's demise, Du Bois lamented, was a consequence of "election frauds of the South." His words, however, came years after Black Populism's rise and fall. This is to say, African Americans in the rural South would largely go at building their movement without the support of northern black leaders.[20]

Left to fend for themselves, many rural southern African Americans looked to escape the hostilities and lack of opportunities in the region and hope for better conditions elsewhere. But unlike the exodus of the late 1870s, which saw a movement largely west, the new one would continue—uninterrupted—for decades to come, and mostly directed to the north. What became a mass outpouring of rural black southerners to northern urban centers would reshape the political, economic, and cultural contours of the North. Soon, the "Great Migration" would usher landmark political developments in the twentieth century: industrial unionism, the New Deal, and a transformation of a largely black Republican electoral base to African Americans becoming a key constituency of the northern Democratic Party.[21]

With the collapse of Black Populism and the reassertion of the Southern Democracy, many African Americans left the South. They did so just as African Americans had done a generation earlier with the collapse of Reconstruction. The second time, however, was on a significantly larger scale. Beginning as a trickle in the 1890s, black migration to the North grew into a steady flow by the first decades of the twentieth century. The Great Migration first saw the movement of African Americans from rural areas to cities in the South; from southern cities African Americans moved north. African Americans, as individuals and families, moved from Atlanta, Birmingham, Memphis, and Norfolk, up to Chicago, Pittsburgh, Cleveland, and Harlem. Between 1880 and 1910, it is estimated that 537,000 black men and women from the South moved to the North.[22]

The advent of World War I accelerated black migration to northern cities with increased demand for labor. Hundreds of thousands of mostly white workers left their jobs to serve in the armed forces. Meanwhile, European immigration into the United States slowed down. The combination brought tens of thousands of African Americans into jobs from which they had been either previously barred from entering or only occupied in small numbers. Adding to the drive northward was a boll weevil infestation of the cotton crop, which destroyed harvests throughout the Black Belt. The infestation created even greater economic hardship for African Americans in the South, prompting further migration. By 1930 it is estimated that an additional 1.5 million African Americans left the South. They entered a range of urban-based work, including industrial labor. The massive demographic shift to the North would help usher in some of the most critical political developments at the twentieth century, including industrial unionism, the New Deal, and the modern civil rights movement.[23]

In the South, the ideal set forth of a "New South"—the development of a manufacturing region mirroring the Northeast—would manifest itself only in a few areas. These areas included Birmingham, with its iron industry, and parts of North Carolina's Piedmont, with its furniture-making factories. By and large, however, the South remained a labor-intensive, low-technology, agricultural region well into the twentieth century. While increasing numbers of African Americans in the South owned land—at least through the first decade of the twentieth century—it tended to be less valued, low-yielding property at considerable distances from railroad stops. By the turn of the century nearly one out of four black southerners owned at least some of the land they worked; this meant that three-quarters of African Americans still did not own land. Black landownership was lowest in the Black Belt—that is, areas of high cotton growth, where African Americans comprised large populations working on antebellum-style plantations.[24]

Despite the growth in black landownership the single largest group of rural African Americans in the South at the turn of the century remained sharecroppers: 670,000 men and women, or 75 percent of the rural black population, with agricultural workers accounting for fewer than 5 percent.[25] The consolidation of the best land into the hands of wealthier white farmers in the early twentieth century, through a combination of inequitable trading practices, financial discrimination, inflated interest rates, and the advent of new mechanization (mechanical reapers and harvesters), along with falling crop prices, would drive tens of thousands more African Americans off the land, abandoning agriculture and migrating out of the region.

Paradoxically, despite the increased migration of African Americans out of the South, large parts of the region, especially rural areas, became overcrowded. The largest families in the nation were southern based, averaging five persons per household. With a 2.1 percent rate of growth, southern population increase was double that of the Northeast.[26] As Edward Ayers notes, "The rural South became caught in a demographic and economic vise. Growing numbers of people tried to make a living on the land, but the crop they grew paid an ever-declining return precisely because so many more people were growing it." He continues, "the average size of Southern farms shrank every year as parents divided old farms for their children and as sons turned to the only alternative to going to town or moving away: starting out as a tenant on someone else's land."[27] While some Black Populists joined the Great Migration in search of economic (and political) opportunities, most—like the majority of African Americans in the South—were forced to accommodate to southern white supremacy, which entailed both economic and political dependency.[28]

A number of Black Populist leaders affiliated with the Colored Alliance, the People's Party, or both were killed during the course of the movement. Oliver Cromwell was murdered by white supremacists in Mississippi in 1889; Ben Patterson was killed by white planters in Arkansas in 1891; and Jim Kennard and Jack Haynes were both murdered by the White Man's Union in Texas in 1899. Dozens of other black leaders, whose names have been lost or remain undiscovered, but whose existence can be inferred from existing records of violence in the region, were also killed; hundreds more—such as local leaders Lewis Jones of North

Carolina's Colored Alliance or Henry Doyle of Georgia's People's Party—were either assaulted or narrowly escaped assassination.[29]

Other Black Populist leaders retreated from the fray before being physically harmed. The details are not clear, but a combination of threats on leaders and their families, financial strain, and other related pressures forced many to retreat. After helping to establish the national People's Party in 1892, Colored Alliance leaders Walter Pattillo of North Carolina, William Warwick of Virginia, and John L. Moore do not appear in records indicating their involvement in the movement. By 1892, Humphrey, the most notable white leader in the movement, had served as the Colored Alliance's chief spokesperson for six years. Like Pattillo and Warwick, Humphrey largely disappears from the record after 1892.[30]

Pattillo, Warwick, Moore, and Humphrey, along with other leaders, continued their work as farmers, educators, and ministers (the three most prominent lines of work among Black Populist leaders).[31] Other African American leaders in the movement migrated—or escaped—to the North to pursue careers in journalism and politics in less hostile environments. After serving as an assistant enrolling clerk for the People's Party in Kansas, Lutie Lytle studied law and became the first woman to teach law in the South. She moved to New York and became a member of the Women's Federation, which advocated women's suffrage. By the 1920s she had become a supporter of Marcus Garvey, the Jamaican-born leader of the Universal Negro Improvement Association and founder of contemporary Black Nationalism.[32]

Most African Americans stayed in the South and attempted to cope with the political and economic conditions of Jim Crow. While Booker T. Washington did not support the People's Party, he may have been speaking indirectly to African Americans who had politically asserted themselves when he stated, "'Cast down your bucket where you are'—cast it down in making friends in every manly way of the people of all races by whom we are surrounded ... In all things that are purely social [black and white southerners] can be as separate as the fingers, yet one as the hand in all things essential to mutual [economic] progress." At least publicly, he cautioned against political activity. He urged accommodation instead and, in particular, self-improvement along the lines of what the Colored Alliance had advocated in its declaration of principles over a decade earlier: "To educate the agricultural classes in the science of economic government in a strictly non-partisan spirit ... To aid its members to become more skillful and efficient workers."[33]

Nevertheless, Booker T. Washington secretly financed several campaigns and legal cases against electoral discrimination. In 1900 he raised money to challenge the constitutionality of a grandfather clause in the new Louisiana state constitution. The constitution allowed illiterate white men to vote if their grandfathers were qualified to vote, yet African Americans were excluded from voting based on the same principal. In 1903 and 1904 Washington also funded the legal challenges *Giles v. Harris* and *Giles v. Teasley* against discriminatory voter registration practices in Alabama. The Supreme Court went on to throw out both *Giles* cases on technicalities. Washington's covert actions speak to the multiple ways in which African Americans in the New South had to negotiate their political environment. They often did so by publicly stating what white southerners wanted to hear, while privately carrying out the work deemed necessary to support African Americans' interests.[34]

John B. Rayner of Texas had come into Black Populism as the movement turned toward the electoral arena. He was active in the People's Party from 1892 through its collapse. Unlike most Black Populists, much is known about his career beyond the movement. After leaving the Texas People's Party, Rayner remained in the South and founded two black vocational schools. He returned to the Republican Party in 1912, wrote newspaper articles, and campaigned against Prohibition (a reversal of his earlier position).[35] While Rayner worked publicly for accommodation—currying favor with the lumber magnate John Henry Kirby, who contributed to his educational projects and occasionally employed him as a labor recruiter—he privately wrote of "the white man's hallucinated idea of his race superiority."[36] Rayner worked in the Texas Law and Order League and became grand master of the United Brothers of Friendship, one of a number of black fraternal orders. Toward the end of his life he wrote editorials pressing for African Americans to serve in the armed forces during World War I. He died of natural causes in his home in Calvert, Texas, in 1918.[37]

South Carolina's George Washington Murray, who had helped to lead the Colored Alliance in the state and worked on behalf of black political interests via the Republican Party, became a successful inventor of agricultural technologies. He received eight patents for his inventions in agricultural implements, including various attachments that could be adapted to a single implement for multiple uses. After serving his terms in Congress where he represented "the toiling and producing millions, who are neither gold bugs nor silver bugs," he moved to Chicago, where he developed a career as a writer and lecturer.[38] Murray—the last African American congressman from South Carolina until the late twentieth century—would also serve as a delegate to several Republican national conventions in the early 1900s. He lived to the age of seventy-three, passing away in 1926.[39]

A number of Black Populist leaders returned to their church base; some pursued divinity school, if they had not yet received such training. Sherman McCrary of South Carolina's Cooperative Workers received a master's degree from Lincoln University's seminary in 1904; he was ordained by the First Colored Baptist

Church in Atlanta before returning to Greer, South Carolina.[40] John S. Jackson of Alabama's Colored Alliance was ordained and joined the Negro Young People's Congress (whose membership included Booker T. Washington). The Georgia People's Party's Henry S. Doyle received a doctor of divinity degree from Ohio Wesleyan University and become pastor of the Colored Methodist Episcopal church, holding important charges in Birmingham, Augusta, and Washington, D.C., and later serving in Shreveport, Louisiana. According to one of Doyle's contemporaries, Channing H. Tobias, "Although the third party movement passed off the scene, Doyle never became reconciled with the Republican Party as a medium through which equal rights for the Negro could be secured . . . the door of the [Democratic Party] was closed against the black man. So Doyle was a partyless man from the time of the dissolution of the Populist movement until he died [in Kerrville, Texas, in 1913]."[41]

W. E. B. Du Bois had taken interest in the rise of the People's Party, and made it part of the subject of his trilogy *The Black Flame*, which was based on interviews and correspondence with members of Doyle's family and friends. In the first book, *The Ordeal of Mansart*, he deals with the role of Doyle in Watson's campaign. Du Bois writes of Doyle's dilemma with the defeat of 1892: "Doyle faded into silence after the campaign of 1892. He had planted the seed. He had given all his strength and risked his life career. His own people distrusted his breach with the Republican Party and his alliance with [disaffected] Democrats and poor whites." When Doyle was pressed by his bishop for his lackluster financial report (having dedicated himself to Black Populism more than the tasks of ministering, including fundraising for his church), the young minister was ordered to Alabama. As Du Bois notes, "Doyle could not rebel. He had a young family. He knew no other work. He bowed his head and went west. Ten years he aroused growing congregations to fervent prayer . . . Then [tuberculosis] crept into his golden voice. Ten more years he fought back its ravages in ever failing effort; until discouraged and forgotten, he died in Texas where the [Colored] Alliance had been born."[42]

Du Bois reached both Tobias, a fellow Black Populist who knew Doyle from attending his church and following his political leadership, as well as Doyle's son, Dr. Bertram W. Doyle, a sociologist trained at the University of Chicago. As it turns out, the younger Doyle taught at Fisk University (where Du Bois had earlier attended). In 1937 Professor Doyle published *The Etiquette of Race Relations in the South: A Study in Social Control*, which was to be long considered the standard treatise on the manners of white supremacy in the South. In the book, Doyle discusses how custom was even more effective than law in controlling social conduct. As he put it, "when in doubt as to what is expected of him, [southern African Americans] will ask what is customary—not what is the law."[43]

Doyle later became a dean at Municipal College in Louisville, Kentucky, and in 1950 was elected bishop of the Christian Methodist Episcopal Church, headquartered in Memphis.[44] As Doyle's trajectory into the mid-twentieth century helps to demonstrate, educational advancement and the church remained central tenets of the black community.

In 1896, after traveling and working around the state Walter Pattillo returned to Granville County, North Carolina, where he was appointed principal of Oxford High School.[45] He also preached at a number of black Baptist churches in the county, including Antioch and First Baptist. In 1906, two years before he died in his home, his alma mater, the Raleigh Theological Institute (Shaw University), honored him for his life's work by awarding him a doctor of divinity degree.[46] Pattillo's son recalled his father's last sermon. It was in the spring of 1908 and Pattillo chose to read the following biblical passage: "Be watchful, stand firm in your faith, be courageous, be strong. Let all that you do be done in love ... I urge you to be subject to such men and to every fellow worker and laborer" (I Corinthians 16:13–16).[47] In choosing this particular passage, Pattillo may have been reflecting on his own experiences during a brief moment when poor black and white people might have come together to make the South anew. His decision to use these particular words might have been his way of paying silent homage to his fellow workers and laborers in their collective crusade while signaling the need for that struggle to carry on in ways that were possible. *A History of the Negro Baptists of North Carolina*, published the same year Pattillo passed away, describes the black minister as "a strong man taken from the ranks, loyal to every interest"—foremost among those interests being those of rural black folk.[48]

If detailed firsthand accounts of Black Populist male leaders remain scant, less still exists on African American women in the movement. Women had been key organizers of the black churches which had been points of departure for the multiple labor unions and farming associations that constituted Black Populism. The particular contributions of black women to Black Populism—whether on their own or in their capacities as the wives, sisters, mothers, or daughters of male participants—remain obscure. Mary Ida (Hart) Pattillo, Winnie A. (Williams) Lowe, Clarissa Rayner, Fannie Munn Shuffer, and other spouses of known Black Populist leaders likely shaped the movement.[49] They may have done so as advisors and confidantes, if not strategists behind the scenes. In a more tangible manner, it is known that African American women were relied upon as financial backers to Black Populist organizations—that is, in addition to being primary sources of support for households.[50] The fact that women constituted such large numbers within the Colored Alliance—at least according to what records exist—suggests not only active participation, but leadership. As one black Baptist male congregant noted of female "officials" in his church, they "exercise an authority, greater in many cases than that of the ministers."[51]

According to Humphrey, women comprised a quarter of the total membership of the Colored Alliance in 1891; many, like their male counterparts, worked as farmers and agrarian laborers. Census records, however, minimize the actual extent of female agrarian labor. Women in rural areas were rarely listed as "farmers" but as "servants" instead. Those who were wage earners had a particularly important role to play in the movement. Many women in the Colored Alliance were tied to the cash economy as rural domestics or petty traders. Their access to cash helped to ensure regular payment of subscriptions and membership dues to the organization that their non-wage-earning male counterparts were often unable to pay.[52] Black women had moreover created their own unions and associations. In the 1880s, laundresses, among others, formed local chapters of the Knight of Labor and were members of other groups that fed the rise of the People's Party. The Women's Christian Temperance Union (WCTU) was part of the coalition of reform groups that founded the national People's Party. Its most prominent black leader, Lucinda Thurman, headed up the WCTU's Department of Colored Workers. Under her leadership the number of southern black chapters, known as the "Thurman union," grew substantially; Texas alone had at least fifteen WCTU chapters and a statewide organization. (Thurman left the organization in 1908 to become president of the National Association of Colored Women.) Finally, as various People's parties were formed across the South, black women both attended and helped to organize rallies for the new "negro party."[53]

The apparent lack of women's involvement in certain types of protest actions points to another set of issues. Black women were, on record, less involved than their male counterparts in strikes and demonstrations involving violence. While women led or participated in boycotts that ultimately did include violence (for instance, during the Leflore County boycott, or earlier still, as Tera Hunter notes of Atlanta's washer women—the "Washing Amazons," led by the "ebony hued damsels" Sarah Collier and Matilda Crawford, among others), they appear to have been less willing than men to engage in direct confrontation with employers or landlords. It seems that the risks and repercussions of such confrontational engagements to families, especially children, weighed more heavily among women than among their male counterparts. But added to this, as Hunter notes, "strikers in Atlanta [also] showed little attachment to prevailing middle-class conventions of femininity." She continues, "As they did on other occasions, working-class women used street fights to settle disputes that jeopardized their unity and engaged in militant resistance." The question among black women, as was the case for black men, was the value of such tactics.[54]

With the coming of Jim Crow, black women assumed new roles, some of which gave them greater voices relative to black men in dealing with white authority. The historian Evelyn Brooks Higginbotham argues that as southern black men were increasingly excluded from official arenas of politics in the 1890s, black women began to serve as "ambassadors" to white society. Not to be overstated—and not as prevalent in rural areas as in urban centers—in certain key respects, black women assumed greater political responsibilities in the closing decade of the century in negotiating the shifting terrain of "race-relations." For their part, white Populist women had been active in their own movement: white Alliance women, for instance, debated the question of female suffrage. A survey of letters published in the Texas-based *Southern Mercury* between 1888 and 1889 indicated that up to 15 percent of (presumably white) women who wrote letters focused on their right to vote. As the historian Marion Barthelme points out, the act of writing about suffrage in a public forum may have represented "the first articulation of feminist consciousness for many rural women."[55] While no such surveys of rural black women exists, given the increasingly marginalized political status of African Americans, the subject of suffrage was undoubtedly of concern and a source of discussion among black women.

The new gender dynamics of the 1890s also enhanced black women's existing involvement in community mobilization through the black churches. African American women had initially come to assume this role during the antebellum era in the antislavery crusades of that period. Free black women helped to gather abolitionist petitions and organized boycotts of slave-made goods; following the war (and joined by newly emancipated black women) their political role continued in the spreading of Union Leagues–Republican Party chapters.[56] Following the collapse of Black Populism, black women became active in both antilynching campaigns, most famously, the one led by Ida B. Wells-Barnett, followed by the National Association for the Advancement of Colored People's campaigning, and the women's suffrage movement. Lutie Lytle had longed to use her legal expertise to help African Americans gain justice, but was unable to find work as an attorney in the South. In her reading, "The anchor of [African Americans] is grounded in the constitution . . . It is the certificate of our liberty and our equality before the law." She planed on giving public lectures in the South in order to "improve [the] condition [of black men and women] as citizens."[57] Her plans changed, however, as she was excluded from practicing law. She and her husband, a minister of the AME church, moved to New York where she advocated women's right to vote through local pro-suffrage groups.[58]

Lytle served one year on Central Tennessee University's law faculty in Nashville before deciding to leave for upstate New York. By 1910 she had moved to Brooklyn where she remarried—to a lawyer this time. She became the first female member of the National Bar Association, the organization of black attorneys. Lytle did not return to Topeka until 1925. Upon her return she addressed a packed audience at St. John's AME Church, the church she had attended in her youth. Lytle spoke about her political history and the limits of the legal profession; she discussed the work of Marcus Garvey and his Universal Negro Improvement Association (UNIA), as well as the advent of the Harlem Renaissance.[59]

While Lytle had been an ardent supporter of women's suffrage, African American women had a particularly difficult time promoting the cause in the South. Southern white women's suffrage leaders argued for a new solution to the "Negro problem." As they saw it, the solution to black men's vote being the deciding (and therefore unacceptable) factor in elections was to enfranchise white women—but to exclude black women.[60] Kate Gordon expressed this view to the *New Orleans Times Picayune* in 1901. A white leader of the women's suffrage movement in Louisiana, Gordon served on the national board of the National American Woman Suffrage Association. As she put it, "[The] question of white supremacy is one that will only be decided by giving the right of the ballot to the educated intelligent white women of the South ... Their vote will eliminate the question of the negro vote in politics, and it will be a glad, free day for the South when the ballot is placed in the hands of its intelligent, cultured, pure and noble womanhood ... The South, true to its traditions, will trust its women, and thus placing in their hands the balance of power, the negro as a disturbing element in politics will disappear."[61]

While black men—the "disturbing element in politics"—were increasingly denied the vote in the South, black women were excluded from the women's suffrage movement. Adella Hunt Logan of Alabama, the daughter of a black/Creek Indian and a wealthy white planter, was not allowed to attend regional white-run women's suffrage conferences—despite being better educated than most of her white counterparts, having even received a master's degree from Atlanta University. Despite her exclusion, Logan, a lifelong member of the National American Woman Suffrage Association, led discussions on women's suffrage at the Tuskegee Institute's Women's Club and published several articles on women's suffrage, including in the *Woman's Journal* and Du Bois's *Crisis* magazine. Her frustration with racism and sexism led to deepening depression; in 1915 she committed suicide.[62]

Ongoing hostility toward African Americans was maddening on a host of levels; it was also dangerous for many black women to the point of being life threatening. Ida B. Wells-Barnett had escaped the South with her life intact; Lutie Lytle left the region under far less pressing conditions than Wells. But for African American women who remained in the South for financial or family reasons, Jim Crow often had grave consequences, as Adela Logan's life attests—despite her being relatively privileged in comparison to most black women. As Higginbotham concludes, "Once black men were denied the suffrage, black women became ever more powerless and vulnerable to southern racial hostility."[63]

Despite southern black women gaining leverage relative to black men as the latter were stripped of their vote at the close of the nineteenth century, all African Americans were further repressed under Jim Crow. Early death due to grinding poverty did not spare the vast majority of black people in the South (as well as hundreds of thousands of poor white southerners). Being of a certain class, race, or gender were among the leading determining factors in one's life expectancy—and the quality of one's life. Disproportionately high infant mortality and reduced life expectancy among southern African Americans was common, to be expected, and the result of material hardships carried from one generation to the next. As Black Populists had been keenly aware, these were political matters, as much as they were economic. They were also matters that would not be easily alleviated, let alone resolved, in their time.[64]

Throughout the first half of the twentieth century, African Americans continued to challenge the Southern Democracy by organizing themselves into various political parties, associations, and labor unions. They did so through a range of organizations: the International Workers Party (IWW), the Socialist Party, the UNIA, and black farmer and sharecropper unions. In the decade following Black Populism, the IWW organized black waterfront and timber workers in Louisiana and east Texas.[65] African Americans had also joined the ranks of the Socialist Party in the South. By 1913, African Americans were members of the third party in Florida, Georgia, Kentucky, Louisiana, Mississippi, Oklahoma, and Tennessee.[66] However, the numbers of black members in the Socialist Party remained small compared to those who joined the UNIA's southern divisions. Of the four hundred UNIA divisions in the South during the late 1910s and early 1920s, over 80 percent came from rural areas. As the historian Steven Hahn notes, "Louisiana ranked first with seventy-five divisions, followed by North Carolina (61), Mississippi (56), Virginia (43), Arkansas (42), Georgia (35), Florida (30), South Carolina (25), and Alabama (14)."[67] African Americans in the South would also reconstitute themselves into agrarian labor unions in the 1930s—notably, the Southern Tenant Farmers' Union, the Louisiana Farmers' Union, and the Communist-led Alabama Sharecroppers' Union.[68] The Sharecroppers' Union carried on the work of the Cotton Pickers' League, which had broken off from the Colored Alliance, to carry out the strike of 1891. Some forty-three years later, during the fall of 1934, nearly one thousand members of the Sharecroppers' Union struck for the same one dollar per hundred pounds picked that had been the goal of the Black Populists—but won.[69]

One of the few southern black agrarian organizations that started in the Black Populist era and continued into the twentieth century was Robert Lloyd

Smith's Farmers' Improvement Society. Smith had been a classmate of South Carolina's Colored Alliance leader George Washington Murray before moving west in the early 1880s. In 1890 Smith founded the Farmers' Improvement Society in Texas, which mirrored the Colored Alliance's demands and practices of "self-improvement," the building of cooperative businesses, and efforts to accumulate land in order to improve the lives of black farmers. As Smith put it, there would be a "second emancipation" with "economic improvement through communal effort." According to the historian Debra A. Reid, by 1891 Smith advocated a "politicized agenda," specifically, to abolish the credit system. By raising foodstuffs at home and purchasing cooperatively, Smith believed black farmers could circumvent the Texas lien law. Reid notes that Smith "recognized the significant third party challenge brewing in the form of the Colored Farmers' Alliance ... and the involvement of African Americans in the People's Party." Smith, however, remained a Republican.[71] Like Murray, Smith pursued, and won, public office as a Republican (Smith served in the Texas state legislature during the mid-1890s).

By 1909 the Farmers' Improvement Society claimed 21,000 members across Texas and had begun organizing in Oklahoma and Arkansas.[72] Smith's perspective of "uplifting the race" along the lines of the Colored Alliance, and later the Tuskegee Institute, was seemingly in contrast to the "militant" demands of northern black leaders and their organizations at the beginning of the new century (such as T. Thomas Fortune's National Afro-American Council). But as the historian Winston James has observed, the mere existence of independent black organizations in the South posed a threat to southern white authority. As the Colored Alliance had demonstrated in the early 1890s, independent black organizations could mobilize African Americans in the electoral arena. From the vantage point of the Southern Democracy, boycotts and strikes led by the Colored Alliance threatened profits, but they could be and were suppressed relatively quickly. The political mobilization of African Americans in alliance with white independents posed a much larger threat.[73]

Because of the threat of a more empowered black electorate in the South, especially in alliance with white independents, the Southern Democracy extended Jim Crow into virtually every aspect of southern life. Beyond African Americans and many poor white southerners being stripped of their vote, not only would public schools and trolleys be segregated, but restrooms, drinking fountains, and even the playing of cards fell under Jim Crow. As the historians Jane Dailey, Glenda Gilmore, and Bryant Simon note, "Jim Crow was not the logical and inevitable culmination of civil war and emancipation, but rather the result of a calculated campaign by white elites to circumscribe all possibility of African American political, economic, and social power."[74] In this way, Jim Crow was a divide-and-conquer strategy to further marginalize African Americans and, in the process, ensure that black and white southerners would not form alliances that could threaten Democratic rule.

It has been either explicitly argued or suggested that Black Populism had helped to bring about Jim Crow.[75] As August Meier phrased it, "in many states constitutional disfranchisement was an aftermath of the agrarian revolt."[76] This is true, insofar as historical causality can be claimed. But it is equally true that Black Populism lay the groundwork for progressive changes in the century that followed. Black Populists, along with their white Populist counterparts, were among the first to advocate on behalf of key economic and political reforms that eventually came to pass. These reforms included regulatory measures against transportation monopolies (the Hepburn Act of 1906 gave the Interstate Commerce Commission greater power to regulate railroads, keeping costs down for small farmers), the Sixteenth and Seventeenth Amendments to the U.S. Constitution (which required the direct election of U.S. senators and a progressive personal income tax, both passed in 1913), federal subsidies for farmers (albeit not until the 1930s through the Farm Securities Administration—although it favored more affluent farmers), and the reinstatement of civil and political rights for African Americans in the South (with the Civil Rights Act of 1964 and the Voting Rights Act of 1965—the principal having been laid in the defeated Lodge Bill of 1891).[77]

Whether through covert organizing or through public efforts, African Americans would continue to pursue independent political action during the first half of the twentieth century—finding, as noted by the historian Robin Kelley, "creative ways to resist and survive the South."[78] Ultimately, it took three generations and a new movement for civil and political rights—the fulfillment of a "Second Reconstruction"—for African Americans to overthrow Jim Crow.[79] As it turns out, a number of the descendents of Black Populist leaders had participated in the civil rights movement of the twentieth century, including Henry S. Doyle's son (Bertram W. Doyle), Jacob J. Shuffer's grandson (George Macon Shuffer Jr.), John B. Rayner's great-grandson (Ahmed A. "Sammy" Rayner Jr.), Walter A. Pattillo's great-grandson (Walter H. Pattillo Jr.), Oliver Cromwell's great-great-granddaughter (Barbara Jeanne Williams), and a distant relative of George Washington Murray (James E. Clyburn). Each had participated in their own way, and at different points—some had done so as scholars (Doyle and Pattillo), in the armed services and as political leaders (Shuffer and Rayner), or as young foot soldiers in the movement (Williams and Clyburn).[80]

Opposing images of Black Populists suggest the very different ways in which they were viewed and understood by their contemporaries—the "sleek, oily, negro" (Pattillo) and the "notoriously bad negro" (Cromwell), lay in sharp contrast with the "black eagle" (Murray) and the "silver-tongued orator of the colored race"

(Rayner). But whether in east Texas's countryside or South Carolina's Low Country, those who organized strikes for higher wages on Louisiana's sugarcane fields or on Arkansas's cotton fields, those who fought with fatal consequences for their economic independence in Leflore, Mississippi, or demonstrated their political independence on the streets of Raleigh, North Carolina, formed part of a broad and vibrant movement of African Americans. Linked by shared circumstances, Black Populists organized their responses to the conditions in which they operated in a multitude of ways; their actions were neither isolated nor anomalous. Rather, they were the manifestations of a regionwide movement which is called here Black Populism in the New South.

Epilogue

So long as we confine our conception of *the political* to activity that is openly declared we are driven to conclude that subordinate groups essentially lack a political life or that what political life they do have is restricted to those exceptional moments of popular explosion. To do so is to miss the immense political terrain that lies between quiescence and revolt.

—James C. Scott, *Domination and the Arts of Resistance*

A century after Black Populists in Raleigh paraded alongside their presidential candidate James B. Weaver in a display of political power, over half a million African Americans cast their ballots for another independent presidential candidate, H. Ross Perot. The Texas billionaire had apparently decided he had had enough of the bipartisan establishment and called upon voters to "turn the government back to the people and take it away from the special interests [i.e., the two major parties]."[1] In all, nearly 20 million voters (approximately 20 percent of the total electorate) came out to the polls in 1992 and cast their vote for Perot, making it the largest electoral outpouring for either an independent or third-party candidate in the nation's history.[2] As in 1892, African Americans were part of the political rebellion.

Challenging the two major parties has been an ongoing, albeit lesser-known feature of black politics since the formation of the Liberty Party in 1840. Frederick Douglass along with black leaders Samuel Ringgold Ward and Henry Highland Garnet stumped on behalf of the pro-abolitionist third party before turning to the Republican Party to advance the antislavery cause. African Americans—largely Republican following the Civil War and then largely Democrat following the modern civil rights movement—have variously used independent politics to advance their interests. As the political scientist Michael Dawson has noted, "Blacks have tended to be loyal to the two major parties. However, specific circumstances have led to active African-American support for third parties. When the two major parties reject African Americans' political goal of inclusion, African Americans seek other political allies."[3]

Epilogue

In the late 1950s and 1960s, the great-grandson of Texas Black Populist John B. Rayner, Ahmed A. "Sammy" Rayner Jr., a Tuskegee airman, carried on the tradition of independent politics. Following the war, Sammy began building an independent black base of support on Chicago's South Side; in 1967 he captured a city council seat. In doing so, he defeated the city's Democratic Party machine, then under the control of Mayor Richard Daley. As the former Student Nonviolent Coordinating Committee leader Stokely Carmichael and the political scientist Charles V. Hamilton described in their book *Black Power*, "In the Sixth Ward, an independent black candidate, Sammy Rayner, defeated an incumbent, machine-backed candidate . . . His victory will begin to establish the habit of saying 'No' to the downtown bosses. In the same way that the black Southerner had to assert himself and say 'No' to those who did not want him to register to vote, now the Northern black voter must begin to defy those who would control his vote."[4]

Sammy's father had moved to Chicago as part of the Great Migration in the 1910s. As was the case in the South, much of the black electorate in the North remained disempowered throughout this period; both Democratic and Republican party machines ruled the cities, dividing territories and populations. After years of saving up and learning the business of funeral homes, the elder Rayner started his own business—the A. A. Rayner & Sons Funeral Home. When Sammy returned from the war, he was among the many black veterans who decried the contradictions of fighting for freedom and democracy overseas while living with the restrictions of segregation and disfranchisement at home. The Rayner family and its business had meanwhile become an important part of Chicago's African American community. As it turns out, the family found itself at the heart of what became a galvanizing event for African Americans across the nation: the lynching of young Emmet Till in 1955. The Rayner family was sought out by Chicago resident Mamie Till, whose son had been killed while visiting family in Mississippi. Mrs. Till insisted on displaying her son's body in an open casket to show the world the horrors of lynching. Like others of his generation, Sammy became politically active.

Years of grassroots organizing went by before Sammy won office. He did so as an independent in 1967 and then quickly joined other African Americans in pursuing a national independent political strategy. Serving on the steering committee of the National Conference for a New Politics, Sammy was among those who tried to recruit Dr. Martin Luther King Jr. to run for president of the United States as an independent. While unsuccessful in that effort, Sammy's independent base-building road to victory served as a model for future independent black political efforts in the post–civil rights era. One person who picked up on this strategy was a young Harvard Law School graduate. In the early 1990s Barack Obama would work in some of the same Chicago communities in which Sammy had worked, building a new independent base of support. Like the legendary Black Populist John B. Rayner and his vocal independent great-grandson, Obama would, in his own way, challenge the Democratic establishment—in his case, rising to the U.S. Senate before making his bid for the nation's highest office as an insurgent candidate.[5]

Obama's stunning 2008 presidential victory grew out of a nationwide movement for political reform. A critical factor in Obama's win was the formation of on-the-ground black and independent alliances that had been in the making since 1988—years before either Obama or Perot had entered the political arena.[6] By the mid-1980s the vision held by some in the African American community to create a national all-black political party, an idea proposed in 1972 at the National Black Political Convention in Gary, Indiana, which Sammy Rayner Jr. had attended with some two thousand other delegates, had effectively run its course.[7] However, the *de facto* strategy coming out of the Gary convention had been to elect more African Americans to office via the Democratic Party. Over the next twenty years thousands of African Americans were elected as Democrats across the country (in 1972 there were 2,264 black elected officials, by 1992 that number had grown to 7,552).[8] Among these elected officials was a distant relative of South Carolina Colored Alliance lecturer George Washington Murray, James E. Clyburn.

Murray had been the last African American from the state to serve in Congress—that is, until Clyburn, who in 1992 became the first African American since his relative to represent South Carolina in Congress. Clyburn had been a foot soldier in the civil rights movement—a key witness in a 1960 Orangeburg civil disobedience case. And like many of his generation, Clyburn joined the progressive wing of the Democratic Party and steadily rose through its ranks. Like Murray, he had been tied to South Carolina's black farming community, serving as executive director of the state Commission for Farm Workers.[9]

Other Black Populist descendents were active in the civil rights movement and in the discussions over strategies for black political empowerment. Barbara Jeanne Williams, the great-great-granddaughter of Mississippi Colored Alliance leader Oliver Cromwell, disagreed with the Democratic strategy coming out of the Gary convention. She was among the mostly younger voices at the national convention that advocated the formation of a multiracial third party (as opposed to an all-black party or staying with the Democrats). For many black political activists in the 1970s and then into 1980s, the question was what kinds of alliances could be built to advance the interests of African Americans that did not rely on the Democratic Party. Dr. Lenora Fulani, a black psychologist and community organizer, urged a multiracial "Two Roads are Better than One" approach; in 1988 she asked voters to support Reverend Jesse Jackson, who was running for president as an insurgent Democrat, but in the likely event that he did not win the party's nomination, that voters support her as an independent candidate.[10] While she received a modest one-quarter of a million votes that year, having become both the first woman and the first African American to appear on the ballot in all fifty states, her little-known run for president helped to establish the fact that there indeed existed a base of black (and other) support for independent politics. A survey by the University of Michigan's Institute for Social Research in 1988 found that upwards of two-thirds of those who had supported Jackson in the primaries would have voted for him as an independent had he decided to run as such. He did not, but four years later the two major parties were challenged by a new voter revolt—one that took much of the nation by surprise.[11]

As it turns out, when Perot launched his presidential campaign in 1992, his attorneys sought counsel from Fulani's in order to learn how to navigate the complicated and restrictive ballot access laws that overwhelmingly favor the two major parties' candidates (for instance, independent and third-party candidates for president need to gather over twenty times the number of signatures than do the two major party candidates to get on the ballot in all fifty states). Not even a white billionaire like Perot could circumvent the rules. Fulani, meanwhile, had already entered the race in 1992, seeking new alliances that could take African Americans in more independent directions. But with Perot's announcement, and the extraordinary resources he could bring to bear in projecting the need for Americans to break free of bipartisan politics (through paid advertising and other publicity), Fulani called on voters to support either herself *or* Perot (an explosive proposition in black and progressive circles given Perot's conservatism on matters of race, women, and labor). Fulani, however, lent her support as a way of building what was ostensibly becoming an independent political movement for reform—one which spanned much of the ideological spectrum, bringing hundreds of thousands, indeed millions of progressives, liberals, and conservatives together under the same banner of "independent." Apparently, such a range of independents could only agree on one thing: the need to reform the existing electoral system so that more voices could be heard—a question of democracy that harkened back to the Black Populists, whose tactics also included different and often contradictory ideological elements in the alliances they formed.[12]

Fulani's support for Perot was reminiscent of Black Populists in another way: African Americans were willing to support white Populist candidates even when the latter did not seek their support—at least, not publicly. While the meeting between Perot's attorneys and Fulani's was done privately, the coming together of his and her networks was notoriously public. It was affected via the national Reform Party, with a variety of local manifestations. A Black Reformers Network was formed in 1995 under Fulani's leadership which linked independent black leaders from around the country, and across the political spectrum, including Harlem physician Dr. Jessie Fields, Reverend Lawrence Anderson of Ohio, Drake Beadle of Illinois's Harold Washington Party, Philadelphia NAACP vice president Juanita Norwood, Maryland labor attorney Diane Williams, and business owner Wayne Griffin of South Carolina. Meanwhile, other independent-minded black leaders were calling for renewed action. In October 1995 the Nation of Islam's Minister Louis Farrakhan stated at the Million Man March he had spearheaded that what was required was "not necessarily a third party, but a third force." The unprecedented gathering in Washington, D.C., brought together the largest number of African Americans to the nation's capital.[13] African Americans, it seemed, were looking for new options at the close of the twentieth century. One road, among a number pursued (from ongoing efforts at black labor unionism to cultural forms of political expression—that is, as part of the "range of black working-class responses as strategies born of specific contexts," as Robin Kelley describes), was independent politics.[14]

An independent movement had emerged out of the "Perot phenomenon" that struggled to give expression in the 1990s to various calls for political reform.[15] State affiliates of the Reform Party pushed for political reforms that included term limits, ballot access and campaign finance reforms, same-day voter registration, and nonpartisan elections; the party even saw some of its candidates win office. In 1998 South Carolina Black Reformer Wayne Griffin won a city council seat against an eight-year Democratic incumbent; meanwhile, Jesse "The Body" Ventura, a former U.S. Marine and television celebrity, won the governorship of Minnesota. Hundreds of party activists ran for office. Partisan politics and ideological purity, however, dominated electoral organizing—and not just major party politics. Both the leadership of the Green and Libertarian parties, the two largest third parties in the nation, besides Reform, for instance, consistently refused to join together against the two major parties, despite common grievances against bipartisan control of the electoral process. It turns out partisanship *within* the national Reform Party (which was made of up a number of competing ideological strains) ultimately proved its undoing.

Factional fights erupted at the 2000 Reform Party presidential nomination in Long Beach, California, which saw Black Reformers and their allies attempt to counter the takeover of the party by conservative political commentator and former Republican presidential candidate, Patrick Buchanan. In a highly controversial move, Fulani (whose significant following within Reform was reflected by having received 45 percent of the vote for vice chair of the national party in 1999) had earlier supported Buchanan's nomination as the Reform Party candidate. However, her support came on the condition that Buchanan would advocate for political reform measures, not his personal conservative social agenda; when he broke his promise, she rallied her supporters to oppose him. In the end, Reform's national effort to bring together a black and independent alliance—not unlike the People's Party a century before—could not be sustained. Partisanship ruled the day. Locally, however, new possibilities presented themselves from years of independent base-building (creating organization, educating voters, and running candidates).[16]

One of the former Reform Party affiliates, the Independence Party of New York, had been building an unusual coalition that brought together African Americans, white, and Latino independents from across the ideological spectrum. The self-styled "anti-party party" was formed in the wake of the 1992 presidential election, and focused almost exclusively on issues of political reform, as opposed to traditional platform planks as seen by the major parties and most other third parties.[17] Over the course of the 1990s, the party grew to become the third largest in New York and soon caused the first of a series of potent challenges to Democratic-rule in New York City. In 2001 the party ran Michael Bloomberg, a media mogul who had formerly been a Democrat but switched his registration to Republican to gain that party's line in a fusion bid with the Independence Party. The Independence-Republican fusion won him the mayoralty. Four years later, running again in a fusion campaign, Bloomberg received upwards of 47 percent of the black vote. African Americans were breaking ranks from the Democratic Party in ways that signaled a political shift in the city. As John Avlon of the *New York Sun* wrote in the fall of 2005, "Something is happening in the African-American community . . . the diversification of the black community economically and politically is changing the landscape. One recent sign of this is the surprising amount of support for Mayor Bloomberg among African-American voters."[18]

Networks of black and white independents in New York and across the nation continued to build support for a political break from the two major parties. Most of those efforts did not take the form of party politics per se, but were focused on bringing together independents into associations of voters that could assert demands for political reform in nonpartisan ways. Such efforts bore fruit during the 2008 presidential election. Black and independent alliances appeared in over two dozen states with open primaries (where one can vote in a party's primary without being registered in that party). These on-the-ground coalitions of mostly black Democrats and white independents would provide the then junior senator from Illinois with his critical margins of victory over the presumed Democratic nominee Senator Hillary Clinton; Obama would go on to defeat his Republican rival, Senator John McCain, becoming the nation's first African American president.

New York Magazine would dub Obama the nation's first "Independent president." It was a description befitting of his unique path to the presidency, having been the outsider, first defeating the Democratic Party establishment candidate, and then winning the general election with the support of black and independent voters.[19] Among independents, Obama received an eight-point margin of victory over McCain; meanwhile, upwards of 98 percent of all black voters voted for him. Some 19.3 million independent voters cast their ballots for Obama, nearly the size of Perot's vote in 1992. The combined votes of African Americans and white independents, moreover, brought him victory in hotly contested battleground states, including Ohio, Pennsylvania, Florida, and Indiana.[20]

For Black Populists in the 1890s, the issue had been how to best use white independents to break up the monopoly of the Democratic Party; in the 1990s, African Americans similarly leveraged support among white independents to challenge the bipartisan establishment.[21] Today, African Americans continue to pursue independent politics, as do former white Perot activists, individual third-party members (including those in the Green, Natural Law, Independence, and Libertarian parties), and voters who choose not to identify with *any* party but may be affiliated with any one of a number of independent voters' associations. African Americans are among a number of such independent associations, including the Georgia Committee of Independent Voters, Independent Alabama, United Independents of Illinois, the Massachusetts Coalition of Independent Voters, North Carolina Independents for Change, and Independent Texans.[22]

In 2008 both Obama and McCain were widely recognized as beneficiaries of independents' support in their respective party primaries. Obama, like McCain, had reached out to independent voters by asking for their support and raising their concerns about partisan-driven politics. On January 25, 2009, five days after Obama's inauguration, a national meeting of independents was held in New York City. Some five hundred independents, over a quarter of whom were black, and arriving from thirty-three states, convened in midtown Manhattan to strategically assess and retool. The conference, entitled "The Post-Election Independent Movement: Principles Intact, Paradigms in Transition, Obama in the White House," was aired on C-SPAN. Fulani figured prominently at the meeting, which featured other leading African Americans, including city councilman and chair of the South Carolina Independence Party Wayne Griffin, Tyra Cohen of North Carolina's Independents for Change, and David Cherry of United Independents of Illinois.[23] While the demands among African Americans have changed over the past century—with a sea change regarding black civil and political rights in the South—the call for political reform today remains at the core of what independents demanded in the 1890s: "equal justice to all and special privileges to none."[24]

Since the collapse of Black Populism, African American farmers have been virtually wiped out of existence. Over the course of the twentieth century African

American farming families were stripped of their land through a combination of outright coercion, the rise of agribusiness, and through Jim Crow–like policies with government subsidies favoring white farmers over black farmers.[25] As a result, the number of African American farmers in the nation fell from nearly one million in 1910 to less than 18,000 today.[26] Like their Black Populist predecessors, black farmers in the early twenty-first century continue to voice their opposition to their communities' political and economic marginalization. Less than two weeks before the January 2009 conference of independents in New York City, a congressional report was issued regarding the plight of black farming communities. After many years of litigation, African American farmers won a decisive victory against the U.S. Department of Agriculture. In 1997, a class-action suit was filed by 94,000 black petitioners against the USDA for discriminatory lending practices. The African American farmers won their case. But compensation payments to the farmers and their families were stopped in 2001 (with 86 percent being denied financial restitution).[27] The case has since resulted in a ruling in which nearly 14,000 black farmers are receiving payment for discriminatory practices made against them between 1983 and 1997. A campaign led by the National Black Farmers' Association (NBFA) calling for full compensation for black farmers beyond 1997, however, was dismissed for lack of standing.[28]

The damage inflicted on rural black communities can never be fully repaired or justly compensated.[29] As John Boyd Jr., the Virginia-based president of the NBFA and a third-generation farmer himself, notes, "the staggering 98 percent decline in black farm ownership does not tell the whole story: when each farm closed, those farmers, their families and their employees all lost a way of life."[30] While voting rights have been guaranteed by the federal government since 1965—with African Americans holding some of the highest offices in the nation, including the highest—and notwithstanding the growth of a visible black middle class over the last half-century, most African Americans remain chronically poor and politically tied to the Democratic Party. Boyd joined others in campaigning across the South in support of Obama's insurgent candidacy in 2008. He had previously noted, "The black vote is totally being taken for granted by the Democratic Party," and pointed to a growing political "shift" among African Americans.[31]

While Boyd was speaking about a shift in black sentiment away from the establishment Democratic Party in rural areas, recent polls suggest a much larger shift underway in the overall black electorate toward political independence and nonpartisan affiliation. According to the Joint Center for Political and Economic Studies nearly 30 percent of African Americans in the nation identify themselves as politically independent—up from 18 percent a decade ago.[32] Polls, however, have not captured the general feeling that those African Americans who voted for Obama for president did not necessarily do so because he is a Democrat, but likely *in spite of* this fact. *New York Magazine*'s characterization of Obama is revealing. Foremost, it speaks to the growing profile of independents in the nation (prior to Perot, independents were largely unreported in the media); but as the *Raleigh News and Observer* noted in 1886, "There is nothing more lonesome or powerless in this world than an independent in an American legislative assembly."[33] The statement could very well be said of President Obama as he struggles to make his multiple cases for reform to Congress.

Historically, independent political movements have been the driving force behind changes in public policy and the law, even if their impact is not immediately felt. The abolition of slavery, the expansion of the right to vote, and the protection of civil rights were all the products of protracted independent-movement building efforts. Individuals are expressions of such movements; some individuals figuring more prominently than others. Whether it be Weaver, Rayner, Fulani, Perot, or Obama, such individuals, and their campaigns, have variously served independent movements since the late nineteenth century. Since that time, the nation has seen the dismantling of Jim Crow, greater political visibility among a segment of the African American community, yet persistent invisibility and poverty for the masses of ordinary black men and women. As we peer into the past, catching glimpses of Black Populism and its organizers' efforts to plant seeds of change, we can only wonder what Black Populists might have thought about the century that has transpired—that is, the individual and collective successes, as well as the setbacks, limitations, and opportunities created, lost, and sometimes found again.

Historiographical Essay

While there are dozens of state-based and regional studies on the white-led Populist movement, there is significantly less scholarship on Black Populism.[1] Several distinguished scholarly works, widely used American history textbooks, and popularly written books encompassing the period and region either entirely omit the work of African American leaders or identify them only as peripheral to the Colored Alliance or the People's Party. For instance, among the sixteen essays in *Black Leaders of the Nineteenth Century*, edited by Leon Litwack and August Meier, not a single scholarly contribution discusses the work of Black Populists. One of the most recent scholarly studies, Joe Creech's *Righteous Indignation: Religion and the Populist Revolution*, notes that "Confederate veteran and Baptist minister Richard Manning Humphrey" established the Colored Alliance, but no mention is made of African American leaders. In terms of the more popular literature, Howard Zinn minimizes the leadership role of African Americans in the Colored Alliance in his widely read *A People's History of the United States*. He writes, "A Colored Farmers National Alliance grew in the South . . . but it was organized and led by whites. There were also some black organizers." Finally, Alan Brinkley's textbook, *American History: A Survey*, now in its tenth edition, while noting "an important black component to the [Populist] movement," describes white Populists as "*accepting* African Americans into the [People's Party]" (emphasis added), leaving out African American participation in establishing the party in the first place.[2]

Intentional or not, the net result of such omissions or mischaracterizations of Black Populism is that the movement has been all but forgotten, with only passing note—if at all—of some of its leaders and activities. Several recent studies, however, have helped to recover and reconstruct the history of rural black political agency in the New South: Steven Hahn's *A Nation Under Our Feet* (2003), Matthew Hild's *Greenbacks, Knights of Labor, and Populists* (2007), Charles Postel's *The Populist Vision* (2007), my own *In the Balance of Power* (2008), and the reissuing of Gerald Gaither's 1977 *Blacks and the Populist Revolt* as *Blacks and the Populist Movement* (2005).[3] Together, and in different ways, these studies begin to counter the generally held view of southern black political *inaction* in the period following the collapse of Reconstruction and the consolidation of Jim Crow.

The historiography of Black Populism begins in the 1930s. The first regional study of African Americans and the Populist movement was written in 1938—a master's thesis by Girard T. Bryant at the University of Kansas entitled "The Populist Movement and the Negro." Since then, there have been only four other full-length regional studies detailing the role of African Americans in Populism: a master's thesis and three doctoral dissertations, one of which was developed into *Blacks and the Populist Revolt* by Gerald Gaither.[4] Among the state-based studies and shorter treatments of Black Populism are five master's theses, seventeen articles in academic journals, and individual chapters in six academic books.[5] There are over one dozen short articles, books, essays, and papers that reference the work of the Colored Alliance and other Black Populist organizations. For instance, there is Ronald Yanosky's illuminating paper, "The Colored Farmers' Alliance and the Single Tax," delivered in Chicago at the 1992 Annual Meeting of the Organization of American Historians, which discusses the differences between the black and white Alliances regarding the issue of private property.[6] To date there are only two biographies of Black Populist leaders: Gregg Cantrell's *Feeding the Wolf: John B. Rayner and the Politics of Race, 1850–1918*, published in 2001, and John F. Marszalek's *A Black Congressman in the Age of Jim Crow: South Carolina's George Washington Murray*, published in 2006.[7]

Since the mid-twentieth century, the role of African Americans in the Populist movement has become more prominent in the overall literature on Populism, mostly as part of an effort by scholars to demonstrate the labor solidarity that existed between black and white southerners. In the 1950s, C. Vann Woodward, whose scholarship continues to serve as the model, if not starting point of New South history, popularized the idea that white Populists were sympathetic toward African Americans.[8] His perspective, however, remained distinctly that of the white Populists and their movement. While Woodward did note in his *Origins of the New South, 1877–1913* that "there is considerable evidence of independence among the Negroes," he would later make plain in *The Burden of Southern History* that Populism was a "native *white* political movement" (emphasis added).[9] Following Woodward, historians such as Norman Pollack (*The Populist Response to Industrial America*), Walter Nugent (*The Tolerant Populists*), and Lawrence Goodwyn (*Democratic Promise*) pointed to the relative openness of the white Populist movement, its democratic tenets, and the unusual (although not unprecedented) "biracial" coalitions in which white Populists participated. Still, the perspective was that of white Populists. As Goodwyn notes, "while much of [the Colored Alliance's] evolution was traceable to the actions of black people, its origins were a result of white radicalism."[10]

Like Woodward, subsequent scholars of the New South—while more attentive to black political activity—continued to relegate African Americans to the periphery of Populism.[11] Consequently, they identify black-white Populist coalitions as having occurred *within* the white movement when in fact they were tactical alliances forged *between* two separate strands of Populism, each with its own organizations, leaders, tactics, and strategic perspectives. Indeed, it is only when Black Populism is viewed as an autonomous movement, having a relationship to white Populism but separate from it, that it becomes possible to understand the formation, character, and fortunes of the coalitions in which rural black and white southerners joined forces, as temporary as they were.

That Black Populism has not been viewed as a movement unto itself—i.e., that it has not been considered a subject of study until relatively recently—helps to explain the scarcity of scholarship on it. As the historian William Gnatz poignantly noted in the early 1960s about African American history, black people were treated in the scholarly literature largely as "pawn[s] in the struggle between white men ... the Negro was not an issue, not an actor in Southern politics."[12] This conceptual problem, reflected in the work of historians up through the turn of the twenty-first century is compounded by the paucity of primary sources detailing Black Populist activities, organizations, leaders, and ideas. The particular difficulties confronted by Black Populists in organizing their movement required covert actions. Consequently, we are left with piecemeal evidence of specific members, the details of their numbers and activities, and the structures of their organizations. As Goodwyn has aptly noted, the actions of these African Americans has been "shrouded in mystery."[13]

Membership lists of Black Populist organizations, their financial records, correspondence, diaries, and minutes of meetings are largely unavailable either because they were destroyed, or, as part of precautionary measures, rarely committed to paper. What exists are remnants—oral histories passed down over the course of several generations, the words of African Americans and their organization's white spokespersons that appear in white Populist newspapers, and a few other written records. While the primary records that have survived, which are mostly known through other contemporary sources, provide key insights into Black Populism, they also limit the scope of our knowledge about the movement. Writing about the relatively scant research conducted on the Colored Alliance, the historian William Holmes notes, "[the] neglect results largely from the fact that the official records and newspapers of the organization have not survived so far as any historian has been able to determine."[14] Along with other kinds of evidence, such documents may very well be uncovered to shed further light on Black Populism. In the course of my own research on Walter Pattillo, I came across an original photograph of the Black Populist leader in the files of a black orphanage which he had helped to establish in Oxford, North Carolina; I gathered oral history from his great-grandson, Dr. Walter H. Pattillo Jr., a retired professor of biology (one among a number of interviews I conducted with descendents of Black Populists); and a letter written by Pattillo in 1899 was passed along to me by a local archivist in the years since I first did archival work in the town near where the minister lived. The letter came from a descendent of one of Pattillo's neighbors in Granville County, Mrs. Julia Gregory, the widow of Dr. F. R. Gregory, a physician from Granville. Her family had carefully kept the letter of condolence sent by Pattillo soon after Dr. Gregory passed away. The letter, along with family oral history, helps to give some insight into Pattillo's strong relationship with members of the white community, even as he built independent black-based institutions.[15]

In addition to Holmes, other historians have pointed to the relative absence of studies on Black Populists and their organizations. In the mid-1990s Herbert Aptheker suggested that a revisionist treatment of the Populist movement from the perspective of the Colored Alliance was an important area of African American history that needed further exploration.[16] Along these lines, in his "Critical Essay on Recent Works" in the 1995 edition of Woodward's *Origins of the New South*, Charles Dew acknowledged the dearth of literature on the Colored Alliance and its leaders. Echoing Holmes and prefiguring Aptheker, Dew asserted that the Colored Alliance has been "almost totally neglected" and concluded that the work of African Americans and Populism "is obviously in need of additional primary investigation."[17]

Gaither and Adams have compiled a valuable annotated bibliography of primary and secondary sources as related to Black Populism. The bibliography could include at least a dozen additional works that have appeared since its publication in 2004. These works entail a sentence here, or a name there, that can add to the rich and complex stories of Black Populists and their collective movement. Some works provide much more: Marszalek's 2006 biography of George Washington Murray provides a detailed account of the life of one of the movement's most prominent leaders. By the amount of interest generated by my own research into Black Populism, I am optimistic that other scholars will continue to build upon the history offered in the present study. Postel's highly acclaimed *The Populist Vision* (winner of both the Bancroft and the Frederick Jackson Turner awards), and his affirmation of there being two separate Populisms—one black, one white—lends tremendous weight to there being an independent black movement worthy of study and consideration. The present study seeks to establish a framework for students and scholars to view and perhaps further pursue the subject of Black Populism themselves. To be sure, such future investigators will quickly discover that there are multiple paths to begin (or continue in) their research and hopefully help advance our historical understanding of the movement. Other photographs, letters, and the like may very well surface in time.

Ultimately, there is a paradox in writing about Black Populism at this historical (historiographical) juncture. On the one hand, the fact that relatively little has been written about the movement leaves much conceptual room in shaping a new understanding of it. On the other, that the archives contain only fragments on the movement's organizations, members, and leaders limit the extent to which incontrovertible assertions can be made about it. By including previously unconsidered and under-considered organizations and leaders as an integral part of Black Populism, the history I offer here may open up new opportunities to, in the words of Aptheker, "determine when it began, when it ended, who the protagonists were, and what was significant about it."[18]

The methodological challenge of deconstructing existing notions of Black Populism, while working with so few sources in creating a new understanding of the movement, has taken me on a journey across the Piedmont of the Upper South, down the Carolinas, through the Black Belt of the Lower South, and up through Middle Tennessee, before heading back to Maryland. I have relied on the works of many others in developing an understanding of Black Populism. While pioneering scholars such as Girard Bryant, Jack Abramowitz, and William Gnatz laid the empirical foundations of Black Populism for the rest of us to challenge and build upon, more recent historians provide us with valuable new syntheses and ways of seeing and grappling with aspects of its emerging history.

Notes

Introduction

1. *Raleigh News and Observer*, September 30, 1892.
2. The description "populist" was initially a term of opprobrium used by opponents of the movement but was subsequently appropriated by advocates of the People's Party. See Edward L. Ayers, *The Promise of the New South: Life after Reconstruction* (New York: Oxford University Press, 1992), 261.
3. *Raleigh News and Observer*, September 30, 1892; *National Economist*, October 8, 1892.
4. Charles Postel, *The Populist Vision* (New York: Oxford University Press, 2007), 26.
5. Ibid., 13, 140–141.
6. Among the most widely known histories of Populism are Lawrence C. Goodwyn's *Democratic Promise: The Populist Moment in America* (New York: Oxford University Press, 1976) and Robert C. McMath Jr.'s *American Populism: A Social History 1877–1898* (New York: Hill & Wang, 1993). Among the latest regional studies of the movement are those by Postel, *The Populist Vision*, Matthew Hild, *Greenbackers, Knights of Labor, and Populists: Farmer-Labor Insurgency in the Late-Nineteenth Century South* (Athens: University of Georgia Press, 2007), and Joseph Gerteis, *Class and the Color Line: Interracial Class Coalition in the Knights of Labor and the Populist Movement* (Durham, NC: Duke University Press, 2007). Recent state studies include James M. Beeby's *Revolt of the Tar Heels: The North Carolina Populist Movement, 1890–1901* (Jackson: University Press of Mississippi, 2008) and Connie Lester's *Up From the Mudsills of Hell: The Farmers' Alliance, Populism, and Progressive Agriculture in Tennessee, 1870–1915* (Athens: University of Georgia Press, 2006).
7. John D. Hicks, *The Populist Revolt: A History of the Farmers' Alliance and the People's Party* (Minneapolis: University of Minnesota Press, 1931), 115; Jack Abramowitz, "Accommodation and Militancy in Negro Life, 1876–1916" (Ph.D. dissertation, Columbia University, 1950); C. Vann Woodward, *Origins of the New South, 1877–1913* (Baton Rouge: Louisiana State University Press, 1995; first published in 1951); Goodwyn, 1976; Jack Abramowitz, "The Negro in the Populist Movement," *Journal of Negro History* 38, no. 3 (1953), 258; William F. Holmes, "The Leflore County Massacre and the Demise of the Colored Farmers Alliance," *Phylon* 34 (September 1973): 267–274; Gerald H. Gaither, *Blacks and the Populist Revolt: Ballots and Bigotry in the "New South"* (University: University of Alabama Press, 1977); Gregg Cantrell, *Kenneth and John B. Rayner and the Limits of Southern Dissent* (Urbana: University of Illinois Press, 1993); Michael B. Ballard, "Colored Farmers' National Alliance and Cooperative Union," in *Encyclopedia of African American Civil Rights*, ed. Charles D. Lowery and John F. Marszalek (Westport, CT: Greenwood Press, 1992), 120.
8. Timothy P. McCarthy, "A Radical Eye: Herbert Aptheker's Anti-Racism," in *Race & Reason*, Institute for Research in African American Studies, Columbia University, New York, Vol. 2 (1995/1996), 22.

9. The term "New South" was first used by Union forces who had taken over Confederate South Carolina; the term was popularized in the mid-1880s by the white Georgia editor Henry Grady, who envisioned an industrialized post-Reconstruction South. The classic history of the period is Woodward's *Origins of the New South*.

10. Joe Creech, *Righteous Indignation: Religion and the Populist Revolution* (Urbana: University of Illinois Press, 2006), 135.

11. *Progressive Farmer*, August 26, 1890; Creech, 2006, 196 n. 12.

12. Douglass Geraldyne Perry, "Black Populism: The Negro in the People's Party in Texas" (M.S. thesis, Prairie View A & M University, Texas, 1945).

13. Omar H. Ali, "Black Populism in the New South, 1886–1898" (Ph.D. dissertation, Columbia University, 2003); Steven Hahn, *A Nation Under Our Feet: Black Political Struggles in the Rural South from Slavery to the Great Migration* (Cambridge, MA: Harvard University Press, 2003).

14. See Postel, 174, 202; Gerald H. Gaither, *Blacks and the Populist Movement: Ballots and Bigotry in the New South* (University: University of Alabama Press, 2005).

15. Ayers, 257; Girard T. Bryant, "The Populist Movement and the Negro" (M.A. thesis, University of Kansas, Lawrence, 1938), 53–66; Ayers, 257; Patrick J. Dickson, "Out of the Lion's Mouth: The Colored Farmers' Alliance in the New South, 1886–1892" (M.P.S. thesis, Cornell University, 2000), 24, 41–42.

16. See Eric Foner, *Reconstruction: America's Unfinished Revolution, 1863–1877* (New York: Harper & Row, 1988), 37–41.

17. Exceptions to this are American history textbooks such as Eric Foner's *Give Me Liberty! An American History* (New York: W. W. Norton & Co., 2009) or African American history–focused textbooks, such as Darlene Clark Hine's *African Americans: A Concise History* (Upper Saddle, NJ: Pearson Education, 2006).

18. Corey D. B. Walker, *A Noble Fight: African American Freemasonry and the Struggle for Democracy in America* (Urbana: University of Illinois Press, 2008), 178.

19. Ayers, 70; Nancy F. Cott, *No Small Courage: A History of Women in the United States* (New York: Oxford University Press, 2004), 296; C. A. Spencer, "Black Benevolent Societies and the Development of Black Insurance Companies in Nineteenth Century Alabama," *Phylon* 46, no. 3 (1985): 254; William Edward Spriggs, "The Virginia Colored Farmers Alliance: A Case Study of Race and Class Identity," *Journal of Negro History* 64, no. 3 (Summer 1979): 203–204; Michael A. Gomez, *Exchanging Our Country Marks: The Transformation of African Identities in the Colonial and Antebellum South* (Chapel Hill: University of North Carolina Press, 1998), 93–101.

20. C. Eric Lincoln and Lawrence H. Mamiya, *The Black Church in the African American Experience* (Durham, NC: Duke University Press, 1990), 17.

21. Quoted in Hahn, 2003, 372. Robin D. G. Kelley notes, "Grass-roots black community organizations such as mutual benefit societies, church groups, and gospel quartets were crucial to black people's survival. Through them, African Americans created and sustained bonds of community, mutual support networks, and a collectivist ethos that shaped black working-class political struggle." Kelley, 1993, 80.

22. Orville Vernon Burton, *In My Father's House Are Many Mansions: Family and Community in Edgefield, South Carolina* (Chapel Hill: University of North Carolina, 1985), 242, 406 n. 69.

23. Roy V. Scott, "Milton George and the Farmer's Alliance Movement," *Mississippi Valley Historical Review* 45 (June 1958): 107 n. 59; Bernice R. Fine, "Agrarian Reform and the Texas Negro Farmers, 1886–1896" (M.A. thesis, North Texas State University, 1971), 81–82; Theodore Saloutos, *Farmer Movements in the South, 1865–1933* (Berkeley and Los Angeles: University of

California Press, 1960), 79; Eric Anderson, *Race and Politics in North Carolina, 1872–1901: The Black Second* (Baton Rouge: Louisiana State University Press, 1981), 331–342.

24. The Colored Farmers Alliance alone claimed over one million members in 1891. See Richard M. Humphrey, "History of the Colored Farmers National Alliance and Co-Operative Union," in *The Farmer's Alliance History and Agricultural Digest*, ed. Nelson A. Dunning (Washington, D.C.: Alliance Publishing Co., 1891), 290.

25. Gaither, 2005, 48.

Chapter One

1. Michael R. Hyman, *The Anti-Redeemers: Hill-Country Political Dissenters in the Lower South from Redemption to Populism* (Baton Rouge: Louisiana State University Press, 1990), 179, 181–183.

2. *Huntsville Gazette*, September 3, 1881.

3. Abramowitz, "Accommodation and Militancy in Negro Life," 1950, 22.

4. *Huntsville Gazette*, September 3, 1881. See Hyman, chapter 8, and "Response to Redeemer Rule: Hill Country Political Dissent in the Post-Reconstruction South" (Ph.D. dissertation, City University of New York, 1986).

5. *Corinth Sub Soiler and Democrat*, quoted in the *Daily Democrat*, September 8, 1881.

6. *Pascagoula Democratic Star*, quoted in the *Daily Democrat*, September 15, 1881.

7. *Huntsville Gazette*, November 12, 1881; *Natchez Daily Democrat*, November 9, 10, 1881; Abramowitz, 1950, 23.

8. *Huntsville Gazette*, November 12, 1881.

9. *Daily Democrat*, November 9, 10, 1881; *Huntsville Gazette*, November 12, 1881.

10. *Tribune Almanac*, 1882, 74, quoted in Abramowitz, 1950, 24.

11. *Greensboro Daily Record*, March 7, August 19, 1892.

12. Foner, 1988, *passim*; W. E. B. Du Bois, *Black Reconstruction in America, 1860–1880* (New York: Simon & Schuster, 1992; originally published in 1935), 580–636.

13. See Julie Saville, *The Work of Reconstruction: From Slave to Wage Laborer in South Carolina, 1860–1870* (New York: Cambridge University Press, 1994), and Michael W. Fitzgerald, *The Union League Movement in the Deep South: Politics and Agricultural Change During Reconstruction* (Baton Rouge: Louisiana State University Press, 1989).

14. Foner, 1988, 564–587.

15. Woodward, 1995, 216.

16. Hahn, 2003, 288.

17. Eric Foner, *Nothing But Freedom: Emancipation and Its Legacy* (Baton Rouge: Louisiana State University Press, 1983), 82.

18. Foner, 1988, 158.

19. Ibid., 124–170, 512–553.

20. Joseph H. Gerteis, "Class and the Color Line: The Sources and Limits of Interracial Class Coalition, 1880–1896" (Ph.D. dissertation, University of North Carolina, Chapel Hill, 1999), 215.

21. Ibid., 194; Ayers, 198; Woodward, 1995, 180–188; Sharon A. Holt, *Making Freedom Pay: North Carolina Freedpeople Working for Themselves, 1865–1900* (Athens: University of Georgia Press, 2000), 58, 86.

22. Belinda Hurmence, ed., *My Folks Don't Want Me To Talk About Slavery: Twenty-one Oral Histories of Former North Carolina Slaves* (Winston-Salem, NC: John F. Blair, 2000), 52.

23. See Ali, 2003, 31. In 1890 approximately 22 percent of black farming families nationally owned their own home (approximately 121,000 out of 550,000 farm homes); Dickson, 92.

24. Postel, 126.

25. Allen W. Jones, "The Role of Tuskegee Institute in the Education of Black Farmers," *Journal of Negro History* 60, no. 2 (April 1975): 252.

26. *Progressive Farmer*, September 23, 1890; Harold G. Sugg, "The Colored Farmers' Alliance, 1888–1892" (M.A. thesis, Old Dominion University, 1971), 1–2; *Harold G. Sugg Papers*, East Carolina University Manuscript Collection.

27. Girard T. Bryant, "The Populist Movement and the Negro" (M.A. thesis, University of Kansas, Lawrence, 1938), 122; Bureau of the Census, *Report on the Productions of Agriculture*, Department of the Interior, 11th Census (Washington, D.C.: Government Printing Office, 1895), 118–119.

28. Nell Irvin Painter, *Exodusters: Black Migration to Kansas After Reconstruction* (New York: Knopf, 1977), 100; Hahn, 2003, 355.

29. Bureau of the Census, *Negro Population 1790–1915* (Washington, D.C.: Government Printing Office, 1918), 65.

30. Hahn, 2003, 355.

31. Frenise Logan, *The Negro in North Carolina, 1876–1894* (Chapel Hill: University of North Carolina Press, 1964), 124–125; Craig Thurtell, "The Fusion Insurgency in North Carolina: Origins to Ascendency, 1876–1896" (Ph.D. dissertation, Columbia University, 1998), 44.

32. See *Appleton's Annual Cyclopaedia and Register of Important Events* (New York: D. Appleton and Company, 1881), 812; Abramowitz, 1950, 12–13.

33. In years to come, some African Americans in Alabama considered emigrating to Mexico. While in Georgia, A.M.E. bishop Henry M. Turner urged migration across the Atlantic to Liberia; see Gaither, 1977, 24, 43–44, 110.

34. *Appleton's Annual Cyclopaedia*, 1885, 357; Foner's *Freedom's Lawmakers: A Directory of Black Officeholders during Reconstruction* (Baton Rouge: Louisiana State University Press, 1996), 171.

35. Hahn, 328.

36. See William Cohen, *At Freedom's Edge: Black Mobility and the Southern White Quest for Racial Control, 1861–1915* (Baton Rouge: Louisiana State University Press, 1991); Perman, 9–36.

37. Phillip S. Foner, *History of the Labor Movement in the United States, Vol. I* (New York, 1947), 477.

38. The proposed federal coinage of silver (at a weight ratio of 16 ounces of silver to 1 ounce of gold) was presented as a solution to the currency problem. "Free silver" became a rallying cry among the heavily indebted rural poor. Goodwyn, 1976, 215–229; Ayers, 266–267, 293–295.

39. Dickson, 33.

40. Ernest W. Winkler, ed., *Platforms of Political Parties in Texas*, No. 53, *Bulletin of the University of Texas, 1916* (Austin: University of Texas Press, 1916), 180.

41. Dickson, 34.

42. Winkler, 1916, 187; Abramowitz, 1950, 22; Alwyn Barr, *Reconstruction to Reform: Texas Politics, 1876–1906* (Austin: University of Texas Press, 1971); Roscoe C. Martin, "The Greenback Party in Texas," *Southwestern Historical Quarterly* 30 (January 1927): 161–177.

43. Lawrence C. Goodwyn, "Populist Dreams and Negro Rights: East Texas as a Case Study," *American Historical Review* 78 (1971): 1435–1456.

44. Paul Horton, "Testing the Limits of Class Politics in Postbellum Alabama: Agrarian Radicalism in Lawrence County," *Journal of Southern History* 57, no. 1 (February 1991): 71, and "Lawrence County Alabama in the Nineteenth Century: A Study in the 'Other South'" (M.A. thesis, University of Texas, Austin, 1985), 108–115; Samuel L. Webb, *Two-Party Politics in the One-Party South: Alabama's Hill Country, 1874–1920* (Tuscaloosa: University of Alabama Press, 1997), 65–66.

45. Hild, 2007, 33–34.

46. Ibid., 30–31.

47. John F. Marszalek, *A Black Congressman in the Age of Jim Crow: South Carolina's George Washington Murray* (Gainesville: University Press of Florida, 2006), 11.

48. Ayers, 46–47; J. Morgan Kousser, *The Shaping of Southern Politics: Suffrage Restriction and the Establishment of the One-Party South, 1880–1910* (New Haven, CT: Yale University Press, 1974), 27.

49. Historical Census Browser, Geospatial and Statistical Center, University of Virginia Library, http://fisher.lib.virginia.edu/collections/stats/histcensus/php/state.php (Accessed June 5, 2009).

50. See James T. Moore, "Black Militancy in Readjuster Virginia, 1879–1883," *Journal of Southern History* 41, no. 2 (1975): 167–186; Charles E. Wynes, *Race Relations in Virginia, 1870–1902* (Charlottesville: University of Virginia Press, 1961); Gerteis, 1999, 200; Thurtell, 3.

51. Hild, 42.

52. *New York Times*, September 28, December 22, 1878; Hild, 39–43; Marszalek, 2006, 11.

53. Manning Marable, *Race, Reform and Rebellion: The Second Reconstruction in Black America* (Jackson: University Press of Mississippi, 2002), 9.

54. Hild, 43.

55. The "invisible institution" was the name used for the black churches in the antebellum South; congregants met late at night (or early in the morning) in the fields. See Albert J. Raboteau, *Slave Religion: The "Invisible Institution" in the Antebellum South* (New York: Oxford University Press, 1980).

56. Gomez, 1998, 80–81, 244–290; see also Sylviane A. Diouf, *Servants of Allah: African Muslims Enslaved in the Americas* (New York: New York University Press, 1998), 71–106.

57. Tiffany Ruby Patterson, *Zora Neale Hurston and a History of Southern Life* (Philadelphia, PA: Temple University Press, 2005), 8, 94–98, 156.

58. See Evelyn Brooks Higginbotham, *Righteous Discontent: The Women's Movement in the Black Baptist Church, 1880–1920* (Cambridge, MA: Harvard University Press, 1993), 5; Joseph W. Creech Jr., "Righteous Indignation: Religion and Populism in North Carolina, 1896–1906" (Ph.D. dissertation, University of Notre Dame, 2000), 43–48.

59. Creech, 2000, 47. For class divisions within black churches (between more middle-class urban churches versus poor rural churches), see Joe Creech, *Righteous Indignation: Religion and the Populist Revolution* (Champaign: University of Illinois Press, 2006), 18.

60. Daniel A. Payne, "Thought About the Past, the Present and the Future of the African M. E. Church," *A. M. E. Church Review* 1 (July 1884): 1–3; see Albert J. Raboteau, "The Black Experience in American Evangelicalism: The Meaning of Slavery," in *African American Religion: Interpretive Essays in History and Culture*, ed. Timothy Earl Fulop and Albert J. Raboteau (New York: Routledge, 1996), 94.

61. The membership figures were taken from the 1890 religious census available through the Inter-university Consortium for Political and Social research in Ann Arbor, Michigan; Ayers, 160–161.

62. See Ayers, "Percentage of Females in Black Population, 1900," 494.

63. Hahn, 232–233.

64. Ayers, 500.

65. Ibid., 418; Louis Harlan, *Separate and Unequal: Public School Campaigns and Racism in the Southern Seaboard States* (New York: Atheneum, 1969), 32–36.

66. Hahn, 233.

67. Creech, 2000, 36.

68. Ibid., 14.

69. See James Brewer Stewart, *Holy Warriors: The Abolitionists and Slavery* (New York: Hill & Wang, 1997), 51–74, and Foner, 1988.

70. Robin D. G. Kelley, *Hammer and Hoe: Alabama Communists During the Great Depression* (Chapel Hill: University of North Carolina Press, 1990); Omar H. Ali, *In the Balance of Power: Independent Black Politics and Third-Party Movements in the United States* (Athens: Ohio University Press, 2008), 101–133.

71. Gerteis, 1999, 215; Sugg, 2; Girard T. Bryant, "The Populist Movement and the Negro" (M.A. thesis, University of Kansas, Lawrence, 1938), 2.

72. Dickson, 68, 71–73.

73. Charles Crowe, "Tom Watson, Populists, and Blacks Reconsidered," *Journal of Negro History* 60 (April 1970): 99–116.

74. *Charleston News and Courier*, October 7, 1886.

75. Melton A. McLaurin, *The Knights of Labor in the South* (Westport, CT: Greenwood Press, 1978), 140.

76. *National Economist*, March 7, 1891; Herbert Aptheker, *A Documentary History of the Negro People in the United States, Vol. 2* (New York: Citadel Press, 1992), 808.

77. *Southern Mercury*, July 2, 1891.

78. Terrence V. Powderly, *Thirty Years of Labor, 1859–1889* (Columbus, OH: Excelsior Publishing House, 1889), 653.

79. Ayers, 215–216.

80. Solon Buck, *The Agrarian Crusade: A Chronicle of the Farmer in Politics* (New Haven, CT: Yale University Press, 1920), 116. See also Gaither, 2005, 9; Ayers, 214–215; Abramowitz, 1950, 28; Roy V. Scott, "Milton George and the Farmer's Alliance Movement," *Mississippi Valley Historical Review* 45 (June 1958): 107 n. 59.

81. *New Orleans Picayune*, October 3, 1873.

82. Matthew Hild, *Greenbackers, Knights of Labor, and Populists: Farmer-Labor Insurgency in the Late Nineteenth-Century South* (Athens: University of Georgia Press), 13.

83. Curley Daniel Willis, "Grange Movement in Louisiana" (M.A. thesis, Louisiana State University, 1935), 16; D. Sven Nordin, *Rich Harvest: A History of the Grange, 1867–1900* (Jackson: University Press of Mississippi, 1974), 32–33; Theodore Saloutos, "The Grange in the South, 1870–1877," *Journal of Southern History* 19, no. 4 (November 1953): 476–478.

84. *Houston Post*, December 13, 1891; Cantrell, 1993, 321 n. 12; Gaither, 2005, 20–21; *State Wheel*, May 7, 1888; Paul Horton, "Testing the Limits of Class Politics in Postbellum Alabama: Agrarian Radicalism in Lawrence County," *Journal of Southern History* 57, no. 1 (February 1991): 76.

85. William Gnatz, "The Negro and the Populist Movement in the South" (M.A. thesis, University of Chicago, 1961), 33; Horton, 74.

86. *Alabama State Wheel*, February 1, 1888.
87. Ibid., April 26, 1888.
88. Horton, 74.
89. Abramowitz, 1950, 28; *Huntsville Gazette*, May 9, 14, December 13, 27, 1892.
90. Connie L. Lester, *Up From the Mudsills of Hell: The Farmers' Alliance, Populism, and Progressive Agriculture in Tennessee, 1870–1915* (Athens: University of Georgia Press, 2006), 83–86.
91. Joseph Gerteis, *Class and the Color Line: Interracial Class Coalition in the Knights of Labor and the Populist Movement* (Durham, NC: Duke University Press, 2007), 43; William F. Holmes, "The Demise of the Colored Farmers' Alliance," *Journal of Southern History* 41, no. 2 (May 1975): 188.
92. There is a photograph of the minister available through *Documenting the American South* (University of North Carolina, Chapel Hill Libraries). See *Sermons, Addresses and Reminiscences and Important Correspondence, With a Picture Gallery of Eminent Ministers and Scholars* (Nashville, TN: National Baptist Publishing Board, 1901), http://docsouth.unc.edu/church/morris/ill254.html (Accessed June 5, 2009).
93. *Indianapolis Freeman*, April 4, 1891; *Arkansas Democrat*, July 23, 1890; *Eminent Ministers and Scholars*, 254; *African American Biographical Database*, http://aabd.chadwyck.com/ (Accessed June 5, 2009).
94. George W. Lowe to William Coppinger, September 19, 1891; quoted in Kenneth B. Barnes, *Journey of Hope: The Back-to-Africa Movement in Arkansas in the Late 1800s* (Chapel Hill: University of North Carolina Press, 2004), 59, 211 n. 26.
95. Holmes, 1975, 188.
96. Gaither, 2005, 10 and 270 n. 39; *Weekly Toiler*, July 4, 1888.
97. Ibid., July 18, 1888.
98. Ibid., October 7, 1888.
99. Lester, 84–85.
100. See Sidney H. Kessler, "The Organization of Negroes in the Knights of Labor," *Journal of Negro History* 37, no. 3 (July 1952): 248.
101. Ayers, 216.
102. McLaurin, 1978, 139.
103. Ibid., 135, 138. Knights of Labor, *Records of the Proceedings of the General Assembly, 1885*, 204.
104. Ray Marshall, "The Negro in Southern Unions," in *The Negro and the American Labor Movement*, ed. Julius Jacobson (Garden City, NY: Anchor Books, 1968), 133; McLaurin, 1978, 136.
105. *Huntsville Gazette*, February 27, June 12, 1886; Kessler, 255.
106. McLaurin, 1978, 137. Selected letters from January 13, 1886, to April 6, 1887, in *Terrence V. Powderly Papers*, Catholic University of America Library, Washington, D.C.
107. Former Knights general secretary John H. Haynes provided the 60,000-membership figure in 1886; Frank Ferrell provided the 400 "all-Negro locals" figure; Kessler, 272; Gerteis, 2007, 41.
108. Postel, 39.
109. McLaurin, 1978, 136, 148.
110. Powderly, 1889, 654–655; Belton to Powderly, November 15, 1886, *Powderly Papers*.
111. *New Orleans Weekly Pelican*, February 26, 1887; *Cleveland Gazette*, March 19, 1887; *Washington Bee*, October 3, 10, 1885; *Journal of United Labor*, July 10, September 10, 1885; January 10, March 10, April 10, May 10, June 10, October 10–25, 1886; Kessler, 258–259.

112. Robert C. McMath Jr., *Populist Vanguard: A History of the Southern Farmers' Alliance* (Chapel Hill: University of North Carolina Press, 1975), 44; Melton McLaurin, "The Knights of Labor in North Carolina Politics," *North Carolina Historical Review* 49, no. 1 (1972): 308–314; Robert C. McMath Jr., "Southern White Farmers and the Organization of Black Farm Workers: A North Carolina Document," *Labor History* 18, no. 1 (Winter 1977): 116.

113. Hild, 2007, 95, 161.

114. Letter to the editor, "Persecution," from Oxford, NC, May 20, 1887, in *Journal of United Labor*, June 11, 1887; Doc. 4 in Philip S. Foner and Ronald L. Lewis, eds., *The Black Worker: A Documentary History from Colonial Times to the Present, Volume III: The Black Worker During the Era of the Knights of Labor* (Philadelphia: Temple University Press, 1978), 274.

115. *Journal of United Labor*, June 11, 1887; Kessler, 262–263; McLaurin, 1978, 142.

116. H. H. Perry to Elias Carr, May 2, 1890, *Elias Carr Papers*, East Carolina University Manuscript Collection, North Carolina.

117. Kelley, 1991, 1. N.B. In some records Nicholas Stack's last name appears as "Stock."

118. *Birmingham Iron Age*, July 27–August 28, 1887; McLaurin, 1978, 146.

119. McLaurin, 1978, 146; Kessler, 1952, 255 n. 32.

120. McLaurin, 1978, 131–132; Kessler, 248–276.

121. McLaurin, 1972, 306.

122. McMath Jr., 1975, 163.

123. Gerteis, 1999, 215; Sugg, 2; Philip J. Wood, *Southern Capitalism: The Political Economy of North Carolina, 1880–1980* (Durham, NC: Duke University Press, 1986), 112.

124. Quoted in Dolores E. Janiewski, *Sisterhood Denied: Race, Gender, and Class in a New South Community* (Philadelphia: Temple University Press, 1985), 20. See also McMath Jr., *Southern White Farmers*, 117–119, and McLaurin, 1972, 308; Thurtell, 85.

125. Kenneth Kann, "The Knights of Labor and the Southern Black Worker," *Labor History* 18, no. 1 (Winter 1977): 66. Despite the strike being crushed, African Americans continued to organize themselves through the Knights. As Matthew Hild notes, in 1887 African Americans "comprised a significant portion of the Knights' membership in Arkansas." Hild, 2007, 90.

126. McLaurin, 1978, 141; Kessler, "Negroes in the Knights," 268–270.

127. *New York Freeman*, October 8, 1887; McLaurin, 1978, 142; Kessler, 264.

128. See "Lynchings, by State and Race, 1882–1968," Tuskegee Institute Archives, Alabama (February 1979); Stewart E. Tolnay and E. M. Beck, *A Festival of Violence: An Analysis of Southern Lynchings, 1882–1930* (Urbana: University of Illinois Press, 1995).

129. McLaurin, 1978, 141, 144.

130. McMath Jr., 1977, 117.

131. McLaurin, 1978, 138.

132. McMath Jr., 1977, 118–119.

133. Ibid, 115–117.

134. Kessler, 269.

135. Bruce E. Baker, "The 'Hoover Scare' in South Carolina, 1887: An Attempt to Organize Black Farm Labor," *Labor History* 40, no. 3 (1999): 262. See also Baker's "The First Anarchist That Ever Came to Atlanta," in *Radicalism in the South Since Reconstruction*, ed. Chris Green, Rachel Rubin, and James Smethurst (New York: Palgrave/Macmillan, 2006), 39–55.

136. Baker, "The First Anarchist That Ever Came to Atlanta"; *Preamble and Declaration of Principles of the Co-Operative Workers of America*, North Carolina State Archives (Catawba County records, Series C.R. 021, Box 928.3, Folder: Secret Political Organizations, 1887).

137. Baker, 1999, 264.

138. Quoted in *Greenville News*, July 1, 1887; Foner, 283.

139. Ibid.

140. Saville, 1994, 116; Michael W. Fitzgerald, *The Union League Movement in the Deep South: Politics and Agricultural Change During Reconstruction* (Baton Rouge: Louisiana State University Press, 1989).

141. Baker, 1999, 264–265; Omar H. Ali, "Standing Guard at the Door of Liberty: Black Populism in South Carolina, 1886–1897," *South Carolina Historical Magazine* 107, no. 3 (2006): 190–203.

142. Terrence V. Powderly, *Constitution of the General Assembly, District Assemblies, and Local Assemblies of the Order of the Knights of Labor in America* (Marblehead, MA: Statesman Publishing Co., 1883); Baker, 1999, 262.

143. Kessler, 267–268.

144. The Lincoln Seminary College archives lists Isham as Sherman's father; Lincoln Seminary "Biographical Catalogue," 1918, 75. *African American Biographical Database* (Accessed June 5, 2009).

145. *Charleston News and Courier*, July 3, 1887 (from the *Greenville News*, July 1, 1887); U.S. Congress, *Testimony Taken by the Joint Select Committee to Inquire into the Conditions of Affairs in the Late Insurrectionary States (The Ku Klux Klan Conspiracy)* (Washington, D.C.: Government Printing Office, 1872), 538.

146. *Greenville Enterprise and Mountaineer*, July 6, 1887.

147. Baker, 1999, 266.

148. "Hoover" spelled his name with only one "o," but most references to him (contemporary and since) spell it with two. See Letter to Terence V. Powderly, May 22, 1886 (Reel 16, *Powderly Papers*); Baker, 1999, 261.

149. *Charleston News and Courier*, July 3, 6, 1887; *Greenville News*, July 1, 1887.

150. *Greenville Enterprise and Mountaineer*, July 6, 1887; Baker, 1999, 274.

151. *Greenville Enterprise and Mountaineer*, September 28, 1887; Spartanburg *Carolina Spartan*, September 28, 1887.

152. *Charleston News and Courier*, July 6, 1887.

153. Baker, 1999, 281.

155. Ibid., 277.

155. *Athens Weekly Banner-Watchman*, May 24, 1887.

156. *Columbia Daily Register*, July 1, 1887; *Atlanta Constitution*, March 13, 1889.

157. Gaither, 1977, 8.

158. Baker, 1999, 271; *Greenville Enterprise and Mountaineer*, July 3, 1889.

159. Plummer wrote of uniting the strength of the black and white organization by sharing resources. The article, which was reprinted in both the *National Economist* and subsequently in the *Nation*, was originally written for the Colored Alliance's principal newspaper, the *National Alliance*; *The Nation*, February 13, 1890.

160. *Florida Dispatch*, October 17, 1887.

161. Bryant, 14–15; *Florida Dispatch*, October 17, 1887.

162. Constitution of the National Farmers' Alliance and Industrial Union, 1889; See Dunning, 1891; Frank M. Drew, "The Present Farmers Movement," *Political Science Quarterly* 6, no. 2 (June 1891): 282–310. For the exclusionary clause listed in North Carolina's white Alliance, see Article 4, Section 1, in the Farmers' State Alliance of North Carolina, *Secretary-Treasurer's Records*, Minutes, 1887–1893, 31, North Carolina State Archives.

163. *Weekly Toiler*, January 23, 1889; Gaither, 1977, 19.

Chapter Two

1. See Acts of Incorporation, United States of America (Office of the Record of Deeds, Washington, D.C.), book 4, folio 354. The term "Colored Alliance" will be used to describe the consolidation of several groups bearing variations of the name Colored Farmers Alliance.
2. Humphrey, 1891, 288.
3. Ibid.; Holmes, 1975, 189; Dickson, 71–73; George Macon Shuffer Jr., *My Journey to Betterment* (New York: Vantage Press, 1999), 1–2.
4. See *Charter of The Alliance of Colored Farmers of Texas*, filed in the Department of State, February 28, 1887, microfilm accessed at Corporations Section, Secretary of State, Austin, TX; Dickson, 58 n. 8. Gaither, 2005, 7.
5. Lawrence D. Rice, *The Negro in Texas, 1874–1900* (Baton Rouge: Louisiana State University Press, 1971), 179.
6. In addition to the Houston and Lee County–based Colored Alliances, there was a "Texas Colored State Alliance" formed in Robertson County in June 1887. That organization was led by C. H. Hammond, H. Lockhart, and G. G. Giddings—serving as president, secretary, and treasurer, respectively. See Dickson, 94–95.
7. Holmes, 1975, 188.
8. *National Economist*, January 25, 1890; *Nation*, February 13, 1890.
9. *Atlanta Constitution*, December 4, 1890; *Raleigh Progressive Farmer*, December 23, 1890.
10. *Cleveland Gazette*, July 18, 1891; Abramowitz, 1950, 30.
11. See Ayers, 154–155; Alex Lichtenstein, *Twice the Work of Free Labor: The Political Economy of Convict Labor in the New South* (London: Verso, 1995), 73–104.
12. Postel, 41.
13. *Atlanta Constitution*, April 3, 1888; Bryant, 23.
14. Goodwyn, 1976, 122.
15. Colored Farmers' National Alliance and Co-Operative Union, *Ritual of the Colored Farmers' National Alliance and Co-Operative Union of the United States* (Houston: Culmore Bros., circa 1889).
16. See Humphrey, 288–292; Spriggs, 194–195; Gaither, 1977, 1–16.
17. See Articles VIII and IX in *Constitution of the Colored Farmers' National Alliance and Co-operative Union of the United States* (Houston: J. J. Pastoriza, circa 1889).
18. Gerteis, 2007, 43.
19. *Ritual of the Colored Farmers' National Alliance and Co-Operative Union of the United States* (Houston: Culmore Bros., circa 1889), 9.
20. Humphrey, 288.
21. Kerr-Ritchie, 204.
22. Humphrey, 289.
23. Holmes, 1975, 187.
24. *Weekly Toiler*, July 1, 1888; Gaither, 1977, 7.
25. Kerr-Ritchie, 204.
26. *National Economist*, April 4, 1891 (reprinted excerpt from the *National Alliance*).
27. Humphrey, 290.
28. Goodwyn, 1976, 120; Dickson, 91.
29. Gaither, 2005, 19; Postel, 42.
30. Dickson, 92.
31. *Southern Mercury*, December 13, 1888; Girard T. Bryant, "The Populist Movement and the Negro," 23.

32. *Progressive Farmer*, July 31, 1888; *Houston Post*, February 5, 18, 1892; Cantrell, 1993, 207; Marszalek, 2006, 18; Gerteis, 2007, 231 n. 84; George B. Tindall, *South Carolina Negroes, 1877–1900* (Columbia: University of South Carolina Press, 2003), 118.

33. Hahn, 2003, 461.

34. Spriggs, 194.

35. Holmes, 1975, 187; Dickson, 140.

36. Floyd J. Miller in "Black Protest and White Leadership: A Note on the Colored Farmer's Alliance," *Phylon* 33, no. 2 (1972): 170; Yanosky, 4; Postel, 202–203.

37. Patrick Dickson notes, "Evidence of the Colored Alliance's political platform [demonstrates] that despite its claims to be apolitical, the group consistently spoke out on matters it believed affected its membership." He further notes, "In doing so, the Colored Alliance set itself apart not only from the white Alliance . . . but also from Booker T. Washington's accommodationist approach to black advancement." Dickson, 105.

38. Foner and Lewis, 1978, 423.

39. Vera Lee Kearl Marshall, ed., *Proud to Remember* (Provo, UT: Brigham Young University Press, 1964), 16–18, noted in Dickson, 76.

40. Davis, 648; Miller, 170. Houston County, where Humphrey settled in Texas, saw a steady flow of African Americans following Emancipation. By the mid-1880s Humphrey joined nearly 8,000 African Americans in the county, many farming land of their own. Dickson, 64.

41. Hild, 2007, 105.

42. Miller, 171.

43. Hild, 2007, 105–106.

44. See Winkler, 1916, 262–263; William Warren Rogers, *The One-Gallused Rebellion: Agrarianism in Alabama, 1865–1896* (Baton Rouge: Louisiana State University Press, 1970); Yanosky, 1–13.

45. *Galveston Daily News*, October 14, 31, 1888.

46. See U.S. congressional biography of William Harrison Martin, Library of Congress. *Biographical Directory of the United States Congress*, http://bioguide.congress.gov/scripts/biodisplay.pl?index=M000203 (Accessed June 5, 2009).

47. *Galveston Daily News*, October 14, 31, 1888; Secretary of State of Texas, Report, 1888, 162, quoted in Miller, 171.

48. Humphrey, 288–292; Humphrey's congressional testimony to the U.S. Senate Committee on Agriculture and Forestry in 1890 appeared in the *National Economist*, June 7, 1890.

49. Goodwyn, *The Populist Moment*, 122.

50. For a critical discussion about the limitations of the concept and usage of "race" in American history, see Barbara J. Fields, "Ideology and Race in American History," in *Region, Race, and Reconstruction: Essays in Honor of C. Vann Woodward*, ed. J. Morgan Kousser and James M. McPherson (New York: Oxford University Press, 1982), 143–177.

51. Shuffer, 1–2; Dickson, 71–73; George M. Shuffer Jr., personal communication on July 16, 2003.

52. See Robert C. McMath Jr., "The Farmers Alliance in the South: The Career of an Agrarian Institution" (Ph.D. dissertation, University of North Carolina, Chapel Hill, 1972), 247–251; McMath Jr., 1975, 33; Miller, 172.

53. See *New York Times*, September 9, 1891.

54. Melton A. McLaurin, *The Knights of Labor in the South* (Westport, CT: Greenwood Press, 1978), 142; Bryant, 65.

55. Omar H. Ali, "The Making of a Black Populist: A Tribute to the Rev. Walter A. Pattillo," *Oxford Public Ledger*, March 28, 2002 (121, no. 25); Alan Keith-Lucas, *A Monument to Black Initiative and Courage: Central Children's Home, 1883–1990* (Lexington, NC: Wooten, 1991); Moses W. Williams and George W. Watkins, *Who's Who Among North Carolina Negro Baptists* (Alexandria, VA: Chadwyck-Healey, 1940), 344.

56. 1880 U.S. Census, Granville, NC, Film 1254965, T9–0965, 483C. Pattillo's great-grandson, Dr. Walter H. Pattillo Jr., at his home in Durham, North Carolina, personal communication on July 14, 2001. Dr. Pattillo Jr., retired as a professor of biology from North Carolina Central University, generously shared with me a family album of marriages, births, and deaths.

57. Creech, 2006, 196 n. 12.

58. Tiffany Ruby Patterson, *Zora Neale Hurston and a History of Southern Life* (Philadelphia, PA: Temple University Press, 2005), 112.

59. LaRue P. Cunningham, "The Negro in Granville County, North Carolina, As Reflected in the Oxford Public Ledger and Other Related Sources, 1880–1900" (M.A. thesis, Atlanta University, 1972), xi; Barnetta McGhee White's *In Search of Kith and Kin: The History of a Southern Black Family* (Baltimore, MD: Gateway Press, 1986), 11.

60. See C. Eric Lincoln and Lawrence H. Mamiya, *The Black Church in the African American Experience* (Durham, NC: Duke University Press, 1990), 20–75.

61. Claude R. Trotter et al., *A Splendid Enterprise: History of the General Baptist State Convention of North Carolina* (Raleigh, NC: Irving-Swain, 1999), 257.

62. Williams et al., 345; J. A. Whitted, *A History of the Negro Baptists of North Carolina* (Raleigh, NC: Edwards & Broughton Print Co., 1908), 193.

63. *Oxford Torchlight*, June 26, 1883.

64. Robert W. Winston, *It's a Far Cry* (New York: Henry Holt, 1937), 161; William A. Mabry, *The Negro in North Carolina Politics Since Reconstruction* (Durham, NC: Duke University Press, 1940), 22–28.

65. The orphanage was renamed the Central Children's Home in the early twentieth century; Pattillo was described as its "magnanimous spirit." See Keith-Lucas, 1991; Williams et al., 1945; Ali, 2002; *Raleigh News and Observer*, September 18, 1886.

66. Robert C. McMath Jr. contends that Pattillo had some involvement in North Carolina's Knights of Labor, but does not provide a source; McMath Jr., *American Populism*, 172.

67. Williams et al., 345.

68. Gaither, 1977, 12; Abramowitz, 1950, 30.

69. William W. Rogers, "The Negro Alliance in Alabama," *Journal of Negro History* 45, no. 1 (January 1960): 39–40; *National Economist*, March 14, 1889.

70. *Raleigh Progressive Farmer*, December 4, 1888; *Richmond Dispatch*, August 19, 1891; Woodward, 1951, 192.

71. Thurtell, 82, 165. Craven County was itself 65 percent African American; Bureau of the Census, *Negro Population 1790–1915* (Washington, D.C.: Government Printing Office, 1918); Thurtell, 165 n. 15.

72. W. A. Pattillo to Elias Carr, May 2, 1891, *Carr Papers*; J. J. Rogers to Elias Carr, April 30, 1891, *Carr Papers*; Thurtell, 84.

73. Thurtell, 82, 84.

74. W. A. Pattillo to Elias Carr, June 24, 1890, and June 9, 1891, *Carr Papers*; Lala Carr Steelman, *The North Carolina Farmers Alliance: A Political History, 1887–1893* (Greenville: East Carolina University Press, 1985), 178; Thurtell, 83.

75. W. A. Pattillo to Elias Carr, May 12, 1891, *Carr Papers*.

76. Joe Creech, *Righteous Indignation: Religion and the Populist Revolution* (Urbana: University of Illinois Press, 2006), 135.

77. Rogers, 1960, 41; Miller, 172.

78. Thomas E. Watson, "The Negro Question in the South," *Arena* 6 (October 1892): 548.

79. William F. Holmes, "The Southern Farmers' Alliance and the Jute Cartel," *Journal of Southern History* 60 (February 1994): 59.

80. Ibid., 67 n. 28.

81. Ibid., 77.

82. Kimberly S. Hanger, *A Medley of Cultures: Louisiana History at the Cabildo* (Louisiana State Museum & Louisiana Museum Foundation, 1996), 18. See also *National Economist*, October 11, 1890; *Cleveland Gazette*, August 30, 1890; Holmes, 1973, 269.

83. *National Economist*, June 7, 21, August 23, September 6, December 23, 1890; John D. Hicks, "The Subtreasury: A Forgotten Plan for the Relief of Agriculture," *Mississippi Valley Historical Review* 15 (December 1928): 355–373. Kelley, 1990, 53–54.

84. *National Economist*, June 7, 1890.

85. Ibid.

86. *Richmond Planet*, August 15, 1891; Gerteis, 2007, 182; Kerr-Ritchie, 204.

87. *Richmond Dispatch*, August 11, 1891.

88. Jeffrey R. Kerr-Ritchie, *Freedpeople in the Tobacco South: Virginia, 1860–1900* (Chapel Hill: University of North Carolina Press, 1999), 205; *Virginia Sun*, June 1, 1891.

89. Spriggs, 195–196; Kerr-Ritchie, 205.

90. Barbara Jeanne Williams, the great-great-granddaughter of Oliver Cromwell, shared her family stories and documents with me on August 15, 2001, at her home in Chicago, Illinois.

91. Nicholas Lemann, *The Promised Land: The Great Black Migration and How it Changed America* (New York: Vintage Books, 1992), 9–10; Holmes, 1973, 270.

92. *New Mississippian*, September 4, 1889.

93. Steven Edward Cresswell, *Rednecks, Redeemers, and Race: Mississippi After Reconstruction* (Jackson: University Press of Mississippi, 2006), 62–63; Holmes, 1973, 267–274.

94. *Atlanta Constitution*, September 2, 1889; Holmes, 1973, 271.

95. *St. Louis Post-Dispatch*, September 7, 1889.

96. Charles Hillman Brough, "The Clinton Riot," in the *Publications of the Mississippi Historical Society*, Vol. 4, ed. Franklin L. Riley (Oxford, MS: 1906), 53–63; *Mississippi in 1875: Report of the U.S. Congressional Committee to Inquire into the Mississippi Election of 1876 with Testimony and Evidence* (Washington, D.C.: Government Printing Office, 1876), 2 vols., 466–468.

97. Barbara Jeanne Williams shared this family story with me of Cromwell's final days, which her great-aunt had told her in the late 1970s.

98. *National Economist*, April 11, 1891; Aptheker, 809–810.

99. The bill was named after its Republican congressman sponsor Edwin H. Conger of Iowa. Holmes, 1973; Herman Clarence Nixon, "The Cleavage Within the Farmers Alliance Movement," *Mississippi Valley Historical Review* 15, no. 1 (June 1928): 22–23; *Raleigh Progressive Farmer*, January 6, 1892.

100. The text of the telegram sent by John S. Jackson appears in the *Congressional Record*, 51st Congress, Session 2, 158; *Mobile Daily Register*, December 5, 1890; William W. Rogers, "The Negro Alliance in Alabama," *Journal of Negro History* 45, no. 1 (January 1960): 40.

101. *Congressional Record*, 51st Congress, Session 1; 5789–5793; 6538–6545; 6851; 6869.

102. *Boston Journal*, December 1890; Paul H. Buck, *The Road to Reunion, 1865–1900* (New York: Vintage Books, 1959), 280; Congressional Record, 51st Congress, 1st Session, *passim*; Donald L. Grant, *The Black Experience in Georgia: The Way It Was in the South* (Athens: University of Georgia Press, 2001), 198.

103. *National Economist*, August 2, 1890; William F. Holmes, "The Southern Farmers' Alliance: The Georgia Experience," *Georgia Historical Quarterly* 72, no. 4 (Winter 1988): 649.

104. Gaither, 1977, 63.

105. Ayers, 258; William W. Rogers, "Negro Knights of Labor in Arkansas: A Case Study of the 'Miscellaneous' Strike," *Labor History* 10 (Summer 1969): 498–505.

106. "Negroes Urged to Strike," *New York Times*, September 11, 1891.

107. Kansas City's *American Citizen*, September 11, 1891; *New York Age*, October 3, 1891; Gnatz, 114. Abramowitz, 1950, 26. See *Prices of Farm Products Received by Producers* (Statistical Bulletin 16, U.S. Department of Agriculture, Annual Report for South and Atlantic and Middle South States, Washington, D.C., 1927), 46, 77, 91, 106, 119, 150, 165, 179, 194, 207, 238.

108. Robert C. McMath Jr. lists the following occupations among white officers of the Farmers Alliances in the South in 1890: "Farmer (undifferentiated)" (35.78%), "Small farmer" (8.42%), and "Planter" (23.15%); McMath Jr. 1975, 163.

109. C. Vann Woodward, *Tom Watson: Agrarian Rebel* (New York: Oxford University Press, 1969; first published in 1938), 219; *Raleigh Progressive Farmer*, September 15, 1891; Abramowitz, 1950, 44.

110. Thurtell, 85.

111. *Raleigh Progressive Farmer*, September 15, 1891; *Caucasian*, September 17, 1891; Philip J. Wood, *Southern Capitalism: The Political Economy of North Carolina, 1880–1980* (Durham, NC: Duke University Press, 1986), 26, 111–112.

112. "Cotton Pickers to Strike: Ordered to Stop Work Sept. 12 in all the Southern States," *New York Times*, September 8, 1891.

113. *Cleveland Gazette*, September 26, 1891; Aptheker, 810.

114. Ibid.

115. *Arkansas Gazette*, October 3, 1891, reprinted in Foner and Lewis, 1978, 361–362.

116. Holmes, "The Arkansas Cotton Pickers Strike," 1973, 107–119; Robert C. McMath Jr., "Southern White Farmers and the Organization of Black Farm Workers: A North Carolina Document," *Labor History* 18 (Winter 1977): 117.

117. Dickson, 158.

118. Goodwyn, 122–123.

119. *Atlanta Constitution*, September 1, 12, 1890, and October 6, 1892; Abramowitz, 1953, 259; James C. Bonner, "The Alliance Legislature of 1890," in *Studies in Georgia History and Government*, ed. James C. Bonner and Lucien E. Roberts (Athens: University of Georgia Press, 1940), 163.

120. *National Economist*, March 5, 1892.

121. Miller, 173.

122. See Carl N. Degler, *The Other South: Southern Dissenters in the Nineteenth Century* (Gainesville: University Press of Florida, 2000), 339; Kenneth Coleman, *A History of Georgia* (Athens: University of Georgia Press, 1991), 277.

123. Alexander W. Wayman, *Cyclopedia of African Methodism* (Baltimore, MD: Methodist Episcopal Book Depository, 1882), 58; Yanosky, 9–10.

124. Yanosky, 9–10.
125. Gaither, 1977, 18–20; Dann, 64–68.
126. Ayers, 257; Dickson, 123.
127. "A Complete State Ticket: The People's Party Convention in Florida," *New York Times*, July 22, 1892.
128. *National Economist*, March 7, 1891.

Chapter Three

1. *Atlanta Constitution*, October 25–27, 1892; *Chronicle*, October 26, 1892.
2. Vance to Elias Carr, July 1, 1890, *Carr Papers*.
3. *Virginia Sun*, October 12, 1892; Abramowitz, 1953, 275; and Gaither, 1977, 84.
4. Congressional testimony by Henry S. Doyle in 1896; *Contested Election Case of Thomas E. Watson v. J. C. C. Black* (Washington, D.C.: Government Printing Office, 1896), 669, 683, 717, 781, 793–794; Woodward, 1969, 239–240.
5. Ibid.
6. Watson, 1892, 548.
7. Donald Lee Grant, *The Way It Was in the South: The Black Experience in Georgia* (Athens: University of Georgia Press, 2001), 176–177.
8. Barton C. Shaw, *The Wool-Hat Boys: Georgia's Populist Party* (Baton Rouge: Louisiana State University Press, 1984), 177.
9. Woodward, 1969, 239–240.
10. Robert L. Allen and Pamela P. Allen, *Reluctant Reformers: Racism and Social Reform Movements in the United States* (Washington, D.C.: Howard University Press, 1983), 73. See also Crowe, 1970, 99–116; Abramowitz, 1953, 275.
11. *National Economist*, August 16, 1890; Gerteis, 2007, 45.
12. Foner, 1988, 591–592; Degler, 265.
13. See Blake J. Wintory, "African-American Legislators in the Arkansas General Assembly, 1868–1893," *Arkansas Historical Quarterly* 65, no. 4 (Winter 2006): 385–434.
14. See Aptheker, ed., *Documentary History*, 697–703.
15. McLaurin, 1972, 301; Daniel W. Crofts, "The Black Response to the Blair Education Bill," *Journal of Southern History* 37, no. 1 (February 1971): 41–65.
16. Paul Horton, "Testing the Limits of Class Politics in Postbellum Alabama: Agrarian Radicalism in Lawrence County," *Journal of Southern History* 57, no. 1 (February 1991): 74, 80.
17. *Raleigh News and Observer*, September 12, 18, 1886; Nichols to Powderly, November 26, 1886, Box 22, *Powderly Papers*; McLaurin, 1972, 303–304.
18. Thurtell, 58.
19. *Raleigh News and Observer*, September 18, 1886.
20. Thurtell, 44; Philip Roy Muller, "New South Populism: North Carolina, 1884–1900" (Ph.D. dissertation, University of North Carolina, Chapel Hill, 1971), 80–81; Alan B. Bromberg, "Pure Democracy and White Supremacy, The Redeemer Period in North Carolina: 1876–1894" (Ph.D. dissertation, University of Virginia, 1977), 167–168, 178.
21. Thurtell, 44.
22. Steven Hahn, *The Roots of Southern Populism: Yeoman Farmers and the Transformation of the Georgia Upcountry, 1850–1890* (New York: Oxford University Press, 1983), 284.
23. Gnatz, 38.

24. See Hyman, 1990, 11.

25. J. Morgan Kousser, *The Shaping of Southern Politics: Suffrage Restriction and the Establishment of the One-Party South, 1880–1910* (New Haven, CT: Yale University Press, 1974), 92, 123, 212.

26. See Hahn, 1983, 284.

27. Gnatz, 108–109.

28. C. Vann Woodward, *The Strange Career of Jim Crow* (New York: Oxford University Press, 1974), 59.

29. Gnatz, 109.

30. Thurtell, 64.

31. *Cleveland Gazette*, May 13, 1893; Francis B. Simkins, *The Tillman Movement in South Carolina* (Durham, NC: Duke University Press, 1926), n. 132; Bryant 53; "Richard Carroll Papers," University of South Carolina Society, Manuscripts Collections, www.sc.edu/library/socar/uscs/1998/carrol98.html (Accessed June 5, 2009).

32. Gnatz, 113–114; *National Economist*, September 13, 1890.

33. Dickson, 126.

34. Dann, 65; *National Economist*, April 11, 1891.

35. Coleman, 277,

36. Gerteis, 2007, 46.

37. Spriggs, 198.

38. Gnatz, 10.

39. *Lynchburg Daily Virginia*, August 21, 1890; Spriggs, 194.

40. *New York Sun*, December 4, 1890, quoted in the *New York Age*, December 13, 1890; *National Economist*, December 27, 1890.

41. *Richmond Dispatch*, August 11, 1891.

42. "No Politics, Perhaps," *New York Times*, August 23, 1890.

43. See *Weekly Toiler*, December 18, 1889; Humphrey, 291.

44. Samuel Proctor, "The National Farmer's Alliance Convention of 1890 and Its 'Ocala Demands,'" *Florida Historical Quarterly* 27 (January 1950): 161–167; McMath Jr., 1975, 107.

45. "Proceedings of the Annual Session of the Supreme Council of the National Farmers Alliance and Industrial Union at Ocala, Florida, December 2–8, 1890" (Washington, D.C.: National Economist Publishing Company, 1891); see also Spriggs, 198. Frank Davis, president of the Alabama Colored Alliance, and fellow member J. F. Washington, do not appear as delegates as they were not in favor of electoral action. Goodwyn, 1978, 120; Gaither, 2005, 49.

46. *Atlanta Constitution*, December 4, 5, 1890.

47. *New York Times*, December 3–12, 1890; Abramowitz, 1953, 260 n. 6.

48. Gaither, 2005, 45.

49. *Atlanta Constitution*, December 4, 6–8, 1890; *Indianapolis Freeman*, December 13, 1890; Miller, 173. The People's Party presidential candidate in 1892, James B. Weaver, opposed the Lodge Bill. See August Meier and Elliott Rudwick, eds., *The Making of Black America* (New York: Atheneum, 1969), 33, and Fred Emory Haynes, *James Baird Weaver* (Iowa City: State Historical Society of Iowa, 1919), 302.

50. *Boston Journal*, December 1890; Buck, 1959, 280.

51. *National Economist*, December 20, 1890; Abramowitz, 1953, 262.

52. "Proceedings of the Annual Session of the Supreme Council of the National Farmers Alliance and Industrial Union at Ocala, Florida, December 2–8, 1890" (Washington, D.C.: National Economist Publishing Company, 1891).

53. Buck, 1920, 123.
54. Dunning, 162.
55. *Atlanta Constitution*, December 8, 1890; Spriggs, 200.
56. Spriggs, 153, 162–163. The proceedings at Ocala were also recorded in the *National Economist*, December 13 and 20, 1890.
57. Gnatz, 20.
58. "The Cincinnati Conference: A Convention That Is Likely To See Much Wrangling," *New York Times*, May 18, 1891.
59. Postel, 12; McMath Jr., 1975, Chapter 8; Dickson, 104; *Proceedings of the Confederation of Industrial Organizations, held at Washington, D.C., January 22 to 24, 1891, Powderly Papers*.
60. *New York Times*, May 20, 1891.
61. Postel, 181.
62. *National Economist*, April 11, 1891; Aptheker, 808–810; Gaither, 2005, 43.
63. Gaither, 2005, 43; Helen M. Blackburn, "The Populist Party in the South, 1890–1898" (M.A. thesis, Howard University, 1941), 10; William DuBose Sheldon, *Populism in the Old Dominion: Virginia Farm Politics, 1885–1900* (Princeton, NJ: Princeton University Press, 1935), 66.
64. Gnatz, 10.
65. Abramowitz, 1953, 262.
66. Gnatz, 31; *National Economist*, February 27, 1892.
67. See Abramowitz, 1953, 257–289.
68. *Southern Mercury*, January 10, 1895; Bryant, 68.
69. *People's Party Paper*, February 25, 1892; *National Economist*, February 27, March 5, 1892; Gaither, 1977, 38.
70. *National Economist*, March 5, 1892; Gaither, 1977, 38, 40; William H. Warwick's election as assistant secretary is detailed in the minutes taken at the St. Louis Convention of February 22, 1892, contained in the *National Economist*, March 5, 1892.
71. Abramowitz, 1953, 263; *National Economist*, March 5, 1892.
72. *Virginia Sun*, July 13, 1892; Spriggs, 200; Joseph Gerteis, "Class and the Color Line: The Sources and Limits of Interracial Class Conflict, 1880–1896" (Ph.D. dissertation, University of North Carolina, Chapel Hill, 1999).
73. Hicks, 1931, 435–444; *National Economist*, July 9, 1892.
74. *Topeka Call*, July 24, 1892; Abramowitz, 1953, 278; Gaither, 1977, 41–43.
75. *Topeka Daily Capital*, July 5, 1892; *Topeka Call*, July 24, 1892; Bryant, 66.
76. See Goodwyn, 1976, 215–229; Ayers, 266–267, 293–295.
77. Abramowitz, 1953, 264.
78. Bryant, 70; Abramowitz, 1953, 269.
79. *Southern Mercury*, August 11, 1892.
80. Winkler, 1916, 293, 297; Martin, 41; Abramowitz, 1953, 264, 267–268; Gaither, 2005, 183.
81. Gaither, 2005, 143; Shaw, 58–59; Crowe, 1970, 109; *Atlanta Constitution*, July 10, 1892.
82. *Wilmington Star*, August 1892; Simeon A. Delap, "The Populist Party in North Carolina," *Trinity Archives* 14 (1922): 51.
83. *New York Times*, November 25, 1901.
84. "Arkansas Republicans," *New York Times*, July 28, 1888; Kenneth C. Barnes, *Journey of Hope: The Back to Africa Movement in Arkansas* (Chapel Hill: University of North Carolina Press, 2004), 50–51; Dallas Tabor Herndon, ed., *Centennial History of Arkansas* (Chicago: S. J. Clarke Publishing Co., 1922), 336.

85. Abramowitz, 1953, 266–267; W. Scott Morgan, *History of the Wheel and Alliance and the Impending Revolution* (St. Louis: C. B. Woodward Company, 1891), 335–336.

86. "The Fight for the House," *New York Times*, November 2, 1890.

87. David Y. Thomas, ed., *Arkansas and Its People: A History, 1541–1930* (New York: American Historical Society, 1930), 223.

88. Gnatz, 57.

89. Hild, 2007, 30.

90. *Indianapolis Freeman*, October 4, 1890; Blackburn, 44; Thomas, 239–240.

91. Historians of white Populism offer another perspective: Jeffrey Ostler notes, "The People's Party tried to induce black voters to leave the party of Lincoln by nominating B. F. Foster." Jeffrey Ostler, *Prairie Populism: The Fate of Agrarian Radicalism in Kansas, Nebraska, and Iowa, 1880–1892* (Lawrence: University of Kansas Press, 2007), 125.

92. *Indianapolis Freeman*, September 6, 1890; Morgan County, Kentucky, 1860 Census, District 1, Family Unit 460.

93. *Topeka Call*, August 9, 1891.

94. *Indianapolis Freeman*, December 6, 1890. Polk died of a bladder infection less than three weeks before the 1992 People's Party's national nominating convention; James B. Weaver was nominated as the party's presidential candidate; McMath Jr., 1975, 139.

95. Abramowitz, 1953, 265.

96. Peter H. Argersinger, *The Limits of Agrarian Radicalism* (Lawrence: University Press of Kansas, 1995), 73; Jeffrey Ostler, *Prairie Populism: The Fate of Agrarian Radicalism in Kansas, Nebraska, and Iowa, 1880–1892* (Lawrence: University Press of Kansas, 2007), 10.

97. Argersinger, 46, and Table 2, "Voting Distribution by Town Size, 1890," 67.

98. *Parsons Weekly Blade*, November 12, 1892; *Topeka Call*, November 21, 1892.

99. Blackburn, 27.

100. An illustration of Lytle appears in Booker T. Washington's, *A New Negro for a New Century: An Accurate and Up-to-Date Record of the Upward Struggles of the Negro Race* (Chicago: American Publishing House, 1900), 395.

101. See Noreen R. Connolly, "Attorney Lutie A. Lytle: Options and Obstacles of a Legal Pioneer," *Nebraska Lawyer* (January 1999): 6–12; J. Clay Smith, ed., *Rebel in Law: Voices in History of Black Women Lawyers* (Ann Arbor: University Press of Michigan, 1998); John M. Peterson, "The People's Party of Kansas: Campaigning in 1898," *Kansas History* 13 (1990–91): 235–258; Omar H. Ali, "Lutie A. Lytle," in *African American National Biography*, ed. Henry Louis Gates Jr. and Evelyn Brooks Higginbotham (New York: Oxford University Press, 2008), 344–346.

102. Gnatz, 57.

103. Roscoe C. Martin, *The People's Party in Texas: A Study in Third Party Politics* (Austin: University of Texas Press, 1970), 89, 93.

104. *Southern Mercury*, June 30, 1892

105. Ibid.

106. Abramowitz, 1953, 267.

107. *Southern Mercury*, June 30, 1892.

108. Gaither, 1977, 119; Robert M. Saunders, "The Southern Populists and the Negro in 1892," *Essays in History* 12 (1966–1967): 11 n. 28; *Southern Mercury*, June 30, July 7, 1892.

109. Gaither, 2005, 20–21; Robert Carroll, "Robert Lloyd Smith and the Farmers' Improvement Society of Texas" (M.A. thesis, Baylor University, 1974); Merline Pitre, *Through*

Many Dangers, Toils and Snares: The Black Leadership of Texas, 1868–1900 (Austin, TX: Eakin Press, 1985), 195–205.

110. Shaw, 93 n. 8; Rice, 1971.

111. Gregg Cantrell, *Feeding the Wolf: John B. Rayner and the Politics of Race, 1850–1918* (Wheeling, IL: Harlan Davidson, 2001), 42.

112. Quoted in Ibid., 2–9.

113. Ibid., 10.

114. Ibid., 12.

115. Cantrell, 2001, 7.

116. Anderson, 1981, 4; Cantrell, 2001, 10–11.

117. *Dallas Morning News*, July 31, 1903; Winkler, 1916.

118. Cantrell, 2001, 23.

119. Ibid., 34–38; J. B. Rayner to C. W. Macune, November 12, 1891, *Terrence V. Powderly Papers*.

120. *National Economist*, October 17, 1891.

121. *A History of the Proceedings in the City of New Orleans, On the Occasion of the Funeral Ceremonies in Honor of James Abram Garfield, Late President of the United States, Which Took Place on Monday, September 29th, 1881* (New Orleans, LA: A. W. Hyatt, 1881), 253.

122. Gaither, 2005, 170–171.

123. Ibid., 258–259, see Table XXII, "Voting and Black Population Characteristics for the Louisiana Congressional Election of 1892."

124. Joel M. Sipress, "'The Interests of the White and Colored People of the South are Identical': Populism and Race in Grant Parish, Louisiana," 1–16, unpublished paper delivered at the "Race, Labor, and Citizenship in the Post-Emancipation South" conference in Charleston, South Carolina, on March 12, 2010.

125. Palmer, 53; Natchitoches *Louisiana Populist*, July 5, 1895.

126. *New York Age*, December 13, 1890; Gnatz, 111 n. 3.

127. *Atlanta Journal*, July 20, 1892; Clarence B. Bacote, "The Negro in Georgia Politics, 1880–1908" (Ph.D. dissertation, University of Chicago, 1955), 166; Gnatz, 72; Shaw, 1984, 58–59.

128. *Southern Alliance Farmer*, August 2, 1892, quoted in Norman Pollack, *The Populist Response to Industrial America* (Cambridge, MA: Harvard University Press, 1962), 386–387; Gaither, 1977, 97.

129. *Atlanta Constitution*, May 2, 1892; Gnatz, 80–81.

130. Letters from Channing H. Tobias to W. E. B. Du Bois, July 27, 1949, and Bertram W. Doyle to W. E. B. Du Bois, August 23, 1949, in Herbert Aptheker, ed., *The Correspondence of W. E. B. Du Bois: Volume III Selections 1944–1963* (Amherst: University of Massachusetts Press, 1997), 165–167.

131. W. E. B. Du Bois, *The Black Flame: A Trilogy, Book One, The Ordeal of Mansart* (New York: Mainstream Publishers, 1957), 162. Du Bois's account was based on research conducted over the course of eight years, including correspondence with Channing Tobias and Doyle's son, Dr. Bertram W. Doyle.

132. Aptheker, ed., 1997, 165–167.

133. See *Souvenir; Negro Young People's Congress*, 75, in *African American Biographical Database* (Accessed June 5, 2009).

134. Gnatz, 83, 119.

135. Gerteis, 1999, 223; *People's Party Paper*, October 14, 1892; September 20, 1895; October 25, 1895; March 13, 1896.
136. Woodward, 1969, 239–240; *Election Case of Thomas E. Watson v. J. C. C. Black* (Washington, D.C.: Government Printing Office, 1896), 669, 683, 717, 781, 793–794; *Atlanta Constitution*, October 25–27; *Chronicle*, October 26, 1892.
137. *Southern Mercury*, June 30, 1892.
138. Woodward, 1969.
139. *Wilmington Star*, August 1892; quoted in Delap, 1922, 51; Abramowitz, 1953, 282.
140. Thurtell, 126.
141. See Anderson, 1981; James M. Beeby, "'Equal Rights to All and Special Privileges to None': Grass-Roots Populism in North Carolina," *North Carolina Historical Review* 78, no. 2 (April 2001): 156–186.
142. *State Chronicle*, August 30, 1890, and *Union Republican*, September 4, 1890, noted in Thurtell, 136–137.
143. *Richmond Dispatch*, April 16, 1890; Woodward, 1951, 220.
144. Kousser, 1974, "Strong Party Competition and Heavy Negro Participation in Gubernatorial Races in North Carolina, 1880–1896," Table 7.1, 183.
145. *Tarboro Southerner*, August 13, 1891; Creech, 2006, 135.
146. *State Chronicle*, August 17, 1892; *Caucasian*, August 25, 1892; Anderson, 199; C. C. Cheek to Thomas Settle, October 27, 1892; *Thomas Settle Papers*, Southern Historical Collection, Wilson Library, University of North Carolina, Chapel Hill; Thurtell, 126, 146.
147. Kousser, Table 7.1, 183.
148. *Raleigh News and Observer*, September 30, 1892; *National Economist*, October 8, 1892.
149. Thurtell, 146.
150. *Raleigh News and Observer*, September 30, 1892.
151. Ibid., October 1, 1892.
152. Richard Stiller, *Queen of Populists: The Story of Mary Elizabeth Lease* (New York: Crowell, 1970); Postel, 93.
153. Shaw, 1984, 177.
154. *Raleigh News and Observer*, September 30, 1892.
155. Ibid.; Postel, 100.
156. Kousser, 183.
157. *Contested Election Cases, Martin v. Lockhart* (Washington, D.C.: Government Printing Office, 1895), 176–177; Beeby, 2001, 156–186.
158. Mabry, 35; Abramowitz, 1953, 282.
159. Gnatz, 76.
160. Gerteis, 1999, 162. See also Ayers, *The Promise of the New South*.
161. Lucia E. Daniel, "The Louisiana People's Party," *Louisiana Historical Quarterly* 26 (October 1943): 1080, 1089; Woodward, 1951, 276–277.

Chapter Four

1. Ayers, 295–296; Gerteis, 1999, 163.
2. Abramowitz, 1953, 287.
3. Henry D. Lloyd, "The Populists at St. Louis," *Review of Reviews* 14 (September 1896): 299–300; William L. Katz, *Eyewitness: The Negro in American History* (New York: Pitman Publishing Corporation, 1967), 319; Allen, 1976, 69.

4. Lloyd, 299–300; *St. Louis Globe-Democrat*, July 23, 1896. Letter to Jack Abramowitz from Mr. A. W. Ricker dated December 17, 1947; Abramowitz, 1953, 288.

5. See Ayers, 47, and Michael R. Hyman, *The Anti-Redeemers: Hill-Country Political Dissenters in the Lower South from Redemption to Populism* (Baton Rouge: Louisiana State University Press, 1990), 179, 181–183.

6. Abramowitz, 1953, 287.

7. Postel, 274–275.

8. Gerteis, 1999, 163.

9. Woodward, 1951, 56.

10. *Louisiana Populist*, March 29, May 17, 1895.

11. Woodward, 1971, 276–278; Saloutos, 144–145.

12. Palmer, 53; *Choctaw Alliance*, October 19, 1892, May 2, 1894.

13. Quoted in William Warren Rogers, *The One-Gallused Rebellion: Agrarianism in Alabama, 1865–1896* (Baton Rouge: Louisiana State University Press, 1970), 214, 219.

14. Kousser, 1974, Table 1.6, "Estimated Voting Patterns, by Race," 42; *Virginia Sun*, July 6 and 20, 1892.

15. *New York Times*, May 24, June 13, 1892.

16. Postel, 14; McMath Jr., 1993, 175–176.

17. Quintard Taylor, *In Search of the Racial Frontier: African Americans in the American West, 1528–1990* (New York: W. W. Norton, 1998), 135.

18. Kousser, Table 1.5, "The Opposition at Its Crest in the 1890s"; Hicks, 1931, 263, 337.

19. South Carolina did not have a People's Party ticket in 1894. It was a dissident faction that challenged the regular Democratic Party. See Marszalek, *passim*. As George B. Tindall notes, the state never developed strong independent candidates nor a Populist third party organization; Tindall, 33.

20. Ayers, 278.

21. Studies, such as Kousser (1974), showing in numeric terms the impact of election law changes (for instance the implementation of the "eight box law" in South Carolina in 1882, which cut voter turnout in half), while helpful in understanding the overall impact of a single mitigating factor in the election process, still cannot explain which party black voters would support in a given election; Kousser, 92.

22. *People's Party Paper*, July 27, 1894; Gerteis, 1999, 185, 229.

23. Charles Crowe, "Tom Watson, Populists, and Blacks Reconsidered," *Journal of Negro History* 60 (April 1970): 110.

24. Michael C. Dawson, *Behind the Mule: Race and Class in African-American Politics* (Princeton, NJ: Princeton University Press, 1994), 106.

25. Hyman, 170; Gaither, 1977, 108.

26. Ibid., 98–99, 116–117; *People's Party Paper*, January 20, 1893.

27. *Journal of the Proceedings of the Constitutional Convention of the State of Mississippi* (Jackson, MS: E. L. Martin, 1890), 702.

28. Cresswell, 2006, 124.

29. Kousser, Table 6.2, "An Innoculation against Populism: Effect of Election Law Changes on Turnout and Party Voting in Mississippi, 1888–1895," 144.

30. Cresswell, 2006, 124.

31. *Charleston News and Courier*, October 11, 1892.

32. Kousser, Table 4.4, 92; Table 9.3, 242.

33. *National Economist*, October 8, 1892.

34. Kousser, Table 1.5, "The Opposition Crest in the 1890s," 41.

35. Gnatz, 49.

36. Marszalek, 2006, 8–9.

37. See *Twenty-two Years' Work of the Hampton Normal and Agricultural Institute at Hampton, Virginia* (Hampton, VA: Normal School Press, 1893), 236.

38. William J. Gaboury, "George Washington Murray and the Fight for Political Democracy in South Carolina," *Journal of Negro History* 62, no. 3 (July 1977): 258–269.

39. *Yorkville Enquirer*, September 26, 1888; *Columbia Daily Register*, December 13, 1888; Tindall, 117.

40. *Charleston News and Courier*, April 25, 1889.

41. Ayers, 236; Marszalek, 17–18; Walter B. Edgar, *South Carolina: A History* (Columbia: University of South Carolina Press, 1998), 431–432; Tindall, 57, 117–119.

42. Marszalek, 17–18; Edgar, 1998, 431–432; Tindall, 57, 117–119.

43. Tindall, 118; *Charleston News and Courier*, January 12, September 10, 1891.

44. Letter from George Washington Murray to Booker T. Washington, July 7, 1894, Louis R. Harlan, ed., *The Booker T. Washington Papers*, Vol. 3: 1889–1895; 451–452 n. 1.

45. Tindall, 57 n. 9.

46. Gaboury, 258–259.

47. See, for instance, Holmes, 1973, 273–274, and Dickson, 164.

48. Ali, 2006, 200–203; Gaither, 1977, 95.

49. Gaboury, 262, 266; *Congressional Record*, 54th Congress, 1st Session.

50. *Congressional Record*, 53rd Congress, 1st Session, 860; Gaboury, 258.

51. *Congressional Record*, 53rd Congress, 2nd Session, 2092.

52. J. Morgan Kousser, "The Voting Rights Act and Two Reconstructions," in *Controversies in Minority Voting: The Voting Rights Act in Perspective*, ed. Bernard Grofman and Chandler Davidson (Washington, D.C.: Brookings Institute Press, 1992), 135.

53. Matthew Wasniewski, ed., *Black Americans in Congress, 1870–2007* (Washington, D.C.: Government Printing Office, 2008), 220–226; Gnatz, 49; and George Washington Murray, *Race Ideals: Effects, Cause, and Remedy for the Afro-American Race Troubles* (Princeton, IN: Smith & Sons Publishing Company, 1914), *passim*.

54. Rayford Logan, *The Betrayal of the Negro from Rutherford B. Hayes to Woodrow Wilson* (New York: Da Capo Press, 1997), 91.

55. *Congressional Record*, 53rd Congress, 2nd Session, 2161.

56. Atlanta *People's Party Paper*, July 29, 1892; Palmer, 52 n. 13.

57. Hicks, 263, 337.

58. Black and white population figures available in the U.S. Department of Interior, *Compendium of the Eleventh Census, 1890*, Part I (Washington, D.C.: Government Printing Office, 1892), Table 11, 473; Shaw, 96.

59. See Gaither, "Blacks and the Populist Revolt: Ballots and Bigotry in the New South" (Ph.D. dissertation, University of Tennessee, Knoxville, 1972), 353.

60. Kousser, Table 1.6, "Estimated Voting Patterns, by Race, in Key Gubernatorial Contests During the 1890s," 42.

61. Francis M. Wilhoit, "An Interpretation of Populism's Impact on the Georgia Negro," *Journal of Negro History* 52, no. 2 (April 1967): 118.

62. Shaw, 100.

63. *People's Party Paper*, October 28, 1892.

64. Gaither, 1977, 100–101.

65. Gerteis, 1999, 232.
66. See Gaither, 1977, 97.
67. *People's Party Paper*, September 14, 1894.
68. Kousser, Table 6.1, "Estimated Voting Patterns, by Race, in Key Gubernatorial Contests during the 1890s," 42.
69. *Georgia Baptist* quoted in *Progressive Farmer*, October 30, 1894.
70. *Savannah Tribune*, September 8, 1894; Gnatz, 81.
71. Letter from H. I. Taylor, *People's Party Paper*, September 14, 1894.
72. Gnatz, 77; *Atlanta Journal*, May 17, 1894.
73. *Savannah Tribune*, September 15, 1894.
74. Ibid., September 1, 1894; Gnatz, 121.
75. *People's Party Paper*, August 17, 1894.
76. Ibid., June 22, August 31, 1894; Gnatz, 120.
77. *Atlanta Constitution*, October 4, 5, 1894; Abramowitz, 1953, 275–276.
78. Kousser, 215.
79. Gerteis, 1999, 232, 235; Woodward, 1963, 270.
80. *People's Guide*, quoted in *People's Party Paper*, October 28, 1895; Gaither, 1977, 100.
81. Gerteis, 1999, 235; *People's Party Paper*, September 20, 1894.
82. Gerteis, 1999, 232.
83. *People's Party Paper*, February 16, 1894.
84. *Savannah Tribune*, August 25, September 1, 1894; *People's Party Paper*, May 11, 1894; Gnatz, 79.
85. Abramowitz, 1953, 275.
86. Shaw, 126 n. 6.
87. Atlanta *People's Party Paper*, December 27, 1895; Palmer, 52.
88. Gnatz, 126; Bacote, 215–219; Kousser, Table 7.1, "Effect of Cumulative Poll Tax: Turnout and Estimated Black Turnout in Georgia Compared with Turnout in Ten Other Southern Sates in Presidential Elections, 1876–1908," 212.
89. Jack Bass, *Unlikely Heroes* (Tuscaloosa: University of Alabama Press, 1990), 16.
90. Ayers, 301.
91. See Stewart E. Tolnay and E. M. Beck, *A Festival of Violence: An Analysis of Southern Lynchings, 1882–1930* (Urbana: University of Illinois Press, 1995); National Association for the Advancement of Colored People, *Thirty Years of Lynching in the United States, 1889–1918* (Ayer Company Publishers, 1970; first published in 1919); Sarah A. Soule, "Populism and Black Lynching in Georgia, 1890–1900," *Social Forces* 71, no. 2 (December 1992): 431–449.
92. Ayers, 495.
93. *Raleigh Progressive Farmer*, August 30, 1892; Palmer, 52.
94. Joe Creech, *Righteous Indignation: Religion and the Populist Revolution* (Urbana: University of Illinois Press, 2006), 134; James M. Beeby, "Revolt of the Tar Heelers" (Ph.D. dissertation, Bowling Green State University, 1999), 114–143.
95. Creech, 2006, 136.
96. Thurtell, 52–53
97. Helen Edmonds, *The Negro and Fusion Politics in North Carolina, 1894–1901* (Chapel Hill: University of North Carolina Press, 1951), 16, 30; Gnatz, 40.
98. Edmonds, 27; Gnatz, 43.
99. Thurtell, 46, 48.

100. Palmer, "Appendix F: North Carolina Black Belt Vote," 227.

101. Nathan Carter Newbold, *Five North Carolina Negro Educators* (Chapel Hill: University of North Carolina Press, 1939), 130–132.

102. Gaither, 1977, 91; Thurtell, 132; Democrats in North Carolina fielded a black man, Joe Ray, for township constable in Martin County in 1892 against a white Populist candidate, Joe Swinson, who won; State Executive Committee of the People's Party of North Carolina, *People's Party Handbook of Facts, Campaign of 1898* (Raleigh, NC: Capital Printing Co., 1898), 16.

103. Joseph C. Price, "Does the Negro Seek Social Equality?" *Forum* 10 (January 1891): 562–563; Thurtell, 132–133.

104. Gaither, 1977, 90.

105. Ibid., 90, 92–93.

106. Thurtell, 219.

107. See Eric Foner's *Free Soil, Free Labor, Free Men: The Ideology of the Republican Party Before the Civil War* (New York: Oxford University Press, 1970).

108. Creech, 2006, 135.

109. Thurtell, 52–53.

110. *Contested Election Cases, Martin v. Lockhart*, 176–177. See Beeby, 2001, 156–186.

111. *Martin v. Lockhart*, 21, 120–121, 344–346.

112. Woodward, 1951, 276–277.

113. Thurtell, 213–214; Thurtell draws upon election returns from R. D. W. Connor, ed., *A Manual of North Carolina* (Raleigh: E. M. Uzzelll & Co., 1913).

114. Beeby, 156–186.

115. Gnatz, 43.

116. Thurtell, 12.

117. Abramowitz, 1953, 283; Mabry, 18–22, 36–38.

118. Thurtell, 222.

119. Ayers, 267.

120. Joseph Gregoire De Roulhac Hamilton, *North Carolina Since 1860*, Vol. 3 (Chicago: Lewis Publishing Company, 1919), 248–249; Gaither, 1977, 89.

121. M. C. Birmingham to Butler, December 19, 1896; *Charlotte Observer*, October 29, 31, 1896, Box 4, folder 50, Butler Papers; James L. Hunt, "The Making of a Populist: Marion Butler, 1863–1895," *North Carolina Historical Review* 62 (January 1985): 53–77; (April 1985): 179–202; (July 1985): 317–43; Aptheker, 1992, 808.

122. *National Economist*, March 7, 1891.

123. W. A. Guthrie to Marion Butler, June 7, 1896, Box 2, Folder 29, *Marion Butler Papers*, Southern Historical Collection, Wilson Library, University of North Carolina, Chapel Hill; clipping from *Charlotte Observer* (n.d.) attached; see Gaither, 1977, 89.

124. Kousser, Table 1.6, "Estimated Voting Patterns, by Race," 42.

125. Hugh T. Lefler and Albert Ray Newsome, *North Carolina: The History of a Southern State* (Chapel Hill: University of North Carolina Press, 1963), 519; Gaither, 1977, 93.

126. T. L. Jones to Marion Butler, May 19, 1896, Box 2, Folder 27, *Marion Butler Papers*.

127. Carl N. Degler, *The Other South: Southern Dissenters in the Nineteenth Century* (Gainesville: University Press of Florida, 2000), 360.

128. Ayers, 301.

129. Stephen Kantrowitz, *Ben Tillman and the Reconstruction of White Supremacy* (Chapel Hill: University of North Carolina Press, 2000), 64–71.

130. Ayers, 302.

131. H. Leon Prather, *We Have Taken a City: Wilmington Racial Massacre and Coup of 1898* (Cranbury, NJ: Associated University Press, Inc., 1984); David Cecelski and Timothy B. Tyson, eds., *Democracy Betrayed: The Wilmington Race Riot of 1898 and Its Legacy* (Chapel Hill: University of North Carolina Press, 1998), 95–112.

132. Ida B. Wells, *A Red Record: Tabulated Statistics and Alleged Causes of Lynchings in the United States, 1892–1893–1894*, reprinted in Jacqueline Jones Royster, ed., *Southern Horrors and Other Writings: The Anti-Lynching Campaign of Ida B. Wells, 1892–1900* (Boston: Bedford Books, 1997), 73–157.

133. Cecelski, 24, 25, 30; Ayers, 302.

134. *Daily Record*, August 18, 1898; Degler, 361.

135. Ayers, 301.

136. Degler, 363.

137. Ayers, 301.

138. Woodward, 1951, 261–262; Abramowitz, 1953, 268; Gaither, 1977, 120.

139. Gaither, 2005, 184.

140. *Dallas Morning News*, August 18, 1891; Woodward, 256; Rice, 1971, 69–72, 78; Bruce Palmer, *"Man Over Money": The Southern Populist Critique of American Capitalism* (Chapel Hill: University of North Carolina Press, 1980), 52.

141. Gaither, 1977, 120.

142. Quoted in Cantrell, 2001, 42–43.

143. Rice, 1971, 79.

144. Quoted in Girard T. Bryant, "J. B. Rayner, A Negro Populist," *Negro History Bulletin* 3 (May 1940): 125.

145. Cantrell, 2001, 44.

146. Winkler, 332; quote from Abramowitz, 1953, 270; Roscoe C. Martin, *The People's Party in Texas: A Study in Third Party Politics* (Austin: University of Texas Press, 1970), 133.

147. Cantrell, 2001, 48; Gaither, 1977, 121; Bryant, 125.

148. Gnatz, 118; *People's Party Paper*, April 9, 1894.

149. Rice, 82–84; Palmer, 52.

150. Gaither, 1977, 121; Abramowitz, 1953, 269.

151. Ibid.

152. Kousser, Table 1.6, "Estimated Voting Patterns, by Race," 42; Martin, 210–211; Abramowitz, 1953, 268.

153. Ibid.

154. Gaither, 1977, 121.

155. Goodwyn, 1971, 1443 n. 35.

156. *Galveston News*, November 11, 1882.

157. Goodwyn, 1971, 1438.

158. Ibid., n. 13.

159. Ayers, 301.

160. Goodwyn, 1971, 1438, 1440.

161. Ibid.

162. Ibid., 1441, 1444–1445.

163. Ibid. In 1902 the White Man's Union Association-backed candidates ran completely unopposed.

Notes
Chapter Five

1. Gaither, 2005, 196; see also Foner, 1988, 591–592.
2. *Columbus Advocate*, July 1892; *Topeka Call*, July 24, 1892; Bryant, "The Populist Movement and the Negro," 66; Gaither, 1977, 42; Abramowitz, 1953, 278.
3. *Amoret Chief*, May 29, 1891, quoted in Bryant, 66; Humphrey, 290.
4. See Tali Mendelberg, *The Race Card: Campaign Strategy, Implicit Messages, and the Norm of Equality* (Princeton, NJ: Princeton University Press, 2001), 66.
5. Kousser, Table 6.2, "An Inoculation against Populism: Effect of Election Law Changes on Turnout and Party Voting in Mississippi, 1888–1895," 144.
6. W. Fitzhugh Brundage, ed., *Up from Slavery by Booker T. Washington with Related Documents* (Boston: Bedford, St. Martin's Press, 2003), 9; Hahn, 2003, 445.
7. Kousser, 32, 139–181; Gaither, 2005, 167; See Cohen, 1991; Michael Perman, *Struggle for Mastery: Disfranchisement in the South, 1888–1908* (Chapel Hill: University of North Carolina Press, 2001), 73–74, 88–90. See also Glen Feldman, *The Disfranchisement Myth: Poor Whites and Suffrage Restriction in Alabama* (Athens: University of Georgia Press, 2004).
8. Daniel Brantley, "Blacks and Louisiana Constitutional Development, 1890–Present: A Study in Southern Political Thought and Race Relations," *Phylon* 48, no. 1. (1987): 58; Gaither, 1977, 117–118.
9. Kousser, Table 4.4, "Voting Participation Sliced by Half: Effect of Election Law Changes in South Carolina on Estimated Turnout by Race in Presidential Elections, 1876–1896," 92.
10. Albert B. Gillespie quoted in Woodward, *Origins of the New South*, 1951, 327; *Proceedings of the Constitutional Convention . . . of Virginia*, 1901–1902, II, 3014.
11. Woodward, 1969, 370–371.
12. *Signal*, October 8, 1891; Thurtell, 130.
13. Brundage, 1–19; Woodward, 1951, 338.
14. See Bruce L. Mouser, *For Labor, Race, and Liberty: George Edwin Taylor and the Making of Independent Black Politics* (Madison: University of Wisconsin Press, 2010).
15. Benjamin Quarles, ed., *Narrative of the Life of Frederick Douglass: An American Slave, Written By Himself* (Cambridge, MA: Harvard University Press, 1960), 334–335.
16. Waldo Martin, *The Mind of Frederick Douglass* (Chapel Hill: University of North Carolina Press, 1984), 90, 282; James, 341.
17. *New York Age*, January 25, 1890; Woodward, 1951, 220.
18. James, 351; Abramowitz, 1953, 286.
19. Ray Ginger, *The Bending Cross: A Biography of Eugene Victor Debs* (New Brunswick, NJ: Rutgers University Press, 1949), 151.
20. W. E. B. Du Bois, *Dusk of Dawn: An Essay Toward an Autobiography of a Race Concept* (New York: Schocken Books, 1971), 54; "From McKinley to Wallace: My Fifty Years as an Independent," *Masses-Mainstream* 1, no. 6 (August 1948): 4.
21. Manning Marable, *Race, Reform, and Rebellion: The Second Reconstruction in America, 1945–1990* (Jackson: University Press of Mississippi, 2002), 3–12; Hahn, 2003, 465.
22. Ibid., 464–465. In addition to the over half million African Americans who left the South between 1880 and 1910, 1,243,000 white southerners also left the region during the period; Ayers, 24.
23. William E. Vickery, "The Economics of the Negro Migration, 1900–1960" (Ph.D. dissertation, University of Chicago, 1969), 174–187; Daniel M. Johnson and Rex R. Campbell, *Black Migration in America: A Social Demographic History* (Durham, NC: Duke University

Press, 1981), 62–69; Hope T. Eldridge and Dorothy S. Thomas, *Demographic Analyses and Interrelations*, Vol. 3 of Simon S. Kuznets, *Population Redistribution and Economic Growth: The United States, 1870–1950* (Philadelphia: American Philosophical Society, 1957–1964), 257, 260, 118, 119; Hahn, 2003, 465.

24. Ayers, 208, 514; Richard K. Smith, "The Economics of Education and Discrimination in the U.S. South, 1870–1910" (Ph.D. dissertation, University of Wisconsin, 1973), 81.

25. Ayers, 208.

26. Eldridge, 48.

27. Ayers, 198.

28. Abramowitz, 1953, 286; Booker T. Washington, *A New Negro for a New Century: An Accurate and Up-to-Date Record of the Upward Struggles of the Negro Race* (Chicago: American Publishing House, 1900); Louis R. Harlan, *Booker T. Washington: The Wizard of Tuskegee, 1901–1915* (New York: Oxford University Press, 1986), 202–265.

29. Beeby, 2001, 156. According to family oral history Jacob J. Shuffer was killed by one of his own African American field hands in retaliation for being whipped for drunkenness. The incident speaks to the class differences that sometimes separated black farm owners from black laborers. See Shuffer, 6; Dickson, 169.

30. As was the case with most Black Populists, Humphrey died in obscurity. Patrick Dickson writes, "Sometime after 1900, [R. M.] Humphrey left the Houston area for Brown County, Texas. His wife, Elizabeth, was killed in September of 1902 in a train accident. In the years that followed her death, the Humphrey family frequently appeared in probate court. R. M. was declared a 'habitual drunkard' and 'non compus mentis' by the court." Humphrey died on April 30, 1906, his minor children placed in the guardianship of their older brother. Dickson, 168. Ellis A. Davis and Edwin H. Grobe, eds., *The New Encyclopedia of Texas*, 2 vols. (Dallas: Texas Development Bureau, 1925), 648.

31. There is a record of Rev. John L. Moore serving as secretary of the African Methodist Episcopal Church's Florida conference in Orlando in 1899. See *Centennial Encyclopedia of the African Methodist Episcopal Church* (Philadelphia, PA: Book Concern of the A.M.E. Church, 1916), 387.

32. Ali, "Lutie A. Lytle," in Gates and Higginbotham, 2008, 344–346.

33. Humphrey, 288. There were others who followed the philosophy of self-help, notably the Mississippi-born slave turned farmer, merchant, and business entrepreneur in Arkansas, Scott Bond. See Willard B. Gatewood, ed., *From Slavery to Wealth: The Life of Scott Bond* (Fayetteville, AR: Phoenix International, 2008).

34. Booker T. Washington, *An Autobiography: The Story of My Life and Work* (Atlanta, GA: J. L. Nichols and Company, 1901), 138, 140; Brundage, 2003, 1–19.

35. Rayner served as the chief fundraiser for Conroe College and the Farmers Improvement Society School; he was president of the former; Cantrell, 2001, 95; Jack Abramowitz, "John B. Rayner: A Grass-Roots Leader," *Journal of Negro History* 36, no. 2 (April 1951): 185; Abramowitz, 1953, 271.

36. Abramowitz, 1951, 189.

37. Cantrell, 2001, 32–57.

38. Quoted in Gaither, 2005, 137; *Negro Year Book*, 1914–1915, 284, *African American Biographical Database* (Accessed June 5, 2009).

39. Tindall, 2003, 56–58; Wasniewski, 788.

40. See "Biographical Catalogue," The Lincoln University College Seminary, 1918, 75. *African American Biographical Database* (Accessed June 5, 2009).

41. Letters from Channing H. Tobias to W. E. B. Du Bois, July 27, 1949, and Bertram W. Doyle to W. E. B. Du Bois, August 23, 1949, in Aptheker, 1997, 165–167; see also *Souvenir; Negro Young People's Congress*, 75 in *African American Biographical Database* (Accessed June 5, 2009).

42. W. E. B. Du Bois, *The Black Flame: A Trilogy, Book One, The Ordeal of Mansart* (New York: Mainstream Publishers, 1957), 179.

43. Gary D. Jaworski, *Georg Simmel and the American Prospect* (Albany: State University of New York Press, 1997), 33–34; Doyle, 1937, 161.

44. Letters from Channing H. Tobias to W. E. B. Du Bois, July 27, 1949, and Bertram W. Doyle to W. E. B. Du Bois, August 23, 1949, in Aptheker, 1997, 165–167; Bertram W. Doyle, *The Etiquette of Race Relations in the South: A Study in Social Control* (Chicago: University of Chicago Press, 1937).

45. *Oxford Public Ledger*, January 10, 1896.

46. Ali, 2002. According to Pattillo's great-grandson, Dr. Walter H. Pattillo, the former Black Populist died heavily in debt, leaving his family struggling to pay off what they could (personal communication on July 14, 2001).

47. Quoted in Moses W. Williams and George W. Watkins, *Who's Who Among North Carolina Negro Baptists* (Alexandria, VA: Chadwyck-Healey, 1940), 344–345.

48. John A. Whitted, *A History of the Negro Baptists of North Carolina* (Raleigh, NC: Edwards & Broughton Print Co., 1908), 52.

49. A photograph of Fannie Munn Shuffer taken circa 1938 appears in her grandson George M. Shuffer Jr.'s autobiography *My Journey to Betterment* (New York: Vantage Press, 1999), 3.

50. Holt, 62–63; Tera W. Hunter, *To 'Joy My Freedom: Southern Black Women's Lives and Labors after the Civil War* (Cambridge, MA: Harvard University Press, 1997), 50, 74, 119.

51. Hahn, 233, 533 n. 32.

52. Kerr-Ritchie, 206.

53. Ruth Bordin, *Women and Temperance: The Quest for Power and Liberty, 1873–1900* (New Brunswick, NJ: Rutgers University Press, 1990); Judith N. McArthur, *Creating the New Woman: The Rise of Southern Women's Progressive Culture in Texas, 1893–1918* (Champaign: University of Illinois Press, 1998), 16.

54. Hunter, 74, 89; Humphrey, 1891, 290. Edward J. Blum, *Reforging the White Republic: Race, Religion, and American Nationalism, 1865–1898* (Baton Rouge: Louisiana State University Press, 2005), 203–204.

55. Marion K. Barthelme, *Women in the Texas Populist Movement: Letters to the "Southern Mercury"* (College Station: Texas A & M University Press, 1997), 47–48.

56. Evelyn Brooks Higginbotham, *Righteous Discontent: The Women's Movement in the Black Baptist Church, 1880–1920* (Cambridge, MA: Harvard University Press, 1993), 120–149; Glenda E. Gilmore, *Gender and Jim Crow: Women and the Politics of White Supremacy in North Carolina, 1886–1920* (Chapel Hill: University of North Carolina Press, 1996), 1–30; Hahn, 2003, 462–463.

57. Quoted in the chapter "Chances for Colored Girls" in Frances E. Willard, *Occupations for Women: A Book of Practical Suggestions for the Material Advancement, the Mental, and Physical Development, and the Moral and Spiritual Uplift of Women* (New York: Success Co., 1897), 380.

58. Connolly, 1999, 6–12; Smith, 1998; Kelly P. Finley, "Lytle, Lutie A.," Women's Legal History Biography Project, Robert Crown Law Library, Stanford Law School, 2005, 17, http://womenslegalhistory.stanford.edu/papers05/LytleL-Finley05.pdf (Accessed March 1, 2009).

Notes

59. Smith, 1998, 11–12; Ali, "Lutie A. Lytle," in Gates and Higginbotham, 2008, 344–346. Another Garvey supporter, Henrietta Vinton Davis of New York, had earlier been a member of the People's Party. See Ali, 2008, 117.

60. Marjorie Spruill Wheeler, *New Women of the New South: The Leaders of the Women Suffrage Movement in the Southern States* (New York: Oxford University Press, 1993), 111, 232 n. 34.

61. Quoted in Wheeler, 118, 235 n. 53.

62. Ibid., 100–118.

63. Higginbotham, 4.

64. Hunter, 50.

65. Foner and Lewis, 1978, 419; Philip S. Foner, *Organized Labor and the Black Worker, 1619-1973* (New York: Praeger, 1974), 109, 114–116; Covington Hall, *Labor Struggles in the Deep South and Other Writings*, ed. David R. Roediger (Chicago: Charles H. Kerr, 1999), 1–24.

66. Winston James, "Being Red and Black in Jim Crow America," *Time Longer Than Rope: A Century of African American Activism, 1850–1950*, ed. Charles Payne and Adam Green (New York: New York University Press, 2003), 365; James R. Green, *Grass-Roots Socialism: Radical Movements in the Southwest, 1895-1943* (Baton Rouge: Louisiana State University Press, 1978), 94–110, 148.

67. Hahn, 471.

68. Greta de Jong, "'With the Aid of God and the F.S.A.': The Louisiana Farmers' Union and the African American Freedom Struggle in the New Deal Era," in Payne and Green, 2003, 230–275.

69. Kelley, 1990, 54–56; Dickson 171–172.

70. Debra A. Reid, *Reaping a Greater Harvest: African Americans, the Extension Service, and Rural Reform in Jim Crow Texas* (College Station: Texas A&M University Press, 2007), 1–2.

71. Debra A. Reid, "African Americans, Community Building, and the Role of the State in Rural Reform in Texas, 1890–1930," in *The Countryside in the Age of the Modern State: Political Histories of Rural America*, ed. Catherine McNicol Stock and Robert D. Johnston (Ithaca: Cornell University Press, 2001), 45.

72. Robert Carroll, "Robert Lloyd Smith and the Farmers' Improvement Society" (M.A. thesis, Baylor University, 1974); August Meier, *Negro Thought in America, 1880–1915* (Ann Arbor: University of Michigan Press, 1964), 123–124. Gaither notes that the Farmers' Improvement Society "probably siphoned off members from the declining Colored Farmers' Alliance since the two groups shared similar philosophies." Gaither, 2005, 21.

73. Merline Pitre, *Through Many Dangers, Toils and Snares: The Black Leadership of Texas, 1868–1900* (Austin, TX: Eakin Press, 1985), 195–205; Rice, 79, 110–111, 180–181; Cantrell, 1993, 267–268; Winston James personal communication on December 8, 1999.

74. Jane Dailey, Glenda Elizabeth Gilmore, and Bryant Simon, eds., *Jumpin' Jim Crow: Sothern Politics from Civil War to Civil Rights* (Princeton, NJ: Princeton University Press, 2000), 4.

75. As Robin Kelley notes, "Ironically, segregation facilitated the ... maintenance of the unmonitored, unauthorized social sites in which black workers could freely articulate the hidden transcript. Jim Crow ordinances ensured the churches, bars, social clubs, barbershops, beauty salons, even alleys, remained 'black' space"; Kelley, 1993, 79.

76. August Meier also notes that an initial surge of Jim Crow laws were enacted in southern state legislatures between 1887 and 1891 as white Alliance leaders began winning public offices; Meier, 23.

77. While the Farm Tenant Act of 1937 provided some loans to sharecroppers, tenant farmers, and agrarian laborers for purchasing land, supplies, livestock, and equipment, it largely hurt small farmers; Kelley, 53–54.

78. Ali, 2008, 101–161; Robin D. G. Kelley, *Race Rebels: Culture, Politics, and the Black Working Class* (New York: Free Press, 1996), 77.

79. C. Vann Woodward, *The Strange Career of Jim Crow* (New York: Oxford University Press, 1974), 149–188; Manning Marable, *Race, Reform and Rebellion: The Second Reconstruction in Black America* (Jackson: University Press of Mississippi, 2007), 38–111.

80. I interviewed a number of Black Populist descendents between 2001 and 2009; see Bibliography. Doyle's sociological work on race relations formed part of the discussions that engaged the issue of public school segregation in the 1950s; Pattillo, a biologist in North Carolina, challenged notions of racial inferiority by virtue of his scientific accomplishments; Shuffer, a brigadier general in the U.S. Army, had been instrumental in the practical aspects of desegregation in the military; Rayner, a Tuskegee airman, was active in independent politics in Chicago; Clyburn was involved in the movement while still in his teens in South Carolina; and Williams was part of the tail-end of the movement and focused on feminist struggles thereafter.

Epilogue

1. "Third Clinton-Bush-Perot Presidential Debate," East Lansing, Michigan, October 19, 1992, transcript, John Woolley and Gerhard Peters (The American Presidency Project, University of California, Santa Barbara, 1999–2009); Kristin Huckshorn et al., "Ross Perot: A Man of Dollars and Sense," *Seattle Times*, October 18, 1992.

2. This is in terms of popular votes cast, not percentage, which would have been Theodore Roosevelt's presidential run in 1912 with the Progressive Party.

3. Michael C. Dawson, *Behind the Mule: Race and Class in African-American Politics* (Princeton, NJ: Princeton University Press, 1994), 106; Ali, 2008, 31, 44–56.

4. Stokely Carmichael and Charles V. Hamilton, *Black Power: The Politics of Liberation in America* (New York: Vintage, 1967), 173–177.

5. Charles S. Childs Jr. personal communication on June 26, 2009.

6. Richard Halicks, "Obama's Youthquake: Is the Senator Leading a Movement, or Just an Interesting Campaign?" *Atlanta Journal Constitution*, February 10, 2008.

7. William N. Holmes, *The National Black Independent Political Party: Political Insurgency or Ideological Convergence?* (New York: Garland Publishing, 1999), 47–54.

8. David Bositis, "Black Elected Officials: A Statistical Summary, 2001" (Washington, D.C.: Joint Center for Political and Economic Studies, 2003), 3, 13.

9. Wasniewski, 684–685.

10. "Dr. Lenora Fulani Enters Race for President But Will Quit if Dems Pick Jackson," *Jet* magazine, February 1, 1988.

11. Minority Election Survey, Institute for Social Research, University of Michigan, Ann Arbor, 1988.

12. Omar H. Ali, "Lenora Branch Fulani: Challenging the Rules of the Game," in *African Americans and the Presidency: The Road to the White House*, ed. Bruce A. Glasrud and Cary D. Wintz (New York: Routledge, 2010), 129–146.

13. Ali, 2008, 2–5, 158–159, 163. See transcript of Farrakhan's October 17, 1995, speech at CNN, http://www-cgi.cnn.com/US/9510/megamarch/10-16/transcript/index.html (Accessed July 9, 2009).

14. Kelley, 1996, 230.

15. Ted G. Jelen, ed., *Ross for Boss: The Perot Phenomenon and Beyond* (Albany: State University of New York Press, 2001), xi.

16. Ali, 2008, 158–159.

17. Cathy Stewart, chair of the Manhattan County Independence Party, personal communication on May 16, 2009.

18. John P. Avlon, "Black Voters Declaring Independence," *New York Sun*, October 4, 2005.

19. John Heilemann, "The New Politics: Barack Obama, Party of One," *New York Magazine*, January 11, 2009; "Obama Touts His Outsider Theme," *New York Times*, September 3, 2007; John Avlon, "Obama's Independent Edge," *Real Clear Politics*, April 29, 2008.

20. Omar H. Ali, "Obama and the Generational Challenge," in *The Speech: Race and Barack Obama's "A More Perfect Union,"* ed. T. Denean Shapley-Whiting (New York: Bloomsbury, 2009), 30–31; Jacqueline Salit, "How the Independent Movement Went Left by Going Right: A Special Post-Election Report," *Huffington Post*, January 2, 2009.

21. Ali, 2008, 1–8, 162–168.

22. Courtesy of Nancy Ross and Gwen Mandell, national field coordinators, Committee for a Unified Independent Party, New York, personal communication on March 4, 2009.

23. Salit, "How the Independent Movement Went Left by Going Right," *Huffington Post*, January 2, 2009.

24. Beeby, 2008, 89.

25. Monica Richmond Gisolfi, "From Crop Lien to Contract Farming: The Roots of Agribusiness in the American South, 1929–1939," *Agricultural History* 80, no. 2 (2006): 167–189.

26. Omar H. Ali, "Independent Black Voices from the Late 19th Century: Black Populists and the Struggle Against the Southern Democracy," *Souls: A Critical Journal of Black Politics, Culture, and Society* 7, no. 2 (Spring 2005): 14; John W. Boyd Jr., "Protecting Black Farmers Today," *St. Louis Today*, July 23, 2009.

27. Ali, 2005, 14–15.

28. "The Pigford Case: USDA Settlement of a Discrimination Suit by Black Farmers," Congressional Research Service Report RS20430 (January 13, 2009), http://www.wikileaks.org/leak/crs/RS20430.pdf (Accessed March 2, 2009).

29. See Bruce J. Reynolds, *Black Farmers in America, 1865–2000: The Pursuit of Independent Farming and the Role of Cooperatives*, RBS Research Report 194 (Washington, D.C.: U.S. Department of Agriculture, Rural Business Cooperative Service, 2003), 1–19.

30. John W. Boyd Jr., "Protecting Black Farmers Today," *St. Louis Today*, July 23, 2009.

31. Jamie C. Ruff, "Democrats faulted for weak rural showing," *Richmond Times*, November 8, 2004.

32. Ali, 2008, 173 n. 4; Pew Research Center for People and the Press ("The American Public: Opinions and Values," 2005), Suffolk University Political Research Center noted in Keli Goff, *Party Crashing: How the Hip Hop Generation Declared Political Independence* (New York: Basic Books, 2008), 39; and Columbia University's Center for African American Politics and Society report by Fredrick C. Harris, "Race, Reform, and the 2008 Presidential Process," 2008.

33. *Raleigh News and Observer*, September 18, 1886.

Notes
Historiographical Essay

1. The historiography of white Populism begins with the works of Edward Wiest, John D. Hicks, and William B. Bizzel; Wiest, *Agricultural Organization in the United States* (Lexington: University of Kentucky Press, 1923); Hicks, "The Farmers' Alliance in North Carolina," *North Carolina Historical Review* 2 (April 1925): 162–187; and Bizzel, *The Green Rising; an Historical Survey of Agrarianism, With Special Reference to the Organized Efforts of the Farmers of the United States to Improve Their Economic and Social Status* (New York: Macmillan Company, 1926).

2. Leon Litwack and August Meier, eds., *Black Leaders of the Nineteenth Century* (Chicago: University of Illinois Press, 1991); Joe Creech, 2006, xx; Alan Brinkley, *American History: A Survey, Volume II: Since 1865* (New York: McGraw-Hill, 1999, 10th edition), 676; Howard Zinn, *A People's History of the United States* (New York: Harper Perennial, 1995), 283.

3. See also Anthony J. Adam and Gerald H. Gaither, *Black Populism in the United States: An Annotated Bibliography* (Westport, CT: Praeger, 2004).

4. See Ali, 2003, 11 n. 23.

5. Ibid., 11–12 n. 24; additionally, Bruce E. Baker, "The First Anarchist That Ever Came to Atlanta," in *Radicalism in the South Since Reconstruction*, ed. Chris Green, Rachel Rubin, and James Smethurst (New York: Palgrave/Macmillan, 2006), 39–56, and "Race Progress," in Postel, 2007. These publications do not include my own (Ali, 2005, 2006, 2008); see Bibliography.

6. Ronald Yanosky sent me a revised copy of his paper on July 10, 2003.

7. There is also a biography of Norris Wright Cuney, a leading black Republican figure from Texas who endorsed fusion with the People's Party in 1896, written by his daughter Maud Cuney Hare; *Norris Wright Cuney: A Tribune of the Black People* (New York: Crisis Publishing Company, 1913). In 1995, a new edition of the book was published by Prentice-Hall International with an introduction by Tera W. Hunter.

8. Woodward, 1951. Much of what has been written about Populism over the past half century has either been a direct response to or heavily influenced by Richard Hofstadter's *The Age of Reform: From Bryan to F.D.R.* (New York: Vintage Books, 1955), in which he argues that the Populists were principally motivated by fears of modernity, nostalgia of an agrarian past, racism, and other forms of bigotry. Undermining Hofstadter's central thesis, Postel argues that the Populists were modern in a number of ways. See Postel, 2008, 6.

9. C. Vann Woodward, *The Burden of Southern History* (Baton Rouge: Louisiana State University Press, 1993), 157, and Woodward, 1951, 192.

10. Woodward, 1951, 1969; Norman Pollack, *The Populist Response to Industrial America* (Cambridge, MA: Harvard University Press, 1962); Walter T. K. Nugent, *The Tolerant Populists: Kansas Populism and Nativism* (Chicago: University of Chicago Press, 1963); Lawrence C. Goodwyn, "The Populist Response to Black America," in *Democratic Promise: The Populist Moment in America* (New York: Oxford University Press, 1976); see also Charles Crowe, "Tom Watson, Populists, and Blacks Reconsidered," *Journal of Negro History* 60 (April 1970): 99–116, and Robert Saunders, "Southern Populists and the Negro, 1893–1895," *Journal of Negro History* 54, no. 3 (July 1969): 240–261.

11. Goodwyn, 1976, 118.

12. Gnatz, 1961, 109.

13. Goodwyn, 1976, 122.

14. Holmes, 1975, 187; see also Abramowitz, 1950, 29.

15. Fann Montague of the Richard H. Thornton Library in Oxford, North Carolina, sent me a copy of this letter, dated March 27, 1899.

16. McCarthy, 1995/1996, 22.

17. Woodward, 1951, 542–543.

18. Herbert Aptheker, at his home in San Jose, California, personal communication on January 2, 2002.

Bibliography

Interviews

Charles S. Childs Jr., director of A. A. Rayner & Sons Modern Funeral Service and the first African American elected president of the Illinois Funeral Directors Association (interviewed on June 26, 2009), great-grand-nephew of John B. Rayner, Texas's most important Black Populist leader.
Walter H. Pattillo Jr., retired professor of Biology at North Carolina Central University, Durham, North Carolina (interviewed on July 14, 2001); great-grandson of the Reverend Walter A. Pattillo, North Carolina Colored Alliance state lecturer and delegate to the conventions leading to the national People's Party.
Lawrence L. Reddick III, Bishop of the Christian Methodist Episcopal Church, Birmingham, Alabama (interviewed on June 11, 2009); served as research assistant to former CME Bishop Dr. Bertram W. Doyle (Georgia People's Party leader Henry S. Doyle's son), in the church's Division of Research and History during the summer of 1977.
George Macon Shuffer Jr., brigadier general, U.S. Army, retired, El Paso, Texas (interviewed on July 16, 2003); grandson of Jacob John Shuffer, president and founding member of the Colored Alliance in Texas.
Barbara Jeanne Williams, former Ph.D. candidate in African history, University of Chicago, Chicago, Illinois (interviewed on August 15, 2001); great-great-granddaughter of Oliver Cromwell, leader of Leflore County Colored Alliance boycott in Mississippi.

Manuscript Collections

Marion Butler Papers, Southern Historical Collection, Wilson Library, University of North Carolina, Chapel Hill.
Elias Carr Papers, East Carolina University Manuscript Collection, North Carolina.
Leonidas L. Polk Papers, Southern Historical Collection, Wilson Library, University of North Carolina, Chapel Hill.
Pattillo Family Papers, Private Collection of Dr. Walter H. Pattillo, Durham, North Carolina.
Terrence V. Powderly Papers, Catholic University of America Library, Washington, D.C.
John B. Rayner Papers, Schomburg Center for Research in Black Culture, New York, NY, and Barker Texas History Center, University of Texas, Austin.
Thomas Settle Papers, Southern Historical Collection, Wilson Library, University of North Carolina, Chapel Hill.
Harold G. Sugg Papers, East Carolina University Manuscript Collection, North Carolina.
Thomas E. Watson Papers, Southern Historical Collection, Wilson Library, University of North Carolina, Chapel Hill.

Government Records and Documents

Bureau of the Census. *Granville County, Census of the Population*. Washington, D.C.: Government Printing Office, 1850, 1870.

———. *United States Census of the Population*, 11th Census. Washington, D.C.: Government Printing Office, 1880.

———. *Report on the Productions of Agriculture*. Department of the Interior, 11th Census. Washington, D.C.: Government Printing Office, 1895.

———. *Negro Population 1790–1915*. Washington, D.C.: Government Printing Office, 1918.

Congressional Record. Washington, D.C.: Government Printing Office, 1890–1896.

Contested Election Case of Cyrus Thompson v. John G. Shaw. Third Congressional District of the State of North Carolina, 1895.

Contested Election Case of John E. Fowler v. Charles R. Thomas. Third Congressional District of the State of North Carolina, 1901.

Contested Election Case of Oliver H. Dockery v. John D. Bellamy. Sixth Congressional District of the State of North Carolina, 1899.

Contested Election Cases, Martin v. Lockhart. Washington, D.C.: Government Printing Office, 1895.

Contested Election Cases, Thomas E. Watson v. J. C. C. Black. Washington, D.C.: Government Printing Office, 1896.

Mississippi in 1875: Report of the U.S. Congressional Committee to Inquire into the Mississippi Election of 1876 with Testimony and Evidence. Washington, D.C.: Government Printing Office, 1876.

Prices of Farm Products Received by Producers. Statistical Bulletin 16, Department of Agriculture, Annual Report for South and Atlantic and Middle South States. Washington, D.C.: Government Printing Office, 1927.

U.S. Department of Interior, *Compendium of the Eleventh Census, 1890*, Part I. Washington, D.C.: Government Printing Office, 1892.

Miscellaneous

A History of the Proceedings in the City of New Orleans, On the Occasion of the Funeral Ceremonies in Honor of James Abram Garfield, Late President of the United States, Which Took Place on Monday, September 29th, 1881. New Orleans, LA: A. W. Hyatt, 1881.

Centennial Encyclopedia of the African Methodist Episcopal Church. Philadelphia, PA: Book Concern of the A.M.E. Church, 1916.

Constitution of the Colored Farmers' National Alliance and Co-operative Union of the United States. Houston: J. J. Pastoriza (circa 1889).

Journal of the Proceedings of the Constitutional Convention of the State of Mississippi. Jackson, MS: E. L. Martin, 1890.

Knights of Labor, *Records of the Proceedings of the General Assembly, 1878–1896*.

National Association for the Advancement of Colored People, *Thirty Years of Lynching in the United States, 1889–1918*. Ayer Company Publishers, 1970; first published in 1919.

Preamble and Declaration of Principles of the Co-Operative Workers of America. North Carolina State Archives, Catawba County records, Series C.R. 021, Box 928.3, Folder: Secret Political Organization, 1887.

Proceedings of the Annual Session of the Supreme Council of the National Farmers Alliance and Industrial Union at Ocala, Florida, December 2–8, 1890. Washington, D.C.: National Economist Publishing Company, 1891.

Ritual of the Colored Farmers' National Alliance and Co-Operative Union of the United States. Houston: Culmore Bros. (circa 1889).

Secretary-Treasurer's Records. North Carolina State Archives, Minutes of the Farmers' State Alliance of North Carolina, 31, 1887–1893.

Sermons, Addresses and Reminiscences and Important Correspondence, With a Picture Gallery of Eminent Ministers and Scholars. Nashville, TN: National Baptist Publishing Board, 1901.

State Executive Committee of the People's Party of North Carolina. *People's Party Handbook of Facts, Campaign of 1898*. Raleigh, NC: Capital Printing Co., 1898.

Twenty-two Years' Work of the Hampton Normal and Agricultural Institute at Hampton, Virginia. Hampton, VA: Normal School Press, 1893.

Newspapers

Alabama State Wheel (Alabama)
American Citizen (Missouri)
Amsterdam News (New York)
Arkansas Democrat (Arkansas)
Athens Weekly Banner (Georgia)
Atlanta Constitution (Georgia)
Birmingham Age-Herald (Alabama)
Birmingham Iron Age (Alabama)
Caucasian (North Carolina)
Charleston News and Courier (South Carolina)
Charlotte Observer (North Carolina)
Choctaw Alliance (Alabama)
Cleveland Gazette (Ohio)
Columbia Daily Register (South Carolina)
Columbus Daily Enquirer Sun (Georgia)
Dallas Morning News (Texas)
Dallas Southern Mercury (Texas)
Florida Dispatch (Florida)
Galveston News (Texas)
Greenville News (South Carolina)
Greenville Enterprise and Mountaineer (South Carolina)
Houston Chronicle (Texas)
Houston Post (Texas)
Huntsville Gazette (Alabama)
Indianapolis Freeman (Indiana)
Louisiana Populist (Louisiana)
Lynchburg Daily Virginia (Virginia)
Wisconsin Afro-American (Wisconsin)
Mobile Daily Register (Alabama)
Moulton Advertiser (Alabama)

Natchez Daily Democrat (Mississippi)
National Economist (Washington, D.C.)
New Mississippian (Mississippi)
New Orleans Picayune (Louisiana)
New Orleans Times-Democrat (Louisiana)
New Orleans Weekly Pelican (Louisiana)
New York Age (New York)
New York Freeman (New York)
New York Sun (New York)
New York Times (New York)
Omaha Daily Bee (Nebraska)
Omaha Enterprise (Nebraska)
Oxford Public Ledger (North Carolina)
Oxford Torchlight (North Carolina)
Parsons Weekly Blade (Kansas)
People's Advocate (Washington, D.C.)
People's Party Paper (Georgia)
Raleigh News and Observer (North Carolina)
Raleigh Progressive Farmer (North Carolina)
Richmond Dispatch (Virginia)
Richmond Planet (Virginia)
Savannah Tribune (Georgia)
Southern Mercury (Texas)
St. Louis Globe-Democrat (Missouri)
St. Louis Post Dispatch (Missouri)
Tarboro Southerner (North Carolina)
Topeka Call (Kansas)
Topeka Daily Capital (Kansas)
Topeka Times-Observer (Kansas)
Trinity Archives (North Carolina)
Virginia Sun (Virginia)
Washington Bee (Washington, D.C.)
Weekly Call (Kansas)
Weekly Toiler (Tennessee)
Wilmington Star (North Carolina)

Books

Ali, Omar H. *In the Balance of Power: Independent Black Politics and Third-Party Movements in the United States.* Athens: Ohio University Press, 2008.

Allen, Robert L., and Pamela P. Allen. *Reluctant Reformers: Racism and Social Reform Movements in the United States.* Washington, D.C.: Howard University Press, 1983.

Anderson, Eric. *Race and Politics in North Carolina, 1872–1901: The Black Second.* Baton Rouge: Louisiana State University Press, 1981.

Aptheker, Herbert. *A Documentary History of the Negro People in the United States, Vol. 2.* New York: Citadel Press, 1992.

———, ed. *The Correspondence of W. E. B. Du Bois: Volume III Selections 1944–1963*. Amherst: University of Massachusetts Press, 1997.
Argersinger, Peter H. *The Limits of Agrarian Radicalism*. Lawrence: University Press of Kansas, 1995.
Ayers, Edward L. *The Promise of the New South: Life After Reconstruction*. New York: Oxford University Press, 1992.
Barnes, Kenneth C. *Journey of Hope: The Back to Africa Movement in Arkansas*. Chapel Hill: University of North Carolina Press, 2004.
Barr, Alwyn. *Reconstruction to Reform: Texas Politics, 1876–1906*. Austin: University of Texas Press, 1971.
Barthelme, Marion K. *Women in the Texas Populist Movement: Letters to the "Southern Mercury."* College Station: Texas A & M University Press, 1997.
Bass, Jack. *Unlikely Heroes*. Tuscaloosa: The University of Alabama Press, 1990.
Beeby, James M. *Revolt of the Tar Heels: The North Carolina Populist Movement, 1890–1901*. Jackson: University Press of Mississippi, 2008.
Berlin, Ira. *Slaves without Masters: The Free Negro in the Antebellum South*. New York: Pantheon Books, 1974.
Bizzel, William B. *The Green Rising; an Historical Survey of Agrarianism, With Special Reference to the Organized Efforts of the Farmers of the United States to Improve Their Economic and Social Status*. New York: Macmillan Company, 1926.
Blum, Edward J. *Reforging the White Republic: Race, Religion, and American Nationalism, 1865–1898*. Baton Rouge: Louisiana State University Press, 2005
Bonner, James C., and Lucien E. Roberts, eds. *Studies in Georgia History and Government*. Athens: University of Georgia Press, 1940.
Bordin, Ruth. *Women and Temperance: The Quest for Power and Liberty, 1873–1900*. New Brunswick, NJ: Rutgers University Press, 1990.
Bositis, David A. *Diverging Generations: The Transformation of African American Policy Views*. Washington, D.C.: Joint Center for Political and Economic Studies, 2001.
Brinkley, Alan. *American History: A Survey, Volume II: Since 1865*. New York: McGraw-Hill, 1999 (10th edition).
Brundage, W. Fitzhugh, ed. *Up from Slavery by Booker T. Washington with Related Documents*. Boston: Bedford St. Martin's Press, 2003.
Bryan, William J. *The First Battle: A Story of the Campaign of 1896*. Chicago: W. B. Conkey, 1897.
Buck, Paul H. *The Road to Reunion, 1865–1900*. New York: Vintage Books, 1959.
Buck, Solon J. *The Agrarian Crusade: A Chronicle of the Farmer in Politics*. New Haven, CT: Yale University Press, 1920.
Burton, Orville Vernon. *In My Father's House Are Many Mansions: Family and Community in Edgefield, South Carolina*. Chapel Hill: University of North Carolina, 1985.
Cantrell, Gregg. *Kenneth and John B. Rayner and the Limits of Southern Dissent*. Urbana: University of Illinois Press, 1993.
———. *Feeding the Wolf: John B. Rayner and the Politics of Race, 1850–1918*. Wheeling, IL: Harlan Davidson, 2001.
———. "John B. Rayner: No Outlet on the Road of Hope." In *The Human Tradition in Texas*, ed. Ty Cashion and Jesús F. de la Teja. Wilmington, DE: Scholarly Resources, 2001.
Carmichael, Stokely, and Charles V. Hamilton. *Black Power: The Politics of Liberation in America*. New York: Vintage, 1967.

Ceceliski, David, and Timothy B. Tyson, eds. *Democracy Betrayed: The Wilmington Race Riot of 1898 and Its Legacy.* Chapel Hill: University of North Carolina Press, 1998.
Cohen, William. *At Freedom's Edge: Black Mobility and the Southern White Quest for Racial Control, 1861–1915.* Baton Rouge: Louisiana State University Press, 1991.
Coleman, Kenneth. *A History of Georgia.* Athens: University of Georgia Press, 1991.
Cott, Nancy F. *No Small Courage: A History of Women in the United States.* New York: Oxford University Press, 2004.
Creech, Joe. *Righteous Indignation: Religion and the Populist Revolution.* Urbana: University of Illinois Press, 2006.
Cresswell, Steven Edward. *Rednecks, Redeemers, and Race: Mississippi After Reconstruction.* Jackson: University Press of Mississippi, 2006.
Dailey, Jane, Glenda Elizabeth Gilmore, and Bryant Simon, eds. *Jumpin' Jim Crow: Sothern Politics from Civil War to Civil Rights.* Princeton, NJ: Princeton University Press, 2000.
Dawson, Michael C. *Behind the Mule: Race and Class in African-American Politics.* Princeton, NJ: Princeton University Press. 1994.
Degler, Carl N. *The Other South: Southern Dissenters in the Nineteenth Century.* Gainesville: University Press of Florida, 2000.
Diouf, Sylviane A. *Servants of Allah: African Muslims Enslaved in the Americas.* New York: New York University Press, 1998.
Doyle, Bertram Wilber. *The Etiquette of Race Relations in the South: A Study in Social Control.* Chicago: University of Chicago Press, 1937.
Du Bois, W. E. B. *Black Reconstruction in America, 1860–1880.* New York: Simon & Schuster, 1992 (originally published in 1935).
———. *Dusk of Dawn: An Essay Toward an Autobiography of a Race Concept.* New York: Schocken Books, 1971 (first published in 1940).
———. *The Black Flame: A Trilogy, Book One, The Ordeal of Mansart.* New York: Mainstream Publishers, 1957.
Dunning, Nelson A., ed. *The Farmer's Alliance History and Agricultural Digest.* Washington, D.C.: The Alliance Publishing Co., 1891.
Edgar, Walter B. *South Carolina: A History.* Columbia: University of South Carolina Press, 1998.
Edmonds, Helen G. *The Negro in Fusion Politics in North Carolina, 1894–1901.* Chapel Hill: University of North Carolina Press, 1951.
Feldman, Glen. *The Disfranchisement Myth: Poor Whites and Suffrage Restriction in Alabama.* Athens: University of Georgia Press, 2004.
Fitzgerald, Michael W. *The Union League Movement in the Deep South: Politics and Agricultural Change During Reconstruction.* Baton Rouge: Louisiana State University Press, 1989.
Foner, Eric. *Free Soil, Free Labor, Free Men: The Ideology of the Republican Party Before the Civil War.* New York: Oxford University Press, 1970.
———. *Nothing But Freedom: Emancipation and Its Legacy.* Baton Rouge: Louisiana State University Press, 1983.
———. *Reconstruction: America's Unfinished Revolution, 1863–1877.* New York: Harper & Row, 1988.
———. *Freedom's Lawmakers: A Directory of Black Officeholders During Reconstruction.* Baton Rouge: Louisiana State University Press, 1996.
———. *Give Me Liberty! An American History.* New York: W. W. Norton & Co., 2009.
Foner, Philip S. *Organized Labor and the Black Worker, 1619–1973.* New York: Praeger, 1974.

Foner, Philip S., and Ronald L. Lewis, eds. *The Black Worker: A Documentary History from Colonial Times to the Present: The Black Worker During the Era of the Knights of Labor.* Philadelphia: Temple University Press, 1978.
Franklin, John Hope. *The Free Negro in North Carolina, 1790–1860.* Chapel Hill: University of North Carolina Press, 1995.
Fulop, Earl, and Albert J. Roboteau, eds. *African American Religion: Interpretive Essays in History and Culture.* New York: Routledge, 1996.
Gaither, Gerald H. *Blacks and the Populist Revolt: Ballots and Bigotry in the "New South."* University: The University of Alabama Press, 1977 and 2005 (renamed *Blacks and the Populist Movement: Ballots and Bigotry in the New South*).
Garrow, David J. *Bearing the Cross: Martin Luther King, Jr. and the Southern Christian Leadership Conference.* New York: Harper Perennial, 1999.
Gates, Henry Louis, Jr., ed. *America Behind the Color Line: Dialogues with African Americans.* New York: Warner Books, 2004.
Gates, Henry Louis, Jr., and Evelyn Brooks Higginbotham, eds. *African American National Biography.* New York: Oxford University Press, 2008.
Gatewood, Willard B., ed. *From Slavery to Wealth: The Life of Scott Bond by Dan A. Rudd and Theo. Bond.* Fayetteville, AR: Phoenix International, 2008.
Gerteis, Joseph. *Class and the Color Line: Interracial Class Coalition in the Knights of Labor and the Populist Movement.* Durham, NC: Duke University Press, 2007.
Gilmore, Glenda E. *Gender and Jim Crow: Women and the Politics of White Supremacy in North Carolina, 1886–1920.* Chapel Hill: University of North Carolina Press, 1996.
Ginger, Ray. *The Bending Cross: A Biography of Eugene Victor Debs.* New Brunswick, NJ: Rutgers University Press, 1949.
Glasrud, Bruce A., and Cary D. Wintz, eds. *African Americans and the Presidency: The Road to the White House.* New York: Routledge, 2010.
Goff, Keli. *Party Crashing: How the Hip Hop Generation Declared Political Independence.* New York: Basic Books, 2008.
Gomez, Michael A. *Exchanging Our Country Marks: The Transformation of African Identities in the Colonial and Antebellum South.* Chapel Hill: University of North Carolina Press, 1998.
Goodwyn, Lawrence C. *Democratic Promise: The Populist Moment in America.* New York: Oxford University Press, 1976.
———. *The Populist Moment: A Short History of the Agrarian Revolt in America.* New York: Oxford University Press, 1978.
Grant, Donald Lee. *The Way It Was in the South: The Black Experience in Georgia.* Athens: University of Georgia Press, 2001.
Green, Chris, Rachel Rubin, and James Smethurst, eds. *Radicalism in the South Since Reconstruction.* New York: Palgrave/Macmillan, 2006.
Green, James R. *Grass-Roots Socialism: Radical Movements in the Southwest, 1895–1943.* Baton Rouge: Louisiana State University Press, 1978.
Grofman, Bernard, and Chandler Davidson, ed. *Controversies in Minority Voting: The Voting Rights Act in Perspective.* Washington, D.C.: Brookings Institute Press, 1992.
Hacker, Andrew. *Two Nations: Black and White, Separate, Hostile, Unequal.* New York: Ballantine Books, rev. 1995.
Hahn, Steven. *The Roots of Southern Populism: Yeoman Farmers and the Transformation of the Georgia Upcountry, 1850–1890.* New York: Oxford University Press, 1983.

———. *A Nation Under Our Feet: Black Political Struggles in the Rural South from Slavery to the Great Migration*. Cambridge, MA: Harvard University Press, 2003.
Hall, Covington. *Labor Struggles in the Deep South and Other Writings*. David R. Roediger, ed., Chicago: Charles H. Kerr, 1999.
Hamilton, Joseph Grégoire De Roulhac. *History of North Carolina Since 1860*, Vol. 3. Chicago: Lewis Publishing Company, 1919.
Hanger, Kimberly S. *A Medley of Cultures: Louisiana History at the Cabildo*. Louisiana State Museum & Louisiana Museum Foundation, 1996.
Hare, Maud Cuney. *Norris Wright Cuney: A Tribune of the Black People*. New York: Crisis Publishing Company, 1913.
Harlan, Louis R. *Separate and Unequal: Public School Campaigns and Racism in the Southern Seaboard States*. New York: Atheneum, 1969.
———. *Booker T. Washington: The Wizard of Tuskegee, 1901–1915*. New York: Oxford University Press, 1986.
Harlan, Louis R., and Raymond Smock, eds. *The Booker T. Washington Papers*, Vols. 1–9. Urbana: University of Illinois Press, 1972–1989.
Haynes, Fred Emory. *James Baird Weaver*. Iowa City: State Historical Society of Iowa, 1919.
Herndon, Dallas Tabor, ed. *Centennial History of Arkansas*. Chicago: S. J. Clarke Publishing Co., 1922.
Hicks, John D. *The Populist Revolt: A History of the Farmers' Alliance and the People's Party*. Minneapolis: University of Minnesota Press, 1931.
Higginbotham, Evelyn Brooks. *Righteous Discontent: The Women's Movement in the Black Baptist Church, 1880–1920*. Cambridge, MA: Harvard University Press, 1993.
Hild, Matthew. *Greenbackers, Knights of Labor, and Populists: Farmer-Labor Insurgency in the Late-Nineteenth-Century South*. Athens: University of Georgia Press, 2007.
Hofstadter, Richard. *The Age of Reform: From Bryan to F.D.R*. New York: Vintage, 1955.
Holmes, William N. *The National Black Independent Political Party: Political Insurgency or Ideological Convergence?* New York: Garland Publishing, 1999.
Holt, Sharon Ann. *Making Freedom Pay: North Carolina Freedpeople Working for Themselves, 1865–1900*. Athens: University of Georgia Press, 2000.
Hunter, Tera W. *To 'Joy My Freedom: Southern Black Women's Lives and Labors After the Civil War*. Cambridge, MA: Harvard University Press, 1997.
Hurmence, Belinda, ed. *My Folks Don't Want Me To Talk About Slavery: Twenty-one Oral Histories of Former North Carolina Slaves*. Winston-Salem, NC: John F. Blair, 2000.
Hyman, Michael R. *The Anti-Redeemers: Hill-Country Political Dissenters in the Lower South from Redemption to Populism*. Baton Rouge: Louisiana State University Press, 1990.
Jacobson, Julius, ed. *The Negro and the American Labor Movement*. Garden City, NY: Anchor Books, 1968.
Janiewski, Dolores E. *Sisterhood Denied: Race, Gender, and Class in a New South Community*. Philadelphia: Temple University Press, 1985.
Jaworski, Gary D. *Georg Simmel and the American Prospect*. Albany: State University of New York Press, 1997.
Jelen, Ted G., ed. *Ross for Boss: The Perot Phenomenon and Beyond*. Albany: State University of New York Press, 2001.
Johnson, Daniel M., and Rex R. Campbell. *Black Migration in America: A Social Demographic History*. Durham, NC: Duke University Press, 1981.

Kantrowitz, Stephen. *Ben Tillman and the Reconstruction of White Supremacy.* Chapel Hill: University of North Carolina Press, 2000.
Katz, William L. *Eyewitness: The Negro in American History.* New York: Pitman Publishing Corporation, 1967.
Kazin, Michael. *The Populist Persuasion: An American History.* New York: Basic Books, 1995.
Keith-Lucas, Alan. *A Monument to Black Initiative and Courage: Central Children's Home, 1883-1990.* Lexington, NC: Wooten, 1991.
Kelley, Robin D. G. *Hammer and Hoe: Alabama Communists During the Great Depression.* Chapel Hill: University of North Carolina Press, 1991.
———. *Race Rebels: Culture, Politics, and the Black Working Class.* New York: Free Press, 1996.
Kelsey, Carl. *The Negro Farmer.* Chicago: Jennings & Pye, 1903.
Kerr-Ritchie, Jeffrey R. *Freedpeople in the Tobacco South: Virginia, 1860-1900.* Chapel Hill: University of North Carolina Press, 1999.
Kousser, J. Morgan. *The Shaping of Southern Politics: Suffrage Restriction and the Establishment of the One-Party South, 1880-1910.* New Haven, CT: Yale University Press, 1974.
Kurlander, Gabrielle, and Jacqueline Salit, eds. *Independent Black Leadership in America: Minister Louis Farrakhan, Dr. Lenora Fulani, Reverend Al Sharpton.* New York: Castillo International, 1990.
Lefler, Hugh T., and Albert Ray Newsome. *North Carolina: The History of a Southern State.* Chapel Hill: University of North Carolina Press, 1963.
Lemann, Nicholas. *The Promised Land: The Great Black Migration and How It Changed America.* New York: Vintage Books, 1992.
Lester, Connie L. *Up From the Mudsills of Hell: The Farmers' Alliance, Populism, and Progressive Agriculture in Tennessee, 1870-1915.* Athens: University of Georgia Press, 2006.
Lewinson, Paul. *Race, Class, and Party: A History of Negro Suffrage and White Politics in the South.* New York: Oxford University Press, 1932.
Lichtenstein, Alex. *Twice the Work of Free Labor: The Political Economy of Convict Labor in the New South.* London: Verso, 1995.
Lincoln, C. Eric, and Lawrence H. Mamiya. *The Black Church in the African American Experience.* Durham, NC: Duke University Press, 1990.
Litwack, Leon, and August Meier, eds. *Black Leaders of the Nineteenth Century.* Urbana: University of Illinois Press, 1991.
Logan, Frenise. *The Negro in North Carolina, 1876-1894.* Chapel Hill: University of North Carolina Press, 1964.
Lusane, Clarence. *African Americans at the Crossroads: The Restructuring of Black Leadership and the 1992 Elections.* Boston, MA: South End Press, 1994.
Mabry, William A. *The Negro in North Carolina Politics Since Reconstruction.* Durham, NC: Duke University Press, 1940.
Marable, Manning. *Race, Reform and Rebellion: The Second Reconstruction and Beyond in Black America, 1945-2006.* Jackson: University Press of Mississippi, 2007.
Marshall, Vera Lee Kearl, ed. *Proud to Remember.* Provo, UT: Brigham Young University Press, 1964.
Marszalek, John F. *A Black Congressman in the Age of Jim Crow: South Carolina's George Washington Murray.* Gainesville: University Press of Florida, 2006.
Martin, Roscoe C. *The People's Party in Texas: A Study in Third-Party Politics.* Austin: University of Texas Press, 1970 (first published in 1933).

Martin, Waldo. *The Mind of Frederick Douglass*. Chapel Hill: University of North Carolina Press, 1984.
McArthur, Judith N. *Creating the New Woman: The Rise of Southern Women's Progressive Culture in Texas, 1893–1918*. Champaign: University of Illinois Press, 1998.
McKivigan, John R., ed. *Abolitionism and American Politics and Government*. New York: Garland Publishing, 1999.
McLaurin, Melton A. *The Knights of Labor in the South*. Westport, CT: Greenwood Press, 1978.
McMath, Robert C., Jr. *Populist Vanguard: A History of the Southern Farmers Alliance*. Chapel Hill: University of North Carolina Press, 1975.
———. *American Populism: A Social History 1877–1898*. New York: Hill & Wang, 1993.
Meier, August, and Elliot Rudwick, eds. *The Making of Black America*. New York: Atheneum, 1969.
Meltzer, Milton, ed. *In Their Own Words: The History of the American Negro, 1865–1916*, vol. 2. New York: Thomas Y. Crowell Company, 1965.
Mendelberg, Tali. *The Race Card: Campaign Strategy, Implicit Messages, and the Norm of Equality*. Princeton, NJ: Princeton University Press, 2001.
Morgan, W. Scott. *History of the Wheel and Alliance and the Impending Revolution*. St. Louis: C. B. Woodward Company, 1891.
Mouser, Bruce L. *For Labor, Race, and Liberty: George Edwin Taylor and the Making of Independent Black Politics*. Madison: University of Wisconsin Press, 2010.
Murray, George Washington. *Race Ideals: Effects, Cause, and Remedy for the Afro-American Race Troubles*. Princeton, IN: Smith & Sons Publishing Company, 1914.
Naison, Mark. *Communists in Harlem During the Depression*. New York: Grove Press, 1985.
Newbold, Nathan Carter. *Five North Carolina Negro Educators*. Chapel Hill: University of North Carolina Press, 1939.
Noblin, Stuart. *Leonidas Lafayette Polk: Agrarian Crusader*. Chapel Hill: University of North Carolina Press, 1949.
Nordin, D. Sven. *Rich Harvest: A History of the Grange, 1867–1900*. Jackson: University Press of Mississippi, 1974.
Nugent, Walter T. K. *The Tolerant Populists: Kansas Populism and Nativism*. Chicago: University of Chicago Press, 1963.
Ostler, Jeffrey. *Prairie Populism: The Fate of Agrarian Radicalism in Kansas, Nebraska, and Iowa, 1880–1892*. Lawrence: University Press of Kansas, 2007.
Painter, Nell Irvin. *Exodusters: Black Migration to Kansas After Reconstruction*. New York: Knopf, 1977.
Palmer, Bruce. *"Man Over Money": The Southern Populist Critique of American Capitalism*. Chapel Hill: University of North Carolina Press, 1980.
Patterson, Tiffany Ruby. *Zora Neale Hurston and a History of Southern Life*. Philadelphia, PA: Temple University Press, 2005.
Payne, Charles M., and Adam Green, eds. *Time Longer Than Rope: A Century of African American Activism, 1850–1950*. New York: New York University Press, 2003.
Perman, Michael. *Struggle for Mastery: Disfranchisement in the South, 1888–1908*. Chapel Hill: University of North Carolina Press, 2001.
Pitre, Merline. *Through Many Dangers, Toils and Snares: The Black Leadership of Texas, 1868–1900*. Austin, TX: Eakin Press, 1985.
Pollack, Norman. *The Populist Response to Industrial America*. Cambridge, MA: Harvard University Press, 1962.

Postel, Charles. *The Populist Vision*. New York: Oxford University Press, 2007.
Powderly, Terrence V. *Constitution of the General Assembly, District Assemblies, and Local Assemblies of the Order of the Knights of Labor in America*. Marblehead, MA: Statesman Publishing Co., 1883.
———. *Thirty Years of Labor, 1859–1889*. Columbus, OH: Excelsior Publishing House, 1889.
Prather, H. Leon. *We Have Taken a City: Wilmington Racial Massacre and Coup of 1898*. Cranbury, NJ: Associated University Press, 1984.
Quarles, Benjamin, ed. *Narrative of the Life of Frederick Douglass: An American Slave, Written by Himself*. Cambridge, MA: Harvard University Press, 1960.
Raboteau, Albert J. *Slave Religion: The "Invisible Institution" in the Antebellum South*. New York: Oxford University Press, 1980.
Reid, Debra A. *Reaping a Greater Harvest: African Americans, the Extension Service, and Rural Reform in Jim Crow Texas*. College Station: Texas A&M University Press, 2007.
Rice, Lawrence. *The Negro in Texas, 1874–1900*. Baton Rouge: Louisiana State University Press, 1971.
Riley, Franklin L., ed. *Publications of the Mississippi Historical Society*, vol. 4. Oxford, MS: 1906.
Rogers, William Warren. *The One-Gallused Rebellion: Agrarianism in Alabama, 1865–1896*. Baton Rouge: Louisiana State University Press, 1970.
Royster, Jacqueline, ed. *Southern Horrors and Other Writings: The Anti-Lynching Campaign of Ida B. Wells, 1892–1900*. Boston: Bedford Books, 1997.
Saloutos, Theodore. *Farmer Movements in the South, 1865–1933*. Berkeley and Los Angeles: University of California Press, 1960.
Saville, Julie. *The Work of Reconstruction: From Slave to Wage Laborer in South Carolina, 1860–1870*. New York: Cambridge University Press, 1994.
Schuchter, Arnold. *White Power, Black Freedom: Planning the Future of Urban America*. Boston, MA: Beacon Press, 1968.
Scott, James C. *Domination and the Arts of Resistance: Hidden Transcripts*. New Haven, CT: Yale University Press, 1990.
Sharpley-Whiting, T. Denean, ed. *The Speech: Race and Barack Obama's "A More Perfect Union."* New York: Bloomsbury, 2009.
Shaw, Barton C. *The Wool-Hat Boys: Georgia's Populist Party*. Baton Rouge: Louisiana State University Press, 1984.
Sheldon, William DuBose. *Populism in the Old Dominion: Virginia Farm Politics, 1885–1900*. Princeton, NJ: Princeton University Press, 1935.
Shuffer, George M., Jr. *My Journey to Betterment*. New York: Vantage Press, 1999.
Simkins, Francis Butler. *The Tillman Movement in South Carolina*. Durham, NC: Duke University Press, 1926.
———. *Pitchfork Ben Tillman, South Carolinian*. Baton Rouge: Louisiana State University Press, 1944.
Smith, J. Clay. *Rebels in Law: Voices in History of Black Women Lawyers*. Ann Arbor: University of Michigan Press, 1998.
Smith, Robert C. *We Have No Leaders: African-Americans in the Post–Civil Rights Era*. New York: State University of New York Press, 1996.
Steelman, Lala Carr. *The North Carolina Farmers Alliance: A Political History, 1887–1893*. Greenville: East Carolina University Press, 1985.
Stewart, James Brewer. *Holy Warriors: The Abolitionists and Slavery*. New York: Hill & Wang, 1997.

Stiller, Richard. *Queen of Populists: The Story of Mary Elizabeth Lease.* New York: Crowell, 1970.
Sweet, Leonard I., ed. *The Evangelical Tradition in America.* Macon, GA: Mercer University Press, 1984.
Taylor, Quintard. *In Search of the Racial Frontier: African Americans in the American West, 1528–1990.* New York: W. W. Norton, 1998.
Tindall, George B. *South Carolina Negroes, 1877–1900.* Columbia: University of South Carolina Press, 2003.
Tolnay, Stewart E., and E. M. Beck. *A Festival of Violence: An Analysis of Southern Lynchings, 1882–1930.* Urbana: University of Illinois Press, 1995.
Trotter, Claude R., et al. *A Splendid Enterprise: History of the General Baptist State Convention of North Carolina.* Raleigh: Irving-Swain, 1999.
Walker, Corey D. B. *A Noble Fight: African American Freemasonry and the Struggle for Democracy in America.* Urbana: University of Illinois Press, 2008.
Walton, Hanes, Jr. *Black Political Parties: An Historical and Political Analysis.* New York: Free Press, 1972.
———. *African American Power and Politics.* New York: Columbia University Press, 1997.
Washington, Booker T. *Up From Slavery.* New York, 1956.
———. *A New Negro for a New Century: An Accurate and Up-to-Date Record of the Upward Struggles of the Negro Race.* Chicago: American Publishing House, 1900.
———. *An Autobiography: The Story of My Life and Work.* Atlanta, GA: J. L. Nichols and Company, 1901.
Watson, Thomas E. *The People's Party Campaign Book, 1892: Not a Revolt; It is a Revolution.* New York: Arno Press, 1975 (first published in 1892).
Webb, Samuel L. *Two-Party Politics in the One-Party South: Alabama's Hill Country, 1874–1920.* Tuscaloosa: The University of Alabama Press, 1997.
Wheeler, Marjorie Spruill. *New Women of the New South: The Leaders of the Women Suffrage Movement in the Southern States.* New York: Oxford University Press, 1993.
White, Barnetta McGhee. *In Search of Kith and Kin: The History of a Southern Black Family.* Baltimore, MD: Gateway Press, 1986.
Whitted, John A. *A History of the Negro Baptists of North Carolina.* Raleigh, NC: Edwards & Broughton Print Co., 1908.
Wiest, Edward. *Agricultural Organization in the United States.* Lexington: University of Kentucky, 1923.
Willard, Frances E. *Occupations for Women: A Book of Practical Suggestions for the Material Advancement, the Mental, and Physical Development, and the Moral and Spiritual Uplift of Women.* New York: The Success Co., 1897.
Winkler, Ernest W., ed. *Platforms of Political Parties in Texas,* No. 53, *Bulletin of the University of Texas, 1916.* Austin: University of Texas Press, 1916.
Winston, Robert W. *It's a Far Cry.* New York: Henry Holt, 1937.
Wood, Philip J. *Southern Capitalism: The Political Economy of North Carolina, 1880–1980.* Durham, NC: Duke University Press, 1986.
Woodward, C. Vann. *Tom Watson: Agrarian Rebel.* New York: Oxford University Press, 1969 (first published in 1938).
———. *The Strange Career of Jim Crow.* New York: Oxford University Press, 1974 (first published in 1955).
———. *Origins of the New South, 1877–1913.* Baton Rouge: Louisiana State University Press, 1995 (first published in 1951).

Wynes, Charles E. *Race Relations in Virginia, 1870–1902*. Charlottesville: University of Virginia Press, 1961.
Zinn, Howard. *A People's History of the United States*. New York: Harper Perennial, 1995.

Articles, Essays, and Papers

Abramowitz, Jack. "The Negro in the Agrarian Revolt." *Agricultural History* 24, no. 2 (April 1950): 89–95.
———. "John B. Rayner: A Grass-Roots Leader." *Journal of Negro History* 36, no. 2 (1951): 160–193.
———. "The Negro in the Populist Movement." *Journal of Negro History* 38, no. 3 (July 1953): 257–289.
———. "Crossroads of Negro Thought: 1890–1895." *Social Education* 18, no. 3 (March 1954): 117–120.
Ali, Omar H. "Perot movement." In *History in Dispute: American Social and Political Movements, 1945–2000*, ed. Robert J. Allison. Detroit, MI: St. James Press, 2000.
———. "The Making of a Black Populist: A Tribute to the Rev. Walter A. Pattillo." *Oxford Public Ledger*, March 28, 2002 (121, no. 25).
———. "Independent Black Voices from the Late 19th Century: Black Populists and the Struggle Against the Southern Democracy," *Souls: A Critical Journal of Black Politics, Culture, and Society* 7, no. 2 (Spring 2005): 4–18.
———. "Standing Guard at the Door of Liberty: Black Populism in South Carolina, 1886–1897." *South Carolina Historical Magazine* 107, no. 3 (2006): 190–203.
———. "Lutie A. Lytle." In *African American National Biography*, ed. Henry Louis Gates Jr. and Evelyn Brooks Higginbotham. New York: Oxford University Press, 2008.
———. "Lenora Branch Fulani: Challenging the Rules of the Game." In *African Americans and the Presidency: The Road to the White House*, ed. Bruce A. Glasrud and Cary D. Wintz, 129–146. New York: Routledge, 2010.
———. "Obama and the Generational Challenge." In *The Speech: Race and Barack Obama's "A More Perfect Union,"* ed. T. Denean Shapley-Whiting, 25–39. New York: Bloomsbury, 2009.
Allen, Robert L., and Pamela P. "Self Interest and Southern Populism." In *Reluctant Reformers: Racism and Social Reform Movements in the United States.* Washington, D.C.: Howard University Press, 1983.
Anderson, Eric. "The Populists and Capitalist America: The Case of Edgecombe County, North Carolina." In *Race, Class, and Politics in Southern History: Essays in Honor of Robert F. Durden*, ed. Jeffrey J. Crow, Paul D. Escott, and Charles L. Flynn Jr. Baton Rouge: Louisiana State University Press, 1991.
Ballard, Michael B. "Colored Farmers' National Alliance and Cooperative Union." In *Encyclopedia of African American Civil Rights*, ed. Charles D. Lowery and John F. Marszalek. Westport, CT: Greenwood Press, 1992.
Baker, Bruce E. "The 'Hoover Scare' in South Carolina, 1887: An Attempt to Organize Black Farm Labor." *Labor History* 40, no. 3 (1999): 261–282.
———. "The First Anarchist That Ever Came to Atlanta." In *Radicalism in the South Since Reconstruction*, ed. Chris Green, Rachel Rubin, and James Smethurst. New York: Palgrave/Macmillan, 2006.
Beale, Calvin. "The Negro In American Agriculture." In *The American Negro Reference Book*, ed. John P. Davis. Englewood Cliffs, NJ: Prentice-Hall, 1966.

Beeby, James M. "'Equal Rights to All and Special Privileges to None': Grass-Roots Populism in North Carolina." *North Carolina Historical Review* 78, no. 2 (April 2001): 156–186.
Bowden, Mark. "Pompadour with a Monkey Wrench." *Atlantic Monthly* (July/August 2004).
Brantley, Daniel. "Blacks and Louisiana Constitutional Development, 1890–Present: A Study in Southern Political Thought and Race Relations." *Phylon* 48, no. 1. (1987): 51–61.
Bryant, Girard T. "J. B. Rayner, A Negro Populist." *Negro History Bulletin* 3 (May 1940): 125–126.
Cantrell, Gregg. "John B. Rayner: A Study in Black Populist Leadership." *Southern Studies* 24 (Winter 1985): 432–443.
———. "'Dark Tactics': Black Politics in the 1887 Texas Prohibition Campaign." *Journal of American Studies* 25 (April 1991): 85–93.
Cantrell, Gregg, and D. Scott Barton. "Texas Populists and the Failure of Biracial Politics." *Journal of Southern History* 55, no. 4 (November 1989): 659–692.
Chafe, William. "The Negro and Populism: A Kansas Case Study." *Journal of Southern History* 34 (1968): 402–419.
Connolly, Noreen R. "Attorney Lutie A. Lytle: Options and Obstacles of a Legal Pioneer." *Nebraska Lawyer* (January 1999): 6–12.
Crofts, Daniel W. "The Black Response to the Blair Education Bill." *Journal of Southern History* 37, no. 1 (February 1971): 41–65.
Crowe, Charles. "Tom Watson, Populists, and Blacks Reconsidered." *Journal of Negro History* 60 (April 1970): 99–116.
Daniel, Lucia E. "The Louisiana People's Party." *Louisiana Historical Quarterly* 26 (October 1943): 1055–1149.
Dann, Martin. "Black Populism: A Study of the Colored Farmers' Alliance Through 1891." *Journal of Ethnic Studies* 2 (1974): 58–71.
Dawson, Michael C. "African American Political Opinion: Volatility in the Reagan-Bush Era." In *African American Power and Politics*, ed. Hanes Walton Jr., 135–153. New York: Columbia University Press, 1997.
De Jong, Greta. "'With the Aid of God and the F.S.A.' The Louisiana Farmers' Union and the African American Freedom Struggle in the New Deal Era." In *Time Longer than Rope: A Century of African American Activism*, ed. Charles M. Payne and Adam Green, 230–275. New York: New York University Press, 2003.
Delap, Simeon A. "The Populist Party in North Carolina." *Trinity Archives* 14 (1922): 40–74.
Drew, Frank M. "The Present Farmers Movement." *Political Science Quarterly* 6, no. 2 (June 1891): 282–310.
Du Bois, W. E. B. "From McKinley to Wallace: My Fifty Years as a Independent." *Masses-Mainstream* 1, no. 6 (August 1948): 3–14.
Fields, Barbara J. "Ideology and Race in American History." In *Region, Race, and Reconstruction: Essays in Honor of C. Vann Woodward*, ed. J. Morgan Kousser and James M. McPherson. New York: Oxford University Press, 1982. 143–177.
Fingerhut, Eugene R. "Tom Watson, Blacks, and Southern Reform." *Georgia Historical Quarterly* 4 (Winter 1976): 324–343.
Franklin, John Hope. "The Enslavement of Free Negroes in North Carolina." *Journal of Negro History* 29, no. 4 (October 1944): 401–428.
Gaboury, William J. "George Washington Murray and the Fight for Political Democracy in South Carolina." *Journal of Negro History* 62 (July 1977): 258–269.

Gisolfi, Monica Richmond. "From Crop Lien to Contract Farming: The Roots of Agribusiness in the American South, 1929–1939." *Agricultural History* 80, no. 2 (2006): 167–189.

Goodwyn, Lawrence C. "Populist Dreams and Negro Rights: East Texas as a Case Study." *American Historical Review* 76 (1971): 1435–1456.

Hicks, John. "The Farmer's Alliance in North Carolina." *North Carolina Historical Review* (April 1925): 162–187.

——. "The Subtreasury: A Forgotten Plan for the Relief of Agriculture." *Mississippi Valley Historical Review* 15 (December 1928): 355–373.

Holmes, William F. "The Leflore County Massacre and the Demise of the Colored Farmer's Alliance." *Phylon* 34 (September 1973): 267–274.

——. "The Arkansas Cotton Pickers Strike of 1891 and the Demise of the Colored Farmers' Alliance." *Arkansas Historical Quarterly* 32, no. 2 (1973): 107–119.

——. "The Demise of the Colored Farmers' Alliance." *Journal of Southern History* 41, no. 2 (May 1975): 187–200.

——. "The Southern Farmers' Alliance: The Georgia Experience," *Georgia Historical Quarterly* 72, no. 4 (Winter 1988): 627–652.

——. "The Southern Farmers' Alliance and the Jute Cartel." *Journal of Southern History* 60 (February 1994): 59–80.

Horton, Paul. "Testing the Limits of Class Politics in Postbellum Alabama: Agrarian Radicalism in Lawrence County." *Journal of Southern History* 57, no. 1 (February 1991): 63–84.

Humphrey, Richard M. "History of the Colored Farmers' National Alliance and Co-Operative Union." In *The Farmer's Alliance History and Agricultural Digest*, ed. Nelson A. Dunning, 288–292. Washington, D.C.: Alliance Publishing Co., 1891.

Hunt, James L. "The Making of a Populist: Marion Butler, 1863–1895." *North Carolina Historical Review* 62 (January 1985): 53–77; (April 1985): 179–202; (July 1985): 317–343.

James, Winston. "Being Red and Black in Jim Crow America: On the Ideology and Travails of Afro-America's Socialist Pioneers, 1877–1930." In *Time Longer than Rope: A Century of African American Activism*, ed. Charles Payne and Adam Green, 336–399. New York: New York University Press, 2003.

Jones, Allen W. "The Role of Tuskegee Institute in the Education of Black Farmers." *Journal of Negro History* 60, no. 2 (April 1975): 252–267.

Kann, Kenneth. "The Knights of Labor and the Southern Black Worker." *Labor History* 18, no. 1 (Winter 1977): 49–70.

Kelley, Robin D. G. "'We are not what we seem': Rethinking Black Working-Class Opposition in the Jim Crow South." *Journal of American History* 80, no. 1 (June 1993): 75–112.

Kessler, Sidney H. "The Organization of Negroes in the Knights of Labor." *Journal of Negro History* 37 (July 1952): 248–276.

Kirwan, Albert D. "Apportionment in the Mississippi Constitution of 1890." *Journal of Southern History* 14 (May 1948): 234–246.

Kousser, J. Morgan. "The Voting Rights Act and Two Reconstructions." In *Controversies in Minority Voting: The Voting Rights Act in Perspective*, ed. Bernard Grofman and Chandler Davidson. Washington, D.C.: Brookings Institute Press, 1992.

Kresky, Harry. "A Constitutional Crisis." *The Neo-Independent: The Politics of Becoming* 1, no. 2 (Fall 2004): 11–17.

Lloyd, Henry D. "The Populists at St. Louis." *Review of Reviews* 14 (September 1896): 299–300.

Marshall, Ray. "The Negro in Southern Unions." In *The Negro and the American Labor Movement*, ed. Julius Jacobson. Garden City, NY: Anchor Books, 1968.

Martin, Roscoe C. "The Greenback Party in Texas." *Southwestern Historical Quarterly* 30 (January 1927): 161–177.

McCarthy, Timothy P. "A Radical Eye: Herbert Aptheker's Anti-Racism." *Race & Reason*, Institute for Research in African American Studies, Columbia University, New York, Vol. 2 (1995/1996): 18–22.

McLaurin, Melton. "The Knights of Labor in North Carolina Politics." *North Carolina Historical Review* 49, no. 3 (1972): 298–315.

McMath, Robert C., Jr. "Southern White Farmers and the Organization of Black Farm Workers: A North Carolina Document." *Labor History* 18 (Winter 1977): 115–119.

Miller, Floyd J. "Black Protest and White Leadership: A Note on the Colored Farmer's Alliance." *Phylon* 33, no. 2 (1972): 169–174.

Moore, James T. "Black Militancy in Readjuster Virginia, 1879–1883." *Journal of Southern History* 51 (May 1975): 167–186.

Naison, Mark. "Black Agrarian Radicalism in the Great Depression: The Threads of a Lost Tradition." *Journal of Ethnic Studies* 1, no. 3 (Fall 1973): 47–65.

Nixon, Herman Clarence. "The Cleavage Within the Farmers Alliance Movement." *Mississippi Valley Historical Review* 15, no. 1 (June 1928): 22–33.

Payne, Daniel A. "Thought About the Past, the Present and the Future of the African M. E. Church." *A. M. E. Church Review* 1 (July 1884): 1–3.

Peterson, John M. "The People's Party of Kansas: Campaigning in 1898." *Kansas History* 13 (1990–91): 235–258.

Raboteau, Albert J. "The Black Experience in American Evangelicalism: The Meaning of Slavery." In *African American Religion: Interpretive Essays in History and Culture*, ed. Timothy Earl Fulop and Albert J. Raboteau. New York: Routledge, 1996.

Reid, Debra A. "African Americans, Community Building, and the Role of the State in Rural Reform in Texas, 1890–1930." In *The Countryside in the Age of the Modern State: Political Histories of Rural America*, ed. Catherine McNicol Stock and Robert D. Johnston. Ithaca: Cornell University Press, 2001.

Reynolds, Bruce J. *Black Farmers in America, 1865–2000: The Pursuit of Independent Farming and the Role of Cooperatives*, RBS Research Report 194. Washington, D.C.: U.S. Department of Agriculture, Rural Business Cooperative Service, 2003.

Rogers, William W. "The Negro Alliance in Alabama." *Journal of Negro History* 45, no. 1 (January 1960): 38–44.

———. "Negro Knights of Labor in Arkansas: a Case Study of the 'Miscellaneous' Strike." *Labor History* 10 (Summer 1969): 498–505.

Salit, Jacqueline. "Unpopular Partnerships (Bloomberg's Dilemma)." *The Neo-Independent: The Politics of Becoming* 1, no. 1 (Spring 2004): 13–21.

Saloutos, Theodore. "The Grange in the South, 1870–1877." *Journal of Southern History* 19, no. 4 (November 1953): 473–487.

Saunders, Robert M. "The Southern Populists and the Negro in 1892." *Essays in History* 12 (1966–1967): 7–25.

———. "Southern Populists and the Negro, 1893–1895." *Journal of Negro History* 54, no. 3 (July 1969): 240–261.

Scott, Roy V. "Milton George and the Farmer's Alliance Movement." *Mississippi Valley Historical Review* 45, no. 1 (June 1958): 90–109.

Shapiro, Herbert. "The Populist and the Negro: A Reconsideration." In *The Making of Black America*, ed. August Meier and Elliott Rudwick. New York: Atheneum, 1969.
Soule, Sarah A. "Populism and Black Lynching in Georgia, 1890–1900." *Social Forces* 71, no. 2 (December 1992): 431–449.
Spencer, C. A. "Black Benevolent Societies and the Development of Black Insurance Companies in Nineteenth Century Alabama." *Phylon* 46, no. 3 (1985): 251–261.
Spriggs, William Edward. "The Virginia Colored Farmers Alliance: A Case Study of Race and Class Identity." *Journal of Negro History* 64, no. 3 (Summer 1979): 191–204.
Tindall, George B. "Southern Negroes Since Reconstruction: Dissolving the Static Image." In *Writing Southern History*, ed. Arthur S. Link and Rembert W. Patrick. Baton Rouge: Louisiana State University Press, 1965.
Watson, Richard L., Jr. "From Populism Through the New Deal: Southern Political History." In *Interpreting Southern History*, ed. John G. Boles and Evelyn T. Nolen. Baton Rouge: Louisiana State University Press, 1987.
Watson, Thomas E. "The Negro Question in the South." *Arena* 6 (1892): 540–550.
Wesley, Charles. "The Participation of Negroes in Anti-Slavery Political Parties." In *Abolitionism and American Politics and Government*, ed. John R. McKivigan. New York: Garland Publishing, 1999.
Wilhoit, Francis M. "An Interpretation of Populism's Impact on the Georgia Negro." *Journal of Negro History* 52, no. 2 (April 1967): 116–127.
Wintory, Blake J. "African-American Legislators in the Arkansas General Assembly, 1868–1893." *Arkansas Historical Quarterly* 65, no. 4 (Winter 2006): 385–434.
Woodman, Harold. "Economic Reconstruction and the Rise of the New South, 1865–1900." In *Interpreting Southern History*, ed. John G. Boles and Evelyn T. Nolen. Baton Rouge: Louisiana State University Press, 1987.
Woodward, C. Vann. "Tom Watson and the Negro in Agrarian Politics." *Journal of Southern History* 4 (February 1938): 14–33
———. "The Populist Heritage and the Intellectual." In *The Burden of Southern History*. Baton Rouge: Louisiana State University Press, 1960.
Yanosky, Ronald. "The Colored Farmers' Alliance and the Single Tax." Unpublished paper delivered at the 1992 Annual Meeting of the Organization of American Historians, 1–17.

General References

Adam, Anthony J., and Gerald H. Gaither. *Black Populism in the United States: An Annotated Bibliography*. Westport, CT: Praeger, 2004.
Appleton's Annual Cyclopaedia and Register of Important Events. New York: D. Appleton and Company, 1881 and 1885.
Barkley, Roy R., ed. *The New Handbook of Texas*. Austin: Texas State Historical Association, 1996.
Davis, Ellis A., and Edwin H. Grobe, eds. *The New Encyclopedia of Texas*, 2 Vols. Dallas: Texas Development Bureau, 1925.
Eldridge, Hope T., and Dorothy S. Thomas. *Demographic Analyses and Interrelations*, Vol. 3 of Simon S. Kuznets, *Population Redistribution and Economic Growth: The United States, 1870–1950*. Philadelphia: American Philosophical Society, 1957–1964.

Hill, Kathleen Thompson, and Gerald N. Hill. *The Facts on File Dictionary of American Politics.* New York: Checkmark Books, 2001.

Lowe, W. August, and Virgil A. Clift, eds. *Encyclopedia of Black America.* New York: Da Capo Press, 1984.

National Association for the Advancement of Colored People. *Thirty Years of Lynching in the United States, 1889–1918.* Ayer Company Publishers, 1970 (first published in 1919).

Thomas, David Y., ed. *Arkansas and Its People: A History, 1541–1930.* New York: American Historical Society, 1930.

Thompson, Peter. *Dictionary of American History: From 1763 to the Present.* New York: Checkmark, 2001.

Van West, Carroll, ed. *The Tennessee Encyclopedia of History & Culture.* Knoxville: University of Tennessee Press, 1998.

Wasniewski, Matthew, ed. *Black Americans in Congress, 1870–2007.* Washington, D.C.: Government Printing Office, 2008.

Wayman, Alexander W. *Cyclopedia of African Methodism.* Baltimore, MD: Methodist Episcopal Book Depository, 1882.

Williams, Moses W., and George W. Watkins. *Who's Who Among North Carolina Negro Baptists.* Alexandria, VA: Chadwyck-Healey, 1940.

Dissertations and Theses

Abramowitz, Jack. "Accommodation and Militancy in Negro Life, 1876–1916." Ph.D. dissertation, Columbia University, 1950.

Adams, Olin Burton. "The Negro and the Agrarian Movement in Georgia, 1874–1908." Ph.D. dissertation, Florida State University, 1973.

Ali, Omar H. "Black Populism in the New South, 1886–1898." Ph.D. dissertation, Columbia University, 2003.

Bacote, Clarence B. "The Negro in Georgia Politics, 1880–1908." Ph.D. dissertation, University of Chicago, 1955.

Barnes, Brook. "Triumph of the New South: Independent Movements in the 1880s." Ph.D. dissertation, University of Virginia, 1991.

Beeby, James M. "Revolt of the Tar Heelers." Ph.D. dissertation, Bowling Green State University, 1999.

Blackburn, Helen M. "The Populist Party in the South, 1890–1898." M.A. thesis, Howard University, 1941.

Bromberg, Alan B. "Pure Democracy and White Supremacy, The Redeemer Period in North Carolina: 1876–1894." Ph.D. dissertation, University of Virginia, 1977.

Bryant, Girard T. "The Populist Movement and the Negro." M.A. thesis, University of Kansas, Lawrence, 1939.

Carroll, Robert. "Robert Lloyd Smith and the Farmers' Improvement Society of Texas." M.A. thesis, Baylor University, 1974.

Creech, Joseph W., Jr. "Righteous Indignation: Religion and Populism in North Carolina, 1896–1906." Ph.D. dissertation, University of Notre Dame, 2000.

Cunningham, LaRue P. "The Negro in Granville County, North Carolina, As Reflected in the Oxford Public Ledger and Other Related Sources, 1880–1900." M.A. thesis, Atlanta University, 1972.

Dickson, Patrick J. "Out of the Lion's Mouth: The Colored Farmers' Alliance in the New South, 1886–1892." M.P.S. thesis, Cornell University, 2000.
Fine, Bernice R. "Agrarian Reform and the Texas Negro Farmers, 1886–1896." M.A. thesis, North Texas State University, 1971.
Gaither, Gerald H. "The Negro in the Ideology of Southern Populism, 1889–1896." M.A. thesis, University of Tennessee, Knoxville, 1967.
———. "Blacks and the Populist Revolt: Ballots and Bigotry in the New South." Ph.D. dissertation, University of Tennessee, Knoxville, 1972.
Gerteis, Joseph H. "Class and the Color Line: The Sources and Limits of Interracial Class Coalition, 1880–1896." Ph.D. dissertation, University of North Carolina, Chapel Hill, 1999.
Gnatz, William. "The Negro and the Populist Movement in the South." M.A. thesis, University of Chicago, 1961.
Horton, Paul. "Lawrence County Alabama in the Nineteenth Century: A Study in the 'Other South.'" M.A. thesis, University of Texas, Austin, 1985.
Hyman, Michael R. "Response to Redeemer Rule: Hill Country Political Dissent in the Post-Reconstruction South." Ph.D. dissertation, City University of New York, 1986.
McCain, William David. "The Populist Party in Mississippi." M.A. thesis, University of Mississippi, 1931.
McMath, Robert C., Jr. "The Farmers Alliance in the South: The Career of an Agrarian Institution." Ph.D. dissertation, University of North Carolina, Chapel Hill, 1972.
Muller, Philip R. "New South Populism: North Carolina 1884–1900." Ph.D. dissertation, University of North Carolina, Chapel Hill, 1971.
Perry, Douglass Geraldyne. "Black Populism: The Negro in the People's Party in Texas." M.S. thesis, Prairie View A & M University, Texas, 1945.
Reddick, Jamie Lawson. "The Negro and the Populist Movement in Georgia." M.A. thesis, Atlanta University, 1937.
Reinhart, Cornel J. "Populism and the Black: A Study in Ideology and Social Strains." Ph.D. dissertation, University of Oklahoma, Norman, 1972.
Smith, Richard K. "The Economics of Education and Discrimination in the U.S. South, 1870–1910." Ph.D. dissertation, University of Wisconsin, 1973.
Sugg, Harold G. "The Colored Farmers' Alliance, 1888–1892." M.A. thesis, Old Dominion University, 1971.
Thurtell, Craig M. "The Fusion Insurgency in North Carolina: Origins to Ascendancy, 1876–1896." Ph.D. dissertation, Columbia University, 1998.
Vickery, William E. "The Economics of the Negro Migration, 1900–1960." Ph.D. dissertation, University of Chicago, 1969.
Willis, Curley Daniel. "Grange Movement in Louisiana." M.A. thesis, Louisiana State University, Baton Rouge, 1935.

Index

abolitionist, xiii, 7, 15, 27, 37, 138, 162, 168, 176
Adams, Dudley W., 29
African Methodist Episcopal (AME), 8, 24, 25, 186n33, 209n31
Afro-Brazilian, xiii
Afro-Cuban, xiii
Alabama, 10, 14, 21–23, 26, 30, 31, 33–36, 45, 47, 49, 56, 58, 59, 64, 66, 69, 71, 76, 82, 86–88, 92, 111, 112, 116–19, 121, 135, 145, 152–53, 158, 159, 163, 164, 174, 186n33
Alabama Sharecroppers' Union, 164
Alabama State Wheel, 30, 82
Alexander, S. B., 62
Allen, Andrew, 34
Allen, Henry, 40
Allen, J. W., 30, 59, 82
Alliance Advocate, 54, 61
Alliance Aid of South Carolina, 54, 126
Alliance Light, 54
Alliance Party, 94
Alliance Vindicator, 53, 54
Amendments, to U.S. Constitution, 15, 23, 122, 135, 153, 166
American Colonization Society, 32, 137
Anderson, Lawrence, 172
anti-fusion, 4
Arkansas, 8, 9, 10, 19, 22, 23, 27, 29, 30–33, 35, 36, 38, 47, 49, 71, 73–75, 81, 95, 96, 112, 119, 126, 135, 152, 156, 164, 165, 167, 209n33
Armistead, William, 49
Asberry, Alex, 30, 54
Ashby, Harrison, 146
Atkinson, William Y., 134, 145
Atlanta University, 163
Austin, Edwin, Jr., 66

Baptist Pilot, 60
Barnburner Democrats, 138

Barthelme, Marion, 162
Beadle, Drake, 172
Beasley, D. C., 66
Bernard, James Y., 31, 33
Best, Willie, 18–19
Birmingham, M. C., 141
Black, James C. C., 133
Black Baptist, 24, 25, 30, 41, 59–61, 84, 160
Black Codes, 15
Black Masonry, xiii, 146
Black Nationalism, 157
Black Reformers Network, 171–72
"Black Republicans," 59
Blackman, Eva, 110
Blair Bill, 82
Bloomberg, Michael, 173
Bond, Scott, 209n33
Bowden, J. W., 123
Boyd, John, Jr., 175
Brooks, W. A, 34
Brown, J. W., 32
Bruce, Blanche K., 122
Bryan, William Jennings, 113, 115
Burkitt, Frank, 123
Butler, Marion, 108, 136, 141, 142

Cabel, E. C., 91
cabildos de nación, xiii
Calhoon, S. S., 122
Campbell, W. J., 10, 34, 37, 47
Carothers, Andrew J., 49
Carr, Elias, 36, 62
Carrington, Morris, 147
Carroll, Richard, 84
Carter, J. W., 70
Cassdall, H. D., 91, 92
Central Tennessee University, 162
Chase, P. K., 78, 94–95

Cheatham, Henry P., 136
Cherry, David, 174
Cheshire, J. T., 108
Christian Methodist Episcopal Church, 24, 25, 160
Cincinnati meeting (1887), 56
Cincinnati meeting (1891), 86, 88, 89, 90, 91, 92, 93
Citizens' Alliance, 89
Civil Rights Act (1866), 15
Civil Rights Act (1875), 14, 15, 23
Civil Rights Act (1964), 166
Civil War, xiii, 13, 15, 17, 20, 22, 26, 33, 41, 50, 56, 60, 99, 101, 127, 135, 165, 168
Cleveland, Grover, 127
Clinton, Hillary, 173
Clyburn, James E., 166, 170, 212n80
coach-laws, 8, 26, 70, 135, 140
Cobb, Phoebe, 40, 55
Coffey, George W., 49
Cohen, Tyra, 174
Collier, Sarah, 161
Colored Agricultural Wheels, xiv, 9, 10, 26, 29–34, 37, 41, 47, 48, 56, 59, 74, 81, 82, 95, 96
Colored Alliance, 53
Colored Farmers' Alliance (Colored Alliance), xi, xiv, xvii, 4–11, 26–34, 40–77, 81, 82, 84–93, 95, 98, 99, 103, 141, 165, 178, 211n72
Colored Farmers Association, 29
Colored Farmers Home Improvement Lodge, 49
Colored Farmers' National Alliance and Co-Operative Union, 48, 88. *See also* Colored Farmers' Alliance
Colored Farmers Union, 45, 104
Colored Grange, 8, 29, 30
Colored Methodist Episcopal Church, 106, 159, 160
Colored National Labor Union (CNLU), 33
Colored Orphanage Asylum, 61, 179, 194n65
Confederate army, 57, 70, 71, 73, 89, 93, 95, 124, 177, 184n9
Confederation of Industrial Organizations (CIO), 89
Conger Lard Bill, 69, 76, 195n99
Congress for Racial Equality, xiv

Conly, Jane, 143
convict lease system, 9, 13, 26, 50, 56, 81, 140, 146
Cooperative Workers of America (CWA), xiv, 9, 10, 26, 29, 40–45, 47, 48, 59, 158
Coppinger, William, 32
Cotton Pickers League, 72, 164
Cotton Pickers' Strike, 27, 38, 62, 70, 71, 76, 85, 127
Crawford, Lectured, 74, 81
Crawford, Matilda, 161
Crawley, Newton C., 49
Crisis magazine, 163
Cromwell, Oliver, 10, 11, 55, 57, 67, 68, 151, 156, 166, 170, 195n90, 195n97
crop lien, 17–18, 130, 131
Cuney, Norris Wright, 146, 214n7
Custer, George W., 30–31

Daley, Richard, 169
Dancy, John C., 108
Daniels, Josephus, 82
Darthord, M. C., 30
Davis, Frank, 198n45
Debs, Eugene V., 154
Democratic Party, xiv, 3, 4, 9–11, 13, 15–22, 42, 44, 56, 57, 61, 64, 76, 77, 80, 83–84, 88, 90–96, 101, 102, 106–18, 123, 127–38, 141–47, 151, 152, 155, 159, 169, 170, 173–75, 203n19
Dial, J. M., 68
Dial, Jack, 68
Diggs, Annie L., 110
Disciples of Christ, 21
Donnelly, Ignatius, 91
Dorroh, Allen, 42
Douglass, Frederick, 153, 154, 168
Doyle, Bertram W., 159, 166, 212n80
Doyle, Henry S., 10, 11, 24, 78–80, 90, 94, 105, 106, 111, 157, 159, 160, 166
Du Bois, W. E. B., 8, 106, 154, 159, 163, 201n131

Eagle, James P., 95
Eaton, Allen P., 108–9
education, xiv, 9, 21, 22, 29, 50, 53, 54, 63, 65, 67, 80–82, 108, 120, 121, 124–26, 128, 140, 146, 150, 158, 160
Eldridge, E. S., 98

Elliott, William, 128
Exodus, 19, 24, 97, 101, 154
Exoduster(s), 19, 97, 101

Fairfax, Jacob, 49
Farm Securities Administration, 166
Farmers' Improvement Society, 99, 165, 211n72
Farmers Mutual Benefit Association, 88, 89
Farmers' Union, 9, 45, 46, 58, 76
Farrakhan, Louis, 172
Ferrell, Frank J., 29, 35, 189n107
Field, James G., 93
Fields, Jessie, 172
First Colored Baptist Church (Atlanta), 158–59
Fisher, Abe, 49
Fisk University, 96, 159
Fitzpatrick, I. N., 76
Florida, 10, 11, 22, 24, 26, 28, 34–36, 39, 45–47, 55, 58, 59, 64, 66, 69, 71, 75–77, 86, 91, 119, 127, 141, 152, 164, 174
"Force Bill," 69–70, 118. *See also* Lodge Bill
Fortune, T. Thomas, 154, 165
Foster, Benjamin F., 94, 96–97, 106
Free Soil, 138
Freedman's Bureau, 15, 17
Freeman, George, 40
Fulani, Lenora B., 170–72, 174, 176

Garnet, Henry Highland, 168
Garvey, Marcus, 157, 163, 211n59
General Association of the Colored Baptists, 60
George, Henry, 106
Georgia, 8, 10, 11, 18, 22, 24, 28, 34, 35, 37, 40, 44, 45, 47, 49, 50, 59, 64, 70, 71, 74, 75, 76, 78–81, 83–86, 90–92, 94–95, 105–7, 111–21, 129–35, 145, 147, 152, 157, 159, 164, 174, 184n9, 186n33
Georgia Committee of Independent Voters, 174
Gibson, D. A., 30
Giddings, G. G., 192n6
Glass, Fanny, 40, 55
Glopsy, I., 96
Gordon, Kate, 163

Grand United Order of Good Samaritans, 8
grandfather clause, 84, 135, 152, 157–58
Grange (Patrons of Husbandry), 29, 30, 56
Grant, W. A., 74
Grant, W. J., 124, 127
Graves, Anton, 106
Great Migration, 155, 156, 169
Great Southwest Railroad Strike, 35
Green, Harry C., 66
Green Party, 174
Greenback Labor Party, 20–23, 29, 46, 56, 81, 93, 96, 114
Greenback Party, 3, 13–15, 20–23, 29–30, 46, 56, 75, 82, 93, 101, 102, 147
Gregory, F. R., 180
Gregory, Julia, 180
Griffin, Wayne, 172, 174
Grimes, John Bryan, 40
Guthrie, W. A., 142

Hall, Thomas, 18
Hammond, C. H., 192n6
Hampton, Wade, 124
Hannon, J. H., 108
Hardee, Eli, 40
Harold Washington Party, 172
Harrison, Benjamin, 91
Harrison, Lee, 42
Hart, Mary Ida, 59, 160
Hayes, R. H., 94, 102
Hayes, Rutherford B., 16
Haynes, Jack, 147, 148, 156
Haynes, John H., 189n107
Hepburn Act, 166
Hogg, James, 145
Holloway, C. J., 45
Horton, Adolph, 68
Hover, Hiram F., 40–44, 47, 59, 191n148
Howe, William, 37
Humphrey, Elizabeth, 209n30
Humphrey, Richard M., 11, 49, 52, 53, 55–60, 65, 66, 70, 72, 86, 89, 95, 157, 161, 177, 185n24, 193n40, 193n48, 209n30

Ikard, Robert, 60
Independence Party (New York), 173, 213n17
Independence Party (South Carolina), 174

Independent Alabama, 174
Independent Texans, 174
Indiana territory, 86
International Workers Party (IWW), 164
Interstate Commerce Commission, 166
irmandandes, xiii
Islam, 24
Ivy, Frank B., 66

Jackson, A. W., 38–39
Jackson, Jesse, 170–71
Jackson, John S., 69, 87, 88, 159, 195n100
Jaybird Association, 148
Jayson, Warren, 40
Jennings, Henry J., 94, 98, 106
Jim Crow, xiii, 6, 76, 84, 85, 106, 115, 135, 154, 157, 162–66, 175–77, 211n75, 211n76
Johnson, Andrew, 17
Johnson, Edward A., 108
Johnson, Frank, 34
Jones, Hunter, 40
Jones, Lewis N., 139
Jones, M. F., 87
Jones, T., 49

Kansas, 7, 10, 19, 35, 86, 94, 96, 97, 98, 102, 109, 110, 111, 118, 119, 157, 164
Kennard, Jim, 147, 148, 156
Kentucky, 7, 49, 58, 86, 160, 164
King, Lewis, 40
King, Martin Luther, Jr., 169
Kirby, John Henry, 158
Knights of Labor, xiv, 9, 10, 21, 23, 26, 29, 33–42, 45, 47, 48, 51, 55, 56, 59, 61, 71, 75, 82, 89, 95, 102, 142, 151, 189n107, 190n125, 194n66
Know Nothing Party, 99, 138
Kolb, Reuben, 117, 121, 145
Ku Klux Klan, 42, 68

Landlord-Tenant Act (North Carolina), 72
Langhorne, B., 87
Langley, Isom P., 96
Laurent, L. D., 75, 87, 88, 91, 92, 103
Lawrence, P., 64
Lease, Mary Elizabeth, 109
Lee, Green, 49

Leflore County Massacre, 27, 67–69, 122, 161, 167
Liberia, 19, 32, 186n33
Libertarian Party, 172, 174
Liberty Party, 138
"lily white," 83, 84, 101, 104, 114, 118, 132, 146, 153
Lincoln, Abraham, 17, 83, 129, 200n91
Lincoln University, 158
literacy test, 84, 119, 135, 152
Livingston, Leonidas F., 90
Lockhart, H., 192n6
Lockhart, James A., 139
Lodge Bill, 27, 69, 70, 76, 87, 88, 108, 166, 198n49. *See also* "Force Bill"
Logan, Adella Hunt, 163
Lopez League, 27
Louisiana, 16, 19, 20, 23, 26, 27, 30, 34, 35, 39, 45, 47, 49, 65, 71, 75, 76, 86, 87, 88, 91, 92, 94, 95, 102, 103, 104, 111, 112, 114, 116, 117, 119, 135, 152, 157, 159, 163, 164, 167
Louisiana Farmers' Union (20th century), 164
Love, E. F., 50
Lowe, George W., 10, 30–32, 74, 81, 96, 106
Lowe, Winnie A. (Williams), 160
Lowry, Robert, 68
Loyd, Henry Demarest, 113–14
Lynch, John R., 14, 121, 122
lynching, 39, 73, 78, 81, 84, 106, 120, 127, 132, 135, 140, 142, 143, 144, 148, 154, 162, 169
Lytle, Lutie A., 10, 55, 97, 98, 157, 162, 163, 200n100
Lytle, John, 97–98

Mack, John, 105
Macune, Charles W., 102
Mahone, William, 22
Manly, Alex, 143
Marshall, John, 49
Martin, Charles H., 139
Martin, Waldo, 154
Martin, William H., 57
Martin v. Lockhart, 139
Marx, Karl, 106
Massachusetts Coalition of Independent Voters, 174

Mathews, R. J., 105
Maultshy, D. L., 139
McAllister, 68
McCall, Harry G., 58, 59
McDonald, James G., Jr., 148
McDonald, William, 146–47
McEnery, Samuel D., 39
McCallum, Enoch, 139
McCrary, Aaron, 42
McCrary, Isham, 42, 191n144
McCrary, Sherman C., 10, 40, 42, 47, 158, 191n144
McDowell, John H., 33
McGilbra, Israel, 49
McKinley, William, 115
Middleton, Abraham R., 108
Midland Express, 54
Minnesota, 91, 172
Minor, Lee, 40, 43–45
Mississippi, 10, 11, 13, 14, 15, 20, 22, 23, 27, 28, 31, 38, 49, 55, 61, 67–69, 71, 73, 75, 85, 86, 87, 88, 90, 107, 112, 117, 119, 121–23, 129, 135, 143, 151, 152, 156, 164, 167, 169, 170, 209n33
Missouri, 7, 35, 58, 91, 92, 119
Moise, Edwin M., 127
Montgomery, S. M., 49
Moon, Gale, 40
Moore, John L., 10, 11, 24, 28, 55, 64, 66, 75, 76, 77, 91, 141, 157, 209n31
Morey, William, 91
Morris, Scott, 68
Mott, T. J., 59
Municipal College, 160
Murray, George Washington, 81, 85, 124–29, 151, 153, 158, 165, 166, 170, 180

Nation of Islam, 172
National Afro-American Council, 154, 165
National Alliance, 53, 57, 74, 191n159
National American Woman Suffrage Association, 163
National Association for the Advancement of Colored People (NAACP), xiv, 162, 172
National Association of Colored Women, 161
National Bar Association, 163
National Black Farmers Association (NBFA), 175

National Black Political Convention, 170
National Colored Alliance, 49
National Conference for a New Politics, 169
National Economist, 53, 57, 74, 85, 102, 141, 191n159, 193n48
National Farmers Alliance and Industrial Union, 56, 141
National Negro Liberty Party, 154
National Order of Mosaic Templars of America, 8
"National Union Conference," 89
National Union Labor Party, 56
Natural Law Party, 174
"Negro Domination," 28, 43
"Negro party," 78, 79, 99, 111, 161
"Negro Rule," 28, 79, 122, 144, 145, 148, 152
Negro Young People's Congress, 159
Nelson, Lee, 34, 47
neocolonial, xiii
New York, 44, 89, 114, 157, 162, 173, 174, 175, 211n59
Nichols, J. H., 87, 88
Nichols, John, 82, 95–96
Nichols, Willis, 49
Norris, John D., 87, 88, 124–27
North Carolina, 3, 5, 9, 10, 11, 18, 19, 24, 26, 27, 28, 33–40, 44, 45, 47, 49, 54, 55, 58–63, 66, 71, 72, 75, 78, 81–88, 91, 94, 95, 99, 100, 101, 107–10, 112, 114, 116, 117, 119, 121, 135–43, 147, 148, 150, 152, 155, 157, 160, 164, 167, 174, 179, 212n80, 215n15
North Carolina Independents for Change, 174
Northern, William J., 120
Northern Farmers Alliance (Northern Alliance), 58, 69, 91
Norwood, C. M., 95
Norwood, Juanita, 172

Oates, William, 121
Obama, Barack, 169, 170, 173–76
Ocala meeting (1890), 58, 69, 70, 76, 86–88, 127, 199n56
Odd Fellows, 103
Ohio Wesleyan University, 105, 159
Omaha meeting (1892), 42, 56, 86, 92, 93, 94, 97, 150

Omaha platform, 42
Owens, Riley, 42

Patterson, Ben, 11, 55, 57, 73, 156
Pattillo, Mary Ida (Hart), 59, 160
Pattillo, Walter A., 10, 11, 24, 36, 55, 57, 59–64, 66, 69, 75, 76, 85, 87, 88, 91, 100, 106, 151, 157, 160, 166, 179, 180, 194, 210n46
Pattillo, Walter H., Jr., xvii, 166, 179, 194n56, 210n46
Payne, Daniel A., 25
People's Party, xii, xiv, 3–6, 9–11, 25, 26, 29, 42, 54–56, 58, 59, 75, 77–81, 83, 85–87, 90–112, 113–49, 150–61, 165, 173, 177, 183n2, 198n49, 200n91, 203n19, 211n59, 214n7
Perot, H. Ross, 168, 170, 171, 172, 174, 176
Perry, H. H., 36, 62
Perry, Sam, 40
Peters, J. W., 49
Pickens, James Madison, 21
Pinchback, Pickney B. S., 19, 20
Pledger, William A., 84, 120
Plummer, A. L., 45
Polk, Leonidas L., 62, 71, 97, 136
poll tax, 16, 22, 23, 42, 83, 84, 119, 129, 130, 131, 134, 135, 141, 152
Pope, H. W., 139
Pope, J. W., 108
Powderly, Terrence V., 35, 37
Powell, James H., 85
Power, C. A., 89
Pratt, T. E., 124
Price, Joseph C., 137
Prince Hall Grand Lodges, 7
Prohibition Party, 11, 38–39, 78, 81, 96, 97, 101, 116, 144
Purnell, T. R., 109

Raleigh Theological Institute, 60, 99, 160. *See also* Shaw University
Rayner, Ahmed A., Jr., 166, 169, 170, 212n80
Rayner, Clarissa, 160
Rayner, John B., 10, 11, 24, 94, 99–102, 106, 114, 145–47, 151, 158, 160, 166, 167, 169, 170, 176, 209n35
Rayner, Kenneth, 99, 100
Readjuster Party, 22–23, 67

Reconstruction, xiii, 5, 7, 13, 15–19, 22, 24, 26–28, 31, 36, 41, 42, 46, 69, 70, 79, 81, 83, 100, 101, 111, 115, 122, 124, 127, 130, 139, 140, 142, 152, 154, 155, 166, 177
Red Shirt companies, 17, 23, 124, 142, 143, 148
Redeemer, 16, 19, 22, 23, 28, 29, 114, 124, 144, 147, 152
Reform Party, 171–73
Republican Party, xii, xiv, 3, 4, 9–16, 19, 21–30, 36, 41, 46, 54, 55, 59, 61, 67, 70, 74–85, 90–112, 113–49, 150–62, 165, 168–73, 195n99, 214n7
Revels, Hiram, 122
Richardson, E. A., 71, 90, 91, 105
Ricker, A. W., 114
Robertson, J. W., 34
Rodgers, H. P., 73
Rogers, F. T., 58
Rogers, Joseph J., 54, 58, 62, 66, 86
Roxborough, Charles A., 103, 104, 114
Russell, Daniel L., 142

Saddler, R. M., 49
Sanders, James C., 87, 88
Scott, Garrett, 59, 147, 148, 149
Sewall, Arthur, 115
Shaw University, 60, 99, 100. *See also* Raleigh Theological Institute
Shuffer, Fannie Munn, 160, 210n49
Shuffer, George M., Jr., 166, 193n51, 212n80
Shuffer, Jacob J., 27, 49, 52, 57, 58, 69, 166
Simmons, Lemuel, 139
Singleton, Benjamin, 19
Singleton, Tom, 44
Sisters of Zion, 8
Smalls, Robert, 127
Smith, Adam, 106
Smith, Ezekiel Ezra, 137
Smith, Robert Lloyd, 99
Socialist Party, 116, 154, 164
South Carolina, 8, 10, 11, 16, 19, 22, 23, 26, 29, 33, 34, 38, 40, 43–49, 54, 56, 58, 71–74, 81, 83–89, 112, 114, 117, 119, 121–29, 135, 139, 142, 143, 152, 153, 158, 159, 164, 165, 167, 170, 172, 174, 178, 184n9, 203n19, 203n21, 212n80
Southern Democracy, 17, 29, 50, 67, 69, 75, 77, 90, 94, 112–15, 126, 128, 149, 151–55, 164, 165

Southern Farmers Alliance (Southern Alliance), 31, 38, 46, 58, 61, 62, 69, 71, 75, 76, 77, 88, 89, 90, 91, 97, 107
Southern Tenant Farmers Union, 164
Speer, D. R., 44
Spellman, J. J., 13, 15
Spencer, H. J., 49, 52, 87, 88
St. Cloud, Victor, 38, 59
St. Louis meeting (1889), 86, 87
St. Louis meeting (1892), 58, 86, 91, 92, 93, 110, 199n70
St. Louis meeting (1896), 113, 115
Stack, Nicholas, 36–37, 59, 190n117
Stephens, Uriah, 37
Stevens, William, 121
Stilven, D. H., 98
Streeter, Alson J., 95
Stuart, Cathy, 213n17
Student Nonviolent Coordinating Committee, xiv–xv, 169
subtreasury loan program, 26, 27, 65, 66, 76, 93, 138

Taylor, E. I., 131
Taylor, George Edwin, 154
Teague, William, 146
Telfair, Romeo, 10, 40
tenancy, 13, 18, 35, 56, 72, 107, 130, 132, 139, 156, 212n77
Tennessee, 8, 11, 19, 29–34, 47, 49, 52, 55, 71, 87, 88, 97, 99, 119, 135, 152, 154, 162, 164, 181
Texas, 8, 10, 11, 19–30, 33, 35, 48, 49, 52–57, 59, 69, 71–73, 75, 81, 86–88, 94, 95, 98–102, 107, 111–19, 126, 135, 144–47, 150, 152, 156–69, 209n30, 214n7
Texas Law and Order League, 158
Thompson, C. W., 20
Thompson, Elias M., 139
Thurman, Lucinda, 161
Tilden, Samuel, 16
Till, Emmet, 169
Till, Mamie, 169
Tillman, Benjamin, 84, 114, 123, 127, 128, 129, 143
Tobacco Laborers' Union, 20
Tobias, Channing H., 106, 159
Turner, Anthony, 49

Turner, Henry McNeil, 84, 186n33
Tuskegee Institute, 163, 165

Union army, 3, 31, 93
Union Band of Brothers and Sisters, 8
Union Labor Party, 11, 32, 56, 74, 81, 82, 89, 94–98, 110, 117, 144
Union League, 15, 41, 162
United Brothers of Friendship, 158
United Daughters of Ham, 8
United Friends Association, 8
United Independents of Illinois, 174
United Order of True Reformers, 8
Universal Negro Improvement Association (UNIA), 157, 163, 164

Vance, Ed, 14
Vance, Zebulon, 78
Vaughn, C. A., 32
Ventura, Jesse, 172
Village Improvement Society, 99
Vinton David, Henrietta, 211n59
Virginia, 8, 10, 11, 18, 20, 22, 23, 33, 34–37, 47–49, 54, 55, 58, 62, 66, 71, 75, 85–87, 91–93, 111, 112, 117–19, 124, 152, 153, 157, 164, 175

Wade, Melvin, 101, 102
Walker, Alexander, 34
Walton, S. D., 114, 115
Ward, Samuel Ringgold, 168
Warwick, William H., 10, 11, 55, 57, 66, 67, 75, 85, 87, 88, 91, 92, 114, 157, 199n70
Washington, Booker T., xii, 84, 153, 157, 159, 193n37
Washington, D.C., meeting (1891), 86, 89, 92
Washington, J. F., 198n45
Watson, Tom, 37, 64, 78, 105, 107, 112, 114, 115, 117, 131, 133, 153
Weaver, James B., 3, 92, 93, 109, 111, 116, 136, 151, 168, 176, 198n49, 200n94
Wells-Barnett, Ida B., 143, 154, 162, 163
West Africa, 19, 32
Whig Party, 21, 32, 82, 99, 138
White, E. V., 131
White, Garland H., 137
White, George H., 81
White, W. J., 132

White Leagues, 17
White Man's Union, 148, 149, 156, 207n163
Williams, Barbara Jeanne, 166, 170, 195n90, 195n97
Williams, Diane, 172
Williams, Isaiah D., 124
Williams, Winnie A., 160
Williamson, John H., 108
Wilmington riot, 142–47
Wilson, Anthony, 106
Woman's Journal, 163
Women's Christian Temperance Union (WCTU), 75, 89, 109, 161
Women's Political Council, xiv
Woodward, W. J., 34
World War I, 5, 155, 158

www.ingramcontent.com/pod-product-compliance
Lightning Source LLC
Chambersburg PA
CBHW030340240426
43661CB00052B/1691